BEFORE THE MUSES

AN ANTHOLOGY
OF AKKADIAN LITERATURE

Benjamin R. Foster

VOLUME I: ARCHAIC, CLASSICAL, MATURE

CDL Press
Bethesda, Maryland

Library of Congress Cataloging-in-Publication Data

Foster, Benjamin R. (Benjamin Read)
  Before the muses : an anthology of Akkadian literature /
  Benjamin R. Foster
    p.   cm.
  Includes bibliographical references.
  Contents: v. 1. Archaic, classical, mature — v. 2. Mature, late.
  ISBN 0-9620013-4-1
  1. Akkadian literature — Translations into English. I. Title.
PJ3951.F67 1993
892'.1—dc20   92-42779
                                                            CIP

The preparation of the contents of this volume was made possible
by a grant from the Translations Program of the National Endowment for the Humanities, an independent Federal agency. The
publication of this volume was made possible by a grant from the
Publication Subvention Program of the National Endowment for
the Humanities, an independent Federal agency.

Designed by Karen Polinger Foster and Elizabeth Duncan Lyons.

Printed in Ann Arbor, MI by Cushing-Malloy, Inc.

SBN 0-9620013-4-1

Contents

VOLUME I

GENERAL INTRODUCTION
IN SEARCH OF AKKADIAN LITERATURE

CHAPTER I

THE ARCHAIC PERIOD
(2300 – 2000 B.C.)

CHAPTER II

THE CLASSICAL PERIOD
(2000 – 1500 B.C.)

CHAPTER III

THE MATURE PERIOD
(1500-1000 B.C.)

VOLUME II

CHAPTER IV

THE LATE PERIOD
(1000-100 B.C.)

Abbreviations

AASH	*Acta Antiqua Academiae Scientiarum Hungaricae* (Budapest)
AbB	F. R. Kraus, ed., *Altbabylonische Briefe in Umschrift und Übersetzung* (Leiden, 1964-)
ABL	R. F. Harper, *Assyrian and Babylonian Letters belonging to the Kouyunjik Collection of the British Museum* (London & Chicago, 1892-1914)
ABRT	J. A. Craig, *Assyrian and Babylonian Religious Texts*, 1 (Leipzig, 1895), 2 (Leipzig, 1897)
AfO	*Archiv für Orientforschung* (Graz, Vienna)
AGH	E. Ebeling, *Die akkadische Gebetsserie "Handerhebung" von neuem gesammelt und herausgegeben* (Berlin, 1953)
AHw	W. von Soden, *Akkadisches Handwörterbuch* (Wiesbaden, 1959-1981)
AJSL	*American Journal of Semitic Languages and Literatures* (Chicago)
AMT	R. Campbell Thompson, *Assyrian Medical Texts* (London, 1923)
AnBi	*Analecta Biblica* (Rome)
Ancient Mesopotamia	A. L. Oppenheim, *Ancient Mesopotamia, Portrait of a Dead Civilization*[2] (Chicago, 1977)
ANET[3]	J. B. Pritchard, ed., *Ancient Near Eastern Texts Relating to the Old Testament*[3] (Princeton, 1969)
Annuaire	*Annuaire*, École Pratique des Hautes Etudes, IVe Section: sciences historiques et philologiques (Paris)
AnOr	*Analecta Orientalia* (Rome)
AnSt	*Anatolian Studies* (London)
AOAT	*Alter Orient und Altes Testament* (Neukirchen-Vluyn)
AOATS	*Alter Orient und Altes Testament, Sonderreihe* (Neukirchen-Vluyn)
AOF	*Altorientalische Forschungen* (Berlin)

ARI	A. K. Grayson, *Assyrian Royal Inscriptions* (Wiesbaden, 1972-)
ARM	*Archives Royales de Mari* (Paris)
ARMT	*Archives Royales de Mari, Textes* (Paris)
ArOr	*Archiv Orientální* (Prague)
AS	*Assyriological Studies* (Chicago)
ASKT	P. Haupt, *Akkadische und Sumerische Keilschrifttexte ...* (Leipzig, 1882)
Atrahasis	W. G. Lambert, A. R. Millard, *Atra-ḫasīs, The Babylonian Story of the Flood* (Oxford, 1969)
BA	*Beiträge zur Assyriologie und semitische Sprachwissenschaft* (Leipzig)
Baby-Beschwörungen	W. Farber, *Schlaf, Kindchen, Schlaf! Mesopotamische Baby-Beschwörungen und -Rituale* (Winona Lake, IN, 1989)
BAL	R. Borger, *Babylonisch-assyrische Lesestücke* (Rome, 1963)
BAM	F. Köcher, *Die babylonische-assyrische Medizin in Texten und Untersuchungen* (Berlin, 1963-)
BASOR	*Bulletin of the American Schools of Oriental Research* (New Haven, etc.)
BBR	H. Zimmern, *Beiträge zur Kenntnis der babylonischen Religion* I (Leipzig, 1896), II (Leipzig, 1901)
BBST	L. W. King, *Babylonian Boundary-Stones in the British Museum* (London, 1912)
BE	*The Babylonian Expedition of the University of Pennsylvania* (Philadelphia)
BHLT	A. K. Grayson, *Babylonian Historical-Literary Texts* (Toronto, 1975)
BIN	*Babylonian Inscriptions in the Collection of J. B. Nies* (New Haven)
BiOr	*Bibliotheca Orientalis* (Leiden)
Bit Rimki	J. Læssøe, *Studies in the Assyrian Ritual and Series bît rimki* (Copenhagen, 1955)
BL	S. Langdon, *Babylonian Liturgies* (Paris, 1913)
BM	*Bibliotheca Mesopotamica* (Malibu, CA)

BMS   L. W. King, *Babylonian Magic and Sorcery, being "the Prayers of the Lifting of the Hand"* (London, 1896)

BRM   *Babylonian Records in the Library of J. Pierpont Morgan* (New Haven)

BSD   M. Vogelzang, *Bin šar dadmē, Edition and Analysis of the Akkadian Anzu Poem* (Groningen, 1988)

BSOAS   *Bulletin of the School of Oriental and African Studies* (London)

BWL   W. G. Lambert, *Babylonian Wisdom Literature* (Oxford, 1960)

CAD   *The Assyrian Dictionary of the University of Chicago* (Chicago, 1956-)

CAH3   *The Cambridge Ancient History*3 (Cambridge, 1970-)

Clergé   D. Charpin, *Le Clergé d'Ur au siècle d'Hammurabi (xixe - xviiie siècle av. J.-C.)* (Paris & Geneva, 1986)

Court Poetry   A. Livingstone, *Court Poetry and Literary Miscellanea, State Archives of Assyria* 3 (Helsinki, 1989)

CRRAI 19   P. Garelli, ed., *Le Palais et la royauté, xixe rencontre assyriologique internationale* (1971) (Paris, 1974)

CRRAI 25   H.-J. Nissen, J. Renger, ed., *Mesopotamien und seine Nachbarn, Politische und kulturelle Wechselbeziehungen im Alten Vorderasien vom 4. bis 1. Jahrtausend v. Chr., xxv. rencontre assyriologique internationale* (1978), *Berliner Beiträge zum Vorderen Orient* 1 (Berlin, 1982)

CRRAI 26   B. Alster, ed., *Death in Mesopotamia, xxvie rencontre assyriologique internationale (1979)* (Copenhagen, 1980)

CRRAI 28   *Vorträge gehalten auf der 28. Rencontre Assyriologique Internationale in Wien (1981), AfO Beiheft* 19 (1982)

CRRAI 30   K. R. Veenhof, ed., *Cuneiform Archives and Libraries, Papers read at the 30e rencontre assyriologique internationale (1983)* (Leiden, 1986)

CRRAI 32   K. Hecker, W. Sommerfeld, eds., *Keilschriftliche Literaturen, xxxii rencontre assyriologique internationale (1985), Berliner Beiträge zum Vorderen Orient* 6 (Berlin, 1986)

CRRAI 33	J.-M. Durand, ed., *La Femme dans le proche-orient antique, xxxiiie rencontre assyriologique internationale (1986)*, (Paris, 1987)
CT	*Cuneiform Texts from Tablets in the British Museum* (London)
Devils	R. Campbell Thompson, *The Devils and Evil Spirits of Babylonia* I (London, 1903), II (London, 1904)
Dreams	A. L. Oppenheim, *The Interpretation of Dreams in the Ancient Near East, with a Translation of an Assyrian Dream-book, Transactions of the American Philosophical Society New Series* 46/III (pp. 177-373) (Philadelphia, 1956)
EAK	*Einleitung in die assyrischen Königsinschriften* I = R. Borger, *Erster Teil* (Leiden, 1961), II = W. Schramm, *Zweiter Teil* (Leiden, 1973)
Epik	K. Hecker, *Untersuchungen zur akkadischen Epik*, AOATS 8 (1974)
Explanatory Works	A. Livingstone, *Mystical and Mythological Explanatory Works of Assyrian and Babylonian Scholars* (Oxford, 1986)
FAOS	*Freiburger Altorientalische Studien* (Stuttgart)
GAG	W. von Soden, *Grundriss der akkadischen Grammatik*, AnOr 33 (Rome, 1952)
GETh	R. Campbell Thompson, *The Epic of Gilgamish* (Oxford, 1930)
HBKl	S. Maul, *'Herzberuhigungsklagen,' Die sumerisch-akkadischen Eršahunga-Gebete* (Wiesbaden, 1988)
HKL	R. Borger, *Handbuch der Keilschriftliteratur* (Berlin, 1967-1975)
HSAO	*Heidelberger Studien zum Alten Orient* (Wiesbaden)
HSS	*Harvard Semitic Studies* (Cambridge, MA)
Hymnes	M.-J. Seux, *Hymnes et prières aux dieux de babylonie et d'assyrie* (Paris, 1976)
IEJ	*Israel Exploration Journal* (Jerusalem)
II R	(E. Norris, H. Rawlinson), *The Cuneiform Inscriptions of Western Asia* II (London, 1866)

III R	(G. Smith, H. Rawlinson), *The Cuneiform Inscriptions of Western Asia* III (London, 1870)
I R	(E. Norris, H. Rawlinson), *The Cuneiform Inscriptions of Western Asia* I (London, 1861)
IRSA	E. Sollberger, J.-R. Kupper, *Inscriptions royales sumériennes et akkadiennes* (Paris, 1971)
Ištar und Dumuzi	W. Farber, *Beschwörungsrituale an Ištar und Dumuzi* (Wiesbaden, 1977)
IV R²	(T. Pinches, H. Rawlinson, G. Smith), *The Cuneiform Inscriptions of Western Asia* IV (London, 1891)
JANES	*Journal of the Ancient Near Eastern Society of Columbia University* (New York)
JAOS	*Journal of the American Oriental Society* (New Haven)
JCS	*Journal of Cuneiform Studies* (New Haven, Philadelphia)
JEOL	*Jaarbericht ... van het Vooraziatisch-Egyptisch Genootschap "Ex Oriente Lux"* (Leiden)
JESHO	*Journal of the Economic and Social History of the Orient* (Leiden)
JNES	*Journal of Near Eastern Studies* (Chicago)
JRAS	*Journal of the Royal Asiatic Society* (London)
JSS	*Journal of Semitic Studies* (Manchester)
JTVI	*Journal of the Transactions of the Victoria Institute* (London)
KAH	O. Schrocder, *Keilschrifttexte aus Assur historischen Inhalts, Zweites Heft* (Leipzig, 1922) = WVDOG 37
KAR	E. Ebeling, *Keilschrifttexte aus Assur religiösen Inhalts* (Leipzig, 1915-1923) = WVDOG 28 (= I), 34 (= II)
KAV	O. Schroeder, *Keilschrifttexte aus Assur verschiedenen Inhalts* (Leipzig, 1920) = WVDOG 35
KB	E. Schrader, ed., *Keilschriftliche Bibliothek, Sammlung von assyrischen und babylonischen Texten in Umschrift und Übersetzung* (Berlin)
KBo	*Keilschrifttexte aus Boghazköy* (Berlin)
KUB	*Keilschrifturkunden aus Boghazköy* (Berlin)

LAS	A. Parpola, *Letters from Assyrian Scholars*, 1 = AOAT 5/1 (1970), 2 (Helsinki, 1971)
Literatur	E. Reiner, "Die Akkadische Literatur" in W. Röllig, ed., *Neues Handbuch der Literaturwissenschaft, Altorientalische Literaturen* (Wiesbaden, 1978), 151-210
LKA	E. Ebeling, F. Köcher, J. Jacob-Rost, *Literarische Keilschrifttexte aus Assur* (Berlin, 1953)
LSS (NF)	*Leipziger Semitische Studien (Neue Folge)* (Leipzig)
MAD	I. J. Gelb ed., *Materials for the Assyrian Dictionary* (Chicago)
MAOG	*Mitteilungen der Altorientalischen Gesellschaft* (Leipzig)
Maqlû	K. Tallqvist, *Die assyrische Beschwörungsserie Maqlû* (Leipzig, 1895)
MDOG	*Mitteilungen der Deutschen Orient-Gesellschaft* (Berlin)
MDP	*Mémoires de la Délégation en Perse* (Paris)
Mensch	F. R. Kraus, *Vom mesopotamischen Menschen der altbabylonischen Zeit und seiner Welt*, MKNAW NR 36/6 (1973)
Mésopotamie	J. Bottéro, *Mésopotamie, L'écriture, la raison et les dieux* (Paris, 1987)
MIO	*Mitteilungen des Instituts für Orientforschung* (Berlin)
MKNAW (NR)	*Mededelingen der Koninklijke Nederlandse Akademie van Wetenschappen, afd letterkunde* (Amsterdam) (Nieuwe Reeks)
MSL	*Materialien zum Sumerischen Lexikon* (Rome)
MVAeG	*Mitteilungen der Vorderasiatisch-Aegyptischen Gesellschaft* (Leipzig)
Mythes	J. Bottéro, *Mythes et rites de babylone* (Paris, 1985)
Mythologie	J. Bottéro, S. N. Kramer, *Lorsque les dieux faisaient l'homme, Mythologie mésopotamienne* (Paris, 1989)
Myths	S. Dalley, *Myths from Mesopotamia* (Oxford, 1989)
Nergal	J. Böllenrücher, *Gebete und Hymnen an Nergal*, LSS I/VI (Leipzig, 1904)
OAC	*Orientis Antiqvi Collectio* (Rome)

OECT	*Oxford Editions of Cuneiform Texts* (Oxford)
OLA	*Orientalia Lovaniensia Analecta* (Leuven)
OLZ	*Orientalistische Literaturzeitung* (Leipzig, Berlin)
OrAn	*Oriens Antiqvvs* (Rome)
OrNS	*Orientalia Nova Series* (Rome)
PAPS	*Proceedings of the American Philosophical Society* (Philadelphia)
PBS	*Publications of the Babylonian Section, University Museum, University of Pennsylvania* (Philadelphia)
PHPKB	J. Brinkman, *A Political History of Post-Kassite Babylonia 1158-722 B.C.*, AnOr 43 (1968)
Poetry	E. Reiner, *Your Thwarts in Pieces, Your Mooring Rope Cut, Poetry from Babylonia and Assyria* (Ann Arbor, MI, 1985)
PRAK	H. de Genouillac, *Premières recherches archéologiques à Kich* I (Paris, 1924), II (Paris, 1925)
PSBA	*Proceedings of the Society of Biblical Archaeology* (London)
Quellen	E. Ebeling, *Quellen zur Kenntnis der babylonischen Religion* I = MVAeG 23/I (Leipzig, 1918), II = MVAeG 23/II (Leipzig, 1919)
RA	*Revue d'Assyriologie et d'archéologie orientale* (Paris)
Religions	R. Labat, *Les religions du Proche-Orient asiatique* (Paris, 1970)
RGTC	*Répértoire géographique des textes cunéiformes* (Wiesbaden)
RLA	*Reallexikon der Assyriologie* (Berlin, 1932-)
RO	*Rocznik Orientalistyczny* (Warsaw)
SAHG	A. Falkenstein, W. von Soden, *Sumerische und Akkadische Hymnen und Gebete* (Zurich & Stuttgart, 1953)
Šamaš	A. Schollmeyer, *Sumerisch-babylonische Hymnen und Gebete an Šamaš* (Paderborn, 1912)
SANE	*Sources and Monographs from the Ancient Near East* (Malibu, CA)

ŠÀ.ZI.GA   R. D. Biggs, *šà.zi.ga Ancient Mesopotamian Potency Incantations*, TCS 2 (1967)

SBTU   *Spätbabylonische Texte aus Uruk*, Teil I H. Hunger (Berlin, 1976), Teil II E. von Weiher (Berlin, 1983), Teil III E. von Weiher (Berlin, 1988)

SED   *Studia et Documenta ad Iura Orientis Antiqvi Pertinentia* (Leiden)

SFS   V. Scheil, *Une Saison de fouilles à Sippar* (Cairo, 1902)

Sin   G. Perry, *Hymnen und Gebete an Sin*, LSS 2/IV (Leipzig, 1907)

SRT   C. D. Gray, *The Šamaš Religious Texts* (Chicago, 1901)

STC   L. W. King, *The Seven Tablets of Creation* (London, 1902)

StOr   *Studia Orientalia* (Helsinki)

STT   *The Sultantepe Tablets*, I O. R. Gurney and J. J. Finkelstein (London, 1957), II O. R. Gurney and P. Hulin (London, 1964)

Studies Böhl   M. A. Beek *et al.*, eds., *Symbolæ Biblicæ et Mesopotamicæ Francisco Mario Theodoro de Liagre Böhl Dedicatæ* (Leiden, 1973)

Studies Diakonoff   *Societies and Languages of the Ancient Near East, Studies in Honour of I. M. Diakonoff* (Warminster, 1982)

Studies Finet   M. Lebeau, P. Talon, eds., *Reflets des deux Fleuves, Volume de Mélanges offerts à André Finet, Akkadica Supplementum* VI (Leuven, 1989)

Studies Finkelstein   M. deJ. Ellis, ed., *Essays on the Ancient Near East in Memory of Jacob Joel Finkelstein, Memoirs of the Connecticut Academy of Arts and Sciences* 19 (1977)

Studies Garelli   D. Charpin, F. Joannès, eds., *Marchands, Diplomates et Empereurs, Études sur la civilisation mésopotamienne offertes à Paul Garelli* (Paris, 1991)

Studies Kraus   G. Van Driel *et al.*, ed., *Zikir Šumim, Assyriological Studies Presented to F. R. Kraus on the Occasion of his Seventieth Birthday* (Leiden, 1982)

Studies Moran	I. T. Abusch *et al.*, eds., *Lingering Over Words: Studies in Ancient Near Eastern Literature in Honor of William L. Moran* (Atlanta, 1990)
Studies Oppenheim	*From the Workshop of the Chicago Assyrian Dictionary, Studies Presented to A. Leo Oppenheim* (Chicago, 1964)
Studies Pope	J. H. Marks and R. M. Good, eds., *Love & Death in the Ancient Near East, Essays in Honor of Marvin H. Pope* (Guilford, CT, 1987)
Studies Reiner	F. Rochberg-Halton, ed., *Language, Literature, and History, Philological and Historical Studies Presented to Erica Reiner, American Oriental Series 67* (New Haven, 1987)
Studies Sachs	E. Leichty *et al.*, eds., *A Scientific Humanist, Studies in Memory of Abraham Sachs* (Philadelphia, 1988).
Studies Sjöberg	H. Behrens *et al.*, eds., *Dumu e₂-dub-ba-a, Studies in Honor of Åke W. Sjöberg* (Philadelphia, 1989)
Studies Tadmor	M. Cogan, I. Eph'al, eds., *Ah Assyria ... Studies in Assyrian History and Ancient Near Eastern Historiography Presented to Hayim Tadmor, Scripta Hierosolymitana 33* (1991)
Šurpu	E. Reiner, *Šurpu, A Collection of Sumerian and Akkadian Incantations, AfO Beiheft 11* (1958)
TCL	*Textes Cunéiformes du Louvre* (Paris)
TCS	*Texts from Cuneiform Sources* (Locust Valley, NY)
TIM	*Texts from the Iraq Museum* (Baghdad & Leiden)
TUAT	O. Kaiser, ed., *Texte aus der Umwelt des Alten Testaments* (Gütersloh, 1982-)
TuL	E. Ebeling, *Tod und Leben nach den Vorstellungen der Babylonier* (Berlin & Leipzig, 1931)
UET	*Ur Excavations, Texts* (London)
UF	*Ugarit Forschungen* (Neukirchen-Vluyn)
UFBG	W. Mayer, *Untersuchungen zur Formensprache der babylonischen "Gebetsbeschwörungen," Studia Pohl: Series Maior 5* (Rome, 1976)
Ugaritica	C. F. M. Schaeffer, ed., *Ugaritica* (Paris)

VAB	*Vorderasiatische Bibliothek* (Leipzig)
VAS	*Vorderasiatische Schriftdenkmäler* (Berlin)
V R	(T. Pinches, H. Rawlinson), *The Cuneiform Inscriptions of Western Asia* V (London, 1909)
WdM	H. Haussig, ed., *Götter und Mythen im Vorderen Orient* (Stuttgart, 1965)
WGL	private communication, W. G. Lambert
Witchcraft	I. T. Abusch, *Babylonian Witchcraft Literature, Case Studies* (Atlanta, 1987)
WLM	private communication, W. L. Moran
WO	*Welt des Orients* (Göttingen)
WVDOG	*Wissenschaftliche Veröffentlichungen der Deutschen Orient-Gesellschaft* (Leipzig)
WZKM	*Wiener Zeitschrift für die Kunde des Morganlandes* (Vienna)
YNER	*Yale Near Eastern Researches* (New Haven)
YOS	*Yale Oriental Series* (New Haven)
ZA	*Zeitschrift für Assyriologie und Verwandte Gebiete* (Berlin)
ZATW	*Zeitschrift für die alttestamentliche Wissenschaft* (Berlin)
ZDMG	*Zeitschrift der Deutschen Morganländischen Gesellschaft* (Leipzig)

Preface

Before the Muses introduces modern readers to over three hundred works of Akkadian prose and poetry, including some of the world's oldest literature. Akkadian, the language of ancient Assyria and Babylonia, was written and spoken for nearly 2500 years before the Christian era. Despite the longevity and richness of its written tradition, Akkadian is not widely appreciated today. In large part, this is for want of accessible English translations, such as this anthology is intended to provide.

As in any anthology, text selection was made according to various subjective criteria: inherent interest, intelligibility, completeness, and success in telling a story, or revealing motivation, situation, or mood. For reasons of space, the vast Akkadian scholarly literature of divination, astrology, and philology has not been sampled here; these long texts would require a separate anthology. As for the Gilgamesh Epic, the most widely known of Akkadian literary works, it is readily available in English translations.[1]

Before the Muses begins with a general introduction to the study of Akkadian literature, intended for the reader with no knowledge of the subject. The arrangement of texts into chapters is chronological: Chapter I includes texts from the end of the third millennium B.C.; Chapter II texts from the first part of the second millennium B.C.; Chapters III and IV texts from the middle of the second millennium to the Hellenistic period. Whereas texts may be easily assigned to the first two chapters on the basis of their language, those from later periods are often impossible to date precisely. Hence the decision to place a work either in the third or fourth chapters is often arbitrary.

Certain large blocs of material are grouped together, without regard to their date of composition, as follows: the mythological narrative poems in Chapter III; hymns and prayers without obvious criteria for dating them in Chapter III, alphabetically by deity addressed; proverbs and wisdom literature in Chapter III; post-Classical incantations in Chapter IV, arranged by subject matter.

Each selection includes a brief introduction that gives such information as the historical or cultural setting of the text, its state of preservation, a survey or outline of the contents, and interpretive proposals. The translations are provided with numbered footnotes intended for the general reader. These

---

1. M. G. Kovacs, *The Epic of Gilgamesh* (Stanford, 1989); Dalley, *Myths*, 39-153.

explain terms that the reader might not understand, give the translator's opinion as to some particularly difficult words or lines, note selected variants, and draw attention to parallels found in other texts translated in this anthology. An asterisk (*) in the translation refers to "Notes to the Text" given after the translation. These provide the specialist with a reading or restoration that might not be immediately obvious or acknowledge, where appropriate, indebtedness for understanding of a particular word or passage. The rubric "Text" after the translation gives bibliographical data on the original cuneiform manuscripts and will be of interest only to Assyriologists. The rubric "Edition" refers to publications that may include a transliteration, translation, and commentary on the text. "Translation" refers to other translations of the text that have been consulted.

The next rubric, "Literature," includes two types of material: technical publications that have been useful in preparing the translation, and studies that may be of interest to readers who wish to know more about a particular text. More technical publications are cited in short form, while publications likely to be useful to the general reader are cited in full. The same is true for the footnotes to the introductions and to the general introduction. Citation need not imply my concordance with the author's views.

The glossary of proper names includes names of deities, cities, and other terms that occur generally throughout the book. The work concludes with an index of cuneiform texts, intended for the specialist, and a select, annotated bibliography to guide the general reader who wishes to know more about Akkadian literature. While every effort has been made to include publications that appeared during the decade this work has been in preparation, the ever-increasing flood of material makes completeness impossible.

Reading is a personal and culturally conditioned activity. A reader from one culture can appreciate the figurative language of another only to the extent he is willing to go beyond the familiar. The obstacles are especially great for Akkadian because, unlike other extinct literatures such as Classical Greek, Latin, or Biblical Hebrew, that belong to the cultural heritage of an English-speaking reader, Akkadian has no connection with any living cultural tradition.

Much has been written about the difficulties of translation, especially from extinct languages; I have nothing to add to the eloquence of others on this subject.[1] With a few exceptions, Assyriologists tend to regard translation as a

---

1. G. Steiner, *After Babel: Aspects of Language and Translation* (Oxford, 1975).

necessary evil, a means of presenting their solution to the grammatical, lexical, and semantic problems of an ancient text to the scrutiny of their colleagues.[1] My translations tend to be literal at the expense of English style because I am not confident that, at the present state of knowledge, one can write English and translate from Akkadian at the same time.

If this anthology of translations brings readers and Akkadian texts together once more, however tentative, groping, and unfulfilled the relationship may prove, the translator's efforts will have been successful.

---

1. Remarks on translation by Assyriologists include, *en passant*, Bottéro, *Pour Léon Poliakov* (Paris: 1981), 265f.; Civil, JAOS 103 (1983), 50; Kraus, ZA 43 (1936), 79 note 1 and JESHO 12 (1969), 202-204; W. G. Lambert, *Atrahasis*, 6-7; von Soden, ZA 43 (1939), 305 note 1. Böhl, one of the few Assyriologists to attempt poetic translation, remarks ruefully on the dilemma of the translator caught between an angry Muse and the requirements of strict philology, BiOr 6 (1949), 165. For a stimulating but capricious essay on this topic, see A. L. Oppenheim, "Can These Bones Live?" in *Letters from Mesopotamia* (Chicago, 1964), 54-67.

Acknowledgments

The present work owes much to the scholarship and goodwill of others. As consultant to the National Endowment for the Humanities, W. G. Lambert read critically an early draft of Chapters I and II and part of Chapter III. His numerous annotations, corrections, improved readings, and collations have been decisive in the evolution of this work, far more than the individual acknowledgments in the notes may suggest. Even where I have not followed his advice, I have profited from it. In addition, his own editions of Akkadian literary works have set high standards; I have derived many insights, interpretations, and turns of phrase from his work.

W. L. Moran, also as consultant to the National Endowment for the Humanities, read critically an early draft of Chapters I and II and part of Chapter III. His annotations, advice, and corrections, particularly to Anzu, Atrahasis, and the Creation Epic, have been of great value to me in the preparation of this work.

W. Farber read my treatment of the early incantations in Chapters I and II. With his customary generosity, he shared with me many original readings and suggestions on these difficult texts, which I have gratefully incorporated here.

I thank the following scholars for providing me with collations to manuscripts in the British Museum, London; the Böhl Collection, Leiden; and the Staatliche Museen, Berlin: J. Brinkman, I. Finkel, M. J. Geller, W. G. Lambert, P. Machinist, H. Neumann, M. Stol, and C. B. F. Walker. I thank I. Finkel for allowing me to use his unpublished copy of a literary manuscript, and Béatrice André-Salvini for permission to collate tablets in the Louvre.

The first draft of this work was prepared in 1983 with the help of a translation grant from the National Endowment for the Humanities under the auspices of the American Oriental Society. To S. Insler of the American Oriental Society and to S. Mango, then of NEH, go my warmest thanks for their support at a crucial time, and for their patience with my overly optimistic schedules. I am grateful to the Yale University Graduate School for an Enders Grant that made possible collation of tablets in the British Museum.

While this work utilizes the publications of nearly everyone who has studied Akkadian literature, I would here single out three major sources of guidance. First are the dictionary, grammar, and numerous text editions of W. von Soden, without which a project such as this would be unthinkable. Second is the Chicago Assyrian Dictionary, an inexhaustible treasury of information and source of many new readings, suggestions, and collations. Third are the bibliographical publications of R. Borger; these open the whole of Akkadian literature to the inquirer and are more often consulted than acknowledged.

I thank the numerous students with whom I have puzzled over Akkadian texts and hope that they have learned from the experience as much as I have. I thank as well Ulla Kasten, Gabriella Safran, and the staff of the Yale Babylonian Collection for their continuing assistance and editorial advice.

I am grateful to Karen Polinger Foster for her careful readings of the manuscript and for much assistance throughout the years this work has been in preparation.

Finally, my special appreciation goes to Daniel W. Foster and Timothy Foster, of Rittenhouse Book Distributors Inc., King of Prussia, Pennsylvania, for outstanding bibliographical support in this and other enterprises.

Responsibility for faults of any kind is mine alone.

BRF

General Introduction

In Search of
Akkadian Literature

A. The Akkadian Language

1. SEMITIC LANGUAGES

Akkadian is a member of the Semitic family of languages.[1] Modern Semitic languages, including Arabic, Ethiopic, and Hebrew, are spoken from the Atlantic coast of Africa to the foothills of Iran, and are understood as scriptural and literary languages throughout the world.[2] Ancient Semitic languages, including Akkadian and Aramaic, were mostly spoken in the Near East, with Akkadian at home in Mesopotamia, that is, Assyria and Babylonia.

As a group, Semitic languages exhibit a distinctive morphology.[3] This is characterized by a rich inventory of verbal and nominal patterns, which may imply classes of meaning, such as recurring action. The patterns become lexically specific in combination with roots, which are groups of consonants and associated vowels. These are the primary meaning-bearing elements in Semitic languages.[4] Interaction of root and pattern opens a range of possibilities for expression corresponding to synonyms, modifiers, adverbs, and auxiliaries in English. Thus a sentence in Akkadian poetry or prose must usually be substantially reworded and expanded in length when translated into English. The variety and productivity of these roots and patterns means that Semitic languages are remarkably

---

1. S. Moscati, *An Introduction to the Comparative Grammar of the Semitic Languages* (Wiesbaden, 1969); W. von Soden, "Zur Einteilung der semitischen Sprachen," WZKM 56 (1960), 177-191.

2. For a proposed historical background to this situation, see I. M. Diakonoff, "Earliest Semites in Asia. Agriculture and Animal Husbandry According to Linguistic Data (VIIIth - IVth Millennia B.C.)," AOF 8 (1981), 23-74.

3. E. Ullendorff, "What is a Semitic Language?" OrNS 27 (1958), 66-75; in T. Sebeok, ed., *Current Trends in Linguistics* 6 (The Hague, 1970), 269-273.

4. J. H. Greenberg, "The Patterning of Root Morphemes in Semitic," *Word* 6 (1950), 162-181; B. Landsberger, "Die Gestalt der semitischen Wurzel," *Atti XIX Cong. degli Orientalisti* (1935), 450-452; Goetze, JAOS 62 (1942), 1 note 7.

versatile. They have been used in an extraordinary variety of cultural contexts, from the Bronze Age to the present.

2. AKKADIAN VERNACULAR LANGUAGES

The term "Akkadian" subsumes various languages or dialects that need not all have been mutually intelligible.[1] These may be defined regionally and chronologically as follows:

Old Akkadian (2500-2000 B.C.) is attested in administrative documents, letters, inscriptions, personal names, and a few literary texts (Chapter I). Owing perhaps to the paucity of material, no significant differences have been detected between the form of the language in literary texts and that in any of the other sources for this dialect.[2]

With the turn of the second millennium, one distinguishes two main regional dialects of Akkadian: Assyrian, used in northern Mesopotamia, and Babylonian, used in the south. Assyrian is divided into three chronological phases. Old Assyrian (2000-1750 B.C.) is known mostly from letters and legal documents, as well as a few incantations (Chapter I).[3] Middle Assyrian (1500-1000 B.C.) is known mostly from letters, documents, and a few inscriptions and literary texts (Chapter III).[4] Neo-Assyrian (1000-600 B.C.) is known from royal inscriptions, letters, documents, and literary texts (Chapter IV).[5]

Babylonian, like Assyrian, is divided into three main periods. Old Babylonian[6] (1900-1500 B.C.) and Middle Babylonian[7] (1500-1000 B.C.) are known from letters, documents, and inscriptions, as well as a few literary texts (Chapters II, III). Neo-Babylonian (1000-600 B.C.) is known from letters, documents,

---

1. E. Reiner, *A Linguistic Analysis of Akkadian* (The Hague, 1965), 20-22; "Akkadian," in T. Sebeok, ed., *Current Trends in Linguistics* 6 (The Hague, 1970), 274-303; W. von Soden, *Grundriss der akkadischen Grammatik*, AnOr 33 (1952), 1-4; "Akkadisch," in G. Levi della Vida, ed., *Linguistica Semitice: Presente e Futuro, Studi Semitici* 4 (1961), 33-57; H. Hirsch, "Akkadische Grammatik - Erörterungen und Fragen," OrNS 44 (1975), 245-322.

2. I. J. Gelb, *Old Akkadian Writing and Grammar*[2] (Chicago, 1961).

3. K. Hecker, *Grammatik der Kültepe-Texte*, AnOr 44 (Rome, 1968).

4. W. Mayer, *Untersuchungen zur Grammatik des Mittelassyrischen*, AOATS 2 (1971).

5. S. Ylvisaker, *Zur babylonischen und assyrischen Grammatik, eine Untersuchung auf Grund der Briefe aus der Sargonidenzeit*, LSS 5/VI (1912). This obsolete work mixes observations on Neo-Assyrian and Neo-Babylonian, and is based on a small corpus of letters.

6. The most comprehensive description of Old Babylonian grammar is A. Finet, *L'Accadien des lettres de Mari* (Brussels, 1956). This is designed to be a dialect grammar within Old Babylonian rather than a description of Old Babylonian in general.

7. J. Aro, *Studien zur mittelbabylonischen Grammatik*, StOr 20 (1955).

and literary texts (Chapter IV).[1] During this period and later, Aramaic[2] gradually replaced Akkadian as the common spoken language, though as a scholarly medium Akkadian remained vigorous and productive through Hellenistic times.[3] Late Babylonian (600 B.C. to the Christian era) is often considered more a written than a vernacular language.

In this anthology, four periods of Akkadian literature have been distinguished, corresponding to the following periods of the vernacular language: the Archaic period, including Old Akkadian and Old Assyrian (Chapter I); the Classical period, including Old Babylonian (Chapter II); the Mature period, including Middle Babylonian and Middle Assyrian (Chapter III); and the Late period, including Neo-Assyrian, Neo-Babylonian, and Late Babylonian (Chapter IV).

3. AKKADIAN LITERARY LANGUAGES

In the Classical period of Akkadian literature, corresponding to the Old Babylonian period of the language, literary texts were not written in the same dialect as were letters and documents, but in the Hymnic-Epic dialect, which was differentiated from common speech grammatically and lexically. The Babylonians believed that literature required a special idiom, using grammar, vocabulary, and even spelling removed from common usage. The origin of this dialect is unknown. It may in part have been a survival or imitation of Old Akkadian, in part a regional dialect of Babylonian generalized because of its prestige into a literary language, in part poetic neologisms. One may also consider it a fabricated antique style deemed appropriate for higher expression.[4]

---

1. See above, p. 2 note 5, and N. Woodington, "A Grammar of the Neo-Babylonian Letters of the Kuyunjik Collection" (dissertation, Yale University, 1982).

2. For remarks on the history and significance of Aramaic, see R. A. Bowman, "Arameans, Aramaic, and the Bible," JNES 7 (1948), 65-90; F. Rosenthal, "Aramaic Studies during the Past Thirty Years," JNES 37 (1978), 81-91; S. P. Brock, "Three Thousand Years of Aramaic Literature," *Aram* 1 (1989), 11-23. For Akkadian and Aramaic, see S. Kaufman, *The Akkadian Influences on Aramaic*, AS 19 (1974) and p. 698 note 2.

3. Sachs, AOAT 25 (1976), 379-398; M. J. Geller, "More Graeco-Babyloniaca," ZA 73 (1983), 114-120, an Akkadian incantation with a Greek transliteration perhaps dating to the first century A.D. See also p. 698 note 3.

4. W. von Soden, "Der hymnisch-epische Dialekt des Akkadischen," ZA 40 (1932), 163-227; ZA 41 (1933), 90-183, 236; B. Groneberg, "Untersuchungen zum hymnisch-epischen Dialekt der altbabylonischen literarischen Texte," (disssertation, Münster, 1971); "Terminativ- und Lokativadverbialis in altbabylonischen literarischen Texte," AfO 26 (1978/79), 15-29; A. Poebel, *Studies in Akkadian Grammar*, AS 9 (1939), 71-74; Kraus, *Mensch*, 38.

In the Middle and Late periods of Akkadian literature, corresponding to the Middle Babylonian and Assyrian, Neo-Babylonian and Neo-Assyrian periods of the language, another literary dialect called Standard Babylonian was used. Though influenced by the vernacular speech habits of the times and regions in which it was used, Standard Babylonian dialect tended to be consistent in its grammatical and lexical differentiations for more than a thousand years. "Standard" here means use of a traditional poetic style and inventory of linguistic differentiations; it does not imply existence of an inherited corpus of literary texts that had to be imitated by later generations. The Standard dialect had a wider diffusion and longer life than the Hymnic-Epic dialect, and was an accepted medium of scholarly and literary expression throughout Western Asia from the fifteenth through the fourth centuries B.C.[1]

Late Babylonian refers to another variety of Akkadian, in use from about 600 B.C. until the disappearance of Akkadian as a living and scholarly language during the Hellenistic period. In its literary form, this dialect was characterized by a deliberately archaizing style, as seen for example in the prayers in the names of the Neo-Babylonian monarchs (Chapter IV).

All of these literary dialects were Babylonian in origin, and were used in Assyria during the Mature and Late periods of Akkadian literature. Although Assyrian literature could have distinctive stylistic features (see Chapter III, Introduction), no Assyrian literary dialect evolved.

4. AKKADIAN WRITING AND LITERACY

Akkadian was mostly written using a stylus that made wedge-shaped impressions upon soft clay tablets.[2] This form of writing is referred to as "cuneiform," after the Latin word *cuneus* "wedge(-shaped)." It was probably invented by the Sumerians, a non-Semitic people living in southern Mesopotamia, who used it to write their own language, Sumerian, after about 3000 B.C.[3] Cuneiform writing

---

1. B. Groneberg, *Syntax, Morphologie und Stil der jungbabylonischen 'hymnischen' Literatur*, FAOS 14 (Stuttgart, 1987), 1: 1-21.

2. D. O. Edzard, "Keilschrift," RLA 5, 544-568; M. Powell, "Three Problems in the History of Cuneiform Writing: Origin, Direction of Script, Literacy," *Visible Language* 15 (1981), 419-440.

3. For the earliest development of writing, basic studies include, P. Amiet, "Il y a 5000 ans les Élamites inventaient l'écriture," *Archaeologia* 12 (1966), 20-22; A. LeBrun and F. Vallat, "L'Origine de l'écriture à Suse," *Cahiers de la Délégation Archéologique Française en Iran* 8 (1978), 11-59; S. Lieberman, "Of Clay Pebbles, Hollow Clay Balls and Writing: A Sumerian View," AJA

was subsequently adapted for Akkadian and other languages, including Elamite in Iran and Hittite in Anatolia. While writing seems to have evolved for administrative purposes,[1] it soon acquired commemorative and expressive functions. Indeed, non-administrative texts, including incantations and word lists, figure among the earliest cuneiform documents.[2]

Individual characters in this writing system were composed using one to a dozen or more wedge-shaped marks. Even in its earliest known form, the writing system was complicated, using hundreds of characters. Some signs were used for writing words, some for syllables, and most for both.[3] The same sign could be used to write different words or sounds; conversely, different signs could be used to write the same words or sounds. Individual signs could be modified or combined with others to produce units different in significance from their components taken singly. The result was that cuneiform required more effort to master than the alphabetic writing systems that were to develop centuries later. Like other complex writing systems, cuneiform was endowed by its users with a body of esoteric cultural lore all its own.[4]

The extent of literacy in ancient Mesopotamia is unknown. To read letters and documents, knowledge of two to three hundred characters was adequate,[5] but there is no way of knowing what percentage of the population possessed this basic literacy. Most modern scholars believe that few people were literate in any given period of Mesopotamian history. Perhaps businessmen, priests, administrators, rulers, and other members of the elite could read and write, even if, like their modern counterparts, they generally used professional scribes for official matters.

---

84 (1980), 339-358; D. Schmandt-Besserat, "The Earliest Precursor of Writing," *Scientific American* 238 (1978), 50-59; "An Archaic Recording System and the Origin of Writing," SMS 1/2 (1977), 1-32. For later adaptions of writing, see M. W. Green, "The Construction and Implementation of the Cuneiform Writing System," *Visible Language* 15 (1981), 345-372; J. Bottéro, "De l'aide-mémoire à l'écriture," *Actes du colloque international de l'université* Paris VII; *Écritures, systèmes idéographiques et pratiques expressives* (Paris, 1982), 13-35. See also the volume "Early Writing Systems" = *World Archaeology* 17/3 (1986), where more bibliography can be found.

1. H. Nissen *et al.*, eds., *Frühe Schrift und Techniken der Wirtschaftsverwaltung im alten Vorderen Orient* (Berlin, 1990).

2. H. Nissen, "The Archaic Texts from Uruk," *World Archaeology* 17/3 (1986), 317-334; M. Civil and R. D. Biggs, "Notes sur des textes sumériens archaïques," RA 60 (1966), 1-16.

3. See I. J. Gelb, *A Study of Writing* (Chicago, 1963), 60-72.

4. J. Bottéro, "Les Noms de Marduk, l'écriture et la 'logique' en Mésopotamie ancienne," *Studies Finkelstein*, 5-28.

5. G. Buccellati, "Comparative Graphemic Analysis of Old Babylonian and Western Akkadian," UF 11 (1979), 90-99; see in general Edzard, RLA 5, 561-562.

Access to more elaborate Akkadian literary and scholarly writings required a high level of training and skill, involving memorization of lists of characters and their significances, both practical and theoretical,[1] and study of Sumerian. Although Sumerian had probably died out as a living, spoken language during the first half of the second millennium B.C., it continued to be used as a literary and scholarly language until the Hellenistic period.[2] In addition, the literate scholar had to become versed in the techniques and approaches of Mesopotamian scholarship. These had pronounced influence on the character of Akkadian literature, tending to weight it in favor of the learned and esoteric.[3]

There is some evidence for more popular forms of literature, such as love songs, fables, proverbs, and folk tales. Such texts are less common than those requiring a high degree of cultural competence to appreciate (see Chapter III).

B. Rediscovery of Akkadian Literature

1. Loss and Rediscovery

Akkadian has been a dead language for more than two millennia. After its disappearance in the Hellenistic period, Akkadian was forgotten until its rediscovery by European scholars in the nineteenth century.[4] This means that the reader

---

1. A. Cavigneaux, *Die sumerisch-akkadischen Zeichenlisten, Überlieferungsprobleme* (dissertation, Munich, 1976); "Lexikalische Listen," RLA 6, 609-641; I. M. Diakonoff in *Istorija Lingvističeskih učenij: Drevnij Mir* (Moscow, 1980), 17-37. See in general E. Reiner, ed., "La Linguistica del Vicino e Medio Oriente" in G. C. Lepschy, ed., *Storia della Linguistica* I (Bari, 1990).

2. The date of the disappearance of Sumerian as a living language is disputed. For this topic and its related ethnic questions, see J. Bottéro, "Sumériens et 'accadiens' en Mésopotamie ancienne," *Modes de contact et processus de transformation dans les sociétés anciennes, Actes du Colloque de Cortone* (Rome, 1983), 7-21; J. Cooper, "Sumerian and Akkadian in Sumer and Akkad," OrNS 42 (1973), 239-246; W. Heimpel, "Sumerische und akkadische Personennamen in Sumer und Akkad," AfO 25 (1974/7), 171-174; F. R. Kraus, *Sumerer und Akkader: Ein Problem der altmesopotamischen Geschichte*, MKNAW NR 33 No. 8 (1970). The writer has offered evidence that Sumerian was a living, spoken language in Sumer at least through the Sargonic period, OrNS 57 (1982), 297-304.

3. W. von Soden, "Leistung und Grenze sumerischer und babylonischer Wissenschaft," *Die Welt als Geschichte* 2 (1936), 411-464, 509-557; republished in *Libelli* 142, Wissenschaftliche Buchgesellschaft (Darmstadt, 1965), after p. 21; A. L. Oppenheim, "The Position of the Intellectual in Mesopotamian Society," *Daedalus* 104/2 (1975), 37-46; H. Limet, "Le Sécret et les écrits, Aspects de l'esotérisme en Mésopotamie ancienne," in *Les Rites d'initiation, Actes du Colloque de Liège et de Louvain-la-Neuve 20-21 Novembre 1984* (Louvain-la-Neuve, 1986), 243-254.

4. Various aspects of Babylonian culture survived in other languages and cultures, but not in

of Akkadian has no recourse to a living or continuous cultural tradition, but must piece together whatever evidence the tablets provide.

As early as 1692, the word "cuneiform" was coined to apply to the distinctively Mesopotamian style of writing observed on stone reliefs and clay tablets brought back to Europe by travelers to the Near East.[1] But no one could read this writing or knew what language it represented. In 1842 an English adventurer named A. H. Layard[2] began digging at the mound of Nineveh in Assyria, near modern Mosul, Iraq, and was rewarded with innumerable finds, among them thousands of tablets written in cuneiform script. These proved to be the remains of a great library of ancient Mesopotamian literature, dating to the seventh century B.C. Interest in the contents of these documents heightened as scholars throughout Europe worked on deciphering the writing system and the texts it preserved.[3]

Akkadian was soon recognized as a Semitic language, and a flurry of publications appeared clarifying the meaning of signs, words, and whole texts. After 1850, lengthy connected texts in Akkadian could be read. Thus far, decipherment of Akkadian was primarily of interest to a small community of competitive savants. A single event brought Akkadian to the attention of the general public, and galvanized public opinion about the significance of the recovery of Akkadian literature.

This was George Smith's discovery in 1872 of an Akkadian flood story with unmistakable parallels to the Biblical one, although pagan deities and a flood hero other than Noah were its *dramatis personae*.[4] That an ancient tablet from a Mesopotamian mound could yield data directly relevant to European cultural and religious tradition stunned thinkers of the time. The independence and authority of the Bible had to be reevaluated. Indeed, controversy on this subject continues to the present, mostly on the margins of serious scholarship.

their original languages. For discussion of this question, see for example, O. Neugebauer, "The Survival of Babylonian Methods in the Exact Sciences of Antiquity and Middle Ages," PAPS 107 (1963), 528-535; G. Komoróczy, "Ein assyrischer König in der arabischen Überlieferung," AOF 1 (1974), 153-164.

1. For the earliest history of cuneiform studies, see S. Pallis, *The Antiquity of Iraq* (Copenhagen, 1956), 55-65.

2. G. Waterfield, *Layard of Nineveh* (New York, 1968).

3. Among the numerous accounts of the decipherment of cuneiform, the most detailed are Pallis, *Iraq* (note 26), 94-158; C. Fossey, *Manuel d'Assyriologie* I (Paris, 1904); see also Borger, *Persica* 7 (1975/78), 1-216.

4. G. Smith, PSBA, December 3, 1872.

Following Smith's discovery, Akkadian literature was accorded special consideration for the light it seemed to shed on the Hebrew Bible and the accounts of Babylonian and Assyrian history preserved in ancient Greek and Latin authors. Early studies of Akkadian literature were replete with identifications in Akkadian texts of Biblical and Classical personalities and events, most of which are now rightly abandoned and forgotten. Even today, new tablet discoveries elicit hasty Biblical comparisons, many of which have to be abandoned upon reflection.[1] On the other hand, informed comparison and contrasting of Mesopotamian cultural remains with those of the Hebrew Bible continues to flourish and to yield important insights.[2]

2. MAJOR SOURCES

The principal collections of Akkadian literary manuscripts are as follows:

(1) The Nineveh library recovered by Layard and subsequent excavators is the largest source of Akkadian literary texts.[3] Most of its tablets date to the seventh century B.C. and include scholarly editions of texts prepared for the library, assembled by order of the reigning Assyrian king, Assurbanipal. These scholarly editions preserved many texts much older than Assurbanipal's time. Originally the library may have held five to six thousand manuscripts, most of them works of scholarship dealing with magic, divination, lexicography, or ritual. Only a small number were purely literary works, that is, narrative prose and poetry of a mythological, legendary, historical, religious, or epic character.[4] Many manuscript tablets were broken into small fragments

---

1. For an essay on this topic, see J. J. Finkelstein, "Bible and Babel, A Comparative Study of the Hebrew and Babylonian Spirit," *Commentary* 26 (1958), 431-444. The main focus of Biblical analogy has been the Akkadian myths and legends, as well as documents of the Neo-Babylonian period and texts from Nuzi, Mari, Ugarit, and Ebla. See J. van Seters, *Abraham in History and Tradition* (New Haven, 1975), 5ff. and B. Eichler, "Nuzi and the Bible: A Retrospective," *Studies Sachs*, 107-119.

2. W. W. Hallo, *The Book of the People* (Atlanta, 1991), with extensive bibliography; W. G. Lambert, "Old Testament Mythology in Its Ancient Near Eastern Context," *Supplements to Vetus Testamentum* 40, 124-143.

3. C. B. F. Walker, "The Kouyunjik Collection of Cuneiform Texts: Formation, Problems, and Prospects," in F. M. Fales and B. J. Hickey, eds., *Austen Henry Layard tra l'Oriente e Venezia* (Rome, 1987), 183-193.

4. Oppenheim, *Ancient Mesopotamia*, 16f. He estimates the "tablets" (as literary units, not manuscripts) in the library as follows: omens (300), sign and lexical lists (200), bilingual

when the library was destroyed by the conquering Medes in the late seventh century B.C.

(2) Excavations at Assur[1] uncovered several hundred Akkadian literary tablets and fragments, some dating to the latter part of the second millennium B.C., the majority to the first millennium B.C. In many cases, these duplicate or parallel compositions known from Assurbanipal's library. The Assur tablets are not from a single library; many seem to have been the personal property of scholars whose homes lay near the royal palace.

(3) Excavations at Sultantepe (ancient Huzirina) in Turkey have revealed about two hundred tablets and fragments dating to the eighth century B.C. and forming a single library.[2] Like the Assurbanipal and Assur collections, this consists primarily of scholarly works, with some important literary manuscripts as well. Most of these duplicate or parallel works known from Assur and Nineveh.[3]

(4) Numerous literary and scholarly texts have been found at Uruk, mostly dating from the sixth to the fourth centuries B.C. These were found at various places in the ruins, and so do not constitute a single collection. Many of these duplicate texts already known from the collections mentioned above.

devotional texts (100), conjurations (70), "literature" (30-40). Allowing for additional material, he reckons about 1500 tablets, many in multiple copies, for a total number of lines approaching 200,000. Weidner estimated the manuscript count at 5000 items, AfO 16 (1952/3), 198; see also Hallo, IEJ 12 (1962), 22. For the formation of this library, see Weidner, AfO 16 (1952/3), 197-198; S. Parpola, "Assyrian Library Records," JNES 42 (1983), 1-29; Lieberman, *Studies Moran,* 308ff.

1. W. Andrae with B. Hrouda, *Das Wiedererstandene Assur*[2] (Munich, 1977). A brief account of the publication of the tablet finds is found on pp. 315-318. See in detail O. Pedersén, *Archives and Libraries in the City of Assur* (Uppsala, 1985). Additional information is provided by A. K. Grayson, "Antiquities from Assur: A Brief Description of their Fate with Special Reference to the Royal Inscriptions," *Annual Review of the Royal Inscriptions of Mesopotamia Project* 1 (1983), 15-18.

2. O. R. Gurney, J. J. Finkelstein, P. Hulin, STT; O. R. Gurney, "The Assyrian Tablets from Sultantepe," *Proceedings of the British Academy* 41 (1955), 21-41; for identification of the site, E. Gordon, JCS 21 (1967), 85-88.

3. E. Reiner and M. Civil, "Another Volume of Sultantepe Tablets," JNES 26 (1967), 177-211, especially pp. 177-180.

(5) In 1986, discovery of a large library of cuneiform tablets at Sippar was announced. This library, dating to the Persian period, contains many well-preserved literary and scholarly texts, and promises to be as important as the library of Assurbanipal for the reconstruction of Akkadian literature.[1] Few of these manuscripts were available for study at the time of writing (see III.17, IV.16).

(6) In addition, scattered Akkadian literary manuscripts are known from temples and private houses at Babylon, Nimrud, Kish, Borsippa, Ur, Larsa, Tell Harmal (ancient Shaduppum), Mari, Susa, and other sites.[2]

From this it is plain that most of our knowledge of Akkadian literature is owed to collections from only a few sites, and mostly from first millennium manuscripts that may often be late copies or reworkings of earlier texts. Important evidence is missing. The most significant lack is any large group of literary tablets from Babylon, the cultural center of Mesopotamia from the middle of the second millennium B.C. through the Persian period. A further gap is the paucity of manuscripts from the Mature period of Akkadian literature, 1500-1000 B.C., when one assumes that many of the works known from Assur and Nineveh were cast in their form now known.

3. PUBLICATION AND TRANSLATION

The journey from an ancient clay manuscript to a modern translation can be long, often entailing numerous individual contributions over many years. Ancient tablets are usually broken into many pieces that may be dispersed among different collections. Fragments of the same tablet may be published by different people years apart before recognition that the pieces join. Ancient manuscripts themselves were sometimes incomplete, for apparently Mesopotamian students began copying certain major works, then moved on to others, often without finishing the ones they had begun.[3]

1. *Iraq* 49 (1987), 248f.
2. For Babylon, see van Dijk, VAS NF 8 (1987). For Kish, see Genouillac, PRAK. For Ur, see the analysis by D. Charpin, *Le Clergé d'Ur au siècle d'Hammurabi (xixe - xviiie siècles av. J. -C.)* (Geneva & Paris, 1986). For an Akkadian literary text said to have come from Susa, see below, III.23. An early incantation from Susa is treated below, I.3. For Tell Harmal, see T. Baqir, *Sumer* 5 (1949), 35f.; A. Goetze, *Sumer* 14 (1958), 1ff.; M. de J. Ellis, JCS 26 (1974), 133. These literary texts are for the most part difficult to read and understand; they include the legend of Sargon (II.12a).
3. Reiner, *Literatur*, 157.

Publication of cuneiform tablets is a slow and demanding task. Ideally, this begins with preparation of a precise hand-drawn facsimile of the original by someone thoroughly familiar with its contents, who reproduces as accurately as possible the intent of the original scribe and the present state of the tablet. Even within the small domain of Assyriology, few scholars have the ability and opportunity to undertake such epigraphic work, so publications vary widely in their reliability and completeness. Furthermore, scholarly courtesy prevailing in the discipline forbids use of a manuscript in which another scholar has previously expressed interest. The result is that for some texts treated in this anthology there are additional manuscripts or restoring fragments that could not be used here.

Anthologies of Akkadian literature in translation have appeared since the end of the nineteenth century. The reader who compares some of the renderings offered here with those found in earlier anthologies may feel uneasy or even shocked at the discrepancies he will find, especially if he follows one large text through several anthologies. This means that understanding of texts has improved, not that such wide differences in translation are still acceptable today. In general, anthologies more than thirty years old are out of date and cannot be profitably consulted by one unfamiliar with the original texts. With the continual discovery of new material and the publication of dictionaries and other reference works, knowledge of Akkadian is growing faster than knowledge of Greek, Latin, or Biblical Hebrew; thus obsolescence of translations is far more rapid in Assyriology than in comparable disciplines.

The earliest anthologies in western European and American scholarship include E. Schrader's *Die Keilschriften und das alte Testament* (1872), with subsequent editions and English translations appearing in 1883, 1885, 1888, and 1903; G. Smith's *Chaldaean Genesis* (1875); H. Winckler, *Keilinschriftliches Textbuch zum alten Testament* (1892, 1903, 1909); and H. Gressmann, A. Ungnad, and H. Ranke, *Altorientalische Texte und Bilder zum alten Testament* (1905, revised 1906, 1916, 1930; English translation 1911). A scholarly edition of Mesopotamian mythological texts by P. Jensen, *Assyrisch-babylonische Mythen und Epen* (1901), was the basis for many later treatments of these texts. A French anthology was offered by C.-F. Jean, *La Littérature des Babyloniens et des Assyriens* (1924), replaced by R. Labat's chapter in *Les Religions du Proche-Orient asiatique* (1970) and J. Bottéro and S. N. Kramer, *Lorsque les dieux faisaient l'homme* (1988). English translations include E. Wilson, *Babylonian and Assyrian Literature* (1901); R. F. Harper, *Assyrian and Babylonian Literature: Selected Translations* (1904); R. W.

Rogers, *Cuneiform Parallels to the Old Testament* (1912, 1926), and G. Barton's *Archaeology and the Bible* (1916).

The German and English anthologies with Biblical emphasis were superseded in 1950 by a collection of translations from various ancient Near Eastern languages, *Ancient Near Eastern Texts Relating to the Old Testament* (revised 1955, 1969), edited by J. B. Pritchard. This volume made available a large body of reliable translations with comments by leading authorities. The Akkadian literary material was treated by E. A. Speiser, with updating and revision, as well as later additions, by A. K. Grayson and R. D. Biggs. Speiser's felicitous translation of Semitic idiom into good English is enviable, and I have consulted his versions with admiration. A new German anthology, *Texte aus der Umwelt des Alten Testaments*, began publication in fascicles in 1982, with contributions by various scholars.

Two anthologies of Akkadian in translation have appeared in Russian: *Poetry and Prose of the Ancient East* (1973), with contributions by V. Afanasieva, I. M. Diakonoff, and W. Schileiko, and a volume by Afanasieva and Diakonoff entitled *I Reveal unto You a Hidden Word* (1981), a fresh treatment of thirty-nine Akkadian literary texts with introduction and notes. Several collections have appeared in Italian, for example, G. Furlani, *Miti Babilonesi e Assiri* (1956) and G. R. Castellino, *Testi sumerici e accadici* (1977). Anthologies have appeared in Danish, Dutch, Czech, and other languages, but I have not systematically consulted them.

More restricted collections of translations have also appeared. Particularly noteworthy are A. Schott–W. von Soden's translation of Gilgamesh (1934, 1958, 1982); W. G. Lambert's treatment of *Babylonian Wisdom Literature* (1960) and *Atrahasis* (1969); W. von Soden and A. Falkenstein's *Sumerische und Akkadische Hymnen und Gebete* (1953); and M.-J. Seux's *Hymnes et prières aux dieux de Babylonie et d'Assyrie* (1976). I have profited greatly from all these works.

The standards of scholarly acknowledgment among translators are lower than in other areas of humanistic research. Some of the general anthologists cited above have published under their own names translations that are substantially the work of others, even to the precise wording. Since it is often impractical to determine who first established the meaning of a given line, the custom has grown of acknowledging only deviations from certain standard translations or editions, though this means that often those who have done the most work are acknowledged the least. I have cited editions and translations that I have found useful in preparing this work. In general, translations and readings taken from dictionaries are not acknowledged.

From the foregoing account of the recovery, publication, and interpretation of Akkadian literature, one will see that a literary history of Akkadian is at present impossible. Most attempts are little more than an inventory of available texts with interpretive remarks.[1] Some more specialized studies, however, have treated the dynamics, themes, and contexts of Akkadian literature.[2]

C. POETRY AND PROSE

1. LINGUISTIC DIFFERENTIATION

Most of the texts in this anthology can, in modern terms, be broadly defined as literary on the basis of certain linguistic differentiations, both grammatical and lexical, that Mesopotamians considered marks of formal written expression. These linguistic features cannot for the most part be made visible in translation. Not all linguistically differentiated texts are here considered literary, but this criterion has proved helpful in making an initial selection. On the other hand, a few non-literary texts, such as letters, are included for reasons explained with each example.

The texts selected here can be divided into prose and poetry on the basis of how their language is deployed. One does not know if the Greco-Roman distinction between the two, that prose was to be read but poetry was to be sung or performed, is meaningful for Akkadian. There are good reasons to believe that some Akkadian literary works were sung or performed.[3] In any case, poetry has an apparent, if difficult to define, verse structure and meter.

---

1. B. Meissner, *Die babyonisch-assyrische Literatur* (Wildpark-Potsdam, 1927); O. Weber, *Die Literatur der Babylonier und Assyrer, ein Überblick* (Leipzig, 1907).

2. For the general reader, the essays of Lambert, BWL, 1-20; Oppenheim, *Ancient Mesopotamia*, 228-275; Reiner, CAH³ 3/2, 293-321, and W. Röllig, "Literatur," RLA 7, 48-66, are particularly recommended. Much information will be found in H. Hirsch and others, *Kindlers Literaturlexikon*. Another survey is offered by G. Rinaldi, *Storia delle Litterature nell'antica Mesopotamia* (Milan: 1961). Hecker's *Epik* contains a rich collection of data and observations on Akkadian poetics, and is indispensable to any student of that subject, but will prove daunting reading to the non-Assyriologist.

3. II.1 has unusual spellings that possibly suggest some performance technique; II.6 has Sumerian liturgical indications. See further von Soden, ZA 71 (1982), 165.

2. VERSE STRUCTURE

As for verse structure,[1] individual lines of poetry generally consist of complete sentences or thoughts. Each line tends to be divided into halves, sometimes indicated, especially in later manuscripts, by a blank space in the middle of the line. Each half line tends to consist of three or four words, and the line is divided so as to allow patterning of stress units. Lines of poetry often come in pairs (distiches), which can be related to each other by sound, stress patterning, and meaning. Meaning is developed in the half line, whole line, distich, or larger unit by parallelism.[2]

3. PARALLELISM

This refers to repeated formulation of the same message such that subsequent encodings of it restate, expand, complete, contrast, render more specific, complement, or carry further the first message. The following example from Text II.1, lines 1-4, illustrates this:

> Sing of a goddess, most awe-inspiring goddess,
> Let her be praised, mistress of people,
>> greatest of the Igigi-gods.
> Sing of Ishtar, most awe-inspiring goddess,
> Let her be praised, mistress of women,
>> greatest of the Igigi-gods.

The parallelism is developed in each half line, beginning with the goddess being characterized as "most awe-inspiring." In successive lines, the name Ishtar replaces the generic term "goddess," and "people" is rendered more specific by "women," since particular needs of women are referred to later in the poem.

---

1. Hecker, *Epik*, 101-141.

2. Detailed discussion, with examples, by Hecker, *Epik*, 142-151. There is a vast literature on this subject, especially in the field of Biblical Hebrew. Discussion and extensive bibliography will be found in J. Kugel, *The Idea of Biblical Poetry* (New Haven, 1981); M. P. O'Connor, *Hebrew Verse Structure* (Winona Lake, IN, 1980); E. L. Greenstein, "How does Parallelism Mean?" in *A Sense of Text: The Art of Language in the Study of Biblical Literature, Jewish Quarterly Review Supplement* (1982), 41-70; A. Berlin, *The Dynamics of Biblical Parallelism* (Bloomington, IN, 1985), who draws attention to the use of parallelism in prose.

Here is a second example from Text III.14, Tablet I, lines 89-94:

> My slave cursed me openly in the assembly (of gentlefolk),
> My slave girl defamed me before the mob.
> An acquaintance would see me and make himself scarce,
> My family set me down as an outsider.

In this case, totality is conveyed by inclusive contrasts: male/female; upper classes/rabble; acquaintance/family; denunciation by inferiors /avoidance or snubbing by equals. Furthermore, the people concerned are ranked in successive lines from least to most intimate, as if in a series of concentric circles shrinking around the speaker.

Parallelism can be reinforced by internal rhyme of syllables, single consonants, or vowels.[1] Alliteration, with or without parallel formulations, was a favored resource of the Akkadian poet.[2] Chiasm and "word picturing" were occasionally resorted to, both to reinforce parallelism with dynamic contrast and to add a physical dimension to encoded meaning.[3] Expansion and elaboration of these and other devices and figures are characteristic of how Akkadian poetic language was artificed and manipulated.[4]

4. REPETITION

Whereas parallelism usually implies reformulation of a thought in different words, repetition implies restatement *verbatim*, or with only slight changes. Extensive use of repetition in Akkadian narrative shows it to be a favored device of story-telling. Repetition lengthens narrative to allow development of details and injection of subjective elements that might otherwise burden a continuous narrative too heavily. Akkadian repetition has its modern counterpart in passages of description, judgment, exposition, and comment that interrupt the flow of narrative discourse.[5]

---

1. Hecker, *Epik*, 139-140; see also Foster, JAOS 103 (1983), 126-128. Predominance of the vowel sound /u/ in certain poetic passages could be used to convey solemnity, for example, Erra and Ishum (IV.16) Tablet I line 132, which reads: *ultu ullû aguguma ina šubtiya atbuma aškuna abūbu* "Once long ago indeed I grew angry, left my dwelling, and caused the deluge!"

2. Hecker, *Epik*, 131-140. A good instance is *naḫlaptu apluḫti pulḫātu ḫalipma*, III.17 Tablet IV line 57.

3. Hecker, *Epik*, 144; Foster, *Studies Finkelstein*, 80 note 15; JAOS 103 (1983), 127.

4. The fullest discussion is Hecker, *Epik*, with many examples.

5. For further discussion of repetition, see Hecker, *Epik*, 56ff., 154-160.

Repetition was also used to achieve specific narrative effects, especially in dramatic scenes. An example is the siege of Enlil's household by the strikers in Atrahasis (II.39a), Tablet I lines 70ff. The poet emphasizes the major turns of events by continued repetition of sets of lines in stacatto succession, typically with a spoken and a narrated version of the same passage (compare II.39a Tablet II lines 43-46, 57-62, 70-73, 80-84, 93-96; see also below, E.3). When negotiations between the two sides begin, the pace becomes more leisurely, with lengthier segments of text forming the units of repetition.

In another instance, Ishtar's realization of the true nature of Saltu in Agushaya (II.6 Tablet II ii 13ff.) is twice stated without variation, as if to stress that this is an important moment in the story. In a more elaborate example, the lengthy repetitions of the first half of the Creation Epic (III.17) convey the deliberate and ineffectual proceedings of the older generation of gods, as opposed to the rapid, non-repetitive passages in which youthful Marduk takes charge.

5. METER

Though Akkadian poetry has meter, the same metrical pattern is seldom found many lines in succession. There is uncertainty as to whether metrics were based on syllables, ideas or thought units, some type of quantitative stress, or combinations of these possibilities.[1]

6. WORDPLAY

Perhaps the most difficult aspect of Akkadian poetry for a western reader to appreciate is the importance of paranomasia or wordplay, as this can often be a primary message-bearing device. Suspect as a game in western poetic tradition, paranomasia was often used in Akkadian for serious and significant communication. Wordplay could convey an association that extended beyond the purely phonological or semantic, and was considered a useful expository tool. Wordplay could even depend on spelling rather than pronunciation.[2] In most such instances, direct translation is impossible.

---

1. See W. von Soden, "Untersuchungen zur babylonischen Metrik, Teil I," ZA 71 (1982), 161-204, who works with accentuation scansion.

2. See p. 5 n. 4.

7. PROSE STYLE

Akkadian prose is distinguished from poetry by its absence of short, balanced, metrical lines, although prose can have rhythm. Parallelism is less developed than in poetry, and may be absent altogether. Figure and ornament are sparser than in poetry and fall into more standardized patterns.[1] Sentences can be longer and more complicated than in poetry.

One of the most characteristic devices of ornamented prose, well attested in Akkadian commemorative inscriptions, is the use of numerous and often lengthy dependent clauses that lead up to a climactic statement conveyed by the main verb.[2] While in a broad sense this practice mirrors a basic property of Akkadian syntax, whereby the main verb comes at the end of a sentence, it offers great rhetorical possibilities for unfolding of narrative by presenting a sequence of events climaxing in a main one.

8. FORMULAE AND WORD PAIRS

Akkadian shares with many literatures a tendency to use repeatedly certain literary formulae, especially in narrative poetry, as well as fixed epithets for certain gods and cities. Furthermore, when certain words occur in a literary context, certain other words, usually synonymous or parallel in meaning, can be expected to occur also, as with English "kith," which is normally paired with "kin." This aspect of parallel, symmetrical style is well known in other Semitic litera-tures such as Ugaritic and Biblical Hebrew.[3]

Examples of formulae, pairs, and established sequences found in the texts translated here include "dreams, signs, portents" (III.44b line 48); "my (personal) god and goddess" (III.44b line 5, compare the expansion of this pair in III.44c 16-17); and commonly occurring contrasting or complementary pairs

---

1. Simile is particularly common in commemorative prose, though less so in letters. See D. Marcus, "Animal Similes in Assyrian Royal Inscriptions," OrNS 46 (1977), 86-106 and below, p. 18 note 1.

2. For this commemorative style, see for example the royal inscription of Samsuiluna, IRSA, IVC7d, and for later aspects, A. K. Grayson, "Assyrian Royal Inscriptions: Literary Characteristics," OAC 17 (1981), 35-47.

3. See Avishur, UF 7 (1975), 13ff. *Stylistic Studies of Word-Pairs in Biblical and Ancient Semitic Literatures*, AOAT 210 (1984); Craigie, *Semitics* 5 (1979), 48-58; Grave, OrNS 51 (1982), 171 note 51; Berlin, *Parallelism* (p. 14 note 3) 65ff. and "Parallel Word Pairs: A Linguistic Explanation," UF 15 (1983), 7-16.

such as "days" and "years" (III.45b line 18); "night" and "day" (III.14 Tablet I lines 119-120). One of the most difficult word pairs to translate is the pair "heaven and earth." The Akkadian word for "earth" could also mean "netherworld," and in many instances it is impossible to be sure which was meant. In the translations, I have chosen "netherworld" for the second member of this pair, unless I was confident that "earth" was meant. See further III.50.

9. SIMILE AND METAPHOR

Simile and metaphor lie at the heart of figurative language. Similes in Akkadian[1] are easily recognized by use of "like": "He split her in two like a fish for drying" (III.17 Tablet IV line 137); "[The speech] of my lips was senseless, like a moron's" (III.14 Tablet I line 117). Their content and structure can be complex and worthy of independent study: "The citizenry of Babylon, like reeds in a thicket, had no one in charge" (IV.16 Tablet IV line 6); "Like a young man who has shed blood, who wanders alone in a swamp, whom a pursuer has overtaken, and whose heart is pounding ..." (IV.5 line 69); "Alas for Babylon, that I tended like a thriving orchard, but whose fruit I could not taste" (IV.16 Tablet IV line 42).

Metaphors[2] are also a rewarding study. Some are clichés of little literary value ("dead metaphors"). For example, "shepherd" is a cliché for king, as in III.17 Tablet VII line 148. In this case, however, the metaphor is revitalized in the same line by adding "herdsman," not a common metaphor for king. Others are more creative efforts: "The speech on their lips is a fire breaking out" (IV.4c line 6); "May his joyful songs be the prick of a thorn" (IV.4e line 29); "My friend became a malignant demon" (III.14 Tablet I line 85); "A woman is a sharp iron dagger that slashes a man's throat" (IV.18 line vi); "The writhing (armies) will writhe, two women giving birth, bathed in blood" (II.16a episode D). Simile and metaphor are particularly common in proverbs, as for example, "A household without a master is a woman without a husband" (III.16d line 1). Combinations of simile and metaphor are found, such as, "Death, as if on a

---

1. Mayer, UFBG, 367; S. Ponchia, "Analogie, metafore e simultudini nelle iscrizioni reali assire: semantica e ideologia," OrAn 26 (1987), 223-255; G. Buccellati, "Towards a Formal Typology of Akkadian Similes," AOAT 25 (1976), 59-70; see also page 17 note 1.

2. There is no systematic treatment of metaphor in Akkadian. Examples are discussed by W. G. Lambert in M. Minden *et al.*, eds., *Figurative Language in the Ancient Near East* (London, 1987), 25-39.

day of thirsting, slakes itself at the sight of the warrior" (III.1 v line 52'); "He is shod with the netherworld, as with sandals" (III.25 line 134). While both simile and metaphor are visible in translation, their import sometimes escapes the modern reader.

D. AUTHORS AND REDACTORS

1. AUTHORSHIP

For the majority of Akkadian literary works, the names of their authors are unknown.[1] This does not mean that they lacked authors but that the authors' name has been lost. Certain compositions show enough individuality in terms of language, art, content, and unity of purpose to suggest that they were primarily the work of one author, even if changes appeared in the text later.[2] Furthermore, some of these same texts contain passages that imply or insist that this is the case and give the reader to understand that the circumstances of authorship are crucial to evaluating the text in question. Such passages give clues for understanding Mesopotamian notions of authorship.[3]

The most important texts that refer to authorship are Erra and Ishum (IV.18), Tablet V lines 39-51; the Creation Epic (III.17), Tablet VII lines 145-162; Atrahasis (II.39a), Tablet III col viii lines 9-16; and Agushaya (II.6), col viii lines 22-26. Various other passages allude to authorship, referring either to divine approval of the text or the skill used to compose it. These include the hymn to Ishtar of the Classical period (II.1) stanza xiv, and two compositions ascribed to Assurbanipal (IV.4c, f). Some texts name the author either in the course of the narrative (III.14) or in acrostics (III.25, 45e; IV.17).

These passages suggest the existence of a Mesopotamian literary tradition wherein the author described the genesis, divine approval, composition, authorship, and traditing of his text.

---

1. See Hallo, IEJ 12 (1962), 13-16; Hecker, ArOr 45 (1977), 249-251; W. G. Lambert, "Ancestors, Authors, and Canonicity," JCS 11 (1957), 1-14, 112; "A Catalogue of Texts and Authors," JCS 16 (1962), 59-77; Rochberg-Halton, JCS 36 (1984), 135-137; Geller, BSOAS 53 (1990), 209-213.

2. This obviously subjective judgment is occasionally hinted at by others, e.g., Landsberger, JNES 20 (1961), 154 note 2, who refers to the "odd and confused diction of the poet" (of the Creation Epic), and Reiner, JNES 17 (1958), 41, who refers to the "awkwardness of the scribe-poet" (of Erra and Ishum).

3. B. Foster, "On Authorship in Akkadian Literature," *Annuario del Istituto Orientale di Napoli* 51/1 (1990), 17-32.

Genesis. All examples imply or state divine inspiration for the text in more or less ambiguous terms. In the case of Erra and Ishum, the text was "revealed"; in the Creation Epic, the text was proclaimed during a ceremony, and was "explained" by the author. In the Agushaya poem and the hymn to Ishtar, the author's participation was indistinguishable from that of the god of wisdom himself, or at least the god "caused it to be." In both Atrahasis and Agushaya, ambiguity as to whether a god (first person) or the poet (third person) is speaking may be intentional.

Approval. In the cases of Erra and Ishum, the Creation Epic, and the Ishtar hymn, a god heard and approved the texts. In Erra and Ishum, the author insists that he did not alter the text from its original inspired form. In the Creation Epic, the poet is concerned that future generations will understand the text correctly. In Atrahasis the text is made into a command of Enlil by the artful Ea. In the Vision of the Assyrian Prince (IV.5), the scribe assures the reader that he remembered the prince's discourse accurately.

Composition is called "composing," "discoursing," "writing down," "being made." With the exception of Erra and Ishum, the precise manner of composition and the respective roles of inspirer and inspired are left unclarified.

Authority for the text is granted in the form of divine approval. Such authority is referred to in Erra and Ishum, the Creation Epic, and implied in Atrahasis. The text can have life-giving (Ishtar hymn) or apotropaic powers (Erra and Ishum). Its peculiar status as a "sign" of a god is found in Agushaya and Erra and Ishum. In the Creation Epic, the text is glorified as a key for humankind to understand Marduk's reorganized universe. Erra and Ishum and the Creation Epic are acts of mercy by a god, in the case of the former by a protagonist (Ishum), in the case of the latter by Marduk himself.

Traditing and dissemination of texts are referred to in Erra and Ishum, the Creation Epic, Agushaya, and Atrahasis both synchronically and diachronically: "all people" are supposed to hear them, as well as succeeding generations.

Mesopotamian poetic tradition had therefore a notion of individual inspiration and authorship, which could be used as a literary device. Whereas modern literary tradition stresses the individual's importance as a matrix of creative impulse, Mesopotamian artistic tradition tended to stress the outside source of the inspiration that lent each work its uniqueness. Indeed, authors themselves stressed their works' inspired uniqueness by dwelling on the time or occasion of their composition. In some instances (Creation Epic, Erra and Ishum), the text was seen as an event of cosmic importance; the text became the climax of the events it narrated. In addition, the divine authority of the composition made it a source of blessing, security, well-being, and knowledge.

2. CREATIVITY

Already in the Archaic period, one can point to efforts at creativity and originality.[1] Whereas early Sargonic commemorative inscriptions are highly stylized and convey only simple statements of royal military victories, together with assertions of divine favor, the inscriptions of Naram-Sin have long, complicated sentences in a florid rhetorical style (see Introduction to I.1).

The Classical period of Akkadian literature seems to have been a time of singular creativity, as though a vigorous literature was in formation. Atrahasis, for instance, is a poetic masterpiece. It sets forth the history and life cycle of mankind in relation to divine history, using traditional materials in a highly original manner. The nocturnal prayer of a lonely and reflective diviner (see To Gods of the Night, II.34) contains unusual passages whose lyricism was imitated in later prayers.

Perhaps most characteristic of the creativity of the Mature period of Akkadian literature (Chapter III) were large, composite compositions, which, despite their varied source material, emerged with a unity of theme and intent that made the whole greater than the sum of the parts. Examples include Ishtar Queen of Heaven (III.26) and the Shamash Hymn (III.32). The creativity of this period was marked by great experimentation with language. This included use of rare, dialectal, and scholarly words, elaborate and intricate metaphors, refinements of parallelism, and academic Sumerian loanwords. The Creation Epic (III.17) and the Poem of the Righteous Sufferer (III.14) are good examples of this type of composition.

Experimentation with established forms produced long texts in various combinations of hymnic, confessional, narrative, scholarly, and didactic styles (for example, Kurigalzu and the Ishtar Temple [III.10], the Marduk Prophecy [III.13], Ishtar Queen of Heaven [III.26]). The frequent combination of incantation and prayer is another example of this mature, derivative style (below, D.3). Specific political conditions occasioned a flowering of literature centering on Marduk, the Babylonian national god; see Nebuchadnezzar I and His Times (III.12d, e); the Epic of Creation (III.17), and the Marduk Prophecy (III.13).

---

1. See K. Hecker, "Tradition und Originalität in der altorientalischen Literatur," ArOr 45 (1977), 245-258; Hallo, IEJ 12 (1962), 18-21.

Creativity in the Mature period was not restricted to specific genres. Among the scores of Akkadian prayers, for example, is one that seems consciously to have taken all the clichés of the genre and molded them into an original, moving composition (Against Marduk's Anger [III.44a]).

Other instances of creativity are found in the works of beginners or brilliant youngsters whose technical competence may not be equal to their literary ambitions. These works may present flaws of diction, usage, and perhaps a certain untidiness (III.43b, 46b). Yet along with such blemishes, one finds a high level of feeling and originality, coupled with either the self-absorbed, amazed sensuality of newly discovered emotions or the pedantic rhetoric of the excited novice.[1] The Faithful Lover (II.9) may be a text of this type. Perhaps such puerile eloquence is satirized in At the Cleaners (II.7).

Humor opens infinite ranges to an original and satirical thinker.[2] The spoof incantation against a bleating goat (II.32) develops well-established magical themes and language in a ridiculous way, and was surely the product of some earthy mind wearied of magical lore. At the Cleaners (II.7) and the Gilgamesh Letter (IV.20) are likewise humorous texts. When humor shades off into satire, an elusive genre, a text such as the Dialogue of Pessimism (IV.18) results.

One must mention as well the brilliance of an individual who produces a text that is at once recognized as a masterpiece and becomes a classic. Such a person was Kabti-ilani-Marduk, author of Erra and Ishum, one of the most original and experimental Akkadian narrative texts (IV.16). This poet produced a narrative piece that, apart from its theological and spiritual profundity, can be read as a textbook of the possibilities available in Akkadian poetic tradition.

The long life span of Akkadian literary tradition did not rob it of feeling and originality. To the Late period date various royal prayers, some strongly felt and couched in sonorous prose. These combine intricacy of syntax with fine balancing of parallel rhetorical units (see IV.6-9).

3. INTERTEXTUALITY

Defining relationships between texts is a crucial problem in the study of any literature, including Akkadian. The texts in this anthology illustrate various types of intertextual relationships.

1. Held, JCS 15 (1961), 2.
2. B. Foster, "Humor and Cuneiform Literature," JANES 6 (1974), 69-85.

Two simple cases occur with Archaic period texts. The Old Akkadian letter I.8 contains phraseology, perhaps humorously intended, found in exorcisms more than a millennium later.[1] Likewise, the magical phraseology of the Old Akkadian love charm (see I.7) is echoed in the Old Babylonian love charm II.33b. It is no coincidence that both these examples involve magical language, for magical phraseology shows remarkable durability in Mesopotamian tradition.

The Classical period provides the oldest version of various compositions known from later periods in different forms. Some are magical spells, for example II.14a, of which several later versions are known. Others are narrative, for example Atrahasis (II.39), a version of which was incorporated into the Late Assyrian Gilgamesh epic. The Mature period versions of Anzu (III.21), Etana (III.22), and the Cuthaean Legend of Naram-Sin (III.7b) were built on Classical versions of the same narratives.

Intertextual relationships between Classical and later hymnography and prayers are less amply attested, though the Literary Prayer to Marduk (III.29) is thought to have a Classical forerunner. Were the extant corpus of Classical hymnography and prayers greater, more connections might be found; the few well-preserved Classical hymns do not have extant descendants.

An unusual type of intertextuality occurs in certain composite literary texts of the Mature period (see III.26-30). These combine several independent compositions, perhaps with new material added. The results are long, complicated texts that are not sustained by a narrative thread. Intertextual tradition also combines narrative with hymnography. This is known in the Classical period (Agushaya Poem II.6) and in the Mature period (Poem of the Righteous Sufferer III.14).

Another distinctively Mesopotamian form of intertextuality is imbedding of monumental and archival texts, often unaltered, in literary works.[2] Kudur-Nahhunte and His Times (III.11), for example, includes what may be actual royal letters within its poetic narrative. Other literary texts were composed outright in a pseudo-monumental style (for example, the Cuthaean Legend of Naram-Sin [III.7b]). Conversely, genuine monumental texts can make literary allusions, such as the inscription of the Chaldaean king Merodach-Baladan which quotes Erra and Ishum.[3]

1. Thureau-Dangin, RA 23 (1926), 23ff.
2. Hallo, AS 20 (1975), 195-196.
3. J. Brinkman, *Prelude to Empire* (Philadelphia, 1984), 49 note 230.

Borrowings between scholarly literature and belles lettres provide further examples of intertextual relationships. Belles lettres may borrow from omen series, either in specific content or general style.[1] Omens are referred to in apotropaic prayers (see, e.g., III.50a, c, d, f); the style and diction of omen apodoses can be documented in texts with prophetic or apocalyptic passages.[2] Dualities such as "favorable/unfavorable," basic to divination, appear as tropes in Akkadian literature in such forms as "good times/bad times," or "successful/unsuccessful kings."[3] Such dualities may acquire lives of their own independent of genuine historical traditions worked into literary compositions. To take another example, descriptions of suffering in laments, confessional texts, and medical incantations may draw on medical diagnostic treatises (see the Poem of the Righteous Sufferer [III.14]).

Some of the works translated here, especially incantations, devotional texts, and hymns, are excerpted from larger contexts such as rituals. It is not certain in most cases whether the incantation or hymn was composed for the ritual, or whether it existed independently and was inserted in the ritual later. Occasionally the same text can appear in different ritual contexts and with different applications. Ritual or apotropaic significance was sometimes assigned to certain narrative or literary texts after they were written or in the texts themselves (IV.16).[4]

The Creation Epic (III.17), which probably dates to the Mature period, is a particularly apt subject for intertextual study, for it draws on a variety of Akkadian and Sumerian traditions. These include narrative poems about the god Ninurta,[5] whose deeds are assigned to Marduk in the Creation Epic. The episode of the creation of mankind is drawn from Atrahasis or a similar text; lists of divine names form a basis for the episode of the fifty names of Marduk.[6]

---

1. J. J. Finkelstein, "Mesopotamian Historiography," PAPS 107/6 (1963), 461-472; A. K. Grayson, "Divination and the Babylonian Chronicles," CRRAI 14 (1965), 69-76; P. Michalowski, "Adapa and the Ritual Process," RO 41 (1980), 77-82.

2. A. K. Grayson, "Akkadian Prophecies," JCS 18 (1964), 7-30; W. W. Hallo, "Akkadian Apocalypses," IEJ 16 (1966), 231-242; R. D. Biggs, "More Akkadian Prophecies," Iraq 29 (1969), 117-132; W. G. Lambert, *The Background of Jewish Apocalyptic* (London, 1978).

3. H. G. Güterbock, "Die Historische Tradition und ihre literarische Gestaltung bei Babyloniern und Hethitern bis 1200," ZA 42 (1934), 1-91; 44 (1938), 45-149; Oppenheim, OrNS 5 (1936), 203-208.

4. E. Reiner, "Plague Amulets and House Blessings," JNES 19 (1960), 148-155; W. G. Lambert, "Myth and Ritual as Conceived by the Babylonians," JSS 13 (1968), 104-112.

5. W. G. Lambert, "Ninurta Mythology in the Babylonian Epic of Creation," CRRAI 32 (1985), 55-60.

6. W. G. Lambert, "Götterlisten," RLA 3, 473-479.

In its turn, the Creation Epic exercised considerable influence on later Akkadian literature. Late devotional compositions allude to or quote the epic (III.44b, 44e, 44f, 46a; IV.4e). One cannot demonstrate that in every case the epic was the source and the other text the borrowing, but there are usually circumstantial reasons for taking this to be the case. For example, Against Illness (III.44b) alludes to the epic half a dozen times in the space of ten lines. The allusions are highlighted by being concentrated in a single passage, with no further allusions to be found in the text thereafter. They refer to Marduk's power as slayer of Tiamat and his role as a vegetation and fertility deity. Prince of the Gods (III.44f) contains numerous allusions, direct and indirect, to the epic, and indeed, so far as preserved, reads like a meditation on the larger text.

Nergal the Warrior (III.46a) is a less clear case. Line 4, for example, alludes to the Six Hundred, who are said to be organized by Marduk in the epic (Tablet VI line 44); the "pitiless deluge-weapon" also recalls the epic (Tablet IV line 49); and the gods take to "secret places," as do the defeated gods in the epic. Since these are stock expressions, one could argue that they show common use of well-known material rather than borrowing. However, Sublime Nergal (III.46c) quotes the epic (Tablet I line 94) in a context making so little sense that one may conclude that this was lifted as a memorable line from the epic and misapplied in the Nergal hymn.

A lengthy hymn to Marduk offered in the name of Assurbanipal (IV.4e) is filled with allusions to the epic. The author of the hymn seems to have recognized that the author of the epic assigned to Marduk various triumphs hitherto ascribed to Ninurta, but went further than his source, assigning to Marduk even the killing of the Anzu-bird, a feat generally ascribed to Ninurta or Ningirsu (see III.22).

Peculiar intertextual problems are presented by the Compound Acrostic Prayer to Nabu (III.45d). This poem makes Nabu, Marduk's son, into the Marduk of the gods, just as in the epic Marduk was made into the Enlil of the gods. An explication of certain names of Nabu follows, using some of the same names assigned to Marduk in the epic. Marduk is finally equated with Qingu, the enemy he defeated in the epic. This shows that borrowed material could be used with intentions quite different from those of the source.

E. READING AKKADIAN LITERATURE

Akkadian literature offers a special challenge to the critical reader. Modern literary criticism seldom confronts fragmentary texts in incompletely understood languages, or compositions with centuries-long, complicated histories of textual development. Many of the usual topics for critical study in modern literature are not useful avenues of approach to Akkadian. Approaching these texts from a European tradition, the reader may find them in comparison lifeless, stereotyped, and without apparent form, color, or internal development. The following remarks are intended to orient the reader who wishes to approach these texts from a theoretical or critical standpoint, but who finds himself groping for landmarks on apparently featureless terrain.

1. TIME

Time, a major preoccupation of European literary tradition, is seldom a central issue in Akkadian literature. The Babylonian concept of time was linear rather than cyclical.[1] Time was concrete and calendrical, the sum total of days, months, and years.[2] Normal time and normal human lifespans were thought to have existed only since the Flood.[3] Prior to the Flood, the synchronism of biological and calendrical time was different, in that human beings were thought to have lived impossibly long lives.[4]

Akkadian literature offers in many instances a subjective evaluation of periods of time.[5] The past was considered especially fit for inquiry, because mankind

1. W. G. Lambert, "History and the Gods: A Review Article," OrNS 39 (1970), 170-177, esp. 175. For a general discussion of Mesopotamian concepts of time, see I. S. Klotchkoff, *Duhovnaja Kul'tura Vavilonii: Čelovek, Sud'ba, Vremja* (Moscow, 1983), and his "Vosprijatie vremeni v drevnej Mesopotamii," *Narody Azii i Afriki* (1980), 91-102; M. Liverani, "La valutazione qualitiva del tempo," in S. Moscati, ed., *L'Alba della Civiltà* (Torino, 1976), 3: 462-476.

2. Klotchkoff, *Kul'tura* (note 1), 15-21; see also W. W. Hallo, "Dating the Mesopotamian Past," *Bulletin of the Society for Mesopotamian Studies* (Toronto, 1982), 7-18; "The Nabonassar Era and other Epochs in Mesopotamian Chronology and Chronography," in *Studies Sachs*, 175-190; E. Otto, "Zeitvorstellungen und Zeitrechnung im alten Orient," *Studium Generale* 19 (1966), 743-751. This deals mostly with Egyptian matters, but offers some interesting proposals.

3. A. Malamat, "Longevity: Biblical Concepts and Some Ancient Near Eastern Parallels," CRRAI 28 (1981), 215-224; J. Klein, "The 'Bane of Humanity': A Lifespan of One Hundred Twenty Years," *Acta Sumerologica* 12 (1990), 57-70.

4. Jacobsen, JBL 100 (1981), 520-521.

5. For mythological time, see Klotchkoff, *Kul'tura* (above, note 1), 25; Otto, "Zeitvorstellungen" (note 2), 750. For the past as the usual setting of Akkadian literature, at least in the Classical period, see Kraus, *Mensch*, 133-134.

and human institutions were viewed as products of specific past events. Akkadian literature generally portrays the past as better than the present. Accordingly, the best hope for man was to re-create the past.

Intimately connected with this judgment of the past is the notion of destiny, one's past experienced as one's future. Indeed, destiny in Mesopotamian thought and literature tends to take the place of time as found in European literature.[1] Destiny was either an impersonal necessity, such as death, or it was personified as a Fate, seen as willful and capricious, hence something that could be manipulated or avoided. Especially in narrative poetry, destiny is a frequently developed theme, while the passage of time, as understood in modern literature, is used primarily for rhetorical devices.[2]

Examples of such devices include long spans of time correlated with great distance or unusually prolonged suffering, as in the Poem of the Righteous Sufferer (III.14), and short spans of time used to imply heroic achievement, as in III.6 line 23.[3] Characters do not age in Akkadian literature, though they can grow wiser, and their only acknowledgment of biological time is to contrast the rashness of youth with the measured reason of maturity (see An Old Man's Prayer, III.45b).[4]

The Mesopotamian scheme of solar and lunar time affects Akkadian literature. Certain events are peculiar to the night (dreams, visions, watching); others are characteristic of the morning (revelations, action, understanding). Night may have been viewed as the beginning of the day rather than the end of it, although this point is disputed. The Mesopotamian day and night were divided into watches composed of "double hours," three of the night and three of the day.[5]

Babylonian thought correlated time and space, in that units of time also served as units of distance, distance being expressed in terms of the time elapsed

---

1. This is the central thesis of Klotchkoff's *Kul'tura* (note 1), which I have adopted here in its essentials.

2. Compare G. Furlani, "Sul concetto del destino nella religione babilonese e asira," *Aegyptus* 9 (1928), 205-239; S. Langdon, "The Semitic Goddess of Fate, Fortuna-Tyche," JRAS 1930, 21-29; H. Zimmern, "Šimat, šim, tyche, manat," *Islamica* 2 (1926/7), 574-584; F. Rochberg-Halton, "Fate and Divination in Mesopotamia," CRRAI 28 (1981), 363-371.

3. H. Tadmor, "History and Ideology in the Assyrian Royal Inscriptions," OAC 17 (1981), 14ff.; *Iraq* 35 (1973), 143.

4. Klotchkoff, *Kul'tura* (p. 26 note 1), 28-30.

5. S. Smith, "Babylonian Time Reckoning," *Iraq* 31 (1969), 74-81; R. K. Englund, "Administrative Timekeeping in Ancient Mesopotamia," JESHO 31 (1988), 121-185.

in making normal progress from one point to another.[1]

Some authors were concerned with the relationship between narrative and event, and so experimented with narrative time. In an interesting passage in Erra and Ishum, event and discourse coexist while Erra narrates in the present certain deeds he is doing (see IV.16).

2. PLACE

The spatial background of Akkadian literature tends to be bare, almost schematic. For example, frequent reference is made to upper and lower worlds, but no further information is given as to precisely what is meant by these terms. In this anthology, the distinction is generally rendered "heaven and netherworld," though others render "heaven and earth." It is often not clear whether earth or netherworld is intended (see III.50). In the realm of human affairs, major divisions of scene are between city (civilization) and steppe (wilderness). With a few exceptions,[2] Akkadian literature presupposes an urban environment. The major Mesopotamian cities were viewed by their denizens as the source and center of civilization. Nippur, for example, according to an ancient metaphor, was the meeting place or linkage between the upper and lower worlds.[3]

Of all the aspects of the Mesopotamian city — political, economic, commercial, and cultic — literature tends to emphasize the city as cult center. Within cities, the scene of action is often vague. The street or market was generally a locus of hostility and threats, the congregating place of the rabble, and, in a persistent motif, the scene of prostitution or rape (see the incantations IV.32a, 39a, 44d; Atrahasis [II.39d] Tablet I line 275).[4] The house was the vulnerable center of family life, sometimes the setting for heights of human happiness or depths of human misery. Threats, attacks, or intrusions were most keenly felt at home and were anxiously warded off (see the diviner's prayers II.35; the Poem of the Righteous Sufferer [III.14] Tablet I line 62, Tablet II line 96; the Counsels of Wisdom [III.16a] 66, 72; the Wisdom of Ugarit [III.16b] 12; the Shamash Hymn [III.32] 135ff.).

1. W. al-Jadir, "The Concept of Time and Space in Ancient Mesopotamia," *Sumer* 31 (1975), 327-343.

2. E. Reiner, "City Bread and Bread Baked in Ashes," *Languages and Areas: Studies Presented to George V. Bobrinskoy* (Chicago, 1967), 116-120.

3. For the early background of this concept, see W. G. Lambert, BSOAS 1976, 430; Jacobsen, JNES 5 (1946), 136-137.

4. See also Foster, *Studies Pope,* 23, 26f.

Outside the relative security of the city, the wilderness was generally seen as the hostile and dangerous abode of wild beasts and lawless men, full of real and potential threats. One traversed it in fear and risk (see To Gods of the Night [II.34a]; the Instructions of Shube-Awilim [III.16b] 12; the Shamash Hymn [III.32] 135ff.). Yet the Sacrificial Gazelle (III.51d) is remarkable for its lyrical portrayal of wild animal life as symbolic of ritual purity. Texts such as the Shamash hymn (III.32) use city and wilderness as inclusive contrasts to encompass the whole world.

Mesopotamians believed that the world was flat, disk-shaped, and surrounded by mountains and salt water beyond the edge of the land. Above the sky and below the earth was fresh water.[1] The sun's daily journey took him across the sky and then at night through "innermost heaven."[2] The physical organization of heaven and the netherworld seems to have been visualized in terrestrial terms, though the details vary from source to source. Thus the divine abodes of heaven and hell had gates, courtyards, throne rooms, dining halls, bathing chambers, and so forth. The human denizens of the netherworld lived in darkness and squalor.[3]

The world was divided into a center and four world regions, corresponding to the four cardinal points.[4] The mountains that bordered these regions were portrayed as seats of hostility and bestial human existence, as in the Hunter (III.6). Forests too were threatening in Akkadian literature (see Sargon, King of Battle [II.12a]).

The rivers that crossed the world regions were alternately life-giving and destructive, depending on their flood crest. There is no serene reliance on a river as unfailing provider, as is usually the case with the Nile in Egyptian literature.[5]

Like the rivers, the weather was capriciously destructive or beneficial. Winds and storms are frequently terrifying in Akkadian literature, though gentle breezes could be of good omen (To Adad [III.33]; The Poem of the Righteous Sufferer [III.14] Tablet I line 6).

1. See W. G. Lambert, "The Cosmology of Sumer and Babylon," in C. Blacker and M. Loewe, eds., *Ancient Cosmologies* (London, 1975), 42–65.

2. W. Heimpel, "The Sun at Night and the Doors of Heaven in Babylonian Texts," JCS 38 (1986), 127–151.

3. W. G. Lambert, "The Theology of Death," CRRAI 26 (1979), 53–66; esp. 59–60.

4. J.-J. Glassner, "La division quinaire de la terre," *Akkadica* 40 (1984), 17–34; M. Liverani, *Prestige and Interest, International Relations in the Near East ca. 1600–1100 B.C.* (Padua, 1990), 33–65.

5. Jacobsen in H. Frankfort, ed., *Before Philosophy* (Baltimore, 1966), 137–148.

3. SPEECH, ACTION, CLAMOR, SILENCE

The relationship between speech and action in Akkadian narrative offers a fruitful field of inquiry to the critical reader, as it is one aspect of Akkadian literary endeavor that comes through in translation. Akkadian narrative poetry, like other ancient narrative traditions, allots more space to direct speech than to narrative, with emphasis on action rather than description. Direct speech is used to bring about or to explain action, to predict it, or to advance it. Differently from Greek drama, direct speech is seldom used to narrate action beyond the point of view of the audience, Erra and Ishum (IV.16) being a notable exception.

Direct speech is sometimes repeated as narrative. A simple instance is provided by Atrahasis (II.39a) Tablet I, lines 87-90.

> "Nusku, bar your gate,
> "Get your weapons and stand before me."
> Nusku barred his gate,
> Got his weapons and stood before Enlil.

Seen in the context of Atrahasis (II.39a) Tablet I 43-46, 57-62, 70-77, 80-84, 93-96, the pairing of speech and action in this poem serves many purposes, especially emphasis, as the narrative slows and suspense builds up.

In some examples of Akkadian narrative, speech and action are developed as major motifs. Contrasting use of the two is found in the Creation Epic (III.17). In the first part of the poem, emphasis is on repetition of speeches within speeches, suggesting the sluggishness of the older gods. As soon as Marduk receives his charge and is off to battle, action is narrated with scarcely a repetition until the end of the poem. After the climactic battle, Marduk ushers in a new era in which his speech is effective and creative. He commands the reordering of the universe, step by step, and the gods proclaim Marduk's explanatory names in the final two tablets of the work, nearly all of which are direct speech.

Direct speech is normally indicated in Akkadian literature by the expression *pâ(m) epēšu(m)*, literally, "to make a mouth" (in this anthology "make ready to speak"). This may refer to formation of words or thoughts prior to giving them voice, though the expression is often translated by others "open the mouth" (to speak).[1] When this formulaic expression is absent in narrative, the omission is striking, and suggests the speaker's abruptness or excitement.[2]

As for clamor or noise, Akkadian poetic tradition seems ambivalent as to whether it was good or bad.[3] In Agushaya (II.6), clamor is portrayed in negative terms as a kind of violence that the gods wish to suppress. Noise is antithetic to speech, as in Agushaya (II.6) Tablet I vi lines 17ff., where Enki, in order to speak, has to use four different verbs to invoke silence. One may compare the Creation Epic (III.17) Tablet I line 36, where the noise of Tiamat drowns out speech. There, as in Agushaya, noise and clamor suggest violence. On the other hand, in Atrahasis (II.39), clamor, characteristic of developing mankind, seems vital and productive, rather than evil or destructive. It is the bustle and vigorous clamor of the human race that Enlil seeks to destroy.

Silence in Akkadian poetry is eerie and frightening. Helpless and terrified, the gods fall silent in the Creation Epic (III.17) Tablet II line 6, and in the Anzu poem (III.22), when the gods find no recourse against the monstrous bird. Akkadian is rich in words for silence, awe, and fear.[4]

4. VISUAL ASPECTS

One of the most perplexing motifs of Akkadian literature for modern readers is its emphasis on specific visual qualities, variously translated "brilliance," "fearsomeness," "awesomeness," "radiance."[5] Akkadian tradition, apparently borrowing from Sumerian, considers brilliance both visual and tactile. When a person sees something divine, he shrinks back, shades his eyes, and feels physical discomfort caused by intense illumination. Correlation between this sensation and reli-

---

1. See Oppenheim, OrNS 16 (1947), 221 note 2. For a tabulation of Akkadian literary formulae for speaking, see F. Sonnek, "Die Einführung der direkten Rede in der epischen Texten," ZA 46 (1940), 225-235; Hecker, *Epik*, 174ff. A literary analysis has been undertaken by M. Vogelzang, "Patterns Introducing Direct Speech in Akkadian Literary Texts," JCS 42 (1990), 50-70.

2. Foster, *Studies Pope*, 24 note 20. For direct quotations without verbs of speaking, sometimes referred to as "virtual speech," see Gordis, *Vetus Testamentum* 31 (1981), 410-427 (Biblical evidence) and Hecker, *Epik*, 45ff.

3. For widely divergent opinions on the significance of "noise" in Mesopotamian literature, see Oppenheim, OrNS 16 (1947), 210 note 3; Pettinato, OrNS 39 (1968), 184-200, with earlier literature cited p. 173, and Michalowski, *Studies Moran*, 385-388.

4. For silence in Mesopotamian tradition, see E. Reiner, "Dead of Night," AS 16 (1965), 247-251.

5. E. Cassin, *La Splendeur divine, Introduction à l'étude de la mentalité mésopotamienne* (Paris, 1968); A. L. Oppenheim, "Akkadian *pul(u)h(t)u* and *melammu*," JAOS 63 (1943), 31-34.

gious awe means that in Mesopotamian religious expression the numinous is endowed with blinding brilliance, associated not with heat but rather with a gemlike metallic sheen. Akkadian religious poetry is richly laden with this visual imagery, little of which emerges clearly in translation.

In addition to the numinous and physical aspects of brightness, the concept was intimately connected with notions of purity — religious, ritual, or natural.[1] Purity and brightness were interlocking concepts, and the translator has usually to choose one or the other, depending upon which range of associations he wants to suggest. Brightness of visage or complexion was a sign of happiness, good health, and hence well-being and divine favor. Anger or fear was seen as pallor or darkness, both being opposites of brightness (Atrahasis [II.39a] Tablet I line 93; the Descent of Ishtar [III.18] 29; Nergal and Ereshkigal [III.19] iii 22').[2]

5. KNOWLEDGE

Some Akkadian literature, especially didactic pieces such as the Cuthaean Legend (III.7b), was concerned with human knowledge, how it was acquired and what was worth knowing.[3] According to some literary works, knowledge was gained more through experience and suffering than through study or mastery of an art. Indeed, experts are often portrayed in laments as baffled and helpless (Poem of the Righteous Sufferer [III.26] Tablet I line 52, Tablet II lines 6-7). They are sometimes satirized in humorous texts (The Jester [IV.21], Why Do You Curse Me? [IV.25]). Even in their own devotional expressions, scholars profess, *pro forma* at least, the uncertainties besetting many researchers (For Success in Divination [III.36a], For Help in Haruspicy [III.52a]), and the texts offer no example of a learned man resolving a dilemma. At the same time, Akkadian literature, programmatically perhaps, accorded value only to knowledge that was written down and could thus transcend the self and its narrow circles of kin and colleagues to reach across space and time to the seeker after wisdom.[4]

Literary texts show no agreement on what comprised useful knowledge. Wisdom literature stresses the social, economic, and moral value of being trustworthy, industrious, conciliatory, and self-abnegating (Words of the Wise

1. M.-J. Seux, "Pureté et impureté. Mésopotamie," *Supplément au Dictionnaire de la Bible* 9, 450-459.
2. See also G. Dossin, *La paleur d'Enkidou* (Louvain, 1931).
3. Foster, *Studies Pope*, 42.
4. Foster, *Studies Pope*, 22; see further p. 42 note 1.

[III.16], *passim*). Narrative poetry portrays superior knowledge either as direct apprehension of something remote from common experience, or as insight into questions like how and why the human race and human society came into being, whence human authority, why humans are different from gods (Atrahasis [II.39]). Some texts, such as the Old Babylonian Gilgamesh Epic, suggest that wisdom is acceptance of one's lot. They recommend security, prosperity, good name, and family over adventure. Others suggest that adventure leads to knowledge, and a hero is one whose adventure expands human knowledge regardless of the cost to himself.[1]

Adapa (III.20) and Atrahasis (II.39) imply the existence of god-given knowledge beyond the knowledge attainable through human experience. Such knowledge was communicated directly by a great god, typically the god of wisdom, and its possession gave power to achieve immortality, or the next best: understanding of divine intents. Through judicious use of such knowledge, Atrahasis succeeds; for failing to grasp the full implications of his knowledge, Adapa fails. Knowledge apprehended through divine intervention is the subject of the Creation Epic (III.17) and Erra and Ishum (IV.16). Incantations routinely attribute their wording and procedure not to the ministrant but to gods of wisdom or exorcism, thereby claiming to be a kind of divine knowledge.

6. DIVINE IMAGES

Many Akkadian literary works invoke or refer to Mesopotamian cult images, that is, statues of deities. The reader will need to understand the centrality of these images in Mesopotamian religion.[2]

Throughout the period covered by this anthology, the cult image was the most important symbol of the urban or national community. The major gods were, so far as known, represented in anthropomorphic or zoomorphic composite form. The statues dwelt in their temple homes and were fed, entertained, and presented with petitions. They held court, went in procession, decided lawsuits, and exercised on the divine plane all the functions one associates with temporal human rulers.[3]

---

1. See below, Chapter II, Introduction, and p. 63 note 1.
2. A. Spycket, *Les Statues de culte dans les textes mesopotamiens des origines à la Ire dynastie de Babylone* (Paris, 1968); W. W. Hallo, "Cult Statue and Divine Image: A Preliminary Study," in W. W. Hallo *et al.*, eds., *Scripture in Context* II (Winona Lake, IN, 1983), 1–17; J. Renger and U. Siedl, "Kultbild," RLA 6, 307–319.
3. Oppenheim, *Ancient Mesopotamia*, 183–198.

Each major god had but one cult statue and was considered localized in it. Despoilation of an image or its removal from a sanctuary was more than a symbolic disaster; it signified loss of the central cultic focus of the community and opened a way for attack. The importance and centrality of this belief in Akkadian literature is apparent in Agum-kakrime and the Return of Marduk (III.9), Kudur-Nahhunte and His Times (III.11), and Nebuchadnezzar I and His Times (III.12). Some of these are concerned with the plundering of the Marduk sanctuary in Babylon by the Elamites during the eleventh century B.C., told from the point of view of the Babylonians (Nebuchadnezzar and Marduk, III.12e) or Marduk himself (Marduk Prophecy, III.13).

Erra and Ishum (IV.16) describes refurbishment of Marduk's statue. This was a time of crisis, as the author saw it, when the community was vulnerable to threats of all kinds, because Marduk had temporarily ceased carrying out his divine responsibilities. The Love Lyrics of Nanay and Muati (II.10) celebrate installation of an image; Agum-kakrime and the Return of Marduk (III.9) commemorates refurbishment of the statue of Marduk and his consort. Letters were addressed to cult images and were left before them for perusal (see Kussulu to the Moon God [II.36]).

7. DEMONIC BEINGS

Few cultures are so rich in demonic lore as the Mesopotamian. Demons pervaded Mesopotamian religious and artistic expression and formed a counterpart world both to the human race and to the gods.[1] Unlike gods or human beings, demons were classed generically and did not bear personal names. Each class of demon, such as Lamashtu (I.6, II.26, IV.37), had its own arenas of activity. These included disease, domestic misfortune, death, anything affecting the individual (rather than the community as a whole), regardless of age, sex, or place in society. Demons could be male or female, and often came in battalions, each setting upon a separate part of the body or a particular activity, need, or power. The way was opened for them by witchcraft or by a person's own god forsaking him and failing to act. Demons were visualized as creeping through apertures

---

1. See V. Haas, *Magie und Mythen in Babylonien* (Gifkendorf, 1986); "Die Dämonisierung des Fremden und des Feindes im alten Orient," RO 41 (1980), 37-49. In general see A. Farkas *et al.*, eds., *Monsters and Demons in the Ancient and Medieval Worlds, Papers Presented in Honor of Edith Porada* (Mainz, 1987).

into a person's house to snatch, smash, or murder (Against a Poltergeist(?), II.27). They would lie in wait in alleys or desolate spots and seize, twist, numb, or weigh their victim down in order to incapacitate his bodily or mental powers (see the incantations II.15, 26, 27; IV.32c, 37).

Physicians and exorcists tried to ease suffering by using incantations, medical treatments, and sympathetic magic. Examples of the incantations used to such ends are found in II.14-30 and IV 30-44. Their accompanying magical and medical lore belong to the realm of Mesopotamian expository scholarship.[1] The best of the incantations portray movingly the anxiety felt by the threatened person. Numerous texts seek to prevent and redress the actions of hostile demonic powers, some clearly defined, others less specific. These texts offer insights into Mesopotamian psychology.[2]

Since illness was thought to be caused by demons, it was considered symptomatic of divine disfavor. Demons peopled the Mesopotamian world in great number, and their baleful presence is felt throughout Akkadian literature.

8. PERSONAL DEITY AND GOOD FORTUNE

For most people, the great deities of the Mesopotamian urban sanctuaries seemed as remote as kings. Hence, the individual looked to a personal deity, usually referred to simply by the generic terms "god" or "goddess," who was responsible for the person's success and well-being.[3] Disaster awaited a person forsaken by his individual divine protector, for he was liable to any harm that divine, human, or demonic will could inflict upon him. Religious and penitential literature are rife with address to the personal deity, in terms sometimes pathetic, sometimes reproving, seeking to placate or shame the god or goddess into alleviating some misfortune (see To a Personal God [III.49], compare II.38). The suppliant promises in return for help to praise the deity's name and to glorify his greatness.

1. For discussion of Mesopotamian medical practice, see E. K. Ritter, "Magical-Expert (=*āšipu*) and Physician (= *asû*): Notes on Two Complementary Professions in Babylonian Medicine," AS 16 (1965), 299-321; R. D. Biggs, "Medicine in Ancient Mesopotamia," *History of Science* 8 (1969), 94-105. See also Chapter IV, Introduction and p. 693 note 8.

2. J. V. Kinnier-Wilson, "An Introduction to Babylonian Psychiatry," AS 16 (1965), 289-298 and p. 694 note 5. For observations on pharmacology, see H. Limet, "Croyances, superstitions et débuts de la science en Mésopotamie ancienne," *Oikumene* 5 (1986), 67-90.

3. T. Jacobsen, *The Treasures of Darkness* (New Haven, 1976), 155-160.

A more intimate benefactor was a person's genius. This bestowed the qualities now referred to as talents or gifts.[1] The genius's protective counterpart was the guardian spirit, now referred to as instinct and self-preservation, which enhanced a person's capacity to avoid harm.[2] Outward signs of genius and guardianship included prosperity, high office, economic success, a large family, respect in public thoroughfares, government buildings, or assembly places of the worthy, a circle of admiring friends and colleagues, robust health, radiance of countenance (see above, E.4), and authoritative presence. Loss of such attributes implied either insufficient wardenship by one's divine protector or some external cause: black magic, a sin of omission or commission, or divine disfavor (compare the Poem of the Righteous Sufferer [III.14] Tablet I lines 43ff., 79ff.).

9. DIVINATION

Divination was the central intellectual discipline and most highly esteemed branch of Mesopotamian academic achievement during the period covered by this anthology.[3] Its status in Mesopotamian thinking was comparable to that of scholarship or science in our own. Divination comprised a body of knowledge, as well as techniques for gaining access to this knowledge, applying it, and increasing it.

Many divinatory techniques were based on systematic observation and record-ing of the environment. The method involved first listing observed phenomena, then pairing what was observed with prognoses in the form "If x (is observed), y (is the consequence or implication)." Observations were made of astronomical and atmospherical phenomena, as well as everyday events in the home or street, such as the scuffling of a gecko or the location of a potsherd in a ditch. They could also include characteristics and behavior of people or animals. Data gained by observation were expanded by analogic and associative

---

1. Oppenheim, *Ancient Mesopotamia*, 198-206.

2. W. von Soden, "Die Schutzgenien Lamassu und Schedu in der babylonisch-assyrischen Literatur," BaM 3 (1964), 148-156; B. Groneberg, "Eine Einführungsszene in der altbaby-lonischen Literatur: Bemerkungen zum persönlichen Gott," CRRAI 32 (1985), 93-108, with extensive bibliography; R. Albertz, *Persönliche Frommigkeit und offizielle Religion: religionsinterner Pluralismus in Israel und Babylon* (Stuttgart, 1978).

3. The best survey of Mesopotamian divination is J. Bottéro, "Symptomes, signes, écritures," in J. P. Vernant, ed., *Divination et rationalité* (Paris, 1974), 70-197, with extensive bibliography and examples; see also Oppenheim, *Ancient Mesopotamia*, 206-227. For further discussion, see Chapter IV, Introduction.

reasoning. To the diviner, all the world was his purview, and divination the one universal science.[1]

Other divinatory techniques were based on eliciting phenomena useful to the diviner. Most often referred to in the texts translated here is haruspicy, divination by examining the liver and inner organs of sacrificed animals, especially sheep and goats.[2] Owing to the expense involved, sacrificial divination was for the wealthy, and the prognoses often pertained to affairs of state or matters of interest to the highly placed. Other forms of divination, such as pouring oil upon water to observe its configurations, occasionally occur in literature (see Agum-kakrime and the Return of Marduk [III.9]).[3] The prayers offered by sacrificial diviners while they waited for the gods to implant the message in the exta became a distinct genre (see the diviners' prayers II.34, III.36, 52). Literary texts sometimes show consultation with diviners as recourse for the perplexed or as a meritorious proceeding (Cuthaean Legend of Naram-Sin [III.7b iii]).

F. FORMATION OF AKKADIAN LITERATURE

1. CATEGORIES

Five broad categories of Akkadian literature are recognized here: celebratory, didactic, narrative, effective, and expressive. These do not necessarily correspond to ancient classifications, about which little is known. Some texts may belong to more than one category.

Celebratory refers to two main groups of texts in Akkadian, one dealing with the human sphere, the other with the divine. Texts referring to human affairs can be commemorative in origin and form. Many of these perpetuate the memory of a royal personage and some specific deed he did. Such texts tend to favor prose over poetry. They give the royal name, titulary, information pertaining to a king's parentage or ancestry, or, if that information is not given, why he is the legitimate king; an account of some deed, either in the first or third person; and a concluding statement, often with reference to some monument with which the text is associated. Texts of this type are the principal source of historical information about ancient Mesopotamia. Their primarily commemorative

---

1. Bottéro, "Symptomes" (p. 36 note 3), 99ff.
2. Bottéro, "Symptomes" (p. 36 note 3), 99ff.
3. G. Pettinato, *Die Ölwahrsagung bei den Babyloniern*, Studi Semitici 21-22 (Rome, 1966).

purpose would prevent many modern readers from considering them literature. In addition, many of these are available elsewhere in English translation. For these reasons, they are not included in this anthology (though see Naram-Sin at Armanum [I.1]).[1]

Texts that exemplify interaction between commemorative and literary composition include the legends of Naram-Sin (II.13, III.7b). These legends may have their origin in historical tradition and inscriptions, but soon acquired legendary and exemplary qualities. For example, during his lifetime Naram-Sin was personification of the great warrior king, but after his death he was regarded in Akkadian literature as personification of the hapless sovereign caught up in cosmic events too large for his ken or control.[2]

Other such texts deal with the fall of the Kassite dynasty and the period of Elamite domination in Babylonia, towards the end of the second millennium B.C. (III.11). Still others may refer to a period of Babylonian national revival under Nebuchadnezzar I (see Nebuchadnezzar I and His Times [III.12]; the Marduk Prophecy [III.13] and the Creation Epic [III.17] may belong here). The selections translated here include an actual commemorative text (Nebuchadnezzar in Elam [III.12c]) and literary pieces dealing with the same theme (The War with Elam [III.12b]).

Some apparently commemorative texts are in fact pseudonymous or fictional autobiographies. These are narratives in which a famous ruler from the remote past reflects upon certain critical events of his life. Texts of this type often end with blessings, admonitions, or pseudo-prophecies for the benefit of future generations.[3] Examples of this genre include the Cuthaean Legend of Naram-Sin (III.7b), the Shulgi Prophecy (III.8), the Marduk Prophecy (III.13), and the Birth Legend of Sargon of Akkad (IV.19).

Whereas hymns in honor of kings are a genre well known in Sumerian,[4] they are not so well attested in Akkadian, although many hymns and prayers contain blessings or a petition on behalf of the reigning sovereign (Hymn to Ishtar [II.1], Acrostic Hymn to Marduk [IV.4d]).

---

1. Grayson, ARI; Sollberger-Kupper, IRSA; J. Cooper, *Sumerian and Akkadian Royal Inscriptions* (New Haven, 1986).

2. J. -J. Glassner, *La Chute d'Agadé, l'événement et sa mémoire*, Berliner Beiträge zum Vorderen Orient 5 (Berlin, 1986).

3. H. Galter, "Probleme historischen-lehrhaften Dichtung in Mesopotamien," CRRAI 32 (1985), 71-79; T. Longman, *Fictional Akkadian Royal Autobiographies* (Winona Lake, IN, 1991).

4. C. Wilcke, "Hymnen B," RLA 4, 539-544.

Texts dealing with divine deeds include hymns that glorify signs of the divine nature and, in some instances, refer to specific deeds. Though these latter passages often possess narrative character (for example, Agushaya [II.6]), hymnic texts typically begin and end with an invocation of praise, while strictly narrative texts tend to begin with an expression of time or an invocation of the subject.[1]

For the most part, the texts called here hymns or prayers[2] share formal features of both modern genres. Hymns tend to be lyrical expression of praise, together with pleas for general well-being. Prayers tend to be petitions for personal well-being. Hymns of the Classical period favor self-contained lines, in which typically the god being praised is the subject. By contrast, hymns of the Mature and Late periods often contain long series of dependent clauses defining the god's attributes.

Great or literary hymns and prayers (see III.25-31) can be two hundred or more lines in length. These appear in some instances to use material from different sources and periods (Ishtar Queen of Heaven [III.26], Shamash Hymn [III.32]).

Syncretic hymns form a distinctive subgroup (Syncretic Hymn to Marduk [III.44g]). These are hymns that consider separate deities as aspects of the same deity. Some hymns explain divine names in hermeneutic fashion (The Names of Nabu [III.45d], To Marduk Against Illness [III.44b]). Others honor temples (In Praise of Ezida [IV.14]) and cities (In Praise of Babylon [IV.15], In Praise of Arbela [IV.6]). Characteristic of the Mature and Late periods are hymns using acrostics in which the first and occasionally the last signs of lines convey an independent message (Compound Acrostic Prayer to Nabu [III.45c], Acrostic Hymn to Marduk [IV.4d], Acrostic Hymn to Nabu [IV.8k]).

Prayers[3] have a greater variety of forms and uses than hymns. Prayers may be part of commemorative inscriptions (for example, IV.7-11). Personal names of all periods are often prayers in miniature, such as "Shamash-Save-Me" or "Let-Me-Behold-the-Ebabbar-Temple."[4] Unlike hymns, prayers need not be metrical, though they may be drafted in a differentiated prose style similar to that of poetry. Prayers in everyday language could be written out as petitions presum-

---

1. C. Wilcke, "Die Anfänge der akkadischen Epen," ZA 67 (1977), 153-216.
2. W. von Soden, "Hymnen A," RLA 4, 544-548; J. Klíma, "À propos des éléments profanes dans les hymnes et prières mésopotamiens," ArOr 48 (1980), 240-248.
3. W. von Soden, "Gebet II," RLA 3, 160-170.
4. J. J. Stamm, *Die Akkadische Namengebung*, MVAeG 44 (1934), 170, 85.

ably placed in front of a divine statue or read to the god by a statue of the suppliant (II.36-38).[1]

Prayers of diviners are well known from the Classical period on (II.34-35; III.36a, 41b, 47c, 52a etc.). These ask for a clear oracle, for assistance in interpreting it, and occasionally for professional competence and public respect. Some reflect on the silence of night, as the diviner waits to perform his extispicy (To Gods of the Night [II.34, III.45]); others celebrate in sentimental terms the birth and upbringing of the sacrificial beast (The Sacrificial Gazelle [III.51d], The Sacrificial Lamb [III.51e]). Some prayers occur in rituals as appropriate for a specific point in the proceedings (see To Girra [III.40], To Nusku [III.48]). Others were organized into collections dealing with similar themes (To a Personal God [III.49]).

Laments and complaints are less well known in Akkadian than in Sumerian. Indeed, some Akkadian laments may be based on Sumerian prototypes (Lament for a City [II.8]; see also Lament for Tammuz [IV.26]). Most Akkadian examples deal with suffering of an individual, sometimes in narrative form as if a priest is speaking on behalf of the sufferer (Dialogue of a Man and His God [II.5]). In others, the sufferer speaks for himself (Literary Prayer to Ishtar [III.28]).

A distinct genre known as *šu-illa*, "lifting of the hand," is called the incantation prayer because it unites prayerful appeal with the direct efficacy of a spell (III.33, 34, 35, 36b, 37b, c etc.).[2] These compositions are addressed to a wide range of deities and often enumerate specific evils that the text is supposed to ward off, including the evil portended by such diverse events as a solar eclipse and an infestation of red ants.

Incantation prayers typically open with an invocation and praise of the divinity, often with a long series of attributive clauses. There follows a self-presentation of the speaker, wherein he may state his name and parentage. He then turns to his lament, describing first his unhappiness in general terms, then detailing his specific distress, such as estrangement from his personal deity, his fear of evil omens, social rejection, or victimization by witchcraft. He then acknowledges sins known or not, intentional or not, and pleads for forgiveness. In many such prayers, the petitioner refers to expiatory actions: seeking out the deity, making

---

1. W. W. Hallo, "Individual Prayer in Sumerian: The Continuity of a Tradition," JAOS 88 (1968), 71-89; "Letters, Prayers and Letter-Prayers," *Proceedings of the Seventh World Congress of Jewish Studies, Studies in the Bible and the Ancient Near East* (Jerusalem, 1981), 17-27.

2. Mayer, UFBG; E. Dalglish, *Psalm Fifty-one* (Leiden, 1962), 41ff.

or offering a present, or following some magical or medical procedure. The speaker then turns to his prayer, asking for mercy, blessing, intercession, reconciliation, clearance of sin, rehabilitation, averting of the consequences of evil omens, good fortune, long life, and health. Incantation prayers conclude with a promise to praise the god in return for his actions; in some cases other people and gods are said to join in the thanks.

Royal prayers are best known from the second half of the first millennium, from both Babylonia and Assyria. From Assyria come, for example, the short building prayers commissioned by Sargon II for his new capital city at Dur-Sharrukin (IV.2a). Prayers in the name of Assurbanipal may reflect his scholarly interests in that they allude to literary works such as the Creation Epic or are written in a pompous, pedantic style (see IV.4). From Babylonia come prayers in the name of Nabopolassar, Nebuchadnezzar II, Neriglissar, and Nabonidus (IV.6-9) that typically formed part of commemorative building inscriptions. These usually request durability and well-being for the structure concerned, and long life and reign for the ruler and his progeny. Other royal prayers are scattered through the vast corpus of inscriptions. Particular mention should be made of the earlier Assyrian royal prayers, for example those of Assurnasirpal to Ishtar of Nineveh and Arbela, and the bilingual psalm of Tukulti-Ninurta I (III.4, 3).

Other prayers on behalf of the king, particularly of the incantation prayer type, were incorporated into ritual series such as "The House of the Ritual Bath" (Bit Rimki) and "The House of the Ritual Enclosure" (Bit Meseri). A group of these incantation prayers to Shamash, the sun god, is best known (III.50h-l).

While some readers may find perusal of Mesopotamian hymns and prayers tedious, there is in fact no better way to approach Mesopotamian spiritual expression.[1] Each text chosen here offers some individual point of interest or is representative of a type. The wealth of material has made selection difficult. For additional hymns and prayers in translation, the interested reader is referred to more specialized anthologies.[2]

Didactic literature seeks to convey a lesson or significant experience in order to admonish the reader and give him an opportunity to benefit from what he

---

1. T. Abusch, "The Form and Meaning of a Babylonian Prayer to Marduk," JAOS 103 (1983), 3.
2. Seux, *Hymnes*; von Soden, SAHG.

reads.[1] The teaching can be in the form of narrative, exhortation, or proverbial sayings (Words of the Wise [III.16]). Didactic texts usually focus on practical teaching and advice for a successful life, and were directed to all classes of society. Some offer advice to kings or rulers (Cuthaean Legend of Naram-Sin [III.7b iii], Advice to a Prince [IV.12]), others to common folk (Counsels of Wisdom [III.16a]). Didactic literature is concerned with human affairs, either in the interests of social advancement or of gaining divine favor through proper conduct. Didactic compositions tend to be short and simple, without experimentation in form or medium. Typical cachets include a sage old man offering advice to a youth (Wisdom of Hatti [III.16c]), or the survivor of a trying experience relating what befell him for the admonition of others (Cuthaean Legend of Naram-Sin [III.7b iii]).

An important subgroup of Akkadian didactic literary texts deals with the question of divine justice.[2] Why do apparently righteous people suffer while obviously evil ones prosper? Perhaps the most elaborate example of this type is the Poem of the Righteous Sufferer (III.14). This suggests that divine justice metes out both reward and punishment, and that rescue from seemingly undeserved suffering is itself a sign of divine power. The Theodicy (IV.17) treats the question in dialogue form; a sufferer and a friend debate with courtesy and passion, the friend taking the position that the sufferer must have sinned somehow, for none can know what the gods require. The Dialogue Between a Man and His God (II.5) may belong to this genre insofar as it deals with suffering and redemption, though there is no indication that the sufferer presumes himself sinless (see also A Sufferer's Salvation [III.15]). Of course the problem is raised in other texts such as prayers (Who Has Not Sinned? [III.49d]).

There are also proverbs, sayings, and short compositions of moral and rhetorical character that seek to entertain and educate at the same time. Most of these are Sumerian, often with an Akkadian translation. Native Akkadian proverbs

1. For discussion of "wisdom" in ancient Mesopotamian tradition, see W. G. Lambert, BWL, 1ff.; E. A. Speiser, *Oriental and Biblical Studies* (Phildelphia, 1967), 305ff.; Gordon, BiOr 17 (1960), 123; J. J. A. van Dijk, *La Sagesse suméro-accadienne, recherches sur les genres littéraires des textes sapientaux avec choix de textes* (Leiden, 1953); R. F. G. Sweet, "The Sage in Akkadian Literature: A Philological Study," in J. G. Gammie and L. G. Perdue, eds., *The Sage in Israel and the Ancient Near East* (Winona Lake, IN, 1990), 45-65; C. Wilcke, "Göttliche und menschliche Weisheit im alten Orient," in A. Assmann, ed., *Weisheit* (Munich, 1991), 259-270.

2. W. von Soden, "Das Fragen nach der Gerechtigkeit Gottes im alten Orient," MDOG 96 (1965), 41-59; J. Bottéro, "Le Problème du Mal en Mésopotamie ancienne, *Prologue à une étude du 'Juste Souffrant,'*" *Recherches et Documents du Centre Thomas More* no. 15 (1977), 1-43.

are less well known today because they were not studied and copied in Babylonian and Assyrian schools, as were Sumerian proverbs. Most of the examples of native Akkadian proverbs given here are taken from letters (III.16e).

Narrative literature tells a story about gods or people. Unlike didactic texts, narratives can be of considerable length, owing especially to repetition and parallelism. Narrative tends to favor poetry over prose. The purpose of the narrative is sometimes stated, sometimes left to the reader to ascertain. If commemorative texts stress remembrance and didactic texts practical action, narrative texts are intended to deepen knowledge (see above, Section 5).

Narrative texts about gods include divine exaltation (Creation Epic [III.17]) and mythological stories such as the Descent of Ishtar to the Netherworld (III.18) and Nergal and Ereshkigal (III.19). Others tell of heroic divine deeds (Anzu [III.22], The Serpent [III.23], The Lion-Serpent [III.24]). Others show interactions of gods with people (Adapa Story [III.20], Etana [III.21]). Some mythological tales were transmitted as portions of rituals or incantations (Adapa Story [III.20], Against a Mote in the Eye [II.16], Against Toothache [IV.43]). While stories of the gods are now normally read as mythological texts, it is not always clear whether they were primarily mythological in purpose or whether they were simply narrative strategies for authors in a culture that assigned little literary value to the present and empirically recognizable.

Narrative texts focused on human affairs include the legends of ancient kings (II.12, 13; III.7) and the Assyrian royal epics (III.1). The latter are lengthy, often bombastic celebrations of the valor and justice of the Assyrian kings in warfare, of which the best preserved (III.1) deals with a war against Babylonia. The closest Babylonian equivalent is the group of texts centering around Nebuchadnezzar I (III.12). These are both commemorative and justificatory in character.

In *effective literature*, the text itself brings about a consequence. This is different from a petition or prayer, in which the goal of the petition is stated and a particular deity importuned to act on behalf of the petitioner. In contrast, effective literature comprises magical language (incantations or spells) that in and of their own power might cause the desired result.[1] The difference between a prayer and an incantation is often difficult to see, as many texts, especially of the Mature and Late periods, show characteristics of both.[2]

---

1. Reiner in *Le Monde du Sorcier* (Paris, 1966), 69-98.
2. See Mayer, UFBG, 7-13. For Sumerian there is a discussion by M. Cohen, "The Incantation Hymn: Incantation or Hymn?" JAOS 95 (1975), 592-611.

Incantations often apostrophize evil, conjuring it with threats and blandishments, or sometimes ask a deity's help against it, in the manner of a prayer. Incantations sometimes include what has been called the "cosmological motif,"[1] wherein a brief narrative traces the cosmic origins of the evil to be exorcized (Against Toothache [IV.43], Against a Mote in the Eye [II.16, IV.33d]). This may be a means of fixing upon the evil. Incantations are often allusive and associative, such that the thought patterns may not be readily apparent to the modern reader. Sound may be as important as sense; indeed, some incantations include "abracadabra" passages that may either be gibberish or, in some cases, survivals of unidentified languages (see Against Redness [IV.40]).[2] The figurative language used in incantations tends to be of the simple patterns familiar today from nursery rhymes and children's songs.[3] They include, nevertheless, some of the finest poetic passages in Akkadian, for incantations were less pervaded by clichés than other genres.

Expressive literature refers to texts that seek to convey a mood or scene. Whereas narrative works tell a story, expressive texts elicit a reaction to or judgment upon a story, situation, or formal proposition. Expressive texts can be read as humorous, satirical, sad, cynical, or loving, however the reader gauges the author's intent. In this group, emotional reaction, rather than knowledge or commemoration, seems the purpose. Examples include At the Cleaners (II.7), The Faithful Lover (II.9), The Gilgamesh Letter (IV.20), Why Do You Curse Me? (IV.24), The Dog's Boast (IV.25), The Dialogue of Pessimism (IV.18).

2. AKKADIAN AND SUMERIAN

In the development of Akkadian literature, the interdependence of Sumerian and Akkadian was recognized and esteemed by the Mesopotamians themselves. Some Akkadian literary works are imitations, reworkings, or translations of Sumerian prototypes (Lament for a City [II.8], Gilgamesh Tablet XII).[4] Others are based on Sumerian literary forms (Agushaya [II.6]). A rich bilingual tradi-

1. J. J. A. van Dijk, "Le Motif cosmique dans la pensée sumérienne," *Acta Orientalia* 28 (1964), 1-59; J. Bottéro, "Les textes cosmogoniques mineures en langue akkadienne," *Mythes*, 279-328.

2. Van Dijk, YOS 11, 3-4.

3. Reiner, *Poetry*, 94ff.

4. In general, see Hecker, *Epik*, 187ff.; G. Komoróczy, "Akkadian Epic Poetry and Its Sumerian Sources," *AASH* 23 (1975), 41-63; W. von Soden, *Zweisprachigkeit in der geistigen Kultur Babyloniens, Österreichische Akad. der Wissen., Phil.-hist. Klasse, Sitzungsberichte* 235/1 (1960); *Sprache, Denken und Begriffsbildung im alten Orient*, Akademie der Wissenschaften und der Literatur, Mainz, *Abhandlungen der Geistes- und Sozialwissenschaftlichen Klasse* 1973 No. 6.

tion consists of numerous Sumerian texts with Akkadian translations, not always close to the Sumerian, normally in interlinear versions. Some instances, such as the Bilingual Psalm of Tukulti-Ninurta (III.2) and the Seed of Kingship (III.12a), may be simultaneous composition in the two languages, such that the Akkadian is not a translation but the substrate language for the Sumerian. Sumerian cultural tradition also influenced Akkadian literature in ways less easily definable: style, tone, subject matter. The two traditions are so closely connected that one can speak of a hybrid Sumero-Akkadian literary culture, even in the Late period.

3. ORAL TRADITION

There is no concrete indication in Akkadian literary or other texts that oral literature existed, though some scholars believe that oral tradition was important in the formation of Akkadian literature.[1] No "teller of tales" is mentioned in written Akkadian tradition; in fact, little in Akkadian literature compels reconstructing an oral phase or tradition behind it. There were surely popular traditions that were written down less frequently than more formal literature, if at all. Faced with a dearth of evidence, one can say little about the influence of oral tradition on Akkadian literature.[2]

4. WHAT IS AKKADIAN LITERATURE?

Like any other anthology, *Before the Muses* is a modern, personal selection from a large body of writing. Creation of such an anthology raises two important questions. First, can one properly speak of Akkadian literature as a definable group of texts, and if so, what is meant by this concept? Here no simple answer is possible. If, for example, one defines literature as writing published for the

---

1. For a survey of the problem and remarks on the social context of oral tradition in ancient Mesopotamia, see M. Liverani, "Le Tradizioni orali delle fonti scritte nell'antico oriente," in B. Bernardi *et al.*, eds., *Fonti Orali: Antropologia e Storia* (Milano, 1978), 397-406; Y. Elman, "Authoritative Oral Tradition in Neo-Assyrian Scribal Circles," JANES 7 (1975), 19-32; J. Laessøe, "Literacy and Oral Tradition in Ancient Mesopotamia," *Studia Orientalia Ioanni Pedersen septuagenario ... dicata* (Copenhagen, 1953), 205-218; V. K. Afanasieva, "Mündlich überlieferte Dichtung ("Oral Poetry") und schriftliche Literatur in Mesopotamien," AASH 22 (1974), 121-135; Rochberg-Halton, JCS 36 (1984), 130.

2. W. Röllig, "Volksliteratur in mesopotamischer Überlieferung," CRRAI 32 (1985), 81-87; J. Black, "Babylonian Ballads," JAOS 103 (1983), 25-34.

entertainment of a reading public and the support of its author, little in Akkadian could be so considered, for there is no indication of the existence of a reading public or of authors who made their living by writing. But if one deems literature to be writing of artful form, content, and expression, then there is much Akkadian literature, with nearly all the works in this book examples of it. In this sense, Akkadian may be said to have a rich and voluminous literature.

The second question is why the works in this anthology were copied by Mesopotamian scribes, that is, what role did Akkadian literature play in its own cultural environment? In answer to this, it is important to note that many of the texts treated here may have survived not because they were transmitted over many generations as independent works of literature admired for their own sake, but because they formed part of a cluster of cultural concerns that need not, from a modern point of view, be literary in nature. For example, the Creation Epic (III.17) is known to have been recited at the late Babylonian New Year's festival, and the Adapa Story (III.20a) is preserved in a text dealing with dental treatment. Neither context may have been anticipated or intended by the original authors.

In the formation of a corpus of written tradition, the process of transmission itself acts as a determining factor in the survival of texts. In Mesopotamia, survival of a text normally depended upon decisions by successive generations of scholars to recopy it. Most works of the Classical period are known from only one manuscript, though Mature and Late works typically exist in several exemplars. Does this mean that there was a greater fluidity of tradition in the Classical period, whereas by the Mature and Late periods a canonical corpus had been established?[1] Or is this only an indication of how few manuscripts of the Classical period have survived? Certain texts, such as Erra and Ishum, enjoyed wide popularity and distribution even though they were composed at a relatively late date, so the canonical corpus was open to inclusion of new works.

Accordingly, understanding of what Mesopotamians considered literature may be furthered by considering reasons behind scribal decisions to copy and preserve texts. One fruitful line of inquiry has been study of how texts were altered as they were recopied, what elements were added, deleted, expanded,

---

1. For the concept of canonization in cuneiform, see p. 209 note 1; for possible origins of Classical period literature, see W. G. Lambert, "Interchange of Ideas between Southern Mesopotamia and Syria-Palestine as Seen in Literature," CRRAI 25 (1978), 311-316.

simplified, or left intact.[1] Another avenue has been to identify universals of content, language, and form.

With respect to content, many texts were recopied that dealt with the human condition, as it was perceived or how it came to be; others were tradited that told stories about the gods. Heroic (royal) and epic (divine) elements were favored, as was a setting in the remote past. Texts of a topical or historical nature were less likely to be recopied than texts which, though they might use historical events or personalities, were applicable to any period. Sometimes there were regional or local preferences; for example, the Hittites were understandably most interested in Mesopotamian texts concerned with Anatolia.

As for language, poetry was favored over prose, and texts in moderately artificed language found greatest favor. Highly individual linguistic peculiarities tended to be eliminated over time.

With respect to form, texts that lent themselves readily to expansion or shortening seem to have had the best chances of survival. In general, the greater a text's capacity to change in length, without losing its contours, the more likely successive generations were to preserve it.

If there was no broad reading public in the modern sense, then the formation of Akkadian literature must have been in response to the tastes and requirements of a restricted group of literate people. As was noted above (see B.2), different library collections of Akkadian literary manuscripts from the Late period often include the same works. This suggests to some scholars that texts were recopied because they were part of a curriculum of scribal education which evolved during the Mature period. Students were set to copying certain works or excerpts from them as part of their training. Indeed, some scholars consider a putative educational curriculum a primary factor in the survival of Akkadian literature. The selection of works making up such a curriculum must have been guided by a combination of pedagogical, cultural, and ideological factors, and was no doubt heavily influenced by the needs and outlook of literate professional people such as diviners and exorcists. One can speculate that texts were judged in terms of their content, their broad human and professional interest, their challenging but accessible linguistic texture, and their informational and entertainment value.[2]

---

1. See J. Cooper, "Gilgamesh Dreams of Enkidu: The Expansion and Dilution of Narrative," *Studies Finkelstein*, 39-44; "Symmetry and Repetition in Akkadian Narrative," JAOS 97 (1977), 508-512; J. Tigay, *The Evolution of the Gilgamesh Epic* (Philadelphia, 1982); M. Vogelzang, "Kill Anzu! On a Point of Literary Evolution," CRRAI 32 (1985), 61-70.

2. Reiner, *Literatur*, 157; see further p. 207 note 1.

While curricular needs may explain the survival in multiple copies of some texts of the Mature and Late periods, it cannot explain the creative impulse that brought them into being. Akkadian literature was created by the labor, genius, and inspiration of individual writers, working in the favorable cultural environment of ancient Mesopotamian civilization.

CHAPTER I

THE ARCHAIC PERIOD
(2300 – 2000 B.C.)

The earliest known Akkadian literary texts include royal inscriptions of the Sargonic period (ca. 2300-2200 B.C.),[1] school exercises, and a few short magical texts, all written in Old Akkadian.[2]

The Sargonic period began with Sargon's rise from court officer at Kish to ruler of a kingdom stretching east into Iran, west to the Mediterranean and north into Anatolia. This unprecedented achievement changed permanently the Mesopotamian concept of the politically possible. Sargon's accomplishment was regarded with almost superstitious awe, and in later periods fictional stories circulated about his birth and early life (IV.19). His two sons, Rimush and Manishtusu, re-established and continued his military dominion. Inscriptions of Manishtusu were copied, and even forged, in the Late period.[3]

The feats of Sargon's grandson, Naram-Sin, gave this dynasty legendary fascination for Mesopotamians. Naram-Sin turned a series of military conquests into one of history's first empires.[4] He was the first Mesopotamian ruler to proclaim himself a god, because he had defeated a seemingly invincible coalition of enemies. To Naram-Sin and his contemporaries, his victory over overwhelming odds signified divine approval of his empire and the Sargonic way of life.[5] Not long after Naram-Sin's long and brilliant reign, the empire was destroyed

---

1. For historical surveys of the Sargonic period, see C. J. Gadd, "The Dynasty of Agade and the Gutian Invasion," CAH[3], Chapter XIX; J. Bottéro, "Das erste Semitische Grossreich," *Fischer Weltgeschichte* 2 (Frankfurt, 1965), 91-128. The best study of the period is J.-J. Glassner, *La Chute d'Agadé, l'événement et sa mémoire, Berliner Beiträge zum Vorderen Orient* 5 (Berlin, 1986).

2. For a description of Old Akkadian and a comprehensive list of source material, see I. J. Gelb, *Old Akkadian Writing and Grammar*, MAD 2[2] (Chicago, 1961); see also A. Westenholz, "Old Akkadian School Texts, The Goals of Sargonic Scribal Education," AfO 25 (1974/77), 95-110.

3. See *Iraq* 49 (1987), 249, first report of discovery of a Manishtusu inscription in a Neo-Babylonian copy; I. J. Gelb, "The Date of the Cruciform Monument of Maništušu," JNES 8 (1949), 346-348 (Neo-Babylonian forgery).

4. B. R. Foster, "Archives and Empire in Sargonic Mesopotamia," CRRAI 30 (1983), 46-52.

5. A. Westenholz, "The Old Akkadian Empire in Contemporary Opinion," in M. T. Larsen, ed., *Power and Propaganda, Mesopotamia* 7 (Copenhagen, 1979), 107-115.

by a Zagros mountain people called the Guti, whom the Mesopotamians considered barbarous. Some later writers were disposed to find in this a lesson of divine retribution against Naram-Sin himself.[1]

Sargonic imperial ideology affected the evolution of Akkadian art and literature. An imperial, triumphal art[2] flourished under court patronage. Naturalistic, often monumental reliefs, stelae, and statues were distributed throughout the empire evoking the king's triumphs and the death and enslavement in store for his enemies. Artistic conceptualization and iconography were much influenced by the requirements of royal propaganda.

With respect to literature, commemorative inscriptions immortalized the deeds of the king.[3] The earliest examples of this genre gave the ruler's name and titles, followed by brief, formulaic accounts of campaigns, cities taken, and casualties, ending with dedication to a god of some commemorative object, with curses on anyone who would destroy the monument or alter its text. By the time of Naram-Sin, these texts were expanded to include direct speech, descriptive details, and admonitions about the importance of the achievements of the king.[4] An example of such a text is given here (I.1).

Many Sargonic commemorative inscriptions are known only from Old Babylonian scholarly copies, for scribes of the Classical period considered these texts part of their education.[5] The use of these copies is uncertain, though one purpose was preservation of historical tradition about the Sargonic period.[6] In addition, later scribes may have studied the Sargonic inscriptions because in their view, the careers of Sargon and Naram-Sin had historical and exemplary importance.[7]

The deeds of Sargon and Naram-Sin were the basis for later literary composi-

1. J. Cooper, *The Curse of Agade* (Baltimore, 1983), 17-18; Glassner, *Chute d'Agadé* (p. 49 note 1).

2. P. Amiet, *L'art d'Agadé au Musée du Louvre* (Paris, 1976), 9ff.; H. Sauren, "Die Königstheologie in der Kunst des 3. Jahrtausends," OLA 13 (1982), 45-53.

3. For translations, see Sollberger-Kupper, IRSA, 97-114; I. J. Gelb, B. Kienast, *Die altakkadischen Königsinschriften des dritten Jahrtausends*, FAOS 7 (1990), 37ff.

4. Foster, *Annual Review of the Royal Inscriptions of Mesopotamia Project* 8 (1990), 44.

5. Gelb, MAD 2² 7f.; F. R. Kraus, "Altbabylonische Quellensammlungen zur altmesopotamischen Geschichte," AfO 20 (1963), 153-155.

6. W. G. Lambert, BiOr 30 (1973), 357ff., and JAOS 106 (1986), 795 has argued that Old Babylonian literary dialect was descended from Old Akkadian. See also General Introduction, A.3.

7. H. G. Güterbock, "Die historische Tradition und ihre literarische Gestaltung bei Babyloniern und Hethitern bis 1200," ZA 42 (1934), 1-91, 44 (1938), 45-149; Grayson, BHLT, 3-9, with extensive bibliographical references. See also A. K. Grayson, "Akkadian Historiography," OrNS 49 (1980), 140-194; C. Wilcke, "Zur Geschichtsbewusstsein im alten Mesopotamien," *Archäologie und Geschichtsbewusstsein* 3 (Munich, 1982), 31-52.

tions (see II.16, 17; III.7). Some of these were reworkings of actual Sargonic commemorative texts. No such literary compositions are as yet known from the Sargonic period itself.[1] The grandeur and subsequent humiliation of the greatest empire known was a fit subject for reflection for Old Babylonian thinkers: what divine favor and rejection brought about this remarkable event, and what moral lesson could be drawn from it?[2]

Other Old Akkadian texts include incantations, or magic spells, of which Sumerian counterparts are known from the middle of the third millennium on.[3] The three Old Akkadian incantations translated here (I.2-4) were intended to ward off the evil eye and demons, and to attract a woman to a man. Magical procedures were unaffected by the politics of their times and often used the vocabulary and rites of centuries before.

Two Old Assyrian incantations have been included in this chapter (I.6-7) rather than in Chapter II, because they are Pre-Classical in language, though later than the Archaic period. During the nineteenth century B.C., Assyrian merchants maintained a trading colony at Kanesh in Anatolia (near Kayseri in Turkey), where they took part in caravan trade between Anatolia and Assur. These two magic spells probably came from private houses at Kanesh and were the personal property of an exorcist.

1. MAD 1 172, sometimes treated as a literary text, is best understood as a student excerpt copy of a genuine Naram-Sin inscription. The interpretation of it as a legend by Jacobsen, AfO 26 (1978/79), 1ff. is unconvincing. For another Sargonic student copy of a Sargonic royal inscription, compare MAD 1 194 (= Westenholz, AfO 25 [1974/77], 103 no. 14).

2. J. J. Finkelstein, "Mesopotamian Historiography," PAPS 107/6 (1963), 461-472; J. Westenholz, "Heroes of Akkad," JAOS 103 (1983), 327-336.

3. G. Pettinato, "Le collezione en-e-nu-ru di Ebla," OrAn 18 (1975), 329-351; M. Krebernik, *Die Beschwörungen aus Fara und Ebla, Untersuchungen zur ältesten Keilschriftlichen Beschwörungs-Literatur* (Zurich, 1984); D. O. Edzard, *Hymnen, Beschwörungen und Verwandtes (Aus dem Archiv L.2769), Archivi Reali di Ebla, Testi 5* (1984).

A. COMMEMORATIVE INSCRIPTION

I.1 NARAM-SIN AT ARMANUM

This inscription was copied by an Old Babylonian scholar from a stone monument, now lost, in the temple of the moon god Sin at Ur. This evidently showed scenes of the siege of the city Armanum. The complex opening announcement, parallel development and repetition, use of direct speech, and challenge to the future, set this text apart from earlier, more formulaic, Sargonic commemorative inscriptions. Noteworthy is the cosmological portrayal, beginning with the creation of the human race, culminating in Naram-Sin's achievement, and concluding with the establishment of a standard for future kings to measure themselves against.

> (i 1) Whereas, for all time since the formation of humankind there has never been a king who overthrew Armanum and Ebla,[1] with the weapon(?) of Nergal did Naram-Sin, the mighty, open the only path and he (Nergal) gave him Armanum and Ebla. He (Nergal) bestowed upon him the Amanus too, the Cedar Mountain, and the Upper Sea, and, by the weapon of Dagan, exalter of his kingship, Naram-Sin, the mighty, defeated Armanum and Ebla. Then, from the hither face of the Euphrates,[2] he smote the river(-bank) as far as Ulisum,[3] as well as the people whom Dagan had for the first time bestowed upon him, and they bear for him the burden of Ilaba his god. The Amanus too, the Cedar Mountain, he conquered completely.
>
> (ii 29) When Dagan gave the verdict for Naram-Sin, the mighty, and delivered Rish(?)-Adad, king of Armanum, into his power, and he himself had captured him in his (own) entryway,* he (Naram-Sin) made a statue of himself in diorite(?) and dedicated it to Sin.

---

1. The location of Armanum is unknown. The site of Ebla, to the south of modern Aleppo, is being excavated; see P. Matthiae, *Ebla, Un Impero Ritrovato, dai Primi Scavi alle Ultime Scoperte* (1964 -1987) (Turin, 1988). An earlier edition is available in English as *Ebla, An Empire Rediscovered*, trans. C. Holme (New York, 1981). Matthiae believes that the city was destroyed by Sargon, not by Naram-Sin as claimed in this inscription (H. Waetzoldt *et al.*, eds., *Wirtschaft und Gesellschaft von Ebla* [Heidelberg, 1988], 76).

2. That is, the beginning of the alluvium at Sippar.

3. Location unknown, presumably on the Syrian coast.

(iii 17) Thus says Naram-Sin, the mighty, king of the four world regions: "Dagan having given me Armanum and Ebla, and I having captured Rish(?)-Adad, king of Armanum and Ebla, then did I make my image. I (text: he) dedicated it to Sin: let no one do away with my monument! Let my statue stand before Sin and what(?) his god(?) shall grant(?) him, let that be his duty(?).[1] The mission(?) which I went(?) is a great (deed) to distinguish me(?)."[2]

(iv 20) From the fortification wall to the great wall, 130 cubits is the ascent of the citadel, 44 cubits is the ascent of the wall.

(v 1) From the enclosure⋆ wall to the fortification wall, 180 cubits is the ascent of the citadel, 30 cubits is the ascent of the wall.

Total: 404 cubits ascent from the ground to the top of the fortress.

He undermined(?)⋆ the city Armanum.

(vi 1) From the river to the enclosure wall, 196 cubits is the ascent of the citadel, 20 cubits is the ascent of the wall. From the enclosure wall to the fortification wall, 156 cubits is the ascent of the citadel, 30 cubits is the ascent of the wall.

(276 i) Whosoever shall do away with the inscription of Naram-Sin, the mighty, king of the four world regions, and shall set his own name on the statue of Naram-Sin, saying, "It is my statue," or shows it to an outsider and says, "Erase it and set my name (thereon)," may Sin, owner of this statue, and Ishtar-Annunitum, Anu, Enlil, Ilaba, Sin, Shamash, Nergal, Umshu, Ninkarrak, all the great gods lay on him a terrible curse. May he not hold scepter for Enlil nor kingship for Ishtar. May he not come before his god. May Ninhursag and Nintu give him neither heir nor descent. May Adad and Nisaba not let his furrowing flourish. May Enki measure no water to his canals nor broaden his wisdom … May he … no weapon …

(breaks off, rest of text too fragmentary for translation)

Text: Gadd, UET 1 275, 276; Sollberger, UET 8/2 13.
Edition: Foster, JANES 14 (1982), 27-39; Kienast, FAOS 7 (1990), 253-264.
⋆*Notes to Text:* (iii 8) qab_x-*li;* see JANES 14 (1982), 36-37. (v 1) *kà-wi!-im,* reading suggested by K. R. Veenhof. (v 16) Suggestion WGL.

1. Obscure, translation doubtful.
2. Obscure, translation doubtful.

B. OLD AKKADIAN INCANTATIONS

I.2 AGAINST A DEMON

The magician has caught a firm hold on the oppressor.

> I have seized him — like water[1]
> I have blocked him off, like a watercourse —
> Like a dog by his neck,
> Like a whelp by his scruff.
> (incantation)

Text: D. I. Owen, *Neo-Sumerian Archival Texts, Primarily from Nippur* (Winona Lake, IN, 1984) 917.
Edition: See Gelb, MAD 3³, 242.
Translation: Farber, TUAT II/2, 256.

1. As written the line seems to say "I seized him like water," scarcely the simile one expects of a firm grasp, so I assume a "double pivot" construction with the two water similes dependent on "blocked" and the two dog similes dependent on "seized." Differently Farber, "Ich fing ihn wie (mit) Wasser."

I.3 AGAINST THE EVIL EYE

This ritual is an early example of magic in Akkadian. The procedure may involve taking a sheep to the corners of the dwelling of a man afflicted by the evil eye or other black magic, lifting(?) the sheep in each corner of the house to absorb the evil, killing the animal outside, then stuffing its skin with pieces of some plant (for a late parody of this technique, compare The Jester [IV.21] iv). The sheep, together with bits of plants and trees, is then submerged in water. See also IV.31.

> One black virgin ewe: In (each of) the corners of the house he will lift it up(?).* He will drive out the Evil Eye* and the [ ] ... In the garden he will slaughter it and flay its hide. He proceeds to fill it with pieces of ...-plant. As he fills it, he should watch. The evil man [ ] his skin. Let [him] ca[rry (it) to the river], (and) seven (pieces of) date palm, seven (pieces of) oak, and seven (pieces of ...)* let him submerge.

Text: Legrain, MDP 14 90 (p. 123 and plate 11), collated.
Edition: Legrain, MDP 14 90, 123.
Literature: Farber, ZA 71 (1981), 52, and using other suggestions communicated privately.
Notes to Text: (3) Meaning of verb uncertain, construed here as Gt causative of *zqr*, implying some sympathetic activity. The root *zqr* is common for raising of buildings. (4) Following Farber, ZA 71 (1981), 52. (22) *zu-iš-ma-e*, word(s) of unknown meaning.

I.4 LOVE CHARM

The purpose of this love charm is to enable a man to win a woman's favor by magical procedure. I propose the following divisions of the text. (a) The speaker invokes the god of wisdom and incantations, saying that the love charm sits in the lap of the goddess of love, surrounded by aromatic "sap." (b) The speaker sends off two demonic maidens (compare the daughters of Anu in II.20, and the daughters of Ea in I.7)[1] to fetch some of this sap. The speaker asserts control over the woman he desires, apostrophizing her (c). In (d), through vegetation metaphors, the speaker describes his approach towards her and summons her to search for him. Part (e) may be the imagined internal whisperings of erotic desire awakened in the woman by the love charm, while in (f) the spell has taken hold. In the final line, Ea conjures the helpless girl that she find no release from desire till her union with her would-be lover.

(a)

Ea loves the love charm,
The love charm, son of Ishtar,
[Sea]ted on her thighs, in the sapflow of the incense-tree.

(b)

… you two beautiful maidens,
You are come into bloom, you went down to the garden,
To the garden you went down.
You cut the sapflow of the incense-tree.

(c)

I have seized your mouth for saliva![2]
I have seized your lustrous eyes!
I have seized your vulva for urine!

1. For further discussion, see Westenholz, OrNS 46 (1977), 211.
2. For seizing of the mouth, see II.28a; for the wording, compare II.33b.

(d)

I climbed into the garden of the moon[1]
I cut through poplar to her ...
Seek for* me among the boxwood,
As the shepherd seeks for the sheep,
The goat her kid,
The ewe (her) lamb,
The jenny her foal.

(e)

"His arms are two garlands of fruit,*
"His lips are oil and ...-(plant?).[2]
"A cruse of oil (is) in his hand,
"A cruse of cedar oil (is) on his shoulder,"
(So) the love charms have bespoken her,
Then driven her to ecstasy!

(f)

I have seized your mouth for love-making!
By Ishtar and Ishara[3] I conjure you:
May you find no release from me
Till your neck and his neck lie close beside!

Text: Westenholz, OrNS 46 (1977), 200.
Edition: J. and A. Westenholz, OrNS 46 (1977), 198-219.
Literature: Gelb, MAD 5, 7-12; von Soden, ZA 62 (1972), 273-274; W. G. Lambert in M. Minder et al., eds., *Figurative Language in the Ancient Near East* (London, 1987), 37-38, with corrections in *Nabu* 1989/7.
Notes to Text: (d 3) See Lambert, *Figurative Language*, 38. (e 1) See Gelb, *Studies Kraus*, 71f., though I take this as a positive attribute.

1. Obscure. "Garden" presumably means his beloved's sexual parts. As Jacobsen suggests (*Studies Finkelstein*, 63), this may refer to their crescent shape. Mention of the moon god (Sin) might also refer to his role of ruler of the nighttime. For night as the time for sexual adventure, compare "By night there's no prudent housewife, By night no man's wife makes objection" (IV.22).

2. The original uses a word *tibbuttu*, which can mean a kind of plant, a cricket, or a harp — which is meant here is unknown, though the plant seems most likely.

3. Goddess of love; see also p. 168 note 3.

C. OLD AKKADIAN LETTER

I.5 DO NOT SIT ON A CHAIR!

This letter, included here because of its unusual flowery style, requests that someone come quickly. It uses language derived from magical formulae, presumably with humorous intent.

> Thus says Ishkun-Dagan[1] to Puzur-Ishtar: By Ishtar and Ilaba, Ashgi, and Ninhursag, by the king's life and by the queen's life you must swear it! So long as you have not seen my eyes, may you swallow neither bread nor beer! Also, so long as you do not come to me, do not sit on a chair!

Text: Thureau-Dangin, RA 23 (1926), 25.
Edition: Thureau-Dangin, RA 23 (1926), 23-29.
Translation: A. L. Oppenheim, *Letters from Mesopotamia* (Chicago, 1967), 71.

---

1. Ishkun-Dagan may have been a highly placed administrator in the Lagash region about the time of Sharkalisharri (ca. 2217-2193 B.C., see Foster, JNES 37 [1978], 275; Biga, *Rivista degli Studi Orientali* 53 [1979], 204).

D. OLD ASSYRIAN INCANTATIONS

I.6 AGAINST LAMASHTU

The malevolent Lamashtu-demon (see also II.26 and IV.37) is described, though without the counteracting spell.

> She is singular, she is uncanny,   (1)
> She is a child born late in life(?), she is a will-o'-the-wisp,
> She is a haunt, she is malicious,
> Offspring of a god, daughter of Anu.
> For her malevolent will, her base counsel,   (5)
> Anu her father dashed her down from heaven to earth,
> For her malevolent will, her inflammatory counsel.*
> Her hair is askew, her loincloth is torn away.
> She makes her way straight to the person
>   without a (protective) god.
> She can benumb the sinews of a lion,   (10)
> She can ... the sinews of a youngster or infant.

Text: Clay, BIN 4 26.
Edition: von Soden, OrNS 25 (1956), 141-148.
Literature: Farber, ZA 71 (1981), 53, collations p. 72.
Notes to Text: (7) Syntax on the basis of a suggestion by Farber.

I.7 AGAINST DOGS

This fragment opens with magic words, a description of the feared dogs, and a rhetorical question by the exorcist as to whom he shall send for magic, purifying water. For the last motif, common in spells, compare Against a Mote in the Eye (II.16). For other incantations against dogs, see II.22 and compare III.50d.

Damum-damamum![1]   (1)
The black dog lurks on the ruin heap,
It waits for the scattered caravan,
It is on the look-out for the fair young man.
Whom shall I send to the daughters of Ea,
      seven and seven?   (5)
Take your [pots] of carnelian,
And your stands of chalcedony!
Go! [ ] in the river, ... [pure] water
                        (gap of three lines)
Get away, fellow,
Go back to your place!

Text: H. Hirsch, *Untersuchungen zur altassyrischen Religion,* AfO Beiheft 13/14 (1961), 82; Landsberger, JNES 14 (1955), 17; Farber, ZA 71 (1981), 72 (transliteration only), collation in CAD S, 122b.
Edition: Farber, JNES 49 (1990), 305-306.
Translation: Balkan, *Proceedings of the Twenty-second International Congress of Orientalists held in Istanbul September 15 to 22nd, 1951* (Istanbul, 1953), 20-21.

1. Magic words (Farber, ZA 71 [1981], 70) and compare below, IV.40. They resemble the Akkadian word for "blood," and may be derived from it.

CHAPTER II

THE CLASSICAL PERIOD
(2000 - 1500 B.C.)

The selections presented in this chapter date to the Classical or Old Babylonian period, approximately 2000-1500 B.C.[1] Towards the end of the third millennium B.C., political and economic power in southern Mesopotamia passed from Sumerians and Akkadians into the hands of Amorites, Semitic-speaking people of north Syrian origin who entered Mesopotamia, gradually at some times, in floods at others.[2] The various rival dynasties of Mesopotamia and north Syria during the Classical period were mostly of Amorite background. As a new ethnic element in Mesopotamia, Amorites brought with them speech habits, as well as cultural, social, and economic customs different from those previously known there. Classical Babylonian culture and language grew out of Sumerian, Old Akkadian, and Amorite traditions, drawing on elements of each.

Political and social conditions of the Classical period were particularly important for the development of literature.[3] Mesopotamia was divided into rival kingdoms, which constantly conspired and allied against one another in competition for hegemony, control of commerce, and natural resources. The insecurity of the time left an impression on literary works, either directly, as in the City Lament (II.8), or more subtly, as in Agushaya (II.6). Human fortune was portrayed as a chancy progress towards inevitable death. The world was

---

1. General historical surveys of the Old Babylonian period include D. O. Edzard, *Die 'Zweite Zwischenzeit' Babyloniens* (Wiesbaden, 1967), and "Die altbabylonische Zeit," *Fischer Weltgeschichte, Die altorientalischen Reiche* I (Frankfort, 1972), 165-205; W. W. Hallo, *The Ancient Near East, A History* (New York, 1971), 85-103; P. Garelli, *Le Proche-Orient Asiatique* (Paris, 1969), 128-137; H. Klengel, *Hammurapi von Babylon und seine Zeit* (Berlin, 1976); and C. J. Gadd, "Hammurabi and the End of His Dynasty," CAH[3] (1973), 176-227, where references to the abundant literature on this period may be found.

2. For the early history of the Amorites, see G. Buccellati, *The Amorites of the Ur III Period,* Istituto Orientale di Napoli, *Ricerche* I (Naples, 1966); A. Haldar, *Who Were the Amorites?* (Leiden, 1971); I. J. Gelb, "The Early History of the West Semitic Peoples," JCS 15 (1961), 27-48.

3. The standard work on Old Babylonian society, though a challenge to a general reader, is F. R. Kraus, *Königliche Verfügungen in altbabylonischer Zeit*, SED X (Leiden, 1984). See also his work cited below, p. 62 note 2.

not seen as inherently fair or just, for power was to the strong, whatever their moral deserts.[1] One hoped for good health, long life, an abundant family, and financial success (see II.35). Attainment of these goals was seen as a sign of divine favor; illness, ostracism, and defeat indicated divine displeasure, perhaps because of a sin of omission or commission (see II.5). Yet divine favor need not be a matter of justice. Rather, the gods' moods, needs, competition among themselves, and individual abilities influenced human affairs, such that mortals' fortunes were caught in cross currents which they could hardly comprehend, much less control.

Old Babylonian kings called themselves their subjects' shepherds.[2] In daily life, a shepherd protected his animals, nurtured them, allowed them to pasture in safety, and, in return, could discipline them absolutely and gain a reasonable financial return. Whereas Old Babylonian kings used this imagery often, they expressed the profit-taking[3] aspect of kingship only in terms of prosperity for the people.[4] In their commemorative inscriptions, kings were wont to refer to their divine election, as if the gods had chosen them to lead their human flocks. When a dynasty had been established, kings stressed their divine birth, often claiming to be offspring of a "sacred marriage" (see II.11).[5] As responsible agents for the gods, kings administered justice and protected their people from outside threats.

In the realm of belles-lettres, however, limits to the metaphor of king as shepherd were more sharply drawn. Abuse of royal power is touched on directly in Old Babylonian Gilgamesh and satirized in Agushaya (II.6). Literary heroes were often kings or those who sought the impossible. Whereas Babylonians stressed that all human undertaking, no matter how heroic, would end in the

---

1. The best general study of the Old Babylonian period, including its world view, is Kraus, *Mensch*; note also the essay by H. Klengel, "Zur Rolle der Persönlichkeit in der altbabylonischen Gesellschaft," in *Humanismus und Menschenbild im Orient und in der Antike* (Halle, 1977), 109-117.

2. F. R. Kraus, "Das altbabylonische Königtum," CRRAI 19 (1971), 235-261. For literature at the royal court, see G. Komoróczy, "Literatur am Königshof (2. Jahrtausend v. u. Z.)," *Gesellschaft und Kultur im alten Vorderasien, Schriften zur Geschichte des alten Orients* 15 (Berlin, 1982), 155-161.

3. N. Yoffee, *The Economic Role of the Crown in the Old Babylonian Period*, BM 5 (Malibu, 1977).

4. D. O. Edzard, ""Soziale Reformen" im Zweistromland bis ca. 1600 v. Chr.: Realität oder literarischer Topos?" AASH 22 (1974), 145-156.

5. W. W. Hallo, "The Birth of Kings," *Studies Pope*, 45-52; Å. W. Sjöberg, "Die göttliche Abstammung der sumerisch-babylonischen Herrscher," *Orientalia Suecana* 21 (1972), 87-112; J. Klein, "The Birth of a Crownprince in the Temple: A Neo-Sumerian Literary Topos," CRRAI 33 (1986), 97-106.

anonymity of death, they admired heroic effort. In later literature, by contrast, heroic initiative was seen as not only doomed but possibly sacrilegious, in that it ignored the limits set for mortals by their divine creators (see below, III.32a, Adapa Story).[1]

Economic developments during the Classical period include the amassing of real estate as the basis for wealth,[2] money-lending (see II.37), and competition for agricultural labor, acquired either by contract or debt slavery.[3] Trade and commerce brought high returns for high risks.[4] Sometimes kings attempted to regulate and readjust local economies by annulling certain debts and obligations,[5] but military service and corvée were an onus on the population,[6] as aptly portrayed in the opening lines of Atrahasis (II.39a).[7]

In sum, the author of the Classical period saw his world as uncertain and competitive. His society envied the imagined self-assurance of the past. Babylonians cultivated an interest in their past and in the origins of human society (Etana, III.21; Atrahasis, II.39). Ancient documents were studied in Babylonian schools.[8]

Classical Akkadian literature is full of human interest, lively wit, and strong emotion. The satirical (II.7), the self-knowing, the ironic are found (II.6), as well as sensuality (II.2, 10), anguish (II.5, 8), longing (II.9), and tales of adventure (II.12). Subject matter includes the deeds of the gods and their significance

---

1. Kraus, *Mensch*, 130-134; E. Reiner, "The Etiological Myth of the Seven Sages," OrNS 30 (1961), 1-11.

2. For studies of this phenomenon, see E. Stone, "Texts, Architecture and Ethnographic Analogy: Patterns of Residence in Old Babylonian Nippur," *Iraq* 43 (1981), 19-33; D. Charpin, *Clergé; Archives Familiales et Propriété Privée en Babylonie Ancienne; Étude des Documents de "Tell Sifr"* (Geneva, 1980).

3. J. G. Lautner, *Altbabylonische Personenmiete und Erntearbeitverträge*, SED I (Leiden, 1936); H. Klengel, "Die Geschäfte des Babyloniers Balamunamche," *Das Altertum* 19 (1973), 199-207; M. Van de Mieroop, "The Archive of Balmunamhe," AfO 24 (1987), 1-29.

4. W. F. Leemans, *The Old Babylonian Merchant: His Business and His Social Position*, SED III (Leiden, 1950); A. L. Oppenheim, "The Sea-Faring Merchants of Ur," JAOS 74 (1959), 6-17.

5. J. Bottéro, "Désordre économique et annulation des dettes en Mésopotamie à l'époque paléo-babylonienne," JESHO 4 (1961), 113-164; G. Komoróczy, "Zur Frage der Periodizität der altbabylonischen Misharum - Erlasse," in *Studies Diakonoff*, 196-205 (with up-to-date bibliography).

6. D. G. Evans, "The Incidence of Labour-Service in the Old Babylonian Period," JAOS 83 (1963), 20-26.

7. G. Komoróczy, "Work and Strike of the Gods," *Oikumene* 1 (1976), 9-37.

8. F. R. Kraus, "Altbabylonische Quellensammlungen zur altmesopotamischen Geschichte," AfO 20 (1963), 153-155. For bibliography on Babylonian schools, see p. 208 note 4.

for mankind, as in Etana (see III.21), Agushaya (II.6), Atrahasis (II.39); and deeds of men alone, for example, the fighting hero (Legends of Sargonic Kings, II.12-13), and the pretentious fool (II.7).

As in the Archaic period, incantations were considered effective against various problems such as disease (II.14-17, 20-21), discomfort (II.18-19), natural pests (II.22-25), the pangs of parenthood (II.31) and infant death (II.30), the frustration of unrequited desire (II.33), and malice (II.27). Their directness and grim vividness are the more powerful because of the universality of the experience they deal with. There is also a parody on the style (II.32). The poetics of incantations are simple and immediately appealing, whereas more complex works, such as Atrahasis (II.39), show the high refinement and artistic excellence that Classical period poets could achieve.

A. HYMNS

II.1 TO ISHTAR

After the opening invocation, this poem treats first the attractions of Ishtar's body, then focuses upon her features, suffused with pleasure, and her head, which is bedizened with love charms (compare Love Charm, I.4). Mention of her eyes leads to consideration of the well-being her regard can bestow, especially, in the fifth strophe, on a woman who hopes for harmonious love. The poet thinks then of Ishtar's might and splendor — who could withstand such power? This leads to her role as queen of heaven, the morning and evening star; she reigns supreme with her spouse, the sky, and the lesser lights stand before her, partaking of her brilliance. As the gods await her command, the poet introduces the Babylonian king, Ammiditana (ca.1683-1647 B.C.), who bears rich offerings, whose domains she ensures — may his long life be her command.

i

Sing of the goddess, most awe-inspiring goddess,
Let her be praised, mistress of peoples,
     greatest of the Igigi-gods.
Sing of Ishtar, most awe-inspiring goddess; let her be praised,
Mistress of women, greatest of the Igigi-gods.

ii

She is the joyous one, clad in loveliness,
She is adorned with allure, appeal, charm.
Ishtar is the joyous one, clad in loveliness,
She is adorned with allure, appeal, charm.

iii

In her lips she is sweetness, vitality her mouth,
While on her features laughter bursts to bloom.
She is proud of the love charms set on her head,[1]
Fair her hues, full-ranging, and lustrous her eyes.

---

1. The love charm may be visualized as something worn on the head (Westenholz, OrNS 46 [1977], 205-207).

iv

This goddess,* right counsel is hers,
She grasps in her hand the destinies of all that exists.
At her regard, well-being is born,
Vigor, dignity, good fortune, divine protection.

v

Whispers,* surrender, sweet shared captivation,
Harmony too she reigns over as mistress.
The girl who invokes(?) finds (in her?) a mother,
Among women(?) one mentions her, invokes her name.*

vi

Who is it that could rival her grandeur?
Her attributes are mighty, splendid, superb.
Ishtar this is, who could rival her grandeur?
Her attributes are mighty, splendid, superb.

vii

She it is who stands foremost among the gods,*
Her word is the weightiest and prevails over theirs.
Ishtar stands foremost among the gods,
Her word is the weightiest and prevails over theirs.

viii

She is their queen, they relay her commands,*
All of them bow down before her:
They go to her (in) her radiance,*
Women and men fear her too.

ix

In their assembly her utterance is noble, surpassing,
She is seated among them as an equal to Anu their king,
She is wise in understanding and perception.
Together they make their decisions, she and her lord.[1]

1. Anu is meant. "Lord" may be a term of endearment here; see p. 93 note 1.

x

There they sit together on the dais
In the temple chamber, abode of delights,
The gods stand in attendance before them,
Their ears awaiting what those mouths will command.

xi

Their favorite king, whom their hearts love most,
Ever offers in splendor his pure offerings,
Ammiditana offers before them
His personal, pure libation of cattle and fatted lambs.*

xii

She has asked of Anu her spouse long life hereafter for him,
Many years of life for Ammiditana
Has Ishtar rendered to him as her gift.

xiii

By her command she gave him in submission
The four world regions at his feet,
She harnessed the whole of the inhabited world to his yoke.

xiv

What she desires, this song for her pleasure
Is indeed well suited to his mouth,
    he performed for her Ea's own word(s).[1]
When he heard this song of her praise, he was well pleased with him,
Saying, "Let him live long, may his (own) king always love him."[2]

---

1. This refers to the artfulness of the text, which pleases Ea, god of wisdom. See General Introduction D.1.

2. "King" may mean the god of Ammiditana's city, Babylon (so Thureau-Dangin).

O Ishtar, grant long life enduring to Ammiditana,
the king who loves you, (long) may he live!

(its antiphon)[1]

Text: Thureau-Dangin, RA 22 (1925), 170-171.
Edition: Thureau-Dangin, RA 22 (1925), 172-177.
Translation: von Soden, SAHG, 235-237 no. 1; Stephens, ANET[3], 383; Labat, *Religions*, 238-239;
Seux, *Hymnes*, 39-42; Hecker, TUAT II/5, 721-724.
Literature: Hecker, *Epik*, 77-85.
Notes to Text: (iv 1) Or "pure one," Hecker, TUAT II/5, 722 note 13a. (v 1) With von Soden,
ZA 67 (1977), 279; otherwise, "mutual loves." (v 4) Construing *i-ni-ši* as *in(a) išši*. For *iššu* with-
out a doubled consonant, compare *i-ši-i* in line 4. (vii 1) I follow here von Soden's emendation
to *ša!-at*, ZA 40 (1931), 195 note 4. Collation shows the copy to be exact. Hecker's proposal,
Epik, 79 note 2, *ga!-ṣa!-at*, seems to me less likely because of the parallelism of the lines, which
resembles that of ii. (viii 1) Differently Hecker, *Epik*, 80 note 3: "Ihre Königin lassen sie immer-
wieder ihre Weisungen geben." (viii 3) See Hecker, *Epik*, 80 note 3; Mayer, OrNS 56 (1987),
201. (xi 4) I follow here CAD A/1, 336a, emending *ia-li* to *as!-li*; otherwise, perhaps, "stags."

1. This refers to the lines in the ruled-off section. The poem may have been performed or sung
antiphonally.

II.2 TO NANAY

This hymn comprises fourteen preserved strophes. The first six are in the third person, describing the goddess Nanay (here identified with the planet Venus) as a woman, proud, beautiful, and confident, whom the sky god Anu made mistress of the world. In stanzas vi to xi, the poet changes to the second person, as if Anu were speaking, extolling the joy and prosperity she brings, especially to the reigning king, Samsuiluna of Babylon (ca. 1749 - 1712 B.C.). The poet then reverts to the third person, and concludes with a blessing for the king.

The structure, vocabulary, and content of this hymn are similar to those of the Hymn to Ishtar (II.1).

i

To the goddess, sun of her people,
To Nanay pray, and praise her rank:
For she is like the new moon to look on,
Her wondrous features full of brilliance.*

ii

Ever bursting into bloom upon her
Are abundance, self-assurance, sweetness, and charm.
She has showered down j[o]y, laughter, and loveliness:
Nanay has sung of [lo]ve.

iii

Walking ever at her side are sincerity,
[Wel]l-being, vigor, decorum,
[Fu]llness of well-being and vitality.
Her path (in the heavens) is always a propitious sign.

iv

She is b[edecked] with playfulness,
Canny mistress, she knows her powers!
She is lovable as her father could make her,
When she set forth, he himself put love charms round her neck.[1]

1. See above, p. 65 note 1.

v

From among all goddesses great Anu
Her begetter raised high her head.
She is unique, proud, and cherished,
He made her lot exuberance, happiness as her ...★

vi

He drew near her, a happy speech
He made to her, causing her heart to glow,
"You shall be mistress of all the world's inhabitants!
"The people shall look upon your light as the sun's."

vii

"O Capable, ..., Capable Lady,★
"Fierce Irnina, most valiant of the Igigi-gods,
"You are the highest one above them,★
"Among them your names are held high in regard.★

viii

"Shine, let your heart be glad,
"Keep on rejoicing in the shrines!
"May the neighboring districts bring you cedar trees,
"Approach, that they be filled with delight and abundance.

ix

"May your special pleasure, your favorite,
"The king you have designated, Samsuiluna, burn(?) offerings for you,
"Tribute of earth and mountain let him ever set before you,
"Let him make his dwel[ling in joy] before you.

x

"The crook of life to the h[erdsm]an,
"Years of justice and truth,
"A well-founded [throne] ... well-being,
"At your command [   ]."

xi

[　may] he [　　　]
Nanay [　　　] is happy.
In the [　　　　　]
... [　　] ... she desired a hymn of praise.[1]

xii

[　　　　　　　　　]
She named [　her] beloved [king　]
Samsuiluna, her [　　]
She named him [　　]

xiii

She has bestowed in addition upon him
Long life enduring and wealth,
To Samsuiluna, whom she loves,
She has given the sun as a luminary.[2]

xiv

At her command her f[avorite] is ruler
H[igher than any] hero [in] the world,
[　] let him rejoice whom she named
[　] in the [　].

([its] an[ti]phon)[3]

(fragmentary line, then text ends or breaks off)

Text: Zimmern, VAS 10 215.
Edition: von Soden, ZA 44 (1938), 32-35.
Translation: von Soden, SAHG, 237-239 no. 2; Seux, *Hymnes*, 42-45; Hecker, TUAT II/5, 724-726.
Literature: Hecker, *Epik*, 86-88.
Notes to Text: (i 4) With CAD I/J, 43a versus AHw, 287a; Seux, *Hymnes*, 42 note 2. (v 4) Collation CAD N/2, 66a. (vi 1) Seux, *Hymnes*, 44 notes 20-22. (vii 3-4) von Soden, ZA 67 (1977), 280.

1. Probably a reference to this text; see p. 67 note 1.
2. That is, he is a just king.
3. Refers to strophe xiv? See p. 68 note 1.

II.3 TO PAPULEGARRA

The main theme of these pieces, as in other Classical period hymns, is the relationship between a divinity's power and the success and obligations of the ruling king. Some of the imagery may be drawn from the more ancient Sumerian hymnography to Kesh,[1] a sanctuary in Sumer that was sacred to the mother goddess. The tablet from which these passages are taken evidently held the text of three hymns, but owing to breaks it is not clear where the second began or ended, or where the third began.

(three columns of text omitted)

iv

Come, the god [   ], song of praise [   ]
[Let me sing] the splendid god, [who strikes down] enemies,   (20)
[Let me sing] splendid Papulegarra,
    who hunts down the enemy,
[Who ...] the mighty lion, the shepherd of the people.
Who lames the arrogant ... hamstrings the hostile,
He looks in fury upon him, he pours out venom on him [   ]*
The roar of his torrent ... he pours out, venom [he ...]   (25)

(gap)

Spinning whirlwind, [   ] ... [   ]   (30)
Throwstick (spanning) everything [   ] the sky.
Fanged dragon spewing [deadly] foam,*
    Bronze-pointed arrow that opens the bre[ast],
Rainfall on the meadow, which increases ...,
    Yearly breeze that deposits the frost,   (35)
Saw of battle, dagger of onslaught,
    Reaper of battle, threshing flail(?)* of struggle,
Hatchet felling the forest,
    Raging fire whose onslaught is deadly,
Iron meteorite that pulverizes the ground,   (40)

---

1. For Kesh and its literary tradition, see Edzard, "Keš," RLA 5, 571-573. For an English translation of the Sumerian Kesh temple hymn, see Gragg, TCS 3 (1969), 155-188, with important contributions by Edzard, OrNS 43 (1974), 103-113; note also S. N. Kramer, "Keš and its Fate: Laments, Blessings, Omen," *Gratz College Anniversary Volume* (Philadelphia, 1976), 165-175.

Wrecker's bar of the cella: Let me recount his praise!
Swamp fire which has cracked hard ground,
> Has consumed the ... of the plain like thornbushes,*
Trampler of the crooked whose advice is dishonest:
> Papulegarra dumps them into his net! (45)
Rampaging lion, terror(?) of the highway.

> *(gap)*

Set out* a throne that he take his (rightful) place!
May the king take his place whose attributes are purest,
Who knows how to rejoice(?)* in the temple on the festival day,
Let him draw out the limits, let him make walkways,
Let him do what is correct for the temple of the gods, (65)
> Let him set commemorative pegs,[1]
Let him cause a close to be built for Ishtaran,
Let him make a womb for the Mother Goddess.[2]
The Ezuzal, temple of Sugallitu, let him build,
A recumbent bull, a high house(?) let him build. (70)
The temple: let it bear its head high,
> Below, let its roots grasp the netherworld.
The Kesh temple: let its head be raised high,
> Below, let its roots grasp the netherworld.
Above, let its pinnacle rival heaven, (75)
> Below, let its roots grasp the netherworld.
O Papulegarra, hunter,[3] rejoice and be glad.

Text: Pinches, JRAS *Centenary Supplement* (1924), pl. vi–ix after p. 72.
Edition: Pinches, JRAS *Centenary Supplement* (1924), 63–86.
Translation: Seux, *Hymnes*, 46–50; Hecker, TUAT II/5, 728–731.
Literature: von Soden, ZA 71 (1981), 195–197.
Notes to Text: (24, 32) von Soden, ZA 67 (1977), 280. (37, 43) WGL. (61) von Soden, ZA 67 (1977), 280. (63) WGL.

1. That is, let him undertake construction of cult edifices.
2. This may refer to a cult object; see Jacob-Rost and Freydank, AOF 8 (1981), 325–327 with plates XXIII–XXV (inscribed pubic triangle in bronze dedicated to Ishtar, Old Assyrian period, discussed by E. Braun-Holzinger, *Mesopotamische Weihgaben der frühdynastischen bis altbabylonischen Zeit, Heidelberger Studien zum Alten Orient 3* [1991], 379). See also III.43d.
3. Literally: "fisherman." In the Old Babylonian period, fisherman often meant marine or commando; perhaps that is meant here (see E. Salonen, BiOr 25 [1968], 160–162).

II.4 SELF-PRAISE OF ISHTAR

This small fragment is of interest as a self-predication of the warrior goddess. It resembles the portrayal of the goddess in the Agushaya poem (see II.6). Compare also III.25 and IV.23. The change in gender in lines 12 to 13 may refer to the masculine and feminine qualities of the goddess.

(gap)

I rain battle down like flames in the fighting,   (5)
I make heaven and earth shake(?) with my cries,
I ..., I make my feet ...
I, Ishtar, am queen of heaven and(?) earth.
I am the queen, ...
I constantly traverse heaven, then(?) I trample the earth,   (10)
I destroy what remains of the inhabited world,
 I devastate(?) the lands hostile to Shamash.
I am the most heroic of the gods,
 she who slays the inhabited world,
I draw back on its bridle(?), he who slays ...
The [Mo]on-god begot me, I abound in terror!

Text: Zimmern, VAS 10 213.
Edition: Zimmern, *Berichte über die Verhandlungen der Königlichen Sächsischen Gesellschaft der Wissenschaften zu Leipzig, Philosophisch-historische Klasse* 68 (1916), 43.
Translation: von Soden, SAHG, 239-240 no. 3.
Literature: von Soden, RA 52 (1958), 132.

B. NARRATIVE AND LYRIC POETRY

II.5 DIALOGUE BETWEEN A MAN AND HIS GOD

This text is of interest because of its affinities with other Akkadian texts that deal with the problem of guilt and man's relationship to his god (see III.14, III.49d, IV.17).

i

A young man was imploring his god as a friend,	(1)
He was constantly supplicating, he was [praying to?] him.	
His heart was seared, he was sickened with his burden,	
His feelings were somber from misery.	
He weakened, fell to the ground, prostrated himself.	
His burden had grown too heavy for him,	
he drew near to weep.[1]	(5)
He was moaning like a donkey foal separated	
(from its mother),	
He cried out before his god, his master.	
His mouth a wild bull, his clamor two mourners,	
[His] lips bear a lament to his lord.	

ii

He recounts the burdens he suffered to his lord,	(10)
The young man expounds the misery he is suffering:	
"My Lord, I have debated with myself, and in my feelings	
"[ ] of heart: the wrong I did I do not know!	
"Have I [ ] a vile forbidden act?	
"Brother does not de[sp]ise his brother,	
Friend is not calumniator of his friend![2]	(15)
"The [ ] does not [ ]	

(large gap)

---

1. That is, in order to weep near a statue or cult symbol.
2. If the god is a friend, he will not treat the sufferer unjustly (WGL).

iv

(4 lines lost or fragmentary)
"[From] when I was a child until I grew up,
    (the days?) have been long, when ... [ ]?   (25)
"How much you have been kind to me, how much
    I have blasphemed you, I have not forgotten.
"In[stead?] of good you revealed evil, O my lord,
    you made [ ] glow ...[1]
"My bad repute is grown excessive, it ... to (my) feet.
"It [rains] blows on my skull(?).
"Its [ ] turned my mouth ... to gall.   (30)
(large gap)

vii

(4 lines lost)
[ ] he brought him to earth,
[ ] he has anointed him with medicinal oil,
[ ] food, and covered his blotch,★   (45)
He attended him and gladdened his heart,
He ordered the restoration of his good health to him:

viii

"Your disease is under control,★
    let your heart not be despondent!
"The years and days you were filled with misery are over.
"Were you not ordained to live,   (50)
"How could you have lasted the whole
    of this grievous illness?
"You have seen distress, ... is (now) held back.
"You have borne its massive load to the end.
"I flung wide your access(?), the way is open to you,★
"The path is straight for you, mercy is granted you.   (55)
"You must never, till the end of time, forget [your] god
"Your creator, now that you are favored.

1. Possibly a reference to disease (WGL); von Soden (TUAT III/2, 138) sees here a reference to omens.

ix

"I am your god, your creator, your trust,
"My guardians are strong and alert on your behalf.
"The field will open [to you] its refuge.   (60)
"I will see to it that you have long life.
"So, without qualms, do you anoint the parched,
"Feed the hungry, water the thirsty,
"But he who sits there with burning e[yes],*
"Let him look upon your food, melt, flow down,
    and dis[solve].¹
"The gate of life and well-being is open to you!
"Going away(?), drawing near, coming in, going out:
    may you be well!"

Make straight his way, open his path:
    May your servant's supplication reach your heart!

Text: Nougayrol, *Revue Biblique* 59 (1952), plates vii and viii, collated.
Edition: W. G. Lambert, *Studies Reiner*, 187-202 (with collations).
Translation: von Soden, TUAT III/2, 135-140 (whence several readings and interpretations used here).
Literature: von Soden, OrNS 26 (1957), 315-319 (with collations); W. G. Lambert, BWL, 10-11 (= note 11); see also J. J. A. van Dijk, *La Sagesse suméro-accadienne, recherches sur les genres littéraires avec choix de textes* (Leiden, 1953), 120-121; von Soden, MDOG 96 (1965), 47-49; Bottéro, *Annuaire* 1964/5, 128-130.
Notes to Text: (45) von Soden, TUAT III/2, 139. (48) von Soden, TUAT III/2, 139. (54) Wasserman, *Nabu* 1991/109. (64) von Soden, TUAT III/2, 140.

1. Perhaps a reference to an ill-wisher who will see the sufferer's good fortune and melt away magically. For the phraseology, compare III.40b.

II.6 AGUSHAYA POEM

This poem praises the goddess Ishtar, personification of war. She always wants to fight; Ea, god of wisdom, endowed her with terrifying warlike characteristics. When her aggressiveness extends even to his own abode, Ea is angered. He convokes the gods, explains that Ishtar has become intolerable, and suggests that "discord" (Saltu) be created to contend with Ishtar. The gods are unable to produce such a creature, and suggest that Ea do it himself. This he does, apparently by taking some dirt from under his nails and mixing it with spittle.

The resulting creature is hideous, fierce, spoiling for a fight — in short, Ishtar's counterpart. Ea shouts at Saltu over the uproar she is making that her task is to humiliate a certain goddess, whom he calls Irnina; but the poet assures us that Ishtar is meant. Saltu is to rush off, barge in on Ishtar, and challenge her for no apparent reason.

Clever Ea now begins to describe Saltu's prospective opponent; the poet waxes into another lyrical description of Ishtar's prowess, putting his words into the mouth of the god of wisdom himself. Ea is carried away by his paeans to the extent that he pretends to have second thoughts, and says that, after all, Ishtar is too awful an opponent for Saltu to fight and that she had better desist. As Ea had calculated, this stings Saltu into a jealous fury and she marches off in search of Ishtar.

A large section of text is lost here. Apparently Ishtar becomes aware of the move against her, and sends out her messenger, Ninshubur, to find out about this enemy. Ninshubur finds (to his amazement) a likeness of Ishtar herself. He comes back stammering a description of Saltu's behavior, refraining from any reference to her actual appearance. Ishtar flies into a rage.

Again, the text is broken, but when it resumes, Ishtar is accusing Ea of having made this monster. She demands that he dispose of it. Ea replies that as soon as Ishtar changes her behavior, the hideous creature will disappear. He had created Saltu just to show Ishtar what she looks like. He ordains an annual holiday in which people dance madly in the streets in memory of Ishtar/Agushaya, etymologized by the poet as "The Mad Dancer in Battle." Ishtar is mollified by this gesture, overlooking Ea's pointed sarcasm about how foolish these people look dancing. The poet reappears, blending his voice with that of Ea. He turns proudly to the audience and asks god and man to honor his marvelous text.

The poem is divided into ten numbered sections. These may have something to do with its performance: it was perhaps sung, recited in a special way, or even staged dramatically. The antiphons are like the choruses in Greek tragedy in that they can serve as an extra-narrative commentary on the action and the characters, as if speaking for the audience.

This text can be read as a lesson in violence. Wisdom (Ea) shows that valor carried to excess is brutal, indiscriminate, and stupid. True bravery knows restraint and dignity as well.

Tablet I

i

Let me praise the greatest one, the warrior among the gods,
The daughter of Ningal's might and fame let me extol!
Ishtar, the greatest one, the warrior among the gods,   (5)
The daughter of Ningal, let me tell of her might!

Her grandeur is manifest, her ways hard to fathom,   (10)
She is always in battle, cunning is her str[atagem].
[   ]

(several lines lost)

ii

She dances around gods and kings in her manliness.   (1)

(First Section)

She is the pre-eminent of goddesses,
The praises of Ishtar let me sing!   (5)

(its antiphon)

She holds in her grasp all (divine) authority,
She bestows it wherever she wills.
Ishtar holds in her grasp the lead rope of the peoples,   (10)
Her goddesses h[eed] her [command].

[   ] her word
[   ] her command   (15)
[   ] the firstborn
[No] one [   ]

iii

Young men are hacked off as if for spear poles.[1]   (1)

(Second Section)

There is a certain hero, she is unique,
Ishtar is surpassing, she knows how to smite down.   (5)

(its antiphon)

Her feast is the melee, the dancing about of (grim) reaping.[2]
  ... the harvest song(?),
She garners(?) the valorous.   (10)
Ishtar's feast is the melee, the dancing about of (grim) reaping,
  ... the harvest cry(?),
She garners(?) the valorous.

Frenzy in battle, pas[sion] in strife,   (15)
Her l[ot] which he gave her, [Ea's?] task.

(26 lines lost)

iv

The royal scepter, the throne, the tiara,   (1)
Are given to her, all of them are her due.
He gave her bravery, fame, and might,
He surrounded her in abundance with lightning bolts flashing.   (5)

He did twice as much: he turned her (mind)(?) with her
      own frightfulness![3]
He had made her wear awesome radiance, ghastliness, valor —
As for her, she felt that valor,   (10)

---

1. The simile may mean that the young men are lopped off like poles to be made into spears, that is, "cut down to size."

2. This and the following lines compare battle with the harvest: gleaning the enemy, raising the happy cry of the harvester, and bringing home the mown yield.

3. Literally: "changed" her; this usually has a negative connotation in Akkadian, "changed for the worse." The lines may mean that Ea's handiwork was so good that its own violent proclivity drove it beyond its maker's control or intention.

In her heart she schemed battle.
In the dwelling of the leader Ea, look out for her terror!

She is more fearsome than a bull, her clamor like its raging,   (15)
She stood forth with no hindrance, in her might she set forth.
At her uproar Ea, the wise god, became afraid,   (20)
Ea became enraged with her.

(Third Part)

"Hear [me, Great Gods! ...]
"Ishtar is wary [   ]
"[   ]."   (25)

(its antiphon)

(several lines lost)

v

[   ]   (1)
"She [   ]
"Let her be trusty [   ], let her have muscle,
"Let her raise riot, be always ready to fight.   (5)

"Let her be fierce,
"Let her hair [be ext]raordinary,[1]
"More [luxu]riant than an orchard.
"Let her be strong of frame,
"Let her complain, she must be strong,   (10)
"Let her gasp for breath, she shall not tire,
"Let her not hold back her cry day nor night, let her rage!"

(The gods) assembled, debated, they could not do it.   (15)
They replied these words to the leader Ea,
"You are the one suited to do this thing.
"Who else could bring about what you* cannot?   (20)

---

1. Exceptional hairiness was considered a sign of primitive strength.

He heeded the words they answered him,
Ea the wise scraped out seven times
The dirt of his nails.   (25)
He took (it) in his hand, baked(?) it,*
Ea the wise has created Saltu ("Discord").

(Fourth Section)

God Ea has straightaway set to his task,   (30)
He is making Saltu that she fight with Ishtar!

(its antiphon)

Powerful is her form, monstrous are her proportions,   (35)
She is artful as none could rival, she is a fighter.
Discord is her form,[1] monstrous are her proportions,   (40)
She is artful as none could rival, she is a fighter.

Her flesh is battle, the melee her hair.

vi

[   ]   (1)
[   ]
She is surpassing [   ]
She is fierce [   ]
She has extraordinary strength [   ]   (5)

Saltu is girded with combat for clothes,
Her clamor goes up ...
She is strange, terrifying to behold!   (10)
Raging, she takes her stand in the midst of the depths,
The words which come from her mouth go around her.

Ea the lord made ready to speak,
To her, to Saltu, whom he created, he says,
"Keep quiet, listen,   (15)
"Pay heed to what I say, hear my orders,

---

1. Or: "Saltu's form is monstrous in proportions."

"What I tell you, do!   (20)

"There is a certain goddess,
"Whose greatness is surpassing, beyond all goddesses,
"Strange and cunning is her (handi)wo[rk].[1]
"[Her name] is Irnina, she is [   ] in mail,   (25)
"The supreme lady, the capable one, daughter of Ningal.

"I have created you to humiliate her: (30)
"In my cleverness I gave your stature,
         valor, and might in abundance.
"Now be off, go off to her private quarters!   (35)
"You should be girded with awful splendor.
"Bring her out,* 'You there!'
"She will rush out to you, she will speak to you,
"She will demand, 'Now then, woman,
         explain your behavior!'   (40)
"But you, though she be furious, show no respect to her,
"Whatever she utters, answer her never a word.   (45)

"What advantage shall she have of you?
"You are the creature of my power!
"Speak out proudly what is on your tongue,
"As an equal before her."

                    (Fifth Section)

                         vii

... has Saltu taken her stand
While Ea, in the midst of the depths, gives her might.

                    (its antiphon)

1. It is not clear whether this means that she is wondrously formed or that she does wondrous deeds; the latter seems more likely.

So the Extraordinary of Form[1] dispatched Saltu,
Rousing(?) her with insults, contempt, and calumny.
Ea the wise, whose reasoning is extraordinary,   (10)
Goes on to put yet a word (right) to her feelings.

The sign of Ishtar the queen he will give her —
Ishtar, indeed, she is braver than all other goddesses —   (15)
He makes her know her grandeur,
     He well describes to her that prideful self,
This lest she avoid her later.
"She is the ..., the goddess whose commands are might,   (20)
"She is the mistress whose(?) way none has barred.

(gap, traces only)

"You may have much to say ... she is surpassing*
"... [you?] may be fierce, but she is unique in herself.
"She is grander than you are,
     Don't break in(?) to people's house(s).[2]

viii

(gap)

"Tell me of her [mission],
"Speak to me of [   ]
"[   ] her might.

"[   ] ...
"[   ] Ishtar   (10)
"[   ] she is surpassing
"[   ] high
"[   ] ... she is mistress
"[   ] the Capable Lady
"[   ] your [ ] is planned   (15)
"[   ] ... valor
"[   ] she is inimical
"[   ] she is victorious

1. Ea may be meant (Groneberg, 111).
2. Perhaps a saying: "Do not rush in where angels fear to tread."

"She is clad in [whirl]winds,*

"[   ] battle.   (20)

"Her [   ], anger, are the welling-up of the sea,

"Let her but reach you, your speech will [fail],

"[Inscrutable] are the ways of

        the capable mistress of the people!"   (25)

Saltu flew into a rage, her face altered horribly,

She turned, she was lordly(?),

[   ] like a fugitive,

[   ] ...   (30)

[   ] ...

[Ishtar] ... did not know.

(Sixth Section)

Tablet II

i

"Come now [   ]   (1)

"Give a command [   ]

"Prepare [   ]

"In this way(?) [   ] the signs of her strength,   (5)

"Find out all about her, learn of her haunts,

"Bring me her signs, recount to me her behavior."

The giver of orders, the tried-and-true Ninshubur,   (10)

Wise, strong, [   ]

... he[ro],

He went out to the [de]pth(?),

He went alone to [   ] to face her,   (15)

He looked twice when he s[a]w the exceedingly great one!

He heeded her, ...

He examines her form:

"She is b-bizarre in her actions,[1]   (20)

---

1. My interpretation of the presumed speech distortion of Ninshubur, owing to his great terror, here and in the following lines, is considered "*ausserordentlich*" by Groneberg, 131, who prefers to see an extraordinary succession of scribal errors, one per line, of a most unusual graphic and grammatical type.

"She b-behaves unreasoningly ...,*
"In her form she is [m-mighty],
"She makes many c-cries for battle,
"She is adorned with a-awesomeness,
"I-in her onslaught she is t-terrible,*   (25)
"She is [mur]derous, bullying, vicious,
"Has the young man and the maid ...
"[   ] clamor."
So did she learn her sign.

ii

(gap)

Angrily the most capable of the gods, the all-powerful,
    took (the sign),
Proudly in her might, fiercely she drew herself up.
The warrior Ishtar, the most capable of the gods,
    the all-powerful,   (15)
Proudly in her might, fiercely she drew herself up!
In her greatness she grinds up her enemies,   (20)
She turns not back, she is the greatest among goddesses,
She is ..., like a young man!
She says a word, proudly she speaks,   (25)
"These are the signs of her might!?"

(iii, iv, v)

(large gap)

vi

Agu[shaya   ]   (1)
The Capable [Lady,   ]
To Ea [did say,   ]
"Why did you create [Saltu?] against me,   (5)
"Who is [   ] of mouth,
"... [   ]
"The da[ughter of Ningal] is unique,
(fragmentary lines, then gap)

vii

"You made [her] enormity,   (1)

"Saltu has set [her] cla[mor] against me.

"Let her return to her lair!"

Ea made ready to speak and said to Agushaya,

      hero of the gods,   (5)

"As soon as you said it, then I certainly did it.

"You cheer(?) me and cause delight

      at your having done with it.   (10)

"The reason Saltu was made and created is

"That people of future days might know about us.

"Let it be yearly,   (15)

"Let a whirling dance¹ take place in the ... of the year.

"Look about at all the people!

"Let them dance in the street,

"Hear their clamor!   (20)

"See for yourself the intelligent things they do,

"Learn (now) their motivation.

"As for the king who heard (from me?)

"This song, your praise, the sign of your valor,   (25)

"Hammurabi, in whose reign

"This song, this my praise of you(?), was made,²

"May he be granted life forever!

viii

"Your [   ], at your command,

      you have given to Agushaya.   (1)

"Saltu is forced away, (s)he entrusted(?) your ...,   (5)

"For the lioness ...

"Who might indeed accept what I(?) ... in her hand?

"You, I made (it/her?) for you."   (10)

---

1. The whirling dance (*gūštu*) the people perform is a memorial to Agushaya (=Ishtar), here etymologized by the poet as "the whirling dancer." Though this seems to be an etiology for a holiday accompanied by dancing, the passage is obscure.

2. A reference to the poem itself; see General Introduction, D.1.

Let me praise Ishtar, queen of the gods,
Agushaya's might, like the Capable Lady [   ].
(As for) clamorous(?) Saltu, strange of splendor,   (15)
Whom Ea the leader created,
The signs of her might I/he[1]
Made all the people hear,
I/He have made fair her glorification.   (20)

(Tenth Section)

He made her greatness suitable.
The lioness Ishtar quieted, her heart was appeased.

(Its Antiphon)

Now that Agushaya [   ]

Text: Zimmern, VAS 10 214; Scheil, RA 15 (1918), 174-182.
Edition: Groneberg, RA 75 (1981), 107-134.
Translation: Labat, *Religions*, 228-237; Bottéro, *Mythologie*, 204-219; Hecker, TUAT II/5, 731-740.
Literature: Foster, *Studies Finkelstein*, 79-84; Wilcke, ZA 67 (1977), 181-186; Hecker, *Epik*, 88-100.
Notes to Text: (I v 20) Reading *la ka-at!* (WGL). (I v 26) With Bottéro, though the usual word for firing clay is not used. (I vi 37/8) Dtn imperative fem of *āru*, according to von Soden, AnOr 33/47, 106f; perhaps meaning "make her come out for battle." (I vii) Read perhaps *pí-ki lu šu-tam-li te-eg-[ri-tim?]* (I viii 19) With CAD L, 19a. (I viii 21) Reading *ú-ul im-la-al-lik* (Scheil). Groneberg, 126, suggests *ú-ul ša?!-la-al* NIG₂! [GA/BA] *ni-ši*, and translates, "Nicht wird geplündert(?) das Hab(?) der Menschen(?)" (note the unexpected logogram). This is unconvincing. (I viii 25) *atbušša šulmat* for *tebussa šalummat*? (II vii 16) For reasons unclear to me, von Soden and Groneberg reject this reading, RA 75 (1981), 133; ZA 69 (1979), 156, and emend to *gudūtu*, "offering stand." A later grammatical parallel is provided by T. Pinches, *Texts in Babylonian Wedge-writing* (London, 1882), p. 15 no. 4, 7: *araḫ ša balāṭi isinni akīti liššakin nigūtu* (see IV.15); see also Walker, AnSt 33 (1983), 145ff., lines 43ff.

---

1. The Akkadian original is ambiguous as to whether a third or first person verb is meant. As suggested above, General Introduction D.1, this may have been left ambiguous by the poet so that one could not distinguish between his voice and that of the god of wisdom.

II.7 AT THE CLEANERS

A sophomoric fop lectures a cleaner in technical detail as to how to treat his garment. The exasperated cleaner suggests that he lose no time in taking it to the river and doing it himself.

"Come now, Cleaner, let me give you a commission:
    clean my clothes!   (1)
"Don't neglect the commission I am giving you!
"Don't do what you usually would!
"You should lay flat the fringe and the border(?),
"You should stitch the front to the inside,   (5)
"You should pick out the thread of the border.
"You should soak the thin part in a brew,★
"You should strain that with a strainer.
"You should open out the fringes of the ...,
"You should ... with clean water,   (10)
"You should ... as if it were (fine, imported?) cloth.
"In the overnight(?) ...
"In the closed container(?) ...
"You should p[our out] bleach and ...★
"The po[ured-out] ble[ach]   (15)
"You should ... in a mug.
"You may want to ... the ...
"You should [tap it] with a cornel-tree branch,★
"You should [   ] a high(?) stool,
"[You should ...] the woven work with a comb(?),   (20)
"You should split the seam and cool it,
"You should dry it in the cool of the evening.
"Lest the weaving get too stiffened by the sun,
"You should put it in a trunk or chest,
    "Make sure it's cool!
"Carry (this) out, I'll make you very happy fast.   (25)
"You should deliver it to my home, a measure of barley
    will be poured into your lap!"
The cleaner answers him, "By Ea, lord of the washtub,
    who keeps me alive,

"Lay off! Nobody but a creditor or t[ax collector]
"Would have the gall to talk the way you do,
"Nor could anyone's hands do the job!   (30)
"What you ordered me I could not narrate, declaim,
                 speak, or repeat.
'Come now'[1] — upstream of town, at the city's edge,
"Let me show you a place to ...,
"The big job you have on your hands
                 you can set to yourself,   (35)

        'Don't miss your chance, seize the day!'[2]

"Do ease if you please the countless [burdens?]of a cleaner.
"If you can't give yourself more breathing room,
"The cleaner's not yet born who will pay you any mind.
"They'll think you a ninny, so, as they say,
                 you'll get all heated up,*   (40)
"You're headed straight for a fall."*

Text: Gadd, UET 6/2 414.
Edition: Gadd, *Iraq* 25 (1963), 181-188.
Literature: Charpin, *Clergé*, 431-432; Livingstone, AOAT 220 (1988), 175-183.
*Notes to Text: (7) With Livingstone, 180-181. (14) Reading *t[u-ša-a]l*. (18) Reading *tu-ta-a[r-ra-ak]* (WLM). (40) Reading *imeššunikkum libbakami iḫḫammaṭ*, where *-mi* = "they say," a proverbial expression? (41) Literally: "Your body sticks out straight for a reckless deed," presumably a colloquial expression of the ilk "cruising for a bruising."

---

    1. Here the cleaner mimics the customer, as in line 1.
    2. Literally: "The meal must not pass, do come in," perhaps a proverbial expression meaning "*carpe diem*."

II.8 LAMENT FOR A CITY

This fragment may preserve part of a goddess's lament for her destroyed city and lost subjects. The city lament is well known in Sumerian,[1] but unusual in Akkadian. This piece may depend on some lost Sumerian prototype.

(gap)

Who stood where I stand to cry out,	(1')
To cry out like a helpless one on her bed?	
Among the established cities,	
my city has been smashed,*	
Among the established populace,	
my man has gone away!	
Among the gods(?) residing there,	
I too have surely fled!*	(5')
My ewe cries out in the land of the enemy,	
my lamb is bleating,	
My ewe and her lamb they have taken away!	
When my ewe crossed the river,*	
She abandoned(?) her lamb on the bank.	(10')

(gap)

My birds [ ] ...	
Without knowing it they are cutting off their wings!*	
Where is my house that I used to dwell in?	(5')

Text: Gadd, UET 6/2 403.
Edition: None.
Notes to Text: (4') Reading *it!-ta-aḫ-ba-aš*, see AfO 19 (1959/60), 52.153. (5') *aḫtalqu*, affirmative subjunctive? (9') Mayer, OrNS 56 (1987), 204. (rev 4') Suggestions of WGL.

1. For Sumerian lamentations of this type, see R. Kutscher, *O Angry Sea (a-ab-ba ḫu-luḫ-ḫa), The History of a Sumerian Congregational Lament*, YNER 6 (New Haven, 1975), 1-7; M. E. Cohen, "Balag-Compositions: Sumerian Lamentation Liturgies of the Second and First Millennium B.C.," SANE 1/2 (1974); *Sumerian Hymnology: The Eršemma, Hebrew Union College Annual Supplement* 2 (1981), 1-6; *The Canonical Lamentations of Ancient Mesopotamia* (Potomac, MD, 1988), Vol. 1 11-44.

II.9 THE FAITHFUL LOVER

This poem deals with the theme of unequal love. A woman is in love with a boor who has taken up with someone else. Despite his selfishness and abuse, she remains true, and eventually wins her prize back, if only through persistence. This Mesopotamian celebration of the power of love, regardless of the merit of its object, is a compassionate forerunner, full of life and humor, to the portrayal of the woman's dilemma in the Song of Songs. One is also reminded of the second elegy of Theocritus on this topic, though there the woman looks more foolish than here.

i

(He)

Moan on,* don't bother to answer, not so much talking!	(1)
What I have to say is said,	
I haven't changed on your account any opinion that I hold.	(5)
He who sprawls next to a woman treasures up empty air!	
If he doesn't look out for himself,	
he is no man worthy of the name.	

(She)

May my faithfulness stand firm before Ishtar the queen!	
May my love prevail,	(10)
May she who slanders me come to shame!	
Gra[nt that I] charm, seek my darling's favor constantly.*	
By Nanay's command I am still ... [proud],	(15)
Where might my rival be?	

(He)

I remember better than you your old tricks,	
Give up! Be off with you!	
Tell your (divine) counsellor how we've sobered out of it.	(20)

(She)

I'll hang on to you, and this very day	
I shall make your love harmonize with mine.	

I shall keep on praying to Nanay,
I shall have your eternal good will, darling,[1] freely given.　　　(25)

(He)

I shall keep you hemmed in, I shall bank clouds around you,
Let her who supports you take away your ardor.
Put an end to your rash talk, use sane words.　　　(30)

(gap of about 20 lines)

ii

(She)

May the queen Ishtar h[eap] oblivion on
　　th(at) woman, who doesn't (really) love you.
May she, like me, [be burdened] with sleeplessness,
The whole night may she doze off [but start awake].

(He)

I despise a woman who can't seduce me,　　　(10)
I have no desire for her charms,
I wouldn't give her [　].
Talking without [　],
What does it [　]?
I'll silence those women who gossip about [me],　　　(15)
I'll not listen [　]
Wherever [　]
I have [not] cast off the one I love,
What do you keep prying into me for?

(She)

My omens upset me,　　　(20)
My upper lip grows moi[st], while the lower one trem[bles].
I shall hug him! I shall kiss him!
I shall look and look upon [him]!
I shall get what I want, despite those women

---

1. Literally: "my lord," a term of endearment. Compare II.11 line 11; IV.54 line 15 (first noted by Held, JCS 15 [1961], 5, 13-14).

who gos[sip about me].   (25)
And happily, too, I [shall return] to my l[over].
When our sleep [   ]
We shall reach [   ]

(*gap*)

iii

(*gap*)

(*She*)

I am running, but I cannot catc[h up with him]:
She has given him away to Ishtar as a g[ift].   (5)

(*He*)

Just as they keep on telling you,
Y[ou] are not the one and only.
Hold off! I have taken my love away, [I shall] not [return].*
I have taken it away from your body,
I have [taken] my attractions a million leagues away.   (10)

(*She*)

I am pursuing your attractions,
Darling, I am yearning for [your] love!
Since your smiles are [my ...],
Let them be ..., I hope [they] won't ... [   ]
I will complain day and night [   ]   (15)

(*He*)

Again and a thi[rd] time I'll say it,
Have I not [   ] the beloved [   ] to my mouth?
Do take your place at the window,
Go on, catch up to my love!

(*She*)

So very tired my eyes are,   (20)
I am weary for looking out for him.
I keep thinking he will go through my neighborhood,
The day has gone by, where is [my darling]?

(gap of about 15 lines)

iv

(He)

I ... [   ]   (1)
The one and only [   ]
Why [   ]
Come on, let me take [my place]
I shall sit and await if he is on his way to me.   (5)

(He)

I swear to you by Nanay and King Hammurabi:
I am telling you the truth about me,
Your love is nothing more to me
Than anxiety and bother.

(She)

They came down on me because I still trust my lover,   (10)
The women who gossip about me
        outnumber the stars of heaven.
Let them go hide! Let them be scarce!
Right now let them go hide!
I'll stay right here, ever listening for the voice of my darling.   (15)

(He)

My one and only, your face wasn't bad looking before,
When I stood by you and you leaned your [shoul]der
        against me.   (20)
Call you "Sweetie," dub you "Smart Lady."
Say the other woman is our ill omen, Ishtar be my witness!

Text: von Soden, ZA 49 (1950), 168-169.

Edition: von Soden, ZA 49 (1950), 151-194; Held, JCS 15 (1961), 1-26; JCS 16 (1962), 37-39 (with collations).

Translation: Hecker, TUAT II/5, 743-747.

Notes to Text: (i 1) [s]ur-pí, reading Hecker, TUAT II/5, 743 note 1a, though with a different interpretation. (i 13, 15) WGL suggests k[a-a-a]m at the beginning of line 13 and a form of šâmu in the gap of 15. (iii 5) [ú-tar], WGL.

II.10 LOVE LYRICS OF NANAY AND MUATI

This poem celebrates the marriage of Nanay, goddess of love, to Muati, a god about whom little is known. The text opens with Nanay looking favorably upon Babylon and its king.[1] She is drawn to Muati and brings him to live with her there. She offers herself to him; he accepts joyfully. The poet asks the blissful groom to intercede with Nanay for the king. The poet, speaking for the king, praises Muati's newly installed image, vowing that he will complete it perfectly. The final prayer to Nanay is spoken by the poet, the king, and Muati. The king named in the unique manuscript preserving this composition is Abieshuh, king of Babylon (ca. 1711-1684 B.C.).

(obv?)

[   ]   (1)
[   ] best, sweet [   ]
She looked upon Babylon with her favoring eyes [   ]
She blessed [it], she ordered its favor [   ]
Every day [   ] vigor (for) the king who dwells there [   ]   (5)
Nanay [   ] vigor for the king Abieshuh.
She set him in a restful abode [   ].

Attraction, attraction, just as we need [   ]
Be to us the source of joy!
She establishes handsome Muati for us, makes him dwell [   ]   (10)
Love charms will rain down like dew.
[   ] form, he always takes new pleasure in her, thirsting for
        what is hers as for water.
[   ] is sweet:

(She)
[   ] "Here are my charms, arouse yourself,
        let us make love, you and I!"

1. So in this translation; there is no way to be certain which is the obverse and which the reverse of the tablet.

(He)

[   ] "Let me have what I want of your delights!"   (15)

[   ] whatever [   ] he will bring [   ] with her.

(four lines too broken for translation)

[   ] your love like [   ]

[   ] straightaway they [   ] together.

(rev?)

[   ] you ... Nanay, to whom I am entrusted [   ]   (1)

[   ] of your love-making ... [   ]

[   ] O Nanay ... let us make love, you and I.

[   ] may I always stay brilliant.

[   ] well-being, may he himself be shepherd forever.   (5)

May I always do the [of] Abieshuh.

I will speak to her lover [   ],

    She will gladly fill his heart with joy!

I will speak to her lover Muati,

    She will gladly fill his heart with joy!

[O], your love-making is honey,

    The [ch]arm of your love is all one could want of honey.

O Muati, your love-making is honey,

    The [ch]arm of your love is all one could want of honey.

The image that you saw there is a (standing) blade,

    Never to be ... [   ]   (10)

I will make you complete, you whose form is such,

    Filled with joy [   ]

O Muati, you whose form is such,

    Filled with joy [   ]

"Let the king live forever at your (Nanay's) command,

    "Let Abieshuh live forever [at your command!]."

Text: W. G. Lambert, MIO 12 (1966), plates after p. 48.

Edition: W. G. Lambert, MIO 12 (1966), 41-51.

Translation: Hecker, TUAT II/5, 741-743.

II.11 LOVE LYRICS OF RIM-SIN

These love lyrics, partly dialogue and partly the chaffing song of the attendants outside the nuptial chamber, celebrate the springtime new year rite when the king, here Rim-Sin, king of Larsa (ca. 1822–1763 B.C.), has intercourse with a priestess to ensure the fertility of the realm. This rendering owes much to suggestions by Lambert and Moran. All indications of speakers are supplied by the translator.

(Singers)

[For the new] year pregnant girls took away the ...,   (1)
While the slender girl has taken his [fi]ne ...[1]

(He)

The [ras]cal(?)★ has taken power over me.

(She)

[   ], my delightful partner, prevailed over me ...[2]

(Singers, to Her)

You are too joyful(?),★ O my beloved, do not rely on him!   (5)
You are in too great ecstasy, do not put your trust in him!

(She to Him)

Now, you are the one and only, you listened, my lover,
    you fell silent in my presence,
You accepted my entreaties, may your heart be eased for me.
In the assembly, the city, and among the fine(?) people
    you spoke well of me.   (10)
My darling,[3] you made me distinguished,
At a suitable time(?) you [raised] me.★

---

1. Perhaps articles of apparel are referred to, but both words are unclear.
2. Perhaps, "by pleas."
3. Literally: "my lord" (see p. 93 note 1).

(Singers)

On account of (his) consort's eye ...
    he is thrown into confusion.
Yes! It is springtime, for which we will always bless him,
We are indeed yearning to see him, for so long,
    many days, life forever.   (15)
The bearer of happiness to Rim-Sin,
    our Sun God for the new year,
Gives her wine which sparkles in my right hand.*

(She)

"Come here, I want to be embraced,
    as my heart has dictated to me,   (20)
"Let us perform lovers' task, never sleep all night,
"Let both of us on the bed be in the joyful mood
    for love-making!"[1]

(She to Him)

Come together with[2] attractiveness and love-making!
    Sustain yourself with life!
Burn out your desire on top of me!

(He to Her)

My love is poured out for you,
    Take as much as you desire in generous measure.[3]   (25)

(rest fragmentary)

Text: Hussey-van Dijk, YOS 11 24.
Edition: None.
Translation: Hecker, TUAT II/5, 747-750.
Notes to Text: (3) Difficult: [GA-ar]-da-mu iḫ?-ta-bu-ut (WGL). (5) ta-BA-ZI from *peṣû?*
(12) *sí-ma-an tu-ša-[qá]-an-ni* (WGL). (17) WGL.

1. Text: "Let me rejoice happily on the bed, both of us." Perhaps the first part of the line is one speaker, while "both of us" is a reply from another speaker.
  2. Literally: "Mingle yourself with."
  3. Literally: "being dues amassed."

II.12 LEGENDS OF SARGON

(a) SARGON, KING OF BATTLE

Sargon of Akkad (ca. 2334 - 2279 B.C.) was remembered in Mesopotamian tradition as a famous conqueror. Epic poems about his exploits are known from the Classical, Mature, and Late periods (see III.7, IV.19). Sargon, King of Battle deals with an invasion of northern Syria and Anatolia. Two Classical period manuscripts have been combined here as "A" and "B" and divided into arbitrary episodes.

Episode 1 (= A obv i)

(Sargon sets out for Anatolia, crosses the Amanus, and decides to go to Mardaman. He prays to Ishtar for help.)

[   ] ... so he may attain Ishtar's desire.⋆
They [dwe]lt in the land so he might attain Ishtar's [desire].
[While] Sargon dwelt in the land, [his] heroes [wi]th him,
      twelve he chose(?).[1]
He saw the Zubi,[2] he brought his army across,   (10)
He brought his army across the fir-tree (land),⋆
      he conquered the Cedar Mountain.[3]
He took for his weapon the lightning bolt of his [g]od Hanish.
He made his offerings, he prayed,
He invoked the ... in measured words(?),
He invoked in measured words(?), he spoke the name of Irnina. (15)
"O my warriors, I would conquer the land of Maldaman![4]
      Whatever you[5] tell me, I will surely do!
"His warriors,[6] (be they) [m]an, lion, ox,

---

1. An obscure saying about Sargon's "fifty men," (see below, III.19d viii = BWL, 251.10) may allude to this episode. For the topos of the king triumphing alone or with a small force, without waiting for the main mass of his troops, see Oppenheim, JNES 19 (1960), 140.

2. Zubi was the name of a watercourse in Mesopotamia between Sippar and Cutha (RGTC 2, 296), but it is not clear that is intended here; see further Conti, RA 82 (1988), 115ff.

3. The Amanus mountains; compare above, I.1.

4. To be identified with modern Mardin, ancient Mardaman, RGTC 2, 118, and probably the Maribadan conquered by Naram-Sin (Grayson-Sollberger, RA 70 [1976], 125).

5. Addressed to Irnina.

6. The enemy king's.

"Great brace of date fronds(?), murderous ...

Episode 2 (= A obv ii)

(Sequence of at least two speeches, one apparently a warning to Sargon of the difficulties of his projected campaign.) [1]

"Beware!* The land of Mar[da]man [   ]
"Meribarapa king(?)* of Nawal ... [   ]
"Which he has, so let him turn back,
      unless he goes straight(?), wealth [   ]
"..., the ... I tell of [   ] you barred.   (15')
"Beware the river! Bring up this your released (captive)
      [   ] of the road
"You will attack; the lords ... face [   ] head [   ]
"The land which her (Irnina's) awesome sheen has covered,
      [   ]
"Let him ... [   ]
"Guarding the ... [   ]   (20')
"At the place the river goes forth(?)[2] [   ]."
[When the king heard] this speech of his,
          (breaks off)

Episode 3 (= B 1ff.)

(A speech addressed to the soldiers by Sargon?)

"You have given me confidence   (1)
"...
"You open my ears.*
"Courage(?), discipline, fighting spirit, valor,
"Have been ... to you from before,*   (5)
"From of old has bravery been [   ] to you!
"[   ] the abundance we enjoyed,

---

1. Line 1 is plural, referring to the soldiers, and line 2 is singular, perhaps referring to the commander (as in line 10).

2. Naram-Sin made a campaign to the sources of the Tigris and Euphrates (Kienast, FAOS 7 [1990], 87), but the reading here is uncertain.

"[the difficult] road to ..., hurry!
"Approach and seize [   ]

Episode 4 (Direct continuation of preceding + A rev i 1-7)

(A speech by a "commander," perhaps a champion, to his men.)

Now the commander says,   (10)
"Look to yourselves, your attire, your equipment,
"As befits a wilderness, the enemy comes upon you like
          a baneful wind.
"May your mouth set your heart on its course,   (15)
"May your heart set your legs on their course!
"Yes! This is the encounter of valiant men,
"Tomorrow I will lead the battle of Akkadians![1]
"The celebration of the manly will be held,
"The writhing (ranks) will writhe back and forth,   (20)
"Two women giv' ng birth, bathed in their own blood![2]
"[On one side?] c mrades are summoned,
"On the other, ... lies agape!
"And proud the man whose mouth at day
"Was game to respond (like this) to the king for a mission,   (25)
"'They have no opponent in the(ir?) king's army,
"'In all the(ir) ranks none shows pride!'
"(But) on the morrow you will be the one
          to be proud inside the palace,   (30)
"They will surely receive acts of recognition
          on your account.*
"Face the enemy's weapon, our foes are ...   (35)
"I shall sing praises for you,
          may the king make known to you my acclamations(?).*
"Your statue he shall set up in front of their statue(s)!"

1. Or: "of Akkad"?
2. This compares the undulating ranks of fighters to two women in the last, bloody moments
of childbirth.

Episode 5 (Direct continuation of the preceding + B rev i 9'ff.)

(The enemy city [Haššum?] falls without resistance;
the enemy troops are massacred.)

Slumber obliterated their watchfulness,	(40)
(Its very) guardian spirit delivered the city safely to the lord,	
With his own hand he heaped up the army in piles.	
The pastures of them he [filled] with heroes(?).	
Forty thousand, all together(?), [ ]	(45)
Those in the thousand(-ranks), wearing triple ... [ ],	
Those of the head(-ranks?) ... breastplates of gold,	
On the quay of Haššum(?), those dressed in iron,	
ready for harsh treatment,*	(50)
Those dressed in linen, ...*	
Skillful in maneuver, outstanding in valor,	
These men like stars were spread over the field.	(55)

Episode 6 (Direct continuation of preceding)

(Sargon next moves against Simurrum. The terrible forest blots out the sunlight, but heavenly beacons come out to illumine the way. The enemy flees at his approach and Sargon decimates the city and its surroundings.)

As Sargon made his invasion to the land of Uta-rapashtim,	
The very forest might have been his enemy,	
It cast darkness over the sunlight, the sun grew dark!	(60)
(But) many stars* came out and were set towards the enemy.[1]	
At their battle cry the walls(?) of the enemy ...,	(65)
Men,* cattle, and sheep he captured all together.	
At that time he ... the Simurrian ...[2]	
... of the Akkadians ...	
... of the Akkadians ...	(70)

1. This event was often referred to in Classical and later Mesopotamian historical tradition: "The omen of Sargon who underwent darkness but for whom light came out" (AfO 5 [1928/9], 215.7; RA 27 [1930], 149, B.16-17; see Riemschneider, ZA 57 [1965], 130). According to A rev i 6'ff., this happened when Sargon left the land of Alzi and approached the forest.

2. Location uncertain, but often mentioned as a Mesopotamian military objective in the third millennium B.C. (RGTC 1, 143f.). A campaign of Sargon against this city is commemorated in one of his year names: "The year Sargon went to Simurrum" (Kienast, FAOS 7 [1990], 49).

He turned the city into heaps of ruins,
He tore out the palace compound(?) for ... leagues,
The [bo]nes which he did not burn, the rats gnawed.*
Fifty allied cities [   ]   (75)

(gap of about 20 lines)

Episode 7 (A, end)

(Sargon summarizes his victories, and challenges anyone to equal them.)

"[I am Sargo]n   (95)
"[king of Kish]
"[ki]ng.
"I slew [   ]
"[   ]
"I slew [   ]   (100)
"[   ] fate before him.
"I slew Amurru
"I ... [   ]
"I slew Subartu(?)
"I ... [   ]   (105)
"I slew Mutubila(?)
"I ... its [   ]
"[   ]
"I slew Carchemish(?)
"I ... its [   ]   (110)
"I slew [   ]
"I ... its [   ]
"I slew [   ]
"I cut off its ... and imposed mourning.
"I slew ... [   ]   (115)
"[   ]
"I paid close attention.
"After I conquered them, I ... them."
To his [   ]
Sargon informed the army.   (120)
"So there, any king who would rival me,
"Let him go where I have gone!"

Text: A = van Dijk, TIM 9 48; B = Nougayrol, RA 45 (1951), 182-183 (collated).
Edition: Nougayrol, RA 45 (1951), 169-180 (B only).
Literature: von Soden, OrNS 26 (1957), 319-320 (notes and collations to B); J. Westenholz, JAOS 103 (1983), 329ff.
*Notes to Text: (1) ir[nittaša], with WGL. (11) WGL: ⌜ḫa-šu-ra-am?⌝. (12') Reading ú-ṣur. (13') Reading Me-ri-ba LUGAL! Na-wa-al^{ki}, but this is dubious. (21') Or: aš-ru-um zi-i-na-ri "place of a lyre" (WGL). (3) With von Soden, OrNS 26 (1957), 320. The tablet seems to have ga-ap-ša-a; one would expect ra!-ap-ša-a or the like: "wide." There is scarcely room for another sign to the left. (5) x-ta-šar!-ku-nu-ši-im. (31) Tablet: sú-un-ka, "your lap" (= "your sake?"). I take this to refer to erection of a statue (38f.) as an act of public recognition for valor, though divine "signs" or oracles may be referred to. (36) A: li-še-wi-ka "May he make of you ..." (singular). (50) na-ab-zu-ḫa-tim = "acts of rough treatment" (buzzu'u); that is, fitted in iron, they were prepared for the worst, but Sargon smote them down. (53) Copy correct; il-la-ab-[šu] excluded. (61) Text: kakkakkabu, perhaps an intentional reduplication to indicate a large number, otherwise a dittography. (66) B: a-wi!-lí-im (WGL). (74) Foster, RA 77 (1983), 190.

(b) THE SARGON LETTER

This fictitious letter of Sargon of Akkad, studied in Classical period schools (compare the "Gilgamesh Letter" IV.20), calls up Sargon's allies for a campaign against Purushhanda, a city in Anatolia (see Sargon, King of Battle, III.7a(1)).

> To Ilaba-andulshu, Etel-pi-Zababa, Ma[nn]um-mahirshum, Nur-Shuruppak, Gasher-Ulmash, Mahru-Tidnum, Amurru, and ...: Thus Sargon the great lord: Now vow to the warrior Shamash, Ilaba, Zababa, and Hanish to move against Purushhanda, as soon as you see my letter.

Text: Gurney, UET 7 73.
Edition: Wilcke, *Archaeologie und Geschichtsbewusstsein* (Munich, 1982), 51 (= note 67), additional collations communicated privately.
Literature: Hirsch, AfO 25 (1974/77), 192; Kraus, AnSt 30 (1980), 115.

II.13 LEGENDS OF NARAM-SIN

(a) THE SIEGE OF APISHAL

Naram-Sin, king of Agade (ca. 2254-2218 B.C.) appears frequently in Mesopotamian literary and scholarly tradition as the type of the "great king." This fragment of an eight-column tablet preserves part of an epic account of Naram-Sin's war with the city Apishal, the location of which is unknown.[1] The lines that remain deal with the preparations, the march, and the receipt of a message from the king of Apishal. Naram-Sin's vizier advises him to advance, without regard to resistance or flight of the enemy. Naram-Sin sends another message to the king of Apishal, who replies in a servile manner. Naram-Sin may be telling his vizier that he will be king of Apishal after the city is taken. According to later Mesopotamian scholarly tradition, Naram-Sin besieged the city successfully.[2] The text has numerous scribal mistakes. The interpretation of col. viii is uncertain, as verbs of speaking have been omitted.

i

"The way [   ]   (1)
"... a strange and hostile land.
"Depart! Let the paths of the mountain be open to me,
        the marvels of the ...!"
"[I will show] you going to battles, bread baked on coals,
"[   ] drinking from waterskins."   (5)
[Naram-Sin   ] Agade* ...
                (breaks off)

ii

Naram-Sin went on his way,
The god(s) of the land went with him.
The "Vanguard-of-the-Way" was going(?) before him,
"Zababa, splendid of horns,"* behind,   (5)
The emblems of Annunitum and Shi-laba,[3] two by two,

---

1. See Gelb, AJSL 55 (1938), 71-72; Glassner, RA 77 (1983), 10; B. Foster, "Naram-Sin in Martu and Magan," *Annual Review of the Royal Inscriptions of Mesopotamia Project* 8 (1990), 40-42.
2. J.-J. Glassner, "Naram-Sin poliorcète, les avatars d'une sentence divinatoire," RA 77 (1983), 3-10.
3. Literally, "She-is-a-Lion," presumably a name for Ishtar.

At right a flank, at left a flank.*

(gap)

vii

"Your brilliance is fire, your voice is thunder,   (1)
"You are become like a roaring lion,
"Your mouth is a serpent, your talons a stormbird!
"Irnina goes with you,
"You have no rivals, who is like you?   (5)
"Calm yourself, let Ishtar and Ilaba be your friends!
"Pass me by[1] and I will swear an oath to you."
While the messenger was repeating this speech,
He was averted (from his purpose) and stood(?)
  while the words went forth(?),
The angry Enlil[2] was soothed(?), the king grew calm,   (10)
The fire blazing in the hero's heart was put out.
Naram-Sin made ready to speak
And said to his vizier,
"Did you hearken to the declaration of the Apishalian?
"Is what he wrote me acceptable to you?"   (15)
To the Enlil's words the counsellor answered,
Saying to Naram-Sin the noble,
"You are the lord, though it be fierce lions
  or though they betake themselves to caves,

(fragmentary lines, then gap)

viii

[   ] he took an omen,
[   ] morning and night,
[   ] the task all day long.
As he approached, the Enlil sent(?)[3] to the Apishal\<li\>an,
"Naram-Sin has sent you a message,   (5)
"What do you answer the furious king?"

---

1. That is, without attacking the city?
2. Here, as in line 16, Naram-Sin, the first Mesopotamian king to claim divine honors, is meant, not the god Enlil.
3. See note 2, though lines 9ff. may be spoken by Enlil to Naram-Sin.

"I answer him, 'You be my god.'"

"Give me your command, let me meet him with it."

"I have given (it) to you, you shall be lord of Apishal.

"[When you ta]ke your place on the throne,   (10)

"You shall smite(?) the land

(fragmentary lines, gap)

Text: (Güterbock)-Pinches, AfO 13 (1939/41), pl. I-II after p. 48, partial copy only; new copy by Finkel communicated privately.

Edition: Güterbock, AfO 13 (1939/41), 46-49.

Notes to Text: (i 3) The reading *ta-ab-ra-at* GIR$_{17}$.ZAL (see AHw, 1299b) excluded by new copy. Note that logograms are not used elsewhere in the preserved text. (i 6) Or "the Akkadian"? (ii 4) Text: *i-la-ba*. (ii 5) WGL: *e-da-ša!-am qá-ar-ni-in*. (i 7) WGL.

(b) THE GENERAL INSURRECTION (I)

A coalition of Mesopotamian and foreign rulers attacked Naram-Sin. He defeated them in a series of battles which acquired legendary, epic character in the Classical period, if not before. The Classical version of the narrative is closer to historical reality than is the Mature version (III.10b), which converts it into a cautionary tale. But already exaggeration of numbers has set in and Naram-Sin is dealt crushing defeats. The enemy has taken on an outlandish, supernatural character (ii 17′).

i

(i 1) [En]lil (is) his god,* Ilaba (is) the warrior of the go[ds]! Naram-Sin, the mighty king, king of Agade, king of the four quarters of the earth, emissary(?)* of Ishtar and Annunitum, anointed of Anu, general of Enlil, governor for Ilaba, who guards the sources of the Irnina, Tigris, and Euphrates, who manifests the power of his weapon* to all kings:

(10) When the four quarters as one rebelled against me, Kish, Cutha, Tiwa, Urum, Kazallu, Giritab, Apiak, Ibrat, Dilbat, [   ], Uruk, and Sippar as one rebelled against me.

(16) At that time — (although) Sargon my father had defeated Uruk, had established restoration for the Kishites, had shaved off their locks of servitude,[1] had broken their fetters, had taken Lugalzagesi, their oppressor, to Agade, (yet they turned hostile to me in a ... and wicked way!),[2] by the verdict of Ishtar and Annunitum he defeated them in battle ..., and he (Sargon swore by) Ishtar, Ilaba, Shullat and Hanish, Shamash, and Umshu: "Kish is no enemy but a brother to me —" (at that time) Kish assembled between Tiwa and Urum, in Ugar-Sin between Esabad and the temple of Gula,[3] and elected to kingship Iphur-Kish, a Kishite, son of Sumirat-

1. This refers to a lock of hair left on the partially shorn head as a mark of servitude; it may also have meant more generally external indications of misfortune (compare III.14 Tablet IV Episode A line m). For "restoration," see p. 166 note 5.

2. This sentence, occurring in an inferior text, may be misplaced, since the sense requires that the "when" of line 10 be resumed by the main clause of 24. For discussion of the passage, though with a different understanding of the meaning, see Jacobsen, AfO 26 (1978/9), 5.

3. Variant: "Temple of Ninkarrak."

Ishtar, a singer. Puttimatal, king of Simurrum, Ingi, king of the land of Namar, Rish-Adad, king of Apishal, Migir-Dagan, king of Mari, Hupshumkipi, king of Marhashi, Duhsusu, king of Mardaman, Manum, king of Magan, Lugal-anna, king of Uruk, Ir-Enlil, king of Umma, Amar-Enlil, king of Nippur

(gap here in main manuscript, the following from a second)[1]

ii

[Gula-DINGIR king of G]utium, [   ]-el king of Kakmium, [   ]-ael king of Lullu, [   ]-anda king of Hahhu, [   ]-li-DINGIR king of Turukku, [   ]-ha-DINGIR king of Kanesh, [   ]-du-DINGIR king of the Amorites, [   ]-sudan-DINGIR king of Der, [   ]-buna-DINGIR king of Ararru, [   ]-itluh king of the Kassites, [   ]-ibra king of Meluhha, [   ]-duna king of SUKURRU, [   ]-en king of Marhashi, [   ]-shar king of all Elam, [   ]-na-DINGIR king of GIŠ.GI, *(two lines repeated by scribe)* [   ]-ge king of the land of NIN-NU, [Mada]gina king of Armanum, [   ] king of Hana, ... [rose?] against me.

(iii 4') My troops dug pits for [   ] leagues, but he piled up dirt [and got over]. When I heard what he had done, I went looking for him quickly, in my mighty battle [I defeated him]. Where there is a dais of my gods Shullat and [Hanish], where I invoked the Capable Lady, Ishtar [my] m[other], and where I had provided beer in abundance that I [   ], [I defeated] Mengi king of Nagu in my [mighty] battle and brought him to the port of Agade. Gula-DINGIR king of Gutium [   ], whom I had [defeated] in my mighty battle and had let go to his own land to [   ] — He is neither flesh nor blood, but [   ] — in Hawannu, the land of cedars, ... before a great gorge in the mountains [   ]. He seized its entrance and attacked furtively at night. He utterly defeated my troops and [trampled them], [he piled] their corpses in a confusion of burial mounds, their blood [filled] the depressions and ravines! Until sunset, six leagues he [   ] nor did he give respite [   ]. He pursued me and [attacked me furiously], 90,000 of my troops under the command of [   ] he utterly defeated and [trampled]. I [   ] in my 360,000

1. Shorter text ends, after gap, with "[I ra]ised against them nine armies by levy of Akkad."

troops, somebody ... [   ] and relented toward me. For the sake of
Sargon [my father and] the deeds and rites he had performed [   ]
they did not enter Agade [   ] nor did they [   ] to the port of
Agade. [   ] Puzur-Ulmash and Rish-Zababa, [heroes of] Agade
... [   ], [   ] Rish-Zababa ... [A]gade [   ] ... [   ] x+60,000
[of my] troops

(after two fragmentary lines breaks off)

Text: Grayson-Sollberger, Dossin, RA 70 (1976), 109-110, 113-114, 116, 118-119.
Edition: Grayson-Sollberger, RA 70 (1976), 102-128.
Literature: Jacobsen, AfO 26 (1978/9), 102-128.
Notes to Text: (i 1) Text: A.ZU, mistake for DINGIR-*šu*? (i 4) *mušāpi* by etymology should be
"one who makes manifest" (here, warfare?). (i 8) Text: GIŠ.ZU for GIŠ.TUKUL, or perhaps
mistake for DINGIR-*šu* "his god."

(c) THE GENERAL INSURRECTION (II)

This fragment is either a copy of a genuine Naram-Sin inscription, or a literary composition in the spirit of II.13b. I prefer the latter interpretation on the basis of (1) orthography and grammar, which are Old Babylonian rather than Old Akkadian, (2) the capture and release of lines 3-5, suggesting that Naram-Sin was epically patient or stupid, and (3) the fabulous numbers in line 8. Unlike the other literary texts of this type, this one ends in a genuine Old Akkadian curse formula, various corrupt versions of which are known from Classical period copies, and which is refurbished in the Poem of the Righteous Sufferer (III.14) Tablet I line 100. The deities invoked are the same as II.13b lines 21f.

> O Ishtar, Ilaba, Shullat and Hanish, Shamash, and Umshu! Nine times they rebelled against me, nine times I took them prisoner, nine times I let them go free! For the tenth time they rose against me for battle: Banana, the leader(?) of Hariam, (and) 65,000 I smote [in] battle. [The]n did(?) Naram-Sin, [by] the weapon of Ilaba [and the scepter of Enlil, (*gap*).
>
> [Whosoever shall do away with this inscription] (*gap*) May Ea block up(?) his watercourse …, may no grain sprout in his furrow. May Nergal, lord of the weapon, break his weapon. May Shamash, lord of due process [   ].

Text: van Dijk, VAS 17 42.
Edition: None.

C. INCANTATIONS

II.14 AGAINST DISEASE

Incantations and magic rituals were as important in ancient Mesopotamian medical practice as pharmacopoeia and surgical procedure. Some incantations were used for a specific complaint, some for a variety of illnesses.

(a) VARIOUS DISEASES

This incantation is directed against an array of illnesses, the identifications of most of which are unknown. This translation, which freely combines two variant versions (A, B), reflects the mood rather than the medical sense of the text.

Congestion, fever, dizziness, pox,	(1)
Severe collapse, ..., redness,	
Boils, rash, tender sores, scabies,	(5)
Itch, prostration, chills, and arthritis:	
Having come down from the bosom of heaven,[1]	(10)
They made feverish the sheep and lambs,	
They made feverish the infants in the nursemaid's arms.	
Whom shall I send with an order	
To the daughters of Anu, seven and seven,	
The ones whose juglets are of gold,	
whose pots are of pure lapis?	(15)
Let them bring their juglets of gold,	
Their pots of pure lapis,	
Let them draw pure waters of the se[a],	
Let them sprinkle, let them extinguish	(20)
Congestion, fever, dizziness, pox,	
Severe collapse, ..., redness,	
Boils, rash, tender sores, scabies, itch,	(25)
Prostration, chills, ..., and arthritis!	

1. A reads: "ziggurat(? Farber: closed-in place) of heaven" (corrupt?) B: "breast" (or: "leadline"?) of heaven, for which von Soden suggests "Milky Way" (AHw, 1092b). C reads here "stars of heaven," and adds, "Now the earth has received them (the diseases)." See also W. Heimpel, "The Babylonian Background of the 'Milky Way'," *Studies Sjöberg*, 249–252 (later texts only).

Subscription (A):

(This is a sacred incantation of Damu and Ninkarrak.
The spell is not mine,
but it is the spell which Ningirimma,
Ea, and Asalluhi cast and which I took.)

Subscription (B):

([I] exorcise you by the warrior Shamash, ..., Judging God!
[Let] the (illnesses) retreat [to] your grasp.
You are [for]giving: revive him (the patient),
Let me be the one to cast the spell (that cures him).)

Text: Goetze, JCS 9 (1955), 9-10 (=A, B); widely variant parallel, Hussey-van Dijk, YOS 11 8 (C).
Edition: Goetze, JCS 9 (1955), 8-18.
Literature: Farber, ZA 71 (1981), 54; JNES 49 (1990), 307.

(b) ALL DISEASES

I will cast against you the spell
    that drives away all diseases, (1)
Which Enlil lent a hand to, ordainer of destinies,
Let Ea cast against you the spell of life,
Nudimmud and Nammu, together with Ea.
Let Nin-nigerimma, mistress of spells,
    cast the spell against you: (5)
Nin-nigerimma, the mistress of spells, has cast the spell!
The sick man will rise, he is not exhausted by her spell,
Let Ninkarrak swathe you with her gentle hands,
Let Damu make your fatigue pass from you.
As for the gall which stifles, the snatcher Lamashtu,
    dog bite, human teeth, (10)
May Annunitu crush them with her spell,
May Adad, Shamkan, Nisaba, Shamash, and the River,
All the pure gods, be the ones to cleanse you,
Together with(?) Enlil may they cleanse you.
May Twin Son and Twin Daughter, the children of Sin,
    Shamash and Ishtar (15)
...
... be enraged at you!
May the King of the Depths, exorcist of the gods, Holy Ea
Cast for you the spell which cannot be warded off.
May he make the ... pass over, ... your travail. (20)
I cast against you the spell that drives away all diseases.

Text: Figulla, CT 42 32.
Edition: von Soden, BiOr 18 (1961), 71-73.
Literature: Landsberger, MSL 9, 83; Farber, ZA 71 (1981), 55.

II.15 AGAINST DEMONS

Numerous incantations are directed at demons. For discussion of demons, see General Introduction, E.7.

(a) A DEMON

In this spell the magician takes power over the demon. The tablet was found in the royal palace at Mari in Syria.

I have overpowered(?) you like a [   ],   (1)
I have bound you like a f[og?].*
I have cast you on (your) behind [   ],
I have taken a string, I have silenced [your] lips,
I have been pouncing upon you like a wolf,   (5)
I have cast my spittle upon you like a lion.
Let me give a command, may my command p[revail?]
      over* your command,
Let me speak, let my speech be stronger than your speech.
As wild beasts are stronger than cattle,
So may my command be stronger than your command. (10)
As heaven is stronger than earth,
So may my command be stronger than your command.
You have tied your nose to your anus.
So there! Have I not slapped you in the face?

Text: Thureau-Dangin, RA 36 (1939), 12.
Edition: Thureau-Dangin, RA 36 (1939), 10-13.
Literature: Farber, ZA 71 (1982), 53.
Notes to Text: (2) Restoration suggested by CAD K, 253. (7) *e-[te-le-et]*? (Farber).

(b) A SICKNESS DEMON

The sickness demon is enjoined to gobble up his poisonous madness as if it were medicine. The infection he bears will disappear, and the demon will withdraw and lose his magical powers over the sufferer. "Mouth" in line 7 can mean either the demon's power of speech, in which case he can only babble harmlessly, or his actual mouth, in which case he has no teeth with which to set upon his victim.

Let him devour his fury! (1)
Let his infection(?) fall,★ as if it were a plant.★
Let him hide his face! (5)
Let his mouth become as it was the day he was born!

(Spell)

Text: Böhl, BiOr 11 (1954), pl. II (LB 1001).
Edition: Böhl, BiOr 11 (1954), 82–83.
Literature: Farber, ZA 71 (1981), 54.
★*Notes to Text:* (1) Possibly, "befall (him)" (the demon), but omission of a pronominal object and a ventive suggest the rendering given here; compare II.33a lines 7–8. (4) ḫašūtu, a kind of plant used for medicinal purposes, etymologically related to ḫašû, "thyme"(?).

II.16 AGAINST A MOTE IN THE EYE

A mote or sty is magically washed out of a sufferer's eye. The sty is the result of a mote raised in the air when the gods were harvesting. This part is considered spoken in the past, a device reflected in the translation by "they say." By contrast, the effective part of the incantation uses command forms without markers of speech.

Earth, they say, earth bore mud, mud bore stalk,	(1)
Stalk bore ear, ear bore mote.	
(Then) within, they say, the square field of Enlil,	
seven units in area,	(10)
Moon was reaping, Sun was gathering.	
(Then it was), they say,	
that mote entered the young man's eye.	(15)
Whom shall I send with an order to the daughters of Anu,	
To the daughters of Anu, seven and seven?	
Let them bring to me★ [pot?] of carnelian, vessel of	
chalcedony,	(20)
Let them draw up for me pure waters of the sea,	
Let them drive out mote from the young man's eye!	(25)

Text: (Landsberger)-Jacobsen, JNES 14 (1955), 15.
Edition: Jacobsen and Landsberger, JNES 14 (1955), 14-21; Landsberger, JNES 17 (1958), 56-58.
Translation: Bottéro, *Annuaire* 1978/9, 93 = *Mythes*, 286; Farber, TUAT II/2, 272-273.
Literature: Farber, ZA 71 (1981), 54; Stol, *Studies Finet*, 165; Farber, JNES 49 (1990), 305.
★*Notes to Text*: (20) Bottéro understands all the following to be purpose clauses, ending the question on line 27, but I have followed the Jacobsen-Landsberger interpretation; compare II.14a.

II.17 AGAINST INFANT ILLNESS

After an introduction setting forth the place of the worm in creation,[1] the magician identifies it as the cause of the child's illness and casts a spell to destroy it.

> Anu begot heaven, heaven brought forth earth, (1)
> Earth bore stench, stench bore mud,
> Mud bore fly, fly bore worm.
> The worm, daughter of Gula, is clad in a traveling cloak,
> It wears blood on its head ..., (5)
> ... the child's blood, an ember in its eye.*
> He cast the spell, Damu and Gula killed(?) [the worm],
> ... he slaughtered them ... [   ]
> He (the child?) opened his mouth, took the breast,
>   raised his eyes and [saw   ].
> (The spell is not mine: It is the spell of Damu and Gula,
>   Damu [c]ast and I took.)

Text: Hussey-van Dijk, YOS 11 5, 1-8.
Literature: van Dijk, YOS 11, 19; Farber, YOS 11, 61.
Notes to Text: (6) Based on a suggestion by Farber.

1. This cosmological motif is discussed by van Dijk, *Acta Orientalia* 28 (1964), 1ff.

II.18 AGAINST GAS PAINS

Natural atmospheric wind is, of course, beneficial (see line 2), but wind locked up in the human body is harmful. Thus the wind should come out and go to its natural habitat. See also IV.35.

> Go out, wind, Go out, wind! (1)
> Go out, wind, offspring of the gods!
> Go out, wind, abundance of the peoples!
> Go out of the head, wind!
> Go out of the eye, wind! (5)
> Go out of the mouth, wind!
> Go out of the ear, wind!
> Go out of the anus, wind!
> Let the man be released,
> Let him find rest [   ], (10)
> ...

Text: Gurney, OECT 11 3.
Edition: Gurney, OECT 11, 21.
Literature: Farber, ZA 71 (1981), 53 and 54 note 3.

II.19 AGAINST CONSTIPATION

This bilingual incantation is of the "Marduk-Ea" type,[1] a common literary form wherein Marduk, son of Ea, learns of the patient's affliction and turns to his father for advice, but his father politely disclaims superior knowledge. In the end Ea provides the remedy anyway (not translated here).

> The insides (are) sick, covered over like a box,   (1)
> Like water in a river, they know not where they go,
> Like water in a well, they have no flow,
> They are covered over like a brewing vat,
> Food and water cannot enter them.   (5)
> When Marduk has caught sight of them,
> He cries to his father Ea,
> "O My Father, the insides are sick, covered over like a box,
> "Like water in a river, they know not where they go,
> "Like water in a well, they have no flow,   (10)
> "They are covered over like a brewing vat,
> "Food and water cannot enter them!"
> Ea answers Marduk,
> "My Son, what could I know that you do not?
> "What I know, you too know,   (15)
> "What you know, I know.
> "Be it a human, an ox, or a sheep ..."
>
> *(prescription follows)*

Text: Pinches, CT 4 8, 88-5-12,51.
Edition: None.

---

1. See Falkenstein, LSS NF 1 (1931), 44-67. This type is often characterized by graphic description of the patient's ills. For a parody of a common by-form of this kind of incantation (Falkenstein, 67-70), see II.32.

II.20 AGAINST JOINT PAIN(?)

This incantation is against a condition called *maškadu* that seems to have attacked the musculature of cattle. "Joint pain" is simply a guess to provide a meaningful translation.

> Joint pain, [joint pain], joint pain is not *maškadu*,   (1)
> It is Shu'u.[1]
> Its lurking place is the [cattle pen?],
> Its standing place is where the sheep stand,
> It bites as a wolf bites, it springs as an Elamite dog springs,   (5)
> It enters as livestock enters, it leaves as livestock leaves.
> Go out, joint pain, before the flint knife, the scalpel of Gula,
>   gets to you!

Text: Hussey-van Dijk, YOS 11 14, rev 1-6.
Edition: See van Dijk, YOS 11, 23f.

1. Name of a demon (reading Farber). The lines refer to the necessity of invoking the disease demon by its correct name for the magic to be effective (Reiner, *Studies Moran*, 424 note 18).

II.21 AGAINST AROUSAL

"Arousal" may refer to onset of sexual desire or anger.[1] The speaker wishes to drive such feelings from his heart. See also II.33b x-xii.

Arousal is coming upon me like a wild bull,   (1)
It keeps springing at me like a dog,
Like a lion it is fierce in coming,
Like a wolf it is full of fury.   (5)
Stay!* I pass over you like a threshold,
I walk right through you like a flimsy door,
I span you like a doorway.*
I turn back your approach like a hobble,*
I drive out the fieriness of your heart.   (10)

Text: van Dijk, TIM 9 72; compare Finkel, ZA 75 (1985), 184 = Gadd, UET 6/2 399.
Edition: Whiting, ZA 75 (1985), 180-181.
Literature: Farber, ZA 71 (1981), 55; Sigrist, *Studies Pope*, 86; see also II.33b xi.
Notes to Text: (8) See von Soden, AfO 20 (1963), 124; differently Whiting, ZA 75 (1985), 185-186. (9) With Whiting, ZA 75 (1985), 186.

---

1. For this correlation in Hebrew, see Waldman, *Journal of Biblical Literature* 89 (1970), 215-217.

II.22 AGAINST DOGS

These grim descriptions of attacks by rabid dogs, either literally meant or symbolic of the onset of illness, are remarkable for their stark power.

(a) SWIFT DOG

It is fleet of foot, powerful on the run,   (1)
Strong-legged, broad-chested.
The shadow of a wall is where it stands,
The threshold is its lurking place.
It carries its semen in its mouth,   (5)
Where it bit, it left its offspring.[1]
    (Incantation to survive a dog['s bite], incantation of Ea)*

Text: van Dijk, VAS 17 8.
Edition: None.
Translation: Farber, TUAT II/2, 256.
Literature: Farber, ZA 71 (1981), 56; Sigrist, *Studies Pope*, 86; Whiting, ZA 75 (1985), 183; Gurney, OECT 11, 22.
Notes to Text: (7) Compare Farber, ZA 71 (1981), 56 note 4.

---

1. That is, the dog's bite causes its "offspring" (hydrophobia) to grow in the victim.

(b) DOGBITE

It is long of leg,[1] it is swift to run,
It is famished for food, scarcely anything has it had to eat!
Its semen dangles from its fangs,
Where it bit, it left behind its offspring.[2]

(Incantation)*

Text: Böhl, BiOr 11 (1954), pl. II = LB 2001.
Edition: Whiting, ZA 75 (1985), 182-183.
Literature: von Soden, OrNS 25 (1956), 144 note 1; Farber, ZA 71 (1981), 54; Sigrist, *Studies Pope*, 86; Gurney, OECT 11, 22.
**Notes to Text*: (5) tu-en-ne₂-nu-ri, see Farber, ZA 71 (1981), 54.

1. Literally: "knees." "Long" (*urruk*) is similar in sound to "fleet" (*urruḫ*) (II.22a line 1), so may be considered a variant version of the same line.
2. See above, p. 124 note 1.

II.23 AGAINST SNAKES

(a) LURKING SERPENTS

In this incantation, "seize by the mouth" may mean "capturing by spell"; compare I.7 part c, where the same expression is used. The mouth in the Mesopotamian view was the organ of independent action and effectiveness, so "control of the mouth" expresses absolute control. See also II.15b.

I seize the mouth of all snakes, even the viper,*
  Serpent(s) that cannot be conjured: (1)
The "No-One-is-There," the "Vacant Lotter,"
  The "Fish" snake, the "Colored Eyes,"
The "Eel," the "Hissing Snake,"
  The "Hisser," the "Window Snake."
It came in by a crevice,
  It went out by a drain.
It struck the gazelle while it slept,
  It secreted itself(?) in a withered oak.*   (5)
The snake lurks in a beam,*
  The serpent lurks in wool.*
The serpent has six mouths, seven tongues,
  Seven are the poisonous vapors(?) of its heart.*
It is bushy of hair, horrible of feature,
  Its eyes are frightful.
From its mouth a spring issues forth,
  Its spittle* cleaves stone.

     (Incantation)

Text: van Dijk, TIM 9 65, 66.
Edition: None.
Literature: Farber, ZA 71 (1982), 55.
Notes to Text: (1) Apparently the direct object of "seize," though the grammar is difficult. (5) Following CAD A/1, 354. (6) With AHw, 1247b; less likely, "the belt"; Variant: *šu-pa-tim*, perhaps, "pits." (7) Following Reiner, *Literatur*, 191, where this passage is translated. (9) Or: "Upper/higher (parts)" = lips?

(b) SNAKEBITE

A snake is here portrayed with the luminous, smooth, greenish sheen of a reed. Like a reed, the snake's head comes to a point, from which brightness radiates.

Adorned* like a reed, green like Tishpak,[1]	(1)
His snout runs to a point, his mouth is a ball of flame,	
His tongues are glaring light:	
May his glaring lights ... for me.*	(5)

(Incantation to survive snakebite)

Text: van Dijk, VAS 17 4.
Edition: van Dijk, OrNS 38 (1969), 540-541.
Notes to Text: (1) Reading [u]*l-lu-ḫu* with CAD M, 153a. *elēḫu* is often used in connection with hair and is normally a positive attribute. (5) Text: *li-a-PI-ti-a-am*.

1. A warrior and vegetation(?) deity; see Jacobsen, *Oriental Institute Communications* 13 (1932), 51ff.

II.24 AGAINST FLIES

In this spell someone brushes flies away from his head and face. The swarm of
flies is ordered to fly away like the rising of a plague of locusts.

> I have swatted you at the crown,   (1)
> From crown to brow,
> From brow to ear,   (5)
> From ear to nostril of the nose!
> I exorcise you by Ninkarrak:
> You shall rise a locust's rising   (10)
> From his thrashing.

Text: Hussey-van Dijk, YOS 11 6, 1-11.
Edition: See van Dijk, YOS 11, 21.

II.25 AGAINST SCORPIONS

The speaker exudes vitality, like a river overrunning its banks, against the dread scorpion.[1] Just as the onrush of a flooding river overwhelms stationary objects like dust, clods, and tiny plants, so too the speaker will overwhelm the scorpion, even though the scorpion can move about. See also IV.41.

> I spew over myself, I spew over my (own) person,[2]   (1)
> As a river spews over its (own) banks.
> Clod in the roadway, dust of the street,
> Shoot in the inundated field, ... of the orchard,   (5)
> The scorpion is different.★
> It will surely come,★
> It will surely strike,
> It will surely not get away!   (10)

Text: Hussey-van Dijk, YOS 11 2.
Edition: van Dijk, YOS 11, 17.
★*Notes to Text*: (6) *ša-a-nu-ú-ma*. (7) Affirmative subjunctive (WGL).

---

1. For a general discussion of scorpions, see E. Douglas Van Buren, "The Scorpion in Mesopotamian Art and Religion," AfO 12 (1937/9), 1-28.
2. Or, "I engender myself" (Westenholz, OrNS 46 [1977], 214f.).

II.26 AGAINST LAMASHTU

Lamashtu was one of the most dreaded figures in Mesopotamian demonology. She attacked young women and small children. The symptoms of her on-slaught, according to later medical texts, could be jaundice, fever, fits of insanity, chills, paralysis, and intense thirst. She brought complications in pregnancy and delivery, as well as sudden infant death. See also I.6, IV.37, and F. A. M. Wigger-mann *apud* M. Stol, *Zwangerschap en geboorte bij de Babyloniërs en in de Bijbel* (Lei-den, 1983), 95-115; W. Farber, "Lamaštu," RLA 6, 439-446.

(a) ANU BEGOT HER

The first part of the text fixes upon the culprit by telling of her origins and mode of entry into the house. The magician then orders her out of the house to a tortured wandering in the wilderness.

Anu begot her, Ea reared her,	(1)
Enlil doomed her a dog's face.	
She is tiny of hands,	
She is long of finger, long(er still) of nail.	
Her forearms(?) are ...	(5)
She came right in the front door,	
Slithering over the (door)post casing!	
She slithered over the (door)post casing,	
She has caught sight of the baby!	
Seven seizures has she done him in his belly!	
Pluck out your nails! Let loose your arms!	(10)
Before he gets to you, Ea, the warrior, as sage for the task.	
The (door)post casing is big enough for you,	
the doors are open,	
Come then, be gone through the (door)post casing!	(15)
They will fill your mouth with dust, your face with sand,	
With fine-ground mustard seeds they will fill your eyes.[1]	
I exorcise you by Ea's curse: you must be gone!	(20)

---

1. That is, to blind her so she cannot find her way back.

Text: Keiser, BIN 2 72.
Edition: von Soden, OrNS 23 (1954), 337-344.
Literature: Landsberger, JNES 17 (1958), 53 note 7, 57; Farber, ZA 71 (1981), 72.

(b) SHE IS FIERCE

She is fierce, she is wicked, she is [   ],   (1)
She slinks about, she is un[canny].*
Though no physician, she bandages,
Though no midwife, she wipes off the babe.
She reckons the month(s) of pregnant women,   (5)
She likes to block the dilation of women in labor.
She dogs the livestock's footsteps
She spies out the country with plundering fierceness.*
She seizes the young man in the roadway,
The young woman in play,   (10)
The little one from the wet nurse's arms.
When the Two Gods saw her,
They made her go out through the window,
They made her slip out the (door) socket,
They tied her up to(?) a t[amarisk],   (15)
[   ] in the midst of the sea.*
...

(A Spell of [   ])

Text: Hussey-van Dijk, YOS 11 19.
Edition: van Dijk, YOS 11, 25-26.
Notes to Text: (2) *i!-l[a-at]*? (8) Farber. (16) See Farber, YOS 11, 64.

II.27 AGAINST A POLTERGEIST(?)

This spell describes a female demon who invades a house, although the subscription refers to eye disease.

[   ]   (1)
Enmeshing net, closing bird snare,
She went by the babies' doorways and brought rash
    among the babies.   (5)
She went by the door of mothers in childbirth
    and strangled their babies.
She entered as well the jar room
    and smashed the stopper(s).
She demolished the secluded stove,   (10)
She turned the ... house into a ruin.
She even struck the chapel,
    the god of the house has gone out of it.
Slap her in the face! Make her turn away to the hinter(lands?)!
Fill her eyes with salt! Fill her mouth with ashes!   (15)
May the [god?] of the house [by?] me.*
       (Incantation for the [eyes])

Text: Farber, ZA 71 (1981), 62, obv.
Edition: Farber, ZA 71 (1981), 60-71.
Literature: Farber, JNES 43 (1984), 70.
Notes to Text: (16) Reading *le-tu-u-a* [   ].

II.28 AGAINST A NOXIOUS HERB(?)

This incantation refers to a mythical(?) herb, perhaps a metaphor for some malaise, that has upset sun, moon, cattle, and humankind. The magician sends his envoy off to Ea, god of wisdom and magic. The envoy repeats the narrative and receives the ritual to counteract the effects of the plant.

> Sun brought the herb across from the moun[tain],   (1)
> It seized the heart of Sun who brought it across.
> It seized the heart of Moon in heaven,   (5)
> It seized the heart of ox in paddock,
> It seized the heart of sheep in fold,
> It seized the heart of young man in roadway,
> It seized the heart of maiden in play!
> Whom shall I send to the great dweller in the depths (to say),   (10)

(The text repeats itself so far as preserved, then after a break it ends with: "I purified ...")

Text: Hussey-van Dijk, YOS 11 11.
Edition: Farber, JNES 49 (1990), 308-309.
Literature: van Dijk, YOS 11, 22.

II.29 AGAINST A DISEASE OF SHEEP AND GOATS

In heaven [above] a blaze broke out,   (1)
Congestion(?) has fallen upon all the beasts.
It has made feverish kids, lambs,   (5)
And little ones in the wetnurse's arms!
Address[1] this to my mother Ningirimma:
"Let the beasts' faces brighten!
"Let the cattle rejoice!   (10)
"Let the green plants rejoice!
"Let the roadway rejoice!"[2]
I will set for all time sun disks
In the dwellings of the great gods, with loving care.[3]   (15)
          (Incantation for sheep constriction[?])

Text: Hussey-van Dijk, YOS 11 7.
Edition: van Dijk, YOS 11, 21.

1. As Farber suggested to me, the "seven and seven" (see above, II.14a, II.16) are called upon here.
2. This may be a metonym for humankind; compare II.28, line 8.
3. This may refer to a dedication of precious objects secured to the clothing of cult images; see A. L. Oppenheim, "The Golden Garments of the Gods," JNES 8 (1949), 172-193.

II.30 FOR A WOMAN IN LABOR

The perilous journey from the womb to the world was eased by magical rites and words spoken by the midwife. See also IV.48.

(a) SHE HAS NEVER GIVEN BIRTH

In this text, Sun and Moon look with sorrow upon the agonies of the mother, transmuted into a legendary cow (see also III.48b).

The cow was pregnant, the cow is giving birth,	(1)
In the paddock of Shamash, the pen of Shamkan.[1]	
When he saw her, Shamash was crying,	
When the Pure-rited[2] One saw her, his tears came	
flowing down.	
Why is Shamash crying,	
Why are the Pure-rited One's tears flowing down?	
"For the sake of my cow, who has never been breeched!"	
"For the sake of my kid, who has never given birth!"*	(10)
[Whom shall I send with an order to the	
the daught]er(s) of Anu, seven [and seven],[3]	
[May] they [ ] their pots of [ ],	
May they bring this baby straight forth!	
If it be male, like ...	(15)
If it be female, like...[4]	
let it come into the world.	

(Incantation for a woman in labor)

Text: van Dijk, VAS 17 34.
Edition: van Dijk, OrNS 41 (1972), 343-348.
Translation: M. Stol, *Zwangerschap en geboorte bij de Babyloniers en in de Bijbel* (Leiden, 1983), 31.
Literature: van Dijk, OrNS 41 (1972), 339-348; Farber, ZA 71 (1981), 26; Farber, JNES 49 (1990), 308.

1. Shamkan, the cattle god, was son of Shamash (van Dijk, OrNS 41 [1972], 344).
2. An epithet of the moon.
3. Compare II.16.
4. Farber suggests "like a lock-bolt? may it [the baby] drop hither (from the womb) to the ground!"

Notes to Text: (9) See Finkel, AfO 27 (1980), 44 note 12. (10) See AHw, 1420b; WGL suggests: "my unborn calf." (15) Moran, RA 77 (1983), 189 (also, independently, WGL).

(b) THE CHILD'S ARMS ARE BOUND

This incantation asks Asalluhi, god of magic, to save a child stuck in the womb and release him to the waiting midwife.

In the waters of intercourse	(1)
Bone was formed,	
In the flesh of sinews	
Baby was formed.	
In the ocean waters, fearsome, raging,	(5)
In the water of the far-off sea,	
There is the little one, his arms are bound!	
There within, where the sun's eye cannot bring brightness,	
Asalluhi, Enki's son, saw him.	
He loosed his tight-tied bonds,	(10)
He set him on the way,	
He opened him the path.	
"The path is [op]ened to you,	
"The way is [made straight?] for you,	
"The ... physician(?) is waiting for you,	
"She is maker of [bl]ood(?),	
"She is maker of us all."	(20)
She has spoken to the doorbolt, it is released.	
"The lock is [fre]ed,	
"The doors thrown wide,	
"Let him strike [ ],	(25)
"Bring yourself out, there's a dear!"	

Text: Hussey-van Dijk, YOS 11 86, 1-28.
Edition: van Dijk, OrNS 42 (1972), 502-507.

II.31 TO CALM A BABY

Babylonian parents sometimes tried magic words to calm fretting and crying babies. See also IV.49.

> Little one who dwelt in the dark chamber,[1] (1)
> You really did come out here, you have seen the [sunlig]ht.
> Why are you crying? Why are you [fretting]?
> Why did you not cry in there?
> You have disturbed the household god,
>   the bison(-monster) is astir, (saying), (5)
> "Who disturbed me? Who startled me?"
> The little one disturbed you, the little one startled you.
> Like wine tipplers, like a barmaid's child,[2] (10)
> Let sleep fall upon him!
>   (Incantation to calm a little one)

Text: Farber: ZA 71 (1981), 62 rev.
Edition: Farber, ZA 71 (1981), 60-71; *Baby-Beschwörungen*, 34-35.
Literature: Farber, Anthropos 85 (1990), 141ff.

1. Probably, with Farber, 68, a metaphor for the womb.
2. Perhaps a reference to the expected alcoholic intake of a child nursed by a woman of bibulous habits, and the child's resulting stupor.

II.32 AGAINST A BLEATING GOAT

This bilingual parody expresses the murderous rage of a man unable to sleep because of a bleating goat. He claims that Ea, god of wisdom, also disturbed, abruptly sent off the great god Marduk (without the usual consultation), and charged him with silencing the offending animal. Marduk is commanded to insert the goat's own dung into its ear, a sort of "ear-for-an-ear" reprisal in that the goat has filled the sufferer's ears with its plaints. The sleepless one contemplates the goat's demise with relish. He hopes that the gods of livestock will not take this amiss, and expresses confidence that the whole country will erupt with praise and thanksgiving at the awe-inspiring deed.

When the Ea [ ],	(1)
And Enlil [ ],	
On account of what pertained to the b[easts].	
He caught sight of a goat.	
The goat is sick, it cannot [shut?] its mouth(?)!	(5)
The shepherd is disturbed and cannot sleep,	
It disturbs his herdsman,	
Who must go about, day and night, forever herding.*	
When Enki saw it,	
He called the Wise One, sent him off with weighty charge,	(10)
"A goat in pen or fold ... is disturbing me.	
"Go, it must not disturb me!"	
"Take its dung,	
"Stuff it into its left ear,	
"That goat, instead of falling asleep, let it drop dead!"	(15)
May Shamkan, lord of the beasts, hold nothing against me,	
Nor serve me summons for this case.	
Folk and land will sing your praises,	
Even the great gods will praise what you can do!	(20)

Text: Genouillac, PRAK II pl. 3, C1.
Edition: W. G. Lambert, *Studies Garelli*, 415-419.
Literature: Farber, ZA 71 (1981), 53.
Notes to Text: (8) With AHw, 977a.

II.33 LOVE CHARMS

(a) HORNS OF GOLD

Like the Old Akkadian love charm, I.4, this opens with a description of the love charm (a). The speaker hopes that the woman of his choice will remain available (b), and that he can acquire power over her (c). He concludes by apostrophizing her (d). This translation incorporates readings and suggestions by W. G. Lambert. See also IV.45.

(a)

Love charm, love charm!   (1)
Its horns are of gold,
Its(!)* tail of pure lapis,
It is placed in Ishtar's heart.

(b)

I called to her, but she did not come back to me,   (5)
I whistled at her,[1] but she did not look at me.
If she is "consecrated," may her lover fall,
If she has been taken, may her accuser fall.[2]

(c)

(May the) marriageable girl, the free-born young lady,
Fall at my clamor, at my shout.   (10)
May the dough fall from her hands,[3]
May the little boy(?) at her side ... to her.

---

1. This may refer to the prolonged hiss that serves throughout the Near East today as a "wolf whistle."

2. As WGL suggests, this couplet may refer to the speaker's proprietary attitude towards the girl's virginity. If she is pure, may any would-be lover not deflower her; if she has been deflowered, may her accuser not prove his case.

3. This and the next line may refer to domestic tasks, one involving food preparation and the other child care (her younger brother?), that the beloved will be unable to perform while the charm affects her heart.

(d)

You set up your household for your household utensils,★
Look upon me as if (I were) a leash!
Follow me around like a calf!★
Why did you bind your head with my love, like a headband?★

(six lines fragmentary)

Text: Hussey-van Dijk, YOS 11 87.
Literature: Westenholz, OrNS 46 (1977), 206f.
★*Notes to Text*: (3) Text: *zi-ba*-ZI. (d) WGL.

(b) LOOK AT ME!

These spells are intended for men and women in love who wish to attract or to arouse sex partners. Their explicitness can be compared with I.4, II.9, and II.11. References to speakers are supplied by the translator on the basis of grammatical forms in the original that distinguish masculine and feminine. Various Sumerian incantations in this collection have been omitted.

ii

(She)

"With dog slaver, thirst(?), hunger(?),   (1)
"Slap in the face, deflection of eye,
"I have hit you on the head, I have driven you out of your mind!
"Set your thinking to my thinking,
"Set your reason to my reason!   (5)
"I hold you in restraint, as Ishtar held Dumuzi,
"(As) liquor binds him who drinks of her,[1]
"I have bound you with my mouth for breaths,*
"With my vulva for urination,
"With my mouth for spitting,   (10)
"With my vulva for urination.
"May no rival come to you!
"Dog is crouching, pig is crouching,
"You too keep crouching on my thighs!"

(ritual follows)

iii

(She)

"Look at me, feel tension like (a taut harp) string,
"May your heart glow as with liquor,
"Keep bursting forth like the sun upon me,
"Keep renewing yourself for me like the moon,
"... may your love ever be new."

(ritual follows)

---

1. Or, "I have bound you (as) liquor ..."

iv

(She)

"Get your legs underway, Erra-bani,[1]
"Get your middle in motion,
"Let your sinews follow after."

(He)

"Let your heart rejoice,
"Let your spirits be happy,
"I will swell large as a dog!
"Your ... are like a hobble-rope,
"Don't let them go limp(?) on me!"

(Love incantation)

v

(He)

"Stay awake at night,
"Don't go to sleep in the day,
"You shall not sit down nights!"

(Love incantation)

vi

(She)

"Beloved, beloved,
"You, whom Ea and Enlil installed,
"As Ishtar sits on dais,
"As Nanay sits in chamber,
"I close you in!
"High priestesses love burning(?),
"Wives despise their husbands!
"Cut off her stuck-up nose,
"Set her nose under my foot!
"Just as her love was too strong for me,
"So may my love be too strong for her love."

(Love incantation)

---

1. Personal name, whether real or proverbial is unknown.

vii

(He)

"Why are you as hard as a thorn in a thicket,

(She)

"Why is your desire as perverse as a child's?

(He)

"Why is your face so hostile?
"Why am I invisible, do not exist?

(She)

"In your heart lies a dog, lurks a pig,
"You lie down with me and I'll pluck out your bristle,
"Take what you have in your hand and put it into my hand."

(Incantation ...)

viii

(She)

"Where is your heart going?
"Where are your eyes lo[oking]?
"Let [your heart come] to me!
"Let [your eyes look at] me!
"Look at me l[ikc   ]
"Gaze at me [   ]
"You will [hunger for] me like bread,
"You will [thirst for] me like beer.
"...

(Love incantation)

x

(She)

"[Arousal], arousal!
"It ke[eps its place] in his heart.
"Let me give you cool water to drink,
"Let me give you ice and coolants.
"Your heart is vigor, like a wolf,
"Like a lion, may splendor possess you.
"Spring, O arousal of Nanay!"

xi

(She)

"Arousal, arousal!¹
"He [comes upon me] like a wild bull,
"He [keeps springing at me] like a hound,
"L[ike a lion he is furious] in his onset,
"Li[ke a wolf] he goes where he lists.
"…
"I [broke the …] of his heart,
"I will cross him like a bri[dge],
"The Tigris river is under [him].
"Spring, [O arousal] of Nanay!"

xii

(She)

"Arousal, arousal!
"I will step over you like a threshold,
"I will traverse you like open gro[und],
"Spring, O [ar]ousal of Nanay!"

(Incantation, using? a lump of salt)

1. Compare II.21. There the incantation seems to be directed against arousal, unless the last line means that she appeases him; here the same language may be used to wish arousal upon the beloved.

xiii

(She)

"Big mouth, floppy ears, Iddin-Damu,[1]

"Open your mouth like a ...-fish.

"Your heart is a ...-plant.

"I lapped at your heel,

"I took the ...

"I caught your leg.

"Cuddle me like a puppy,

"M[ount] me like a dog!"

(Incantation, using soap-plant)

xiv

(She)

"I have hit you on the head,

"You will squirm around me on the ground like a [   ],

"You will ... the ground like a pig,

"Until I'll have my way, like a child!"

xv

"Both onion and ox stick up a blade,

"As river moistened its banks,

"I make myself moist,

"I make my body moist.

"I have opened my seven doors for you, Erra-bani,

"...

"Bring the constant gnawing of your heart to an end on me!"

Text: Wilcke, ZA 75 (1985), photo opposite p. 208.

Edition: Wilcke, ZA 75 (1985), 198-209.

Notes to Text: (8) W. G. Lambert in M. Minden *et al.*, eds., *Figurative Language in the Ancient Near East* (London, 1987), 38.

1. See p. 142 note 1.

D. PRAYERS AND LETTER PRAYERS

II.34 NOCTURNAL PRAYERS OF DIVINERS

The following two prayers are offered by a diviner to the gods of the night sky
(i) or to the gods of divination, including various nocturnal creatures (ii). The
first is a soliloquy by the diviner as he keeps his lonely vigil: the great gods of
the daytime and mankind in general are all asleep, while he must stay awake
and watch. The only other living creature he sees is a solitary wayfarer. The
diviner prays that the constellations will assist in making the extispicy successful, now that the daytime gods of extispicy, especially the sun, are asleep.

(a) TO GODS OF THE NIGHT

The noble ones are safely guarded(?),* doorbolts drawn,
    rings in place,[1]   (1)
The noisy people are fallen silent, the doors are barred
    that were open.
Gods of the land, goddesses of the land,   (5)
Shamash, Sin, Adad, and Ishtar[2] are gone off to
    the lap of heaven,*
They will give no judgment, they will decide no cases.
Night draws a veil, the palace is hushed,
    the open land is deathly still,   (10)
The wayfarer cries out to[3] a god, even the petitioner
    (of this omen) keeps on sleeping!
The true judge,[4] father to the orphaned,
    Shamash has gone off to his bedchamber.   (15)
May the princely ones[5] of the gods of the night:
    brilliant Girra, warrior Erra,
The "Bow," the "Yoke," Orion, the "Dragon,"

---

1. Variant (b): "Pegs and rings are set."
2. Variant (b): "Adad and Ea, Shamash and Ishtar."
3. Variant (b): "prays to."
4. Variant (b): "true father."
5. Variant (a): "'The Bow', Elamatum, Pleiades, Orion, the 'Dragon', the Great Bear, Lyra,
the 'Bison.'"

The Great Bear, the Lyre, the "Bison,"
    the "Horned Serpent," (20)
Stand by! In the extispicy I perform,
    in the lamb I offer, place the truth!

(b) TO SHAMASH AND GODS OF THE NIGHT

O lofty Shamash, j[udge] Shamash, (1)
O Enki, Ninki, Ala[la, Belili],[1]
Ningizzida prefect [of the (nether)world],*
O ominous malformed creature ... [   ],
O wandering nightfowls [   ], (5)
O Moon, luminary of the [pure] sky:
In the extispicy I perform —

Text: (a) Dossin, RA 32 (1935), 182-183 (34a, b); (b) Schileico, *Izvestija Rossiskoj Akademii Istorii Material'noj Kul'tury* 3 (1924), 144ff. (34a only).
Edition: Dossin, RA 32 (1935), 179-187; von Soden, ZA 43 (1936), 306-308.
Translation: von Soden, SAHG, 274 no. 20; Stephens, ANET[3] 390-391; Oppenheim, AnBi 12 (1959), 295-296; Seux, *Hymnes*, 475-480; Hecker, TUAT II/5, 718-719.
Literature: Oppenheim, AnBi 12 (1959), 289-301 (aesthetic appreciation of 34a); Hirsch, *Kindlers Literaturlexikon* I, 328; von Soden, "Gebet II," RLA 3, 163-164.
Notes to Text: (1) Livingstone, *Nabu* 1990/86. (6) Heimpel, JCS 38 (1986), 130. (3) Restoration WGL.

---

1. Variant (b): "great ones."

II.35 DIURNAL PRAYERS OF DIVINERS

Extispicy, or divination by examination of the entrails of a lamb (exta), required a series of prayers and rituals, culminating in sacrifice and examination of the animal. The prayer and rituals (*ikribu*)[1] are replete with legal imagery: the procedure is a "case"; inducements are offered for a favorable decision; the outcome is a "verdict"; the principal gods concerned are Shamash, god of justice, and Adad, god of thunder. The prayers were intended to attract the god's attention, to enlist his help for proper procedure, and to elicit, if possible, a favorable verdict for the client. Often the specific favorable features of the exta are itemized together with the more general requests of the prayer, as in The Lamb (II.35b) line 16. Where the client's name was to be given, the manuscripts refer to "so-and-so, son of so-and-so."

(a) THE CEDAR

O Shamash, I place in my mouth sacred cedar,   (1)
For you I knot it in a lock of my hair,
For you I place in my lap bushy cedar.

I have washed my mouth and hands,   (5)
I have wiped my mouth with bushy cedar,
I have tied sacred cedar in a lock of my hair,
For you I have heaped up bushy cedar.
Cleansed now, to the assembly of the gods[2]
    draw I near for judgment.   (10)
O Shamash, lord of judgment, O Adad, lord of prayers
    and acts of divination.
In the ritual I perform, in the extispicy I perform,
    place the truth!

O Shamash, I place incense in my mouth,
… sacred cedar, let the incense linger!   (15)

---

1. *Ikribu* is a prayer made in connection with extispicy procedure (I. Starr, *The Rituals of the Diviner*, BM 12 [1983], 45f.). I have translated the word in extispicy prayers as "ritual" (Starr, "extispicy-ritual"), and elsewhere, when it is used as a synonym only, as "prayer."
2. Or: "cleansed for the assembly of the gods."

Let it summon to me the great gods.
In the ritual I perform, in the extispicy I perform,
    place the truth!

O Shamash, I hold up to you water of Tigris and Euphrates,
Which has carried to you cedar and juniper
    from the highlands.   (20)
Wash yourself, O valiant Shamash,
Let the great gods wash with you.
And you too, Bunene, faithful messenger,
Wash yourself in the presence of Shamash the judge.

O Shamash, to you I hold up something choice,   (25)
    ... sacred water for the flour.
O Shamash, lord of judgment,
    O Adad, lord of prayers and divination,
Seated on thrones of gold, dining from a tray of lapis,
Come down to me that you may dine, that you may sit
    on the throne and render judgment!
In the ritual I perform, in the extispicy
    I perform, place the truth!

O Shamash, I hold up to you a lordly tribute,
Which in the ... of the gods to you [   ].   (35)
O Shamash, lord of judgment, O Adad l[ord of acts of]
Divination, seated on thrones of gold,
Dining from a tray of lapis, come down to me
That you may sit on the throne and render judgment!
In the ritual I perform, in the extispicy I perform,
    place the truth!   (40)

O Shamash, I hold up to you seven and seven sweet loaves,
The rows of which are ranged before you.
O Shamash, lord of judgment, O Adad, lord of divination,
Seated on thrones of [gold], dining from a tray of lapis,   (45)
Come [down to me] that you may eat,
That you may sit on the throne and render judgment.

In the ritual I perform, in the extispicy I perform,
    place the truth!

O Shamash, I hold up to you the plentiful yield of the gods,
    the radiance of the grain goddess.   (50)
O Shamash, lord of judgment, O Adad, lord of divination,
In the ritual I perform, in the extispicy I perform,
    place the truth!

O Shamash, I have laid out for you the plentiful yield of
    the gods, the radiance of the grain goddess,
O Shamash, lord of judgment, O Adad,
    lord of prayer and divination,   (55)
In the ritual I perform, in the extispicy I perform,
    place the truth!

Take your seat, O valiant Shamash,
Let there be seated with you the great gods,
Let Anu, father of heaven, Sin, king of the tiara,   (60)
Nergal, lord of weaponry, Ishtar, lady of battle
Be seated with you.
In the ritual I perform, in the extispicy I perform,
    place the truth!

Text: Hussey-van Dijk, YOS 11 22.
Edition: Goetze, JCS 22 (1968), 25-29.
Translation: Seux, *Hymnes*, 467-470; Hecker, TUAT II/5, 719-721.

(b) THE LAMB

[O Shamash, lo]rd of judgment, O Adad, lord of extispicy
 and divination,   (1)
I [hold up] to you a sacred lamb, offspring of a ewe,
 a bright-eyed(?) lamb,
A sacred ...-lamb, curly of fleece, which was appointed(?)
 for this at birth.
Its fleece, which no shepherd plucked, neither right nor left,
 I will pluck for you;
Its fleece of right and left side [I will set out] for you.   (5)
Invite the great gods with resin, let cedar and resin
 invite (all of) you.
In the extispicy I perform, in the ritual I perform,
 place the truth!
[In the matter of?] so-and-so, son of so-and-so, in the lamb
 I offer, place the truth!
[I cal]l* to you, Shamash, I beseech you to cleanse me!
In the lamb I offer, place the truth!
O Shamash, you opened the bolts of heaven's gates, you
 ascended (to this place) a stairway of purest lapis,
Lifting (it) up, you hold a scepter of lapis at your side for the
 case you (gods) judge here.   (10)
The case of the great gods you judge, the case of the wild
 beast you judge, the case of mankind you judge:
Judge this day the case of so-and-so, son of so-and-so,
 on the right of this lamb, on the left of this lamb,
 place the truth!
Come in, O Shamash, lord of judgment; come in, O Adad,
 lord of extispicy rituals and divination; come in, O Sin,
 king of the tiara,
And Ishara, lady of divination, who dwells in the inner
 chamber, Gu'anna, recorder of the gods,
 herald of Anu;
Nergal, lord of the weapon: cause to be present the divinity
 in charge of the extispicy I perform,
 and in the extispicy I perform place the truth!   (15)

In the handiwork of the great gods, in the tablet of the gods,
>   let the "vesicle" be in place.
Let Nisaba, the scribe, write the case down.
Let the divine shepherd bring forward a sheep to the assembly
>   of the great gods, so the ca[se may go we]ll(?).
Let the judges, the great gods, who sit on thrones of gold,
>   who dine from trays of lapis, take their seats before you.
Let them judge the case in justice and righteousness.
Judge this day the case of so-and-so, son of so-and-so.
On the right of this lamb, on the left of this lamb,
>   place the truth!   (20)
I perform this extispicy for the well-being of so-and-so,
>   son of so-and-so, for well-being.

Text: A=Hussey-van Dijk, YOS 11 23; B (parallel)=Nougayrol, RA 38 (1941), 87 AO 7032.
Edition: I. Starr, *The Rituals of the Diviner*, BM 12 (1983), 30-31, 37-38, 44-60 (A); 122-123 (B).
Translation: von Soden, SAHG, 275 no. 21 (B only).
Notes to Text: (9) WGL.

(c) WILL UR-UTU BE ALIVE AND WELL?

This prayer is a general oracular inquiry about the well-being of Ur-Utu, a priest or professional man attached to the local temple in a village near Sippar in the Old Babylonian period. He was presumably one of the leading citizens of the community.

O God, my lord Ninsianna, accept this offering, stand by me when this offering is made, place there an oracle of well-being and life for Ur-Utu, your servant! Concerning Ur-Utu, your servant, who is now standing by this offering, from April[1] 20 until April 20 of the coming year, six times sixty days, six times sixty nights, by command of a god, by command of a goddess, by command of a king, by command of a noble, by command of a commoner, by command of fate or regulation, by any command whatsoever, will Ur-Utu be alive and well? From April 20 until April 20, six times sixty days, six times sixty nights, until next year, will Ur-Utu be alive and well? In his household: his wife, his sons, his daughters, his brother, his sister, his near and distant kin, his neighbor, anyone on (his) street who likes him? In the ritual I perform ... Will Ur-Utu be alive and well? Place an oracle of well-being and life for Ur-Utu!

Text: De Meyer, *Studies Kraus*, 272.
Edition: De Meyer, *Studies Kraus*, 274-277.

1. Text: Nisan, the first month of the Babylonian year (spring).

II.36 KUSSULU TO THE MOON GOD

This bitter harangue, written on a pierced cylinder, is addressed to the Moon God by a certain Kussulu. He loaned money to a certain Elali without a written document, but was instead content with the debtor's four-fold oath in the precinct of the Moon God's temple at Ur, and, apparently, a symbolic gesture.[1] Perhaps Kussulu had wanted to avoid the costs of a scribe and witnesses. The debtor failed to repay. He married and raised a family, although a consequence of breaking an oath was supposed to be infertility. Kussulu had no recourse save a direct appeal to the gods concerned by the broken oath to exercise their power and thereby prove their greatness.

O Nanna, you are king of heaven and earth, I put my trust in you. Elali, son of Girnisa, has wronged me, judge my case!

Having no money, he approached me. He paid his debts with my money. He married, he had a son and daughter. He did not satisfy me, he did not repay my money in full, by his filchings(?) he has wronged me. But I put my trust in Nanna!

In the orchards facing Ekishnugal[2] he swore: "May I be damned if I wrong you!" He swore at the Main Gate, under the weapon which you love, he swore inside the Main Court facing Ekishnugal, facing Ningal of the Egadi, before Ninshubur ... of the Main Court, facing Alamush, before Nanna-Vanguard and Nanna-Reinforcement he swore: "May I be damned if I wrong you or your sons!" He said, "These gods be my witness."

Moreover, in the orchards facing Ekishnugal, before Nanna, before Shamash, he swore this: "May I, Elali, be damned if I wrong Kussulu! May Elali have no heir before Nanna and Shamash (if he wrongs)!"

(One says): "The false swearer (by) Nanna and Shamash shall be a leper, he shall be destitute and not have a male heir." Elali swore by Nanna and Shamash and has wronged me! May Ninshubur,

---

1. Gadd assumes that the oath was the climax of an unsuccessful suit by Kussulu to recover his money from Elali, but there is no mention of a suit at law, nor was there a basis for one, since no loan document had been drawn up.

2. Temple of the moon god at Ur.

master of property rights, stand (as witness), may Nanna and Shamash judge my case! Let me see the greatness of Nanna and Shamash!

Text: Gadd, UET 6/2 402.
Edition: Gadd, *Iraq* 25 (1963), 177-181; Charpin, *Clergé*, 326-329.
Translation: Hecker, TUAT II/5, 750-752.

II.37 UR-NANSHE TO NINSIANNA

This prayer, addressed to the goddess Ninsianna in the form of a letter, complains that she has not been looking after her protégé, Ur-Nanshe.

> Say to Ninsianna, thus says Ur-Nanshe: What have I done to you that [   ]? I cannot hold up my head for misery! For ..., I do not have enough food to eat, nor do I have decent clothes for myself, nor can I limber up my bones with oil. Misery has crept into my heart like a weed(?). I really must complain [   ]

(gap and four fragmentary lines)

Text: Thureau-Dangin, TCL 1 9 = Kraus, AbB 5 (1972), 140.
Edition: Kraus, RA 65 (1971), 27-36.

II.38 APIL-ADAD TO "GOD MY FATHER"

In this letter, addressed to his personal god, Apil-Adad complains of being neglected, and asks him to send a letter to Marduk, god of Babylon.

> Say to God my father, thus says Apil-Adad your servant. Why have you been so neglectful of me? Who might there be to give you a substitute for me? Write to Marduk who loves you, ... my debt.* Let me see your face, let me kiss your feet![1] Consider my family, old and young! For their sakes take pity on me, let your assistance reach me!

Text: Lutz, YOS 2 141 (collated).
Edition: Stol, AbB 9 (1981), 89-91.
Translation: Hecker, TUAT II/5, 752.
Literature: cited by Stol, AbB 9 (1981), 89.
Notes to Text: (11) Previous editors agree on a reading *li-ip-ṭ[ù-ur]*, but collation of the passage by the translator and by R. Marcel Sigrist did not confirm this reading. To me the signs look more like še 60 gur-à[m], as Lutz's copy implies, in which case the issue is a large debt of 60 gur of barley.

1. "Let me see your face," that is, "show yourself capable of doing something." "Let me kiss your feet," that is, "do something that I may have cause to be grateful to you."

E. FLOOD STORY

II.39 ATRAHASIS

Atrahasis is the largest surviving Classical period narrative poem. It sets forth an interpretation of the creation of humanity, the flood, and the origins of human birth, marriage, procreation, and death, all of these themes brilliantly worked out in a cohesive plot.

Humanity was created to provide servants for the gods; birth was instituted to allow them to reproduce. The flood was an attempt at population control when the human race had grown too numerous. When the flood proved too drastic a measure, population control was achieved by forbidding marriage and procreation to certain groups of people, and ordaining mortality for all.

The story is presented here in four versions. The Old Babylonian, or Classical version (II.39a), is based principally on an Old Babylonian manuscript of the seventeenth century B.C. Various other Old Babylonian manuscripts have been incorporated into the translation of this version where possible. The original consisted of three tablets containing 1245 lines of poetry, of which about 60% are preserved in whole or in part.

The Middle Babylonian Version (II.39b), dating to the Mature period, is known in two recensions, a fragmentary manuscript from Nippur (II.39b.1) and a short Atrahasis story from Syria (II.39b.2).

What is called here the Late Assyrian Version (II.39c) is the remains of a first millennium recension of the epic. This was perhaps derived from a Middle Assyrian reworking of the text, and diverges sufficiently from the Old Babylonian text to warrant separate treatment. Other late Assyrian manuscripts preserve text more closely related to the Old Babylonian version, though they diverge in passages. These have been incorporated where possible into the Old Babylonian version, with notes indicating that the relevant manuscripts are later than the Old Babylonian period. The translation of the Late Assyrian version has been keyed to the Old Babylonian text to help the reader who wishes to compare both versions. The later version expanded some episodes, rewrote others, and, in general, levelled out the originality of the older text into a flat, standardized idiom full of repetition. Another version of a part of this story will be found in Tablet XI of the Gilgamesh epic. The Late Babylonian version (II.39d) is known only in fragments.

(a) OLD BABYLONIAN VERSION

(Before mankind existed, the great gods imposed forced labor on the lesser gods.)

When gods were man,[1]   (1)
They did forced labor, they bore drudgery.
Great indeed was the drudgery of the gods,
The forced labor was heavy, the misery too much:
The seven(?) great Anunna-gods were burdening*   (5)
The Igigi-gods with forced labor.
Anu their father was king,
Their counsellor was the warrior Enlil,
Their prefect was Ninurta,
[And] their bailiff(?) [En]nugi.   (10)
They had taken the [   ] ... by the ...,*
They cast lots, the gods took their shares:
Anu went up to heaven,
[Enlil too]k the earth for his subjects(?),*
[The bolt], the closure[2] of the sea,   (15)
[They had gi]ven to Enki the leader.
[The Anunna-gods?] went up to heaven,*
[The gods of the de]pths had descended.
[The Anunna-gods] in the he[ights] of heaven
[Burdened] the Igigi-gods [with forced labor].   (20)
[The gods] were digging watercourses,*
[Canals they opened, the] life of the land.

1. The line is a metaphor (Groneberg, AfO 26 [1978/9], 20), meaning "when gods were (like) men" (in that they had to work). This meaning was already argued, for different reasons, by Lambert, and borne out by a later quotation of this line in a seventh-century B.C. manuscript explicitly as "When the gods like men," (Lambert, OrNS 38 [1969], 533). This does not mean that the gods were actually human beings; rather, they had to work as humans do. Use of singular "man" rather than "men" suggests that the poet sought to make his opening line artful by playing on the words "god" and "man." A different interpretation, whereby "man" meant "boss" and "gods" was taken to be a divine name "Ilu" has been argued by Jacobsen (*Studies Finkelstein*, 117).

2. Literally: "snare," precise sense not clear (Falkenstein *apud* Wilcke, ZA 67 [1967], 160, although I retain Lambert's *ittadnu*). The sea may be portrayed as a gigantic trap, holding all its fish within. In the Late Babylonian version (below, II.39d) the fish break out of the "trap" of the sea, according to Ea, and thus mankind "accidentally" is saved from starvation.

[Those gods] were digging watercourses,
[Canals they opened, the] life of the land.
[The Igigi-gods dug the Ti]gris river,   (25)
[And the Euphrates there]after.
[Springs they opened up from] the depths,
[Wells ...] they established.
[   ] the depth
[   ] of the land   (30)
[   ] within it
[   ] they lifted up,
[They heaped up] all the mountains.
[years] of drudgery,
[   ] the vast marsh.   (35)
They [cou]nted years of drudgery,
[and] forty years,* too much!
[   ] forced labor they bore night and day.
[They were com]plaining, denouncing,
[Mut]tering down in the ditch,   (40)
"Let us face up to our [foreman]* the prefect,
"He must take off (this) our [he]avy burden upon us!
"[ ], counsellor of the gods, the warrior,
"Come, let us remove (him) from his dwelling;
"Enlil, counsellor of the gods, the warrior,   (45)
"Come, let us remove (him) from his dwelling!"
[   ]* made ready to speak,
[And said to the] gods his brethren,
"[   ] the prefect of olden days(?)

(gap of about four lines)

"[   ] let us kill [him]!¹   (a)
"[   ] let us break the yoke!"
[   ] made ready to speak,
[Saying] to the gods his brethren,
"[   ] the prefect of olden days(?) ..."   (e)

---

1. From Late Assyrian fragment (CT 46 7).

"The counsellor of the go[ds], the warrior,
"Come, let us remove (him) from his dwelling.
"Enlil, counsellor of the gods, the warrior,
"Come, let us remove (him) from his dwelling!   (60)
"Now then, call for battle!
"Battle let us join, warfare!"
The gods heard his words,
They set fire to their tools,
They put fire to their spades,   (65)
And flame to their workbaskets.
Off they went, one and all,
To the gate of the warrior Enlil's abode.
It was night, half-way through the watch,   (70)
The house was surrounded, but the god did not know.
It was night, half-way through the watch,
Ekur was surrounded, but Enlil did not know!
Kalkal noticed it and ... [   ],
He touched the bolt and examined the [   ].   (75)
Kalkal woke [Nusku],
And they listened to the clamor of [the Igigi-gods].*
Nusku woke [his] lord,
He got [him] out of bed,
"My lord, [your] house is surrounded,   (80)
"Battle has run right up [to your gate].
"Enlil, your house is surrounded,
"Battle has [ru]n right up to your gate!"[1]
Enlil had [   ] ... to his dwelling.
Enlil made ready to speak,   (85)
And said to the vizier Nusku,
"Nusku, bar your gate,
"Get your weapons and stand before me."
Nusku barred his gate,
Got his weapons and stood before Enlil.   (90)
Nusku made ready to speak,
And said to the warrior Enlil,

---

1. Note the omission of a verb of speaking, indicating excitement and abruptness.

"My lord, your face is (gone pale as) tamarisk,[1]
"Your own offspring! Why did you fear?
"My lord, your face is (gone pale as) tamarisk,   (95)
"Your own offspring! Why did you fear?
"Send that they bring Anu down [here],
"And that they bring Enki be[fore yo]u."
He sent and they brought Anu down to him,
They brought Enki before him.   (100)
Anu, king of [hea]ven, was seated,
The king of the depths, Enki, was [   ].*
With the great Anunna-gods present,
Enlil arose, the debate [was underway].
Enlil made ready to speak,   (105)
And said to the great [gods],
"Against me would they be [rebelling]?
"Shall I make battle [against my own offspring]?
"What did I see with my very own eyes?
"Battle ran up to my gate!"   (110)
Anu made ready to speak,
And said to the warrior Enlil,
"The reason why the Igigi-gods
"Surrounded(?) your gate,*
"Let Nusku go out [to discover it],   (115)
"[Let him take] to [your] so[ns]
"[Your great] command."
Enlil made ready to speak,
And said to the [vizier Nusku],
"Nusku, open [your gate],   (120)
"Take your weapons, [stand before them].
"In the assembly of [all the gods]
"Bow down, stand up, [and expound to them] our [words]:*

    'Anu, [your father],
    'Your counsellor, [the warrior] Enlil,   (125)
    'Your prefect, Ninurta,

---

1. Literally: "your features are tamarisk" (Borger, HKL 2, 158). For the tamarisk as symbolic of pallor born of fear, see III.18 line 29.

'And your bailiff Ennugi have sent me (to say),

"Who [is instigator of] battle?*
"Who [is instigator of] hostilities?
"Who [declared] war,   (130)
"[(That) battle has run up to the gate of Enlil]?"*

[Nusku opened] his gate,
[Took his weapons] and w[ent] ... Enlil.
[In the assembly of a]ll the gods,
[He knelt, s]tood up, expounded the c[omm]and,*   (135)
"Anu, your father,
"[Your counsellor, the] warrior Enlil,
"[Your prefect], Ninurta,
"And [your bailiff] Ennugi [have sent me (to say)]:

'Who is [instigator of] battle?   (140)
'Who is [instigator of] hostilities?
'Who [declared] war,
'[(That) battle has run up to the gate of Enlil]?
'In [   ]
'He trans[gressed the command of] Enlil.'[1]   (145)

"Every [one of us gods has declared] war;
"We have set [   ] in the e[xcavation].
"[Excessive] drudgery [has killed us],
"[Our] forced labor was heavy, [the misery too much]!   (150)
"Now, every [one of us gods]
"Has resolved on [a reckoning?] with Enlil."*
Nusku took [his weapons   ],
He went, he [to his lord],
"My lord, [you sent] me to the [   ],   (155)
"I went [   ]
"I expounded [you]r great [command],
"[trans]gressed it.*

'[Every one of us] gods has declared war,   (160)
'We [have set   ] in the excavation.
'Excessive [drudgery] has killed us,

---

1. See above, Tablet I line 116. Perhaps this was given in Tablet I lines 144f.

'Our forced labor [was heavy], the misery too much!
'[Now, every] one of us gods
'Has resolved on a reckoning(?) with Enlil.'   (165)

When Enlil heard that speech,
His tears flowed.
Enlil ... [   ] his speech(?),
And addressed the warrior Anu,
"I will go up with you, to heaven.   (170)
"Bear your authority, take your power,[1]
"With the great gods in session before you,
"Summon one god, let them put a burial mound over him."
Anu made ready to speak,
And addressed the gods his brethren,   (175)
"Why do we blame them?
"Their forced labor was heavy, their misery too much!
"[Every day   ],
"[The outcry was] loud, [we could] hear the clamor.
[   ] to do,   (180)
[assigned] tasks ..."

(gap)

(The gap in the main edition is partly filled by the following Old Babylonian fragment [CT 44 20, collations Atrahasis, pl. 11]. This suggests that Enki echoes Anu's remonstrances, then goes on to propose creation of man to do the work of the laboring gods.)

Ea made ready to speak,   (a)
And said to the gods [his brethren],
"What calumny do we lay to their charge?
"Their forced labor was heavy, [their misery too much]!
"Every day [   ]   (e)
"The outcry [was loud, we could hear the clamor].
"There is [   ]
"[Belet-ili, the midwife], is present.
"Let her create, then, a hum[an, a man],

---

1. These lines restored from Late Assyrian Version (Lambert, *Atrahasis*, 54).

"Let him bear the yoke [   ],   (j)
"Let him bear the yoke [   ]!
"[Let man assume the drud]gery of god ..."

    (As the main manuscript resumes, Enki is speaking.)

"[Belet-ili, the midwife], is present,
"Let the midwife create ...,   (190)
"Let man assume the drudgery of god."
They summoned and asked the goddess,
The midwife of the gods, wise Mami,
"Will you be the birth goddess, creatress of mankind?
"Create a human being that he bear the yoke,   (195)
"Let him bear the yoke, the task of Enlil,
"Let man assume the drudgery of god."
Nintu made ready to speak,
And said to the great gods,*[1]
"It is not for me to do it,   (200)
"The task is Enki's.
"He it is that cleanses all,
"Let him provide me the clay so I can do the making."
Enki made ready to speak,
And said to the great gods,   (205)
"On the first, seventh, and fifteenth days of the month,*
"Let me establish a purification, a bath.
"Let the one god be slaughtered,
"Then let the gods be cleansed by immersion.
"Let Nintu mix clay with his flesh and blood.   (210)
"Let that same god and man be thoroughly mixed
    in the clay.
"Let us hear the drum for the rest of time,
"From the flesh of the god let a spirit remain,*   (215)
"Let it make the living know its sign,

---

1. Variant omits lines 200-205, thus making Nintu (or Mami's) speech begin in 206.

"Lest he be allowed to be forgotten, let the spirit remain."[1]
The great Anunna-gods, who administer destinies,
Answered "Yes!" in the assembly.   (220)
On the first, seventh, and fifteenth days of the month,
He established a purification, a bath.

They slaughtered We-ilu,[2] who had the inspiration,
    in their assembly.
Nintu mixed clay with his flesh and blood.   (225)
<That same god and man were thoroughly
    mixed in the clay.>
For the rest [of time they would hear the drum],[3]
From the flesh of the god [the] spi[rit remained].
It would make the living know its sign,
Lest he be allowed to be forgotten, [the] spirit remained.   (230)
After she had mixed that clay,
She summoned the Anunna, the great gods.
The Igigi, the great gods, spat upon the clay.
Mami made ready to speak,   (235)
And said to the great gods,
"You ordered me the task and I have completed (it)!
"You have slaughtered the god, along with his inspiration.
"I have done away with your heavy forced labor,   (240)
"I have imposed your drudgery on man.
"You have bestowed(?) clamor upon mankind.[4]
"I have released the yoke, I have [made] restoration."[5]
They heard this speech of hers,

1. I interpret this speech as follows: "Kill the one god (We-ilu) who had the "inspiration" (*ṭēmu*) for the rebellion, purify the executioners, but let a "spirit" (*eṭemmu*) remain from the slain god, this to be part of new-created man (*awēlu*). The pulsation of this spirit will be a perpetual reminder of the dead god."

2. We-ilu may be a play on the Akkadian word for "man" (*awēlu*), as argued, e.g., by K. Oberhuber (*Studies Kraus*, 280).

3. Or heartbeat. For discussion of this passage, see Kilmer, OrNS 41 (1972), 162-166.

4. That is (Pettinato, OrNS 39 [1968], 187 and 189; von Soden, OrNS 38 [1969], 425, AHw, 1128a, and ZA 68 [1978], 67), the only present given to mankind is something to complain of (*rigmu*). Ironically, *rigmu* "clamor" will be the cause for the gods' sending the flood.

5. That is, returned matters to their original state before the great gods had imposed labor on the lesser gods (Charpin, AfO 34 [1987], 37f.).

They ran, restored, and kissed her feet, (saying),   (245)
"Formerly [we used to call] you 'Mami',
"Now let your n[am]e be 'Mistress-of-All-the-Gods' (Belet-kala-ili)."

(Breaks off; for the missing section, which describes the production of seven male and seven female foetuses, see Assyrian Version, col iii, 15'-37'.)

[And the young girl …] her breasts,[1]
[The youth …] a beard,
[And hair …] the cheek of the young man.
[In the   ] … and street   (275)
Wife and husband were [bliss]ful.*
The birth goddesses were assembled,
And Nintu [sat rec]koning the months.
[At the] destined [time] they summoned the tenth month.
The tenth month[2] arrived;   (280)
… opened the womb.
Her face beaming and joyful,
She covered her head
And performed the midwifery.   (285)
She girded (the mother's) middle
As she pronounced a blessing.
She drew (a circle?) with meal and placed the brick,[3]
"I am the one who created, my hands have made it!
"Let the midwife rejoice in the sacrosanct woman's house.[4]   (290)
"Where the pregnant woman gives birth,
"And the mother of the baby is delivered,*
"Let the brick be in place for nine days,

1. The first pair of human beings has grown from babyhood (somewhere after line 32' of the Late Assyrian Version) to adolescence (Tablet I lines 271ff.) and has matured enough to reproduce (Tablet I line 276). In 277ff. the first mother-to-be is about to give birth.

2. 40 weeks = 10 lunar months = 9 calendrical months.

3. The text implies that placing of a brick in the room where a woman was about to give birth was to be a common practice, but it is unknown outside of this composition. For further discussion, see A. Kilmer, "The Brick of Birth," JNES 46 (1987), 211-213.

4. Moran (*Biblica* 52 [1971], 58f. with note 3) suggests that this refers to a woman who has just given birth, so could not have intercourse for a taboo period. The next line refers to resumption of intercourse after delivery.

"Let Nintu, the birth goddess,[1] be honored.   (295)
"Always call Mami their [   ],
"[Always pra]ise the birth goddess, praise Kesh.[2]
"On [the tenth day?], when the bed is laid,
"(Then) let wife and her husband reach bliss together,★   (300)
"At the time for being man and wife,
"They should heed Ishtar in the [   ] ... chamber.
"For the nine days let there be rejoicing,
"Let them [cal]l Ishtar Ishara.[3]
"[   ] at the destined time   (305)

(gap)

(Mankind, now reproducing, is put to work to feed the gods.)

A man [	]
Cleanse the dwelling (?) [	]
The son to [his] father [	] (330)
... [	]
They sat and [	]
He it was who was carrying [	]
He saw and [	]
Enlil [	] (335)
They took up ... [	]★

They made n[e]w hoes and shovels,★
They built the big canal banks.
For food for the peoples, for the sustenance of [the gods]

(large gap)

(Mankind reproduces continuously. Enlil is annoyed by their uproar.)

[Twel]ve hundred years [had not gone by],
[The land had grown wide], the peoples had increased,
The [land] was bellowing [like a bull].
The god was disturbed with [their uproar],   (355)

1. Variant: Belet-ili.
2. Sanctuary of the birth goddess; see p. 72 note 1.
3. Lines 301ff. refer to consummation of marriage (differently Bottéro, "Supersage"). Ishara was another name for Ishtar; see W. G. Lambert, "Išhara," RLA 5, 176-177.

[Enlil heard] their clamor.
[He said to] the great gods,
"The clamor of mankind [has become burdensome to me],
"I am losing sleep [to their uproar].
"[   ] let there be ague ..."   (360)

(three lines lost)

But he, [Atrahasis], his god was Enki,
[He was exceedingly wise].   (365)
He would speak [with his god],
And his god [would speak] with him!
Atrahasis [made] ready to speak,
And said to [his] lord,
"How long [   ]*   (370)
"Will they impose the disease on us [forever]?"
Enki made ready to speak,
And said to his servant,
"The elders ... *
"... in ...   (375)
"[Command]:

   'Let heralds proclaim,
   'Let them raise a loud clamor in the land.*

      "Do not reverence your (own) gods,
      "Do not pray to your (own) goddesses,
      "Seek the door of Namtar,   (380)
      "Bring a baked (loaf) before it.'"

"May the flour offering please him,
"May he be shamed by the gift and suspend his hand."
Atrahasis received the command,   (385)
And assembled the elders to his gate.[1]
Atrahasis made ready to speak,
And said to the elders,
"Elders ...
"[ ] ...   (390)

---

1. There seems to be no way to correlate this line with the instructions in Tablet I line 375.

"[Command]:

   'Let heralds proclaim,
   'Let them raise a loud [clamor] in the land.

      "[Do not reverence] your (own) gods,
      "[Do not] pray to your (own) [goddesses],
      "[Seek] the door of [Namtar],   (395)
      "[Bring a baked (loaf) before it.'"

"May the flour offering please him,
"May he be shamed by the gift and suspend his hand."
The elders heeded [his] words,   (400)
They built a temple for Namtar in the city.
They commanded and the [heralds] proclaimed,
They made a loud clamor [in the land].
They did [not] reverence their (own) gods,   (405)
They did [not] pray to [their (own) goddesses],
They sought [the door] of Namtar,
They [brought] a baked (loaf) before [it].
The flour offering pleased him,
[He was shamed] by the gift and suspended his hand.   (410)
[The ague] left them,
They resumed [their clamor?],

(two lines fragmentary)

Tablet II

i

Twelve hundred years had not gone by,	(1)
The land had grown wide, the peoples had increased,	
The land was bellowing like a bull.	
The god was disturbed by their uproar,	
Enlil heard their clamor.	(5)
He said to the great gods,	
"The clamor of mankind has become burdensome to me,	
"I am losing sleep to their uproar.	
"Cut off provisions for the peoples,	
"Let plant life be too scanty [fo]r their hunger.	(10)
"Let Adad withhold his rain,	
"Below, let the flood not come up from the depths.*	
"Let the wind come to parch the ground,	(15)
"Let the clouds billow but discharge not a drop.	
"Let the field reduce its yields,	
"Let the grain goddess close her bosom.	
"Let there be no rejoicing for them,	(20)
"Let [their faces?] be gloomy,	
"Let there not [ ] ..."	

(gap)

ii*

"[Command:	
'Let heralds proclaim],	
'[Let them make a loud] cl[amor] in the land.	
"Do not reverence your (own) gods,	
"Do not pray to your (own) [goddesses],	(10)
"Seek [the door of] Adad,	
"Bring a baked (loaf) [before it].'"	
"[May the flour offering] please him,	
"May he be shamed [by the] gift and suspend his hand.	(15)
"May he rain down mist in the morning,	

"May he stealthily rain down dew in the night,
"May the fields just as stealthily bear ninefold."*
They built a temple for Adad in the city.   (20)
They commanded and the heralds proclaimed,
They made a loud clamor in the land.
They did not reverence their (own) gods,
They did [not] pray to their (own) goddesses,
They [sought] the door [of Adad],   (25)
[They brought] a baked (loaf) before it.
The flour offering pleased him,
He was shamed by the gift and suspended his hand.
He rained down mist in the morning,   (30)
He stealthily rained down dew in the night,
[The fields just as] stealthily bore ninefold.
[The famine?] left them,
They resumed their [clamor?]   (35)

(gap)

iii

(For another version of what follows, see II.39d.)

(Atrahasis wants to communicate with Enki, but knows that the god is under oath not to speak with him. He sleeps by the water for an indirect communication in dreams.)

[Listening closely for   ] ...   (1)
[He inquired by the   ] of his god.
[Out of] the [ci]ty he set his foot,
Every day he would weep,
Bringing oblations in the morning.   (5)
"My god [would speak to] me, but he is under oath,
"He will [inform] (me) in dreams.
"Enki [would speak to] me, but he is under oath,
"He will [inform] (me) in dreams."*   (10)
[He awaited the com]mand of his god,
[   ] seated, he wept.
He cast [   ],
[Standing or] seated, he wept.

W[hen the river] fell silent,⋆ (15)
Then [ ],
[Hairy hero-men[1] of the river] were visible.
He said to the [hairy hero-men] of the river,
"Let the river take(?) [my ...] and bear (it) away,
"Let it [go] ... (20)
"To the pres[ence of] my [lord].
"May [Enki] see [ ],
"May he [ ]
"In the night I [ ]."
After he p[ut the ... in the river], (25)
[He set his bed] facing the river,
From the bank [ ]
To the depth [ ] went down.
Enki heard [his words],
And [instructed] the hairy hero-men as [follows], (30)
"The man who [ ]
"Let this same one [ ]
"Go, the order [ ]
"[ ] of not [ ] ..."

(gap)

iv

Above [ ] (1)
Below, the flood did not [rise] from the depths.
The womb of earth did not bear,
Plant life did not come forth. (5)
People were not seen about,
The black fields whitened,
The broad plain was filled up with salts.
One year they ate old grain,
The second year they exhausted(?) their stores. (10)
When the third year came,
Their features were distorted from hunger,

---

1. Akkadian *laḫmu*, a kind of hairy, human-shaped creature here associated with Enki; see Wiggermann, JEOL 27 (1981/2), 90-105 (this passage referred to on p. 96).

Their faces were covered, as if with malt,
Life was ebbing, little by little.*
Tall people shriveled in body,   (15)
They walked hunched in the street.
Their broad shoulders became narrow,
Their long stance became short.
The messengers took the command,
They went before the sea,   (20)
They stood and told him,
[Their] orders to Enki the leader,

(fragmentary lines, gap)

v

(gap)

He[1] was filled with anger [at Enki],
"[All we] great Anunna-gods
"Resolved together [on a rule].   (15)
"Anu and Adad watched over [the upper regions],
"I watched over the lower earth.
"Where Enki went,
"He released the yoke, he made restoration.[2]
"He let loose produce for the peoples,[3]   (20)
"He put [shade?] in the glare(?) of the sun."
Enlil [made] ready to speak,
He said to the vizier Nusku,
"Let them bring to me ... sons,[4]
"Let them [send] them into my presence."   (25)

---

1. Enlil.
2. That is, a return to conditions before the attempt to destroy the human race; see p. 166 note 5.
3. I take this speech to mean that Enki loosed a flood of fish upon the land and saved the people from starvation. The trick perhaps lay in the ambiguity of the word: Enki promised to send a flood of fish, which the gods understood to be a flood to overwhelm the land, but which turned out, intentionally no doubt, to be harvest for the starving human race. This may have been the result of Atrahasis' prayer to the river and Enki's instructions to the hairy hero-men. (A different interpretation is found in CAD M/2, 124a.)
4. Compare Tablet I lines 94, 96.

They brought to him ... sons.
The warrior [Enlil] said to them,
"[All we] great Anunna-gods
"Resolved together on a rule.
"Anu and Adad watched over the upper [regions],   (30)
"I watched over the lower earth.
"Where you went[1]
"[You released the yoke], you made restoration.   (1ʹ)
"[You let loose produce for the peoples],
"[You put shade?] in the glare(?) of the sun."

(gap)

vi

(Enlil is explaining to the gods how Enki frustrated his murderous plans.)

"Adad [withheld?] his rain   (10)
"[But   ] filled the fields
"[And] the clouds(?) covered [   ].
"[You (gods) must not] feed his peoples,
"[Nor] supply provisions on which the peoples thrive."
[The god]* fretted for sitting idle,   (15)
[In] the assembly of the gods, worry gnawed at him.
[Enlil] fretted for sitting idle,
[In] the assembly of the gods, worry gnawed at him.

(four lines fragmentary)

(Enlil is speaking.)

"[All we great Anunna-gods]
"[Resolved] together [on a rule],
"Anu and Adad watched over the upper regions,   (25)
"I watched over the lower earth.
"Where you went
"[You] released the yoke, you made restoration.
"[You] let loose produce for the peoples,

---

1. Addressed to Enki, but the addressees of 27 are plural. Compare III.28 Tablet I lines 159ff.

"[You put shade?] in the glare(?) of the sun."   (30)

(gap)

vii

(gap)

"[She? imposed] your drudgery [on man],
"[You] have bestowed(?) clamo[r upon mankind].
"You slaughtered [the god], together with [his inspiration],
"[You] sat down and bath[ed yourselves].
"[   ] it will bring [   ]   (35)
"You resolved on [a rule   ],
"Let (mankind) return to [its] la[ir?].*
"Let us be sure to bind the leader Enki [   ] by an oath
     so that(?) he [   ].
Enki made ready to speak,   (40)
And said to the gods [his brethren],
"Why would you bind me by oath [   ]?
"Am I to bring my hands against [my own peoples]?
"The flood that you are speaking of [to me],
"Who is that? I [do not know].   (45)
"Am I to produce [a flood]?
"The task of that is [Enlil's].
"Let him [   ] choose,
"Let Shullat and [Hanish] go [in front],   (50)
"Let Errakal [tear out] the mooring poles,
"Let [Ninurta] go make [the dikes] overflow.

(small gap)

viii

(large gap)

"Assemble ... [   ]
"Do not obey ... [   ]."
The gods commanded annihilation,
E[nlil] committed an evil deed against the peoples.   (35)

Tablet III

i

Atrahasis made ready to speak,	(1)
And said to his lord,	

(gap)

(Atrahasis has had a dream from Enki, and wishes to know its meaning.)

Atrahasis made ready to speak,
And said to his lord,
"Make me know the meaning [of the dream],
"[ ] let me know,* that I may look out for its consequence."
[Enki] made ready to speak,   (15)
And said to his servant,
"You might say, 'Am I to be looking out while in the bedroom?'*
"Do you pay attention to the message that I speak for you:

    'Wall, listen to me!   (20)
    'Reed wall, pay attention to all my words!
    'Flee house, build boat,
    'Forsake possessions,* and save life.
    'The boat which you build,   (25)
    '[   ] be equal [   ]

(gap)

    'Roof her over like the depths,
    'So that the sun shall not see inside her,   (30)
    'Let her be roofed over fore and aft.*
    'The gear should be very firm,
    'The pitch should be firm, make (her) strong.
    'I will shower down upon you later
    'A windfall of birds, a spate(?) of fishes.'"*   (35)

He opened the water clock and filled it,
He told it (the wall?) of the coming of the seven-day deluge.*
Atrahasis received the command,
He assembled the elders at his gate.
Atrahasis made ready to speak,   (40)

And said to the elders,

"My god [does not agree] with your god,

"Enki and [Enlil] are constantly angry with each other.

"They have expelled me from [the land?].

"Since I have always reverenced [Enki],   (45)

"[He told me] this.

"I can[not] live in [   ]

"Nor can I [set my feet on] the earth of Enlil.

"[I will dwell?] with \<my\> god in(?) the depths."⋆

"[This] he told me [   ] ..."   (50)

(gap of four or five lines)

ii

(gap)

The elders [   ]   (10)

The carpenter [carried his axe],

The reed-worker [carried his stone].

[The rich man? carried] the pitch,⋆

The poor man [brought the materials needed].

(gap)

Atrahasis [   ]

(gap)

Bringing [   ]

Whatever he [had   ]   (30)

Whatever he had [   ]

Pure (animals) he sl[aughtered, cattle] ...⋆

Fat (animals) [he killed, sheep?] ...⋆

He chose [and brought on] board.

The [birds] flying in the heavens,   (35)

The cattle(?) [and   of the cat]tle god,

The [creatures?   ] of the steppe,

[   ] he brought on board

[   ] ...

[   ] he invited his people   (40)

[   ] to a feast.
[   ] his family he brought on board.
While one was eating and another was drinking,
He went in and out; he could not sit, could not kneel,   (45)
For his heart was broken, he was retching gall.
The outlook of the weather changed,
Adad began to roar in the clouds.
The god they heard, his clamor.*   (50)
He brought pitch to seal his door.
By the time he had bolted his door,
Adad was roaring in the clouds.
As the furious wind rose,
He cut the mooring rope and released the boat.   (55)

iii

(four lines lost)

[   ] the storm   (5)
[   ] were yoked
[Anzu rent] the sky with his talons,
[He   ] the land
And broke its clamor [like a pot].   (10)
[   ] the flood [came forth],
Its power came upon the peoples [like a battle].
One person did [not] see another,
They could [not] recognize each other in the catastrophe.
[The deluge] bellowed like a bull,   (15)
The wind [resound]ed like a screaming eagle.*
The darkness [was dense], the sun was gone,
[   ] ... like flies*
[the clamor?] of the deluge   (20)

(two lines fragmentary)

[   ] the clamor of the de[luge]
It was trying [   ] of the gods.
[Enki] was beside himself,   (25)
[That] his sons were carried off before him.
Nintu, the great lady,

Gnawed★ her lips in agony.
The Anunna, the great gods,   (30)
Were sitting in thirst and hunger.
The goddess saw it, weeping,
The midwife of the gods, the wise Mami,
"Let the day grow dark,
"Let it turn back to gloom!   (35)
"In the assembly of the gods,
"How did I agree with them on annihilation?
"Was Enlil so strong that he forced [me] to speak?
"Like that Tiruru, did he make [my] speech confused?[1]   (40)
"Of my own accord, from myself alone,
"To my own charge have I heard (my people's) clamor!
"My offspring — with no help from me —
          have become like flies.★   (45)
"And as for me, how to dwell in (this) abode of grief,
          my clamor fallen silent?★
"Shall I go up to heaven,
"As if to live in a house of [plentiful store]s?★   (50)
"Where has Anu gone to, the chief decision-maker,
"Whose sons, the gods, heeded his command?
"He who irrationally brought about the flood,
"And relegated the peoples to ca[tastrophe]?"

(one line missing)

iv

(gap)

Nintu was wailing [   ]
"...★ gave birth to(?) ...   (5)
"As dragonflies a watercourse, they have filled the sea.★
"Like rafts they lie against the e[dg]e,
"Like rafts capsized they lie against the bank.
"I saw and wept over them,   (10)
"I have exhausted my lamentation for them."

---

1. The meaning of the reference to Tiruru is unknown.

She wept, giving vent to her feelings,
While Nintu wailed, her emotion was spent.
The gods wept with her for the land.   (15)
She had her fill of woe and thirsted for beer.
Where she sat, they too sat weeping,
Like sheep, they filled a streambed.[1]   (20)
Their lips were agonized with thirst,
They were suffering pangs of hunger.
Seven days and seven ni[ghts]
There came the deluge, the storm, [the flood].   (25)
Where it [   ]
[   ] was thrown down

(gap of about twenty-five lines)

v

(gap of twenty-nine lines)

To the [four] winds [   ]   (30)
He cast [   ]
Providing food [   ]
[   ]
[The gods sniffed] the savor,
They were gathered [like flies] around the offering.   (35)
[After] they had eaten the offering,
[Nin]tu arose to rail against all of them,
"Where has Anu come to, the chief decision-maker?   (40)
"Has Enlil drawn nigh the incense?
"They who irrationally brought about the flood,
"And relegated the peoples to catastrophe?
"You resolved upon annihilation,
"So now (the people's) clear countenances are turned grim."   (45)
Then she drew nigh the big ...s*
Which Anu had and ... [   ]*
"Mine is [their] woe! Proclaim my destiny!
"Let him get me out of my misery, let him show me the way(?).   (50)

---

1. The gods are hoping to find water to drink.

"Let me go out ... [   ]

vi

"In [   ]   (1)
"Let [these] flies[1] be jewelry around my neck,
"That I may remember it [every?] day [and forever?]."
[The warrior Enlil] saw the vessel,   (5)
And was filled with anger at the Igigi-gods.
"All we great Anunna-gods
"Resolved together on an oath.
"Where did life(?) escape?*
"How did a man survive the catastrophe?"   (10)
Anu made ready to speak,
And said to the warrior Enlil,
"Who could do this but Enki?
"[   ] he revealed the command."   (15)
[Enki] made ready to speak,
[And said to] the great gods,
"I did it [indeed] for your sakes!
"[I am responsible] for safeguarding li[fe].
"[   ] gods [   ]   (20)
"[   ] the flood
"[   ] brought about
"[O Enlil,   ] your heart
"[   ] and relax.
"Impose your penalty [on a wrong-doer],   (25)
"[For] who is it that disregards your command?[2]
"[   ] the assembly [   ]

(gap)

"[   ] it
"[   ] put,
"[   ] ... my heart."   (40)

---

1. The episode is obscure and seems to contain a play on words. For discussion, see Kilmer, *Studies Reiner*, 175-180.

2. The thrust of the argument may be that he had sworn not to tell mankind of the flood, but did not swear to annihilate life.

[Enlil] made ready to speak,
And said to Ea the leader,
"[Come], summon Nintu the birth goddess,
"[Do you] and she take counsel together in the assembly."
[Enki] made ready to speak,   (45)
And [said to] Nintu the birth goddess,
"[You], birth goddess, creatress of destinies,
"[Establish death] for all peoples!*
"[   ]
"[   ] let there be.   (50)

(one line missing?)

vii

"Now then, let there be a third (woman) among the people,   (1)
"Among the people are the woman who has borne and the
   woman who has not borne.
"Let there be (also) among the people the (she)-demon,[1]
"Let her snatch the baby from the lap of her who bore it,   (5)
"Establish high priestesses and priestesses,
"Let them be taboo, and so cut down childbirth.

(fragmentary lines, then large gap)

viii

(gap)

"How we brought about [the flood],
"But man survived the [catastrophe],   (10)
"You, counsellor of the [great] gods,
"At [your] command have I brought a [   ]* to be,
"This [my] song (is) for your praise.   (15)
"May the Igigi-gods hear, let them extol your great deed
   to each other.
"I have sung of the flood to all peoples:
"Listen!"

---

1. "The-One-Who-Wipes-Out" (family names).

(b) MIDDLE BABYLONIAN VERSIONS

(b.1) NIPPUR EDITION

"[   ] I will explain
"[... a flood] will seize all the peoples at once.
"[   ] before the flood comes forth,
"[Good reeds], as many as there are, should be woven(?),
    should be gathered(?) for it.★   (5)
"[   ] build a big boat.
"Let its structure be [interwoven?] of good(?) reed.
"[   ] let it be a vessel with the name "Guardian of Life."
"[   ] roof it over with a strong covering.
"[Into the boat which] you will make,   (10)
"[Bring aboard] wild creatures of the steppe, birds of heaven.
"Heap up [   ]

(breaks off)

(b.2) AN ATRAHASIS STORY FROM SYRIA

This version of the Atrahasis story was evidently narrated by Atrahasis himself. The tablet was discovered at Ugarit, on the Syrian coast, and dates approximately to the thirteenth century B.C.

> When the gods took counsel concerning the lands, (1)
> They brought about a flood in the world regions.
>
> [ ] would listen [   ]
> [   ] Ea in his heart.
> (5)
> "I am Atrahasis,
> "I was living in the temple of Ea, my lord,
> "And I knew everything.*
>
> "I knew of the counsel of the great gods,
> "I knew of their oath,
>   though they would not reveal it to me. (10)
>
> "He repeated their words to the wall,
>   'Wall, hear [   ]
>
> *(gap)*
>
> *(rev)*
>
> "[   ] the gods life [   ] (1)
> "[   ] your wife [   ]
> "[ ] help and [   ]
> "Life like the gods [you will] indeed [possess]."
>
> *(end of tablet)*

(c) LATE ASSYRIAN VERSION

The Late Assyrian version is a fragmentary, two-tablet edition of the poem. Each tablet had six columns of about sixty lines each. Very little of the second tablet is preserved. The numbering assigned to the tablet lines on Tablet I obverse is for convenience only, as their exact placement is still uncertain. References to the Old Babylonian version are provided in the right margin.

Tablet I

i

[ ] went down	(OB I.19)
[kin]gship of the depths	
[ ] went down	(20)
[kingshi]p(?) of Ea.	
[were dig]ging the river,	
[ ] life of the land.	
[ ] the Euphrates after it	
[ ] from the deep	(25)
They set up their [ ].	

[For ten years?] they bore the drudgery
[For twenty years] they bore the drudgery
[For thirty years] they bore the drudgery
[For forty years] they bore the drudgery.   (30)

[   ] ... they refused(?)★
[   ]

[They were complaining, denoun]cing,
[Muttering down in the di]tch.   (OB I.40)

(fragmentary lines, then gap)

ii

(In this version Nusku makes an additional visit to the rebels after the proposal to slaughter their leader has been made.)

"You [   ]   (OB I.170ff.)
"Take [   ]
"With [the great gods] in session [before you],   (5')
"With Belet-i[li the midwife] in session,
"Summon the one and kill [him]."

Anu made ready to speak, saying [to Nusku],
"Nusku, open your gate, [take] your weapons,
     [stand before them],
"Among all the great gods bow down, [stand up],   (10')
"Say to them [   ],

     'Anu [your father] has sent me,
     'Your counsellor the w[arrior Enlil],
     'Your prefect Ni[nurta and your bailiff? Annugal]:
     'Who is instigator of battle, [who is instigator of hostilities]? (15')
     'Which is the god who made [the war]
     'That battle has run up to [the gate of Enlil]?'"

[When Nusku heard] this,
He to[ok] his weapons [   ].
In the assembly of the great gods [he knelt and stood up],   (20')
[He said] to the[m   ],
"[A]nu [your father has sent me],
"[Your counsellor the warrior] Enlil,
"[Your prefect Ninurta and your bailiff?] Annugal:

     '[Who is instigator of battle? Who is] instigator of hostilities? (25')
     '[Which is the god who made] the war
     '[That battle has run up to] the gate of Enlil?'"

[The great gods] made [ready to speak],
[Saying to Nusku, vizier] of Enlil,   (30')

"[   ]
"[   ]
"[We are the gods, instigators of battle, we] are the gods,
        instigators of hostilities.
"[We are the gods who] made the war,
"[That battle has run unto the gate of] Enlil!"*

(gap)

iii

(large gap)

[   ] Ea said,   (15′)
Ea, [seated before her], was prompting her,
Belet-[ili] was reciting the incantation.
After she had recited her spell,
[She s]pat in her clay.
She pinched off fourteen pieces of clay,
Seven she put on the right,   (20′)
[Seven] on the left.
Between them the brick was placed.*
She ... the headcovering(?)
        and ... the cutter of the umbilical cord,*
She summoned the wise and accomplished
Birth goddesses, seven and seven.   (25′)
Seven produced males,
[Seven] produced females.
The midwife, creatress of destiny —
They will crown(?) them in pairs,[1]
They will crown(?) them in pairs in her presence —   (30′)
Mami laid down the designs for the human race:

"In the house of the pregnant woman about to give birth,
"Let the brick be in place for seven days,
"That Belet-ili, the wise Mami, may be honored.
"Let the midwife rejoice in the house of the woman in labor.

---

1. That is, these foetuses will one day be married, male to female.

"And when the pregnant woman gives birth,   (35′)
"Let the mother of the baby deliver herself.
"A male (baby) to [   ] ...,
"[A female (baby)] ..."

(gap)

iv

[Twelve hundred years had not gone by] (OB I.352)   (1)
The land had grown wide, [the peoples had increased].
He was disturbed [at] their clamor,
[At] their uproar [sleep] could not overcome him.
Enlil convened his assembly,
And said to the gods his sons,   (5)
"The clamor of mankind has indeed become burdensome for me,
"I am disturbed [at the]ir clamor,
"[At] their uproar sleep cannot overcome me.
"Command that there be ague,
"Let contagion diminish their clamor.   (10)
"Let disease, headpain, ague, and malady
"Blast upon them like a whirlwind."

The[y gave the com]mand and there was ague,
Contagion diminished their clamor.
[Dis]ease, headpain, ague, and malady   (15)
Blasted upon them like a whirlwind.

For the destiny of the man, Atrahasis,[1]
Ea, his [god], was heedful.*
Did he not [speak] with his god?
[His god], Ea, spoke with him.   (20)

Atrahasis made ready to speak,
[And said to] Ea his lord,
"Lord, the peoples are groaning,
"Your [disease] is devouring the land.

1. Literally: "The Broad-of-Wisdom-Man," a play on the name and its meaning.

"Ea, lord, the peoples are groaning,   (25)
"[The disease] from the gods is devouring the land.
"[Sin]ce you created us,
"[Will you] remove the disease, headpain, ague, and malady?"

[Ea made ready to] speak, and said to Atrahasis:
"[Command:

    'Let her]alds [proclaim],
    'Let them silence the clamor in the land: (30)

        "[Do not reverence your (own) gods],
        "Do not pray to your (own) goddesses,
        "[   ] observe his rites,
        "[   ] the flour offering
        "[   ] before it
        "[   ] speak a blessing.'"   (35)
"[He will be shamed by the] gift
    [and set aside?] his hand."

[Enlil] convened his assembly, and said to the gods his sons,
"Do not lay contagion upon them (any longer)!*
"[The peo]ples have not dwindled,
    but have become more numerous than before!
"I am disturbed [at] their clamor,   (40)
"[At] their uproar sleep cannot overcome me.
"Cut off provender for the peoples,
"Let plants be scanty in their stomachs.
"Above, let Adad make scarce his rain,
"Below, let (rainfall) be blocked off and raise
    no flood from the depths.   (45)
"Let the fields reduce their yields,
"The grain goddess turn aside her bosom,
"Let the black fields whiten,
"Let the broad plain produce salts,
"Let the earth's womb rebel,
"Let no plants come forth, no grains ripen.
"Let a malady be laid upon the peoples,   (50)

"That the womb be constricted and give no safe birth to a child."

They cut off provender from the peoples,
Plants were scanty in their stomachs.
Above, Adad made scarce his rain,
Below, (the rainfall) was blocked off and raised
     no flood from the depths. (55)
The fields reduced their yields,
The grain goddess turned aside her bosom,
The black fields whitened,
The broad plain produced salts, earth's womb rebelled,
No plants came forth, no grains ripened.
A malady was laid upon the peoples, (60)
So that the womb was constricted
     and gave no safe birth to a child.

v

The bo[lt, the bar of the sea], (1)
[Ea] watched over [together with his plants],
Above, [Adad made scarce his rain],
Below, (rainfall) was blocked off
     [and raised no flood from the depths],
The fields reduced [their yields], (5)
The grain goddess [turned aside her bosom],
[The black fields whitened],
[The broad plain] produced salts, [Earth's womb rebelled],
[No plants] came forth, no grains [ripened].
[A malady was laid upon the peoples]
[That the womb was constricted and gave [no safe birth to a child].
[For one year they ate ...] (10)
[   ]
[When the second year came], they exhausted their stores,
[When the third year] came,
[The peoples' features] were distorted [by hunger].
[When the fourth year came], their [long] legs became short, (15)
[Their broad shoulders] became narrow.
[They walked about hunched] in the street.

[When the fifth year came], daughter saw mother [go in],
[But mother would not] open her door [to daughter].
[Daughter] watched [the scales (when) mother
      (was sold into slavery)],   (20)
Mother watched [the scales (when) daughter
      (was sold into slavery)].
[When the sixth year came], [they served up] daughter for a meal,
[They served up [son for sustenance]:
[They were filled on their own children?],*
One [household] devoured another.
Their [faces] were encrusted [like dead malt].   (25)
[The peoples] were living [on the verge] of death.

[For th]e destiny of the man Atrahasis,
Ea, [his god], was heedful.
Did he not [speak] with his god?
His god Ea spoke with him.   (30)
He left the gate of his god,
He placed his bed facing the river,
But the channels were quiet.

(gap)

vi

[When the second] year [came, they exhausted their stores],   (1)
[When] the third year [came],
The peoples' [features] were distorted by [hunger].
When the fourth year [came], their [long] legs became short,
Their broad [shoulders] became narrow,   (5)
They walked about hunched in the street.
When the fifth year came, daughter saw mother go in,
But mother would not open her door to daughter.
Daughter watched the scales (when) mother
      (was sold into slavery),
[Mother] watched the scales (when) daughter
      (was sold into slavery).   (10)
When the sixth year came, they served up [daughter] for a meal,
They served up son for sustenance:

[They] were filled [on their own children?],∗
One household devoured another.
Their faces [were encrusted] like dead malt.
The peoples [were living] on the verge of [death].   (15)

The command which they received [   ]
They entered and [   ]
The message of Atrahasis [   ]
"Lord, the land [   ]
"A sign [   ]   (20)

(six lines fragmentary)

"Let me go down to the d[ep]ths to dwell in your presence."
One year they ate old grain

(gap)

Tablet II

iii(?)

"Ea, lord, [I heard] you come in,   (OB III i)   (1)
"[I] noticed steps like [your] footsteps."

[Atrahasis] knelt, prostrated himself, stood up [   ],
He made ready [to speak] and said,
"[Lord], I heard you come in,   (5)
"[I noticed] steps like your footsteps.
"[Ea, lord], I heard you come in,
"[I noticed] steps like your footsteps.

"[   ] for(?) seven years,
"Your [   ] has made the weak thirsty.   (10)
"[   ] I have seen your face
"[   ] tell me your (the gods') [   ]."

[Ea] made ready to speak
[And said to] the reed hut,
"[   ] reed hut! reed hut!   (15)
"[   ] pay attention to me!

*(Approximately here goes CT 46 15, another Late Assyrian recension that is
different from this one, but helps to fill the gap.)*

"[   ] let it [   ]   (1')
"[   ] like a circle [   ]
"Let the [roof?] be strong fore and aft,
"[   ] caulk the [boat].
"[Mark] the appointed time of which I send word,   (5')
"Enter [the boat] and shut the boat's door.
"[Bring aboard] it your barley, your goods, your possessions,
"[Your wife], your kith, your kin, and skilled crafts[men].
"[Creatures] of the steppe, all the browsing wild animals
         of the steppe,
"[I] will send to you and they will attend at your door."   (10')

Atrahasis made ready to speak,
And said to Ea, [his] lord,
"Never have I built a boat [   ],
"Draw the de[sign on the gro]und,
"That I may see [the desig]n and [build] the boat."   (15′)
Ea drew [the design] on the ground.
"[   ] my lord, what you commanded [   ]

(breaks off)

(Assyrian recension reverse continues.)

[   ] he put [   ]
[He] entered and sealed up the [boat].
The wind [   ] and brought the wh[irlwind].
Adad mounted the four winds, [his] steeds: (5)
South wind, north wind, east wind, west wind.
Storm, gale, whirlwind, cloudburst,
Ill wind, ..., the winds were rising.
The south wind [   ] arose at his side,
The west wind blasted at his side,   (10)
[   ] went [   ]
[   ] the chariot of the gods [   ]
[It] rushes forward, it kills, it overruns [   ].
Ninurta went and [made] the dikes [overflow],
Errakal tore up [the mooring poles].   (15)
[Anzu rent] the sky with his talons,
[He smashed] the land like a pot, he dispersed its guidance.
[   ] the flood came forth,
Its power came [upon] the peoples [like a battle].

[   ] Anu(?) [   ] the clamor of the flood,   (20)
[   ] terrified the gods.
[Nintu   ] her sons were carried off at her own command.
[   ] her emotion was spent.

(breaks off)

(d) LATE BABYLONIAN VERSION

[Enlil made ready to speak],
Saying to [   ],   (1′)
"[The clamor of mankind] has become [burdensome for me],
"I [am losing sleep] to their uproar.
"Command that [Anu and Adad] watch over [the upper regions],
"That Sin and Nergal guard [the earth in the middle],   (5′)
"That the bolt, the trap [of the sea],
"Ea may watch over together with [his plant life]."

He gave the command: Anu and [Adad] watched
        over [the upper regions],
Sin and Nergal guarded the earth [in the middle],
The bolt, the trap of the sea,   (10′)
Ea guarded together with [his] plant life.
Now Atrahasis, [whose god was Ea],
Had wept every day [   ]
He would bring offerings [   ]
When the channels [   ]   (15′)
He stood at night(?) [by the river?   ]
... [   ]
He said to [the river   ]
"May [the river] take [   ]
"May it be set at the feet of(?) [Ea   ]   (20′)
"May Ea see [   ]
"In the night I [   ]
"After [   ]."

Facing the river [   ]
Facing [   ]   (25′)
To the depth [   ]
[Ea] heard [   ]
And brought the ha[iry hero-men   ]
"The man who [   ]
"[Let] this [   ]   (30′)
"Come, [   ]

(thirteen fragmentary lines, then gap)

ii

(Enlil is speaking.)

"[I commanded that] Anu and Adad watch over
    [the upper regions],
"[That Sin and Nergal] watch over the earth in the middle,
"[That the bolt], the trap of the sea,
"[You should] guard together with your plant life.   (5′)
"[But you let loose] abundance for the peoples!"
[   ] the broad sea
Repeated [the message of] Enlil to Ea:
"[I commanded] that Anu and Adad watch
    over the upper regions,
"[That Sin and Nergal] watch over the earth between,   (10′)
"[That the bolt], the trap of the sea,
"[You should] guard together with your plant life.
"[But you let] loose abundance for the peoples!"
[Ea] made ready to speak,
And [said] to the messenger,   (15′)
"[ ] you commanded, so Anu and Adad watched
    over the upper regions,
"[Sin and Nergal] watched over the earth in the middle,
"[The bolt], the trap of the sea,
"[I] watched over, together with my plant life.
"When [ ] escaped from me,   (20′)
"[ ] a million fish, one million they bore(?).*
"I drew together [the bolt?] of the fish but it went away,
"They broke through the middle of the [trap].

"[After?] I executed the watchmen of the sea,
"I imposed [ ] upon them and punished them.   (25′)
"[After] I had punished them,
"[I repeated it] and imposed the penalty."[1]

---

1. Obscure. What penalty could he lay upon them if they were already executed? Does "them" mean humankind here?

[The   ] took the message.

[   ] the wide sea
[Went] and repeated   (30')
[The message] of Ea to Enlil,
"[ ] you commanded, so Anu and Adad watched
     over the upper regions,
"[Sin and] Nergal watched over the earth in the middle,
"[The bolt], the trap of the sea,
"[I] watched over, together with my hairy hero-men.*   (35')
"When [ ] escaped from me,
"[ ] a million fish, one million they bore(?).
"I drew together [the bolt? of] the fish, but it went away,
"They broke through the middle of the [trap].
"[After?] I had executed the watchmen of the sea,   (40')
"I laid [ ] upon them and punished them.
"After I had punished them,
"[I] repeated it and imposed the penalty."

Enlil made ready to speak,
And said to the assembly of all the gods,   (45')
"Come, all of us, and take an oath to bring a flood."
Anu swore first,
Enlil swore, his son swore with him.

(breaks off)

Text: (a) Clay, BRM 4 1; Lambert and Millard, CT 46 1-4; Lambert, *Atrahasis* plates 1-8; Pinches, CT 44 20. Durand *apud* Groneberg, *Studies Garelli*, 409; W. G. Lambert, *Studies Garelli*, 414 BM 22714b. Some disputed passages in the KU-Ayya manuscript were collated by the writer for this translation. (b.1) Hilprecht, BE 5 1. (b.2) Nougayrol, *Ugaritica* 5 167. (c) King, CT 13 31; CT 15 49; Lambert and Millard, CT 46 5-15; Lambert, *Atrahasis*, Plates 8-11; AfO 27 (1980), 72, 74; BWL, pl. 65; JSS 5 (1960), 116; OrNS 38 (1969), 533. Tablet I i = CT 46 6 + AfO 27 (1980), 72. ii = CT 46 6 + AfO 27 (1980), 72 + *Atrahasis*, xi + Lambert, *Studies Garelli*, 414 K 21851. iii = *Atrahasis*, xii + CT 15 49. iv = CT 15 49 + OrNS 38 (1969), 533 + AfO 27 (1980), 74. v = CT 15 49. vi = CT 13 31 + CT 15 49 + OrNS 38 (1969), 533. Tablet II iii? = JSS 5 (1960), 116. (d) Lambert, *Atrahasis*, pl. 4-5, 9-10.
Edition: (a) Lambert-Millard, *Atrahasis*. A new edition of Tablet I was offered by von Soden, ZA 68 (1978), 50-94. (b.1) Lambert, *Atrahasis*, 126-127. (b.2) Lambert, *Atrahasis*, 131-133. (c) Lambert, *Atrahasis*, 106-115. (d) Lambert, *Atrahasis*, 116-121.

Translation: Lambert-Millard, *Atrahasis*; Bottéro, *Mythologie*, 526-601; Dalley, *Myths*, 1-38.

Literature: The interest aroused by this text has generated a voluminous, often polemic and contradictory literature. The essential philological contributions prior to 1970 are cited line-by-line in Borger, HKL 2, 157-159. His citations are not repeated here, except where controversy continues or to acknowledge suggestions that materially and, I think, correctly altered the Lambert-Millard reading. For the general reader who wishes to delve more deeply into the problems posed by this composition, the following studies will give an idea of the range of opinion on crucial passages and offer interpretations and bibliography. J. Bottéro, "Antiquités Assyro-babyloniennes," *Annuaire* 1967/68, 113-122; "La Création de l'homme et sa nature dans le poème d'Atrahasis," in *Studies Diakonoff*, 23-32; "Le Poème babylonien du 'Supersage'," *Pour Léon Poliakov, La raisonné, mythes et sciences* (Bruxelles, 1981), 257-276, more fully in *Mythologie*, 526-601; T. Jacobsen, "Inuma Ilu awilum," *Studies Finkelstein*, 113-117; A. Kilmer, "The Mesopotamian Concept of Overpopulation and Its Solution as Reflected in the Mythology," OrNS 41 (1972), 160-177; "The Symbolism of the Flies in the Mesopotamian Flood Myth and some Further Implications," *Studies Reiner*, 175-180; G. Komoróczy, "Work and Strike of the Gods, New Light on the Divine Society in the Sumero-Akkadian Mythology," *Oikumene* 1 (1976), 11-37; W. G. Lambert, "A New Look at the Babylonian Background of Genesis," *Journal of Theological Studies* NS 16 (1965), 287-300, more fully in "Babylonien und Israel," *Theologische Realenzyklopaedie* 5, 67-79. For Lambert's answer to emendations of his edition, see OrNS 38 (1969), 533-538; OrNS 40 (1971), 99-101; L. Matouš, "Zur neuern epischen Literatur im alten Mesopotamien," ArOr 35 (1967), 1-25; "Die Urgeschichte der Menschheit im Atrahasis-Epos und in der Genesis," ArOr 37 (1969), 1-7; W. L. Moran, "Atrahasis: The Babylonian Story of the Flood," *Biblica* 52 (1971), 51-61, "The Creation of Man in Atrahasis I 192-248," BASOR 200 (1970), 48-56, "Some Considerations of Form and Interpretation in Atrahasis," *Studies Reiner*, 245-255; S. Picchioni, "Principi di etica sociale nel poema di Atrahasis" OrAn 13 (1974), 83-111; W. von Soden, "'Als die Götter (auch noch) Mensch waren,' Einige Grundgedanken der altbabylonischen Atrahasis-Mythus," OrNS 38 (1969), 415-432, see Or NS 40 (1971), 99-101, and above, "Editions," "Konflikte und ihre Bewältigung in babylonischen Schöpfungs- und Fluterzählungen," MDOG 111 (1979), 1-33 (includes translation of Tablets II and III of the Old Babylonian version). For comparative study, see for example R. Albertz, "Die Kulturarbeit im Atrahasis in Vergleich zur biblischen Urgeschichte," in R. Albertz *et al.*, eds., *Werden und Wirken des alten Testaments, Festschrift für Claus Westermann zum 70. Geburtstag* (Göttingen, 1980), 38-57; H. Kümmel, "Bemerkungen zu den altorientalischen Berichten von der Menschenschöpfung," WO 7 (1973), 25-38; R. Oden, "Divine Aspiration in Atrahasis and in Genesis 1-11," ZATW 93 (1981), 197-216.

Notes to Text: (II.39c) (5) Lambert, JCS 32 (1980), 83-85; Kienast *apud* Pettinato, OrAn 9 (1980), 77; Matouš, ArOr 35 (1967), 6. Some translations read "sevenfold" as referring to the labor (Wilcke, ZA 67 [1977], 157; Bottéro, "Supersage," *ad loc*). (11) For this line, von Soden, OrNS 40 (1971), 100, but denied by Lambert, OrNS 40 (1971), 97. See also Pettinato, OrAn 9 (1980), 77. (14) With Pettinato, OrAn 9 (1980), 77. For a different reading, see von Soden, ZA 68 (1978), 77. (21) For 21-26, I follow von Soden, ZA 68 (1978), 54. (37) von Soden, ZA 68 (1978), 56 suggests 2500 years. (41) von Soden, ZA 68 (1978), 56. (47) Collation by Lambert (*Atrahasis*, pl. xi) excludes restoration of the name of the chief rebel here (compare below, I.223). (77) von Soden, ZA 68 (1978), 58. (102) The reading ʼúʼ-[te-e]q-qí proposed by Schramm *apud* Borger, HKL 2, 158, does not fit the traces (collated). (114) Though this proposal was abandoned by von Soden, ZA 68 (1978), 79, I maintain it here. (123) This restoration has been proposed independently by several translators and documented by Westhuizen, CRRAI 32 (1985), 89-91; compare Bottéro, "Supersage," 269. (128) Lambert, AfO 27 (1980), 73f. (131) Lambert, AfO 27

(1980), 74. (139) See Pettinato, OrAn 9 (1979), 78; Moran, *Studies Reiner*, 249. (152) The proposal of Westhuizen, CRRAI 32 (1985), 91-92 is excluded by collation. (158) Above, to 135. (199) For this passage, I follow many of the proposals made by Moran, BASOR 200 (1970), 48-56; see also G. Pettinato, *Das altorientalische Menschenbild und die sumerischen und akkadischen Schöpfungsmythen* (Heidelberg, 1971), 101ff.; and, Bottéro, CRRAI 26 (1979), 32 and note 81 (see p. 44), also above, "La Création." (206) Variant: "every month" (K 17853 = AfO 27 [1980], 74). (215) Note that the reading *eṭemmu* used here is explicitly denied by von Soden, *Studies Böhl*, 350-352; see ZA 68 (1978), 65f., 80f. Differently Bottéro, "La Création," 26-27. "From" here could mean "by means of." (276) [*li-iḫ*]-*ti-ru!* (compare line 300). (292) Literally: "hollows herself" (*ḫerû* D); Lambert's reading with ḪA, against *erû*, is supported by the Late Assyrian fragment K 17752, AfO 27 (1980), 75. (297) von Soden reads "lege hin die Matte!" in ZA 68 (1978), 68, but I follow Lambert in construing both of the epigraphically difficult readings for the last word in A and E according to the late manuscript P (= CT 46 13 rev 11), which has *ke-e-ša*. (300) Reading *li-iḫ-ti-[ru]*; see Borger, HKL 2, 158; Moran, *Biblica* 52 (1971), 58. (336) von Soden, OLZ 1977, 29. (337) von Soden, ZA 68 (1978), 70. (370) *a-di ma-<ti>-ma* (WLM). (374) von Soden, ZA 67 (1977), 236-237 sees here a second, Hurrian, word for "elder," but this is doubtful. His proposal *i-[bi]* at the end of the line, ZA 68 (1978), 72, has not been adopted here. (377) For a different view, see Moran, *Biblica* 52 (1971), 54. (II i 14) Emending using the parallel passage II iv 2; otherwise, read "gently" for "below" (so, e. g., von Soden, MDOG 111 [1979], 32). (II ii) Lines 7-12 are from JSS 5 (1960), 123, CT 46 41, a first-millennium version; 13-35 from BRM 4 1 and *Atrahasis*, plate 2. (II ii 19) Kraus, RA 69 (1970), 143; earlier references in Borger, HKL 2, 158. (II iii 10) Moran, *Studies Reiner*, 251. (II iii 15) WLM. (II iv) Several readings and interpretations from Groneberg, *Studies Garelli*, 397ff. (II iv 14) Chase, JCS 39 (1987), 241-246; Propp, *Nabu* 1989/68; Groneberg, *Studies Garelli*, 399. (II v 24) Klein, *Nabu* 1990/99, though the restorations proposed there do not fit the copy; Groneberg, *Studies Garelli*, 401ff., with collations. (II vi 17) Veenhof, JEOL 24 (1975/6), 108. (II vii 37) von Soden, OrNS 38 (1969), 430; Moran, BASOR 200 (1970), 54 note 3; Kilmer, *Studies Finkelstein*, 132. (III i 14) Borger, HKL 2, 158. (III i 17) von Soden, OrNS 38 (1969), 431. (III i 24) Hoffner, AOAT 25, 241ff. argues that *ma-ak-ku-ra* refers to "ark," that is, a large boat. This proposal does not take into account the writing *ma-ku-ra* for "ark" in vi 5 of the same manuscript. Compare also CAD M/1, 135. I adopt his understanding of *ubut* in the preceding line. (III i 31) Shaffer, RA 75 (1981), 188; Naster, *Studies Böhl*, 295ff.. (III i 35) Millard, *Iraq* 49 (1987), 63-69. (III i 37) Deller-Mayer, OrNS 53 (1984), 121, but difficult. (III ii 13) Stol, AfO 35 (1988), 78. (III ii 32-33) Based on suggestion of WLM. (III ii 50) WLM. (III iii 16) With von Soden, OrNS 38 (1969), 431. (III iii 18) Or, possibly, "sheep." (III iii 29) *ú-ka-la-la*: difficult. R-stem of *akālu*, built on a D for the two lips? (III iii 40) Moran, JCS 33 (1981), 44. (III iii 45) With WLM; von Soden, MDOG 111 (1979), 29 "über mir"; Lambert, *Atrahasis*, 95 "cut off from me." (III iii 47) *šaḫurru* may be singular here. (III iii 50) Or, possibly, "enemies," (von Soden, OrNS 38 [1969], 432), though the copy favors the former. This is perhaps an ironic reference to starvation. (III iv 5) von Soden, OrNS 38 (1969), 432 reads "two floods"; Lambert, "what?" (III iv 6) For this passage, see Lambert, CRRAI 26 (1979), 57. (III iv 46) *zubu*. Lambert reads "flies," but the word is not written the same way and may conceal some pun; see p. 184 note 1. (III iv 47) The proposal of Saporetti, *Egitto e Vicino Oriente* 5 (1982), 60: *i-ba-an-ˈqaˈ-a[m]*, seems to me unlikely. (III vi 9) Text: ˈpiˈ-*ti-iš-tum*, otherwise unknown; emended by Lambert on the basis of Gilgamesh XI.173. (III vi 48) Lambert, *Mesopotamia* 8 (1980), 58. (III viii 14) *ga[bra]m*(?) "rendition, copy"(??), but this is doubtful. (II 39b.1 5) Emendation von Soden, OrNS 38 (1969), 432; tablet seems to have a corrupt text. (II 39b.2 8) Borger, RA 64 (1970), 189. (II.39c I i 31) For this corrupt line, see most recently

Lambert, AfO 27 (1980), 72. (I ii 8-34) Lambert, AfO 27 (1980), 71ff., *Studies Garelli*, 412f. (I iii 23′) The proposal of Durand, RA 73 (1979), 155 note 6, fails to take into account K 10097 (*Atrahasis*, xi). (I iv 18) See K 10604 = Lambert, OrNS 38 (1969), 533. (I iv 38) K 18479 = Lambert, AfO 27 (1980), 74. (I v 22, vi 12) Differently Klein, *Nabu* 1990/98. (II.39d ii 21′) Borger, HKL 2, 159.

CHAPTER III

THE MATURE PERIOD
(1500 – 1000 B.C.)

The Mature period of Akkadian literature, approximately the second half of the second millennium B.C., has to be considered against a historical background very different from that of the Classical period. Following the fall of the First Babylonian dynasty to the Hittites in the sixteenth century, and the decline, somewhat earlier, of Assyrian military power, a political "dark age" set in, about which little is known.[1] Mesopotamia was ruled in the south by the Kassites, a people of non-Mesopotamian origin, and in Assyria by the Hurrians from their kingdom of Mitanni, centered in the Khabur region.[2] In Anatolia, the Hittites ruled from their capital Hattusha on the central Anatolian plateau.[3]

At the beginning of the Mature period, both Babylonia and Assyria were thus ruled by non-Mesopotamian peoples who were nevertheless under considerable Mesopotamian cultural influence. The Kassites and Hurrians created new political entities whose size and interconnections permitted wide diffusion of Mesopotamian cultural tradition such that, by the end of the second millennium, Akkadian was the lingua franca of the entire Near East. Akkadian inevitably acquired an academic character, especially in regions where the language was not widely understood.

Towards the end of the Mature period, there was a resurgence of Assyrian and Babylonian national feeling. Assyria threw off Hurrian political domination, and embarked on a new imperial phase. In Babylon a native dynasty was re-established under Nebuchadnezzar I.

---

1. A discussion of chronological and historical problems of this period will be found in B. Landsberger, "Assyrische Königsliste und 'Dunkles Zeitalter'," JCS 8 (1954), 31-45, 47-73, 106-133. The term "dark age" refers to modern historical ignorance rather than conditions in the period itself; see T. Mommsen, "Petrarch's Conception of the 'Dark Ages'," Speculum 17 (1942), 226-242.

2. For the Kassites, see J. Brinkman, "Kassiten," RLA 5, 464-473. For the Hurrians, up-to-date bibliography can be found in Revue Hittite et Asianique 36 (1978) and M. T. Barrelet et al., Methodologie et critiques I: problèmes concernant les Hurrites (Paris, 1977).

3. The standard works are A. Goetze, Kleinasien² (Munich, 1957), and O. R. Gurney, The Hittites (Pelican Books, 1952 and following).

Throughout the Mature period, Assyria and Babylonia were political and cultural rivals, though heirs to a common tradition. Each expressed local pride and heritage in literature. Yet so much was Assyria under Babylonian cultural influence that even Assyrian nationalistic literature was written in the Babylonian literary dialect, or sometimes dialectal Sumerian (see General Introduction, A.3).

Notwithstanding this influence, Assyrian hymns, prayers, and psalms (see III.2-4) can have a distinctive regional style, characterized by turgid verbosity and emphasis on the unique importance of Assyrian kingship in the universe. For example, what may be a fragment of a royal hymn in the name of Assur-bel-kala (1074-1057 B.C.) opens as follows:[1]

> To Adad, irrigator of heaven and earth,
> [Who rides] furious storms, thundering to the clamor of [   ],
> Who is possessed of vast terrors
>   [and] awe-inspiring luminosity,
> God without whom no verdicts are established
>   in heaven or netherworld,
> Light, illumination(?) of all peoples,
> For (Adad), who holds the link
>   of heaven and netherworld, his lord:
> Assur-bel-kala, whose name the god invoked
>   from the whole of Assyria,
> Leader and general for the gods [   ],

A typically Assyrian literary genre was the royal epic. The earliest preserved example deals with the exploits of Adad-nerari I (1307-1295 B.C.) against the Kassite king Nazimaruttash (1393-1298 B.C.). The text opens with the fulsome praise of the king characteristic of Assyrian literature:

> Fierce envoy of combat, favorite of the [great?] gods,
> Who winnows the enemy like a pitchfork,
>   who mashes [the ... together like a ...],
> Fierce Adad-nerari, favorite of the [great] gods,
> Who winnows the enemy like a pitchfork,
>   who mashes [the ... together like a ...],
> Trusty herdsman of the black-headed folk,

---

1. Strong, JRAS 1892, 342-343.

shepherd of [the people],
Valiant vanguard of the army, trust of [   ],
Purifier who keeps pure the cleansing rites of the [great] gods,
Reliable administrator of Ekur, favorite of the god [Enlil]:
When Ishtar summoned w[arriors to battle],
She brought down destruction upon me and [   ],
Irnina's heart raged, [she ... for] battle.[1]

Possible models for these royal epics are Babylonian poems of the Classical period about the deeds of the Sargonic kings (see II.12a, 13a). These show that Akkadian epic-style compositions existed by the early second millennium B.C., though none of them is so long as the Assyrian royal epics. The length and complexity of the Adad-nerari epic suggests that it belonged to a fully developed Assyrian royal epic tradition, even though no earlier examples have been preserved.

With respect to Babylonian epic poetry, no Kassite epics concerning the warfare with Assyria are known. Rather, the extant Babylonian texts of comparable style refer to Elam and date near the end of the Mature period (see III.12). These are less bombastic than the Assyrian epics; the lines are shorter and less weighted down with verbiage, the narrative less ponderous. Interesting examples of the Babylonian style are provided by certain texts of the Nebuchadnezzar group (III.12b, c). These have a direct, forceful narrative flow, like the rapid battle narrative of the Creation Epic, Tablet III. The Creation Epic (III.17) itself presents a decidedly Babylonian view of universal history, and so may be considered a nationalistic, political work, despite its theological emphasis.

One can only speculate about the Assyrian attitude towards Babylonian cultural superiority. It may have varied with the personalities and interests of individual kings or court scholars. In the thirteenth century B.C., during the reign of Tukulti-Ninurta I, for example, Assyrian scholars studied Babylonian literary works brought back as booty to Assyria, at the same time cultivating their own distinctive literary style (see III.1).

Evaluation of the literary developments of the Mature period is hampered by a paucity of manuscripts, especially from Babylonia. There is no way to be certain that all the works ascribed here to the Mature period were actually composed

---

1. Text = Schroeder, KAH II 143 = Ebeling, KAR 260; Borger, AfO 17 (1954/6), 369; Köcher, AfO 20 (1963), pl. V (VAT 9820, obv only); VAT 10899 (unpublished), excerpts quoted by Weidner, AfO 20 (1963), 113-115. For this passage, see Wilcke, ZA 67 (1977), 187-191. "Black-headed folk" refers to the Mesopotamians.

then, rather than in the Late or Classical periods. Criteria for dating texts include their language, subject matter, form, and personal names or other historical data within the texts, but these criteria are often debated and interpreted differently by different scholars.[1]

Akkadian literature of the Mature period shows the handiwork of authors deeply interested in words and language as objects of study. Rare words appear in literary texts, some presumably literary words, others dialectal within Akkadian, others drawn from scholarly works (see General Introduction, D.3). Allusive, intricate, and complicated expressions were esteemed (Great Hymn to Nabu [III.31], possibly dating to the Late period). Manuscripts from different repositories were studied and edited.[2] Sumerian was cultivated as a learned, artificial means of expression in literary works, religious observances, royal inscriptions, and devotional inscriptions on cylinder seals.[3] Bilingual Sumero-Akkadian texts were still composed in Assyria (III.2) and Babylonia (III.12d), even though Sumerian was by then long a dead language. Philology flourished, both for its own sake and as a hermeneutic science that was to have a particular impact on literature.[4]

On the level of form, the Mature period sees creative combination of shorter pieces into single composite texts (see Ishtar Queen of Heaven [III.26] and General Introduction, D.3). For the modern reader, these complex works abound in literary and philological difficulties; the existence of ancient commentaries shows that they were not readily accessible to the ancients either. In addition, there is a tendency to organize disparate texts such as omens, lexicography, and magic into standardized series of tablets (see Chapter IV). One senses editors, redactors, and compilers at work along with authors.

Some Assyriologists refer to the organization of ancient Mesopotamian texts

1. The difficulties are discussed by W. von Soden, "Das Problem der zeitlichen Einordnung akkadischer Literaturwerke," MDOG 85 (1953), 14-26; W. G. Lambert, "Zum Forschungsstand der sumerisch-babylonischen Literatur-geschichte," ZDMG Suppl. III/1 (1977), 64-73.

2. For example, the colophon to a manuscript of a hymn states that it was copied from "originals from Nippur and Babylon"; see H. Hunger, AOAT 2 (1968), 30, no. 44 (KAR 15).

3. A. Falkenstein, "Zur Chronologie der sumerischen Literatur, Die nachaltbabylonische Stufe," MDOG 85 (1953), 1-13; S. N. Kramer (with T. Baqir and S. Levy), "Fragments of a Diorite Statue of Kurigalzu in the Iraq Museum," Sumer 4 (1948), 1-39; H. Limet, Les Légendes des sceaux cassites (Bruxelles, 1971), with an important review by W. G. Lambert, BiOr 32 (1975), 219-223.

4. W. von Soden, "Leistung und Grenze sumerischer und babylonischer Wissenschaft," Die Welt als Geschichte 2 (1936), 411-464, 509-557, reprinted in Libelli CXLII (1965).

into standardized form, groups, and series as "canonization."[1] They suggest that during the Mature period texts were "canonized" by making a selection among texts inherited from the past and by discarding material not in agreement with current taste or religious and ethical concepts. Texts so selected were not radically altered from their previous forms, and new material was composed along "canonical" lines. This process is still poorly understood, and use of the term "canonization," with its scriptural overtones, is misleading.

National feeling in Mesopotamia during the Mature period became an important influence on Akkadian literature. In Assyria, literature came to express an imperial ideology for which no clear Babylonian counterpart existed.[2] In both Assyria and Babylonia compositions of a markedly propagandistic character were addressed to the educated, influential class, seeking to sway opinion with theological and ethnocentric terminology.[3]

The emergence of large states in Assyria and Babylonia implied palace-centered governments with international interests, characterized by hierarchy, attempt to control resources, and military adventurism.[4] At the same time, some areas of Mesopotamia may have suffered a decline of population, with settlement patterns tending toward agricultural villages dominated by fortified enclaves. This suggests a wide gulf between a depressed producing population and a military elite.[5] Times were often uncertain, and, outside of the elite, the subject seemed farther from his ruler than in the Classical period. Literature reflected to some degree these realities of Mesopotamian society. The gods, whose order mirrored that of civilized Mesopotamian humanity, seemed

1. W. von Soden, "Zweisprachigkeit in der geistigen Kultur Babyloniens," *Sitzungsberichte der Österreichischer Akademie der Wissenschaften, Philologisch- historische Klasse* 235/1 (1960), 9ff.; W. G. Lambert, "Ancestors, Authors, and Canonicity," JCS 11 (1959), 9; Hallo, AS 20 (1979), 181ff.; van Dijk, *Orientalia et Biblica Lovaniensia* 1 (1957), 6; F. Rochberg-Halton, "Canonicity in Cuneiform Texts," JCS 36 (1984), 127-144; S. Lieberman, "Canonical Official Cuneiform Texts: Towards an Understanding of Assurbanipal's Personal Tablet Collection," *Studies Moran*, 305-336.

2. P. Garelli, "Les empires mésopotamiens," in M. Duverger, ed., *Le Concept d'Empire* (Paris, 1980), 25-43; "La Concept de la royauté en Assyrie," in F. M. Fales, ed., *Assyrian Royal Inscriptions, New Horizons*, OAC 17 (Rome, 1981), 1-11.

3. A. L. Oppenheim, "The City of Assur in 714 B.C.," JNES 19 (1960), 133-147; "Neo-Assyrian and Neo-Babylonian Empires," in H. Lasswell *et al.*, eds., *Propaganda and Communication in World History* (Honolulu, 1979), 1:111-144.

4. B. R. Foster, "The Late Bronze Age Economy: A View from the East," in R. Hägg and N. Marinatos, eds., *The Function of the Minoan Palaces, Proceedings of the Fourth International Symposium at the Swedish Institute in Athens, 10-16 June, 1984*, Skrifter utgivna av Svenska Institutet i Athen 4, XXV (Stockholm, 1987), 11-16.

5. R. McC. Adams, *Heartland of Cities* (Chicago, 1981), 168.

correspondingly more remote and difficult to understand than before, given to harsh punishment of the weak and favoritism of the rich and powerful.[1]

Professionals in divination and the other sciences may have had considerable influence among the elite. Their prayers and rituals tend to focus on the needs and anxieties of the highly placed: generals, courtiers, administrators, the king (see III.36b, 38a, b, 44c, 47b, 50h-l). Naturally professionals asserted the need for their disciplines and formulated elaborate consultative procedures that rendered them indispensable for military and political undertakings, as well as for the day-to-day life of the powerful. These professionals adapted Akkadian written tradition to their needs and ideology.[2] Professionals such as scholars, priests, and singers of laments[3] were presumably responsible for training succeeding generations in literature, the techniques of Mesopotamian philology, editing of texts, historical research, cultivation of rhetoric, and allied disciplines. While schools are known from the Classical period, little is known of them for the Mature period.[4]

Perhaps the most suggestive difference between Akkadian literature of the Classical and Mature periods is the place of mankind in the texts. Whereas in the Classical period man appears as an individual struggling in a difficult world, in the Mature period he is portrayed rather as a mortal lost in a vast, institutionalized cosmos. The hero is now not so much valorous as knowledgeable; the characteristic portrayal of the human plight is not so much servitude to the gods as ignorance and incomprehension of their ways. The exaltation of knowledge is the most salient trait of maturing Akkadian literature.

---

1. T. Jacobsen, *The Treasures of Darkness* (New Haven, 1976), 162ff.

2. A. L. Oppenheim, "The Position of the Intellectual in Mesopotamian Society," *Daedalus*, Spring, 1975, 37-46; J. Pečírková, "Divination and Politics in the Late Assyrian Empire," ArOr 53 (1985), 155-168.

3. M. E. Cohen, *The Canonical Lamentations of Ancient Mesopotamia* (Potomac, MD, 1988), 1:11-44.

4. Charpin, *Clergé*, 482ff.; M. Dandamayev, *Vavilonskie Pisci* (Moscow, 1983), 27ff., 61ff.; A. Falkenstein, "Der babylonische Schule," *Saeculum* 4 (1953), 125-137; S. N. Kramer, "The Sumerian School: A Pre-Greek System of Education" in G. Mylonas, ed., *Studies Presented to David Moore Robinson* (St. Louis, 1961), 238-245; Kraus, *Mensch*, 18ff.; B. Landsberger, "Scribal Concepts of Education" in C. Kraeling and R. McC. Adams, eds., *City Invincible* (Chicago, 1960), 94-102; Å. W. Sjöberg, "The Old Babylonian Eduba," AS 20 (1975), 159-179; H. Vanstiphout, "How Did They Learn Sumerian?" JCS 31 (1979), 118-126; H. Waetzoldt, "Keilschrift und Schulen in Mesopotamien und Ebla," in L. Kriss-Rettenbeck and M. Liedtke, eds., *Erziehungs- und Unterrichtsmethoden im historischen Wandel* (Bad Heilbrunn, 1986), 36-50; "Der Schreiber als Lehrer in Mesopotamien," in J. von Hohenzollern and M. Liedtke, eds., *Magister, Lehrer, Zur Geschichte und Funktion eines Berufstandes* (Bad Heilbrunn, 1989), 33-50.

A. ASSYRIAN POETRY

III.1 TUKULTI-NINURTA EPIC

Tukulti-Ninurta I, a tragic and fascinating Assyrian king of the thirteenth century B.C., began his reign with significant conquests, including parts of northern Syria, Anatolia, and Babylonia. In Babylon he ruled as king for seven years. Royal agents included scholarly and literary manuscripts among the booty brought back from Babylonia. These may have stimulated new literary activity in Assyria and provided writers with new themes and language.

One impressive achievement of this Assyrian renaissance is the bilingual prayer translated below, III.2, which demonstrates a capacity to compose original work in dialectal Sumerian in this period. The text treated here, the epic of Tukulti-Ninurta, is the product of a mature and learned master steeped both in Babylonian and Assyrian tradition. The text presents a distinctive, turgid splendor of language, with rare words and convoluted syntax. The idioms of treaties and diplomacy, penitential psalms and laments, heroic tales, hymnography, and commemorative inscriptions are freely used. One may speculate that the prayer and the epic come from the same hand; close to the troubled monarch was a brilliant scholar and poet whose work appealed to the king's taste. Was it at this man's urging that the tablets were gathered from Babylonia?

In addition to loot and manuscripts, Tukulti-Ninurta brought the statue of Marduk from his temple in Babylon to Assur. The image remained in Assur for a century, to the Babylonians a maddening symbol of their political and military impotence. Furthermore, large numbers of Babylonians and Kassites were resettled in Assyria. The extent to which the king and his scholar attempted to cultivate Babylonian ways and religion at Assur is unknown. Marduk's image was treated with respect. Discontent with the influx of Babylonian ideas into Assyria may have contributed to Tukulti-Ninurta's downfall.

Having reached the natural limits of his conquests early in his reign, Tukulti-Ninurta turned his formidable energies to a massive, even frenetic building campaign. After living in the "Old Palace" at Assur, he reconstructed a palace built by his father, Shalmaneser I. Soon thereafter he cleared a large residential area and built yet another palace with walls to connect it to the fortified sector of the city. Hardly was this done when he began to build a whole new city, Kar-Tukulti-Ninurta, across the Tigris and thus isolated from the traditional capital of the land. There he seems to have shut himself up in suspicion of all around him.

The king's outrageous demands on his subjects for building enterprises opened the way for a successful conspiracy against him led by his own son. Tukulti-Ninurta was seized and murdered in his new palace.

For a portrait of the king and his times, see E. F. Weidner, "Studien zur Zeitgeschichte Tukulti-Ninurtas I.," AfO 13 (1939/41), 109-124. For English translations of his historical inscriptions and relevant passages in the Babylonian chronicles, see Grayson, ARI 1, 101-134. See also the essay on the king's personality by W. von Soden, *Herrscher im alten Orient* (Berlin, 1954), 69-74. Another account will be found by H. Klengel, "Tukulti-Ninurta I., König von Assyrien," *Das Altertum* 7 (1961), 67-77.

i (= K 6007)

(Praises of the god Assur and of the king, Tukulti-Ninurta)

Listen to his praise, the praises of the king of [   ] lords,   (1)
I ex[tol] the [ ] of lord of the world, the Assyrian Enlil,
Let his mighty power, his [   ] be spoken of,
[Hear   ] how great his weapons were over his enemies!
I extol and praise Assur, king of [the gods],   (5)
The great kings also [   ]
Whom [he ...] in the campaign against Kadm[uhi],*
And (whom) by command of the w[arrior] Shamash [he ...],
Aside from the forty kings of [Nairi   ]¹
Whom, in his reign [   ]   (10)
The triumph of his lordship [   ]

(fragmentary lines)

i (= B obv)

(gap)

(Introduction of the protagonist: the valiant Tukulti-Ninurta [in the broken section] and his antagonist, the treacherous Kashtiliash [as the text becomes intelligible]. The Babylonian gods become angry with Kashtiliash and forsake his sanctuaries, a sign of impending doom. After a gap in the text (A obv), there is a fragmentary hymn to Tukulti-Ninurta, with allusions to his birth and upbringing. In i 24' Kashtiliash is referred to again. He disdains his sworn treaty [of friendship and non-aggression?] and plots war.)

[   ] against enemies [   ]
[   ]
[   ] no(?) surviving [   ]
[   ] which cannot be faced [   ]
[   ] the wicked [   ]
[   ] and the disobedient [   ]   (10')
[   ] ... [   ]
[the dis]obedient [   ]
[   ] command [   ]

1. For the incident referred to, see Grayson, ARI 1, 119.

(gap of nine lines)

[   ] and [   ]   (20′)
[   ] to transgress [   ]
[   ] ... [   ]
[   ] ... light [   ]
[   ] the end of the reign of [   ]
[w]arrior of heaven and netherworld.   (25′)
[   ] which he took by force [   ]
[   ] the land which he ruled [   ]
[   ] ... [   ]
[   ] Ishtar, the high point of the land of Akkad [   ]
[fr]om(?) lordship the king of the Kassites   (30′)
[guilt] which cannot be expunged.
[The gods became angry at] the king of the Kassite's betrayal
        of the emblem [of Shamash],
Against the transgressor of an oath, Kashtiliash, the gods
        of heaven and netherworld [   ].
They were [angry] at the king, the land, and the people [   ],
They [were furious and with] the willful one,
        their shepherd.   (35′)
His lordship, the lord of the world,[1]
        became disturbed, so he [forsook] Nippur,
He would not approach [   ] (his) seat at Dur-Kurigalzu.
Marduk abandoned his sublime sanctuary, the city [Babylon],
He cursed his favorite city Kar-[   ].
Sin left Ur, [his] holy place [   ],   (40′)
Sh[amash became angry] with Sippar and Larsa,
Ea [   ] Eridu, the house of wisdom [   ],
Ishtaran became furious w[ith Der   ],
Annunitu would not approach Agade [   ],
The lady of Uruk cast [off her   ]:   (45′)
(All) the gods were enraged [   ]
[   ] on account of the verdict [   ]

(gap)

1. Enlil.

i (= A obv)

[   ] his ..., Assur.
[   ] the gods, lord of judgment,
[   ] he has none to calm him,
[   ] bears him   (5′)
[   ] he made light of the oath of the gods!
[   ] ... defeat,
[Who obeys] the gods' intents on the battlefield,
[   ] he made the weapons glorious.
Glorious is his heroism,
     it [ ] the dis[respectful] front and rear,   (10′)
Incendiary is his onrush,
     it burns the disobedient right and left.
His radiance is terrifying; it overwhelms all foes,
Every pious★ king of the four world regions stands in awe of him.
When he bellows like thunder, mountains totter,
And when he brandishes his weapon like Ninurta,[1]
     all regions of the earth everywhere hover in panic.   (15′)
Through the destiny of Nudimmud, he is reckoned as flesh
     godly in his limbs,★[2]
By fiat of the lord of the world, he was cast sublimely
     from the womb of the gods.
It is he who is the eternal image of Enlil, attentive to the
     people's voice, the counsel of the land,
Because the lord of the world appointed him to
     lead the troops, he praised him with his very lips,
Enlil exalted him as if he (Enlil) were his (Tukulti-Ninurta's)
     own father, right after his first-born son![3]   (20′)
Precious is he in (Enlil's) family,★ for where there is
     competition, he has of him protection.
No one of all kings was ever rival to him,★
No sovereign stood forth★ as his battlefield opponent.
[   ] falsehood,★ crime, repression, wrong-doing,

---

1. An oblique reference to the king's name.
2. Nudimmud = Ea as creator.
3. That is, the god Ninurta (Machinist, diss., 206f.).

[   ] the weighty ... * the divine oath and went
    back on what he swore.   (25′)
[   ] the gods were watching his furtive deed,
[   ] though he was their follower.
[   ] the king of the Kassites made light of what he swore,
He committed a crime, an act of malice.
[Although the one] ... kept changing [   ],
    (the other's) word is sure,   (30′)
[Although the one ...], (the other) is one who pleas
    for divine mercy always.
[   ] and shall not be expunged.
[   ] ... offenses were numerous.
[   ] he turned back on a command
[   ] he spoke hostility   (35′)
[   ] put his trust in ...
[   ] he longed for battle
[   ] stratagem

(fragmentary lines, then gap)

ii (= A obv)

(gap)

(The Assyrians capture Babylonian merchants, who were evidently spying in Assyria, and bring them before the king. He spares them out of respect for international custom. In a prayer to Shamash, god of justice, the king states that he has been faithful to the treaty, explains how it was made, reminds the god that he oversees sworn treaties, and calls on him for a favorable outcome in his contest with the evildoer. In A obv 25′ff. Tukulti-Ninurta sends a message to Kashtiliash, reminding him of the long history of relations between their two lands, and charging him with violation of the treaty. As suggested by Machinist, diss., 237, the letter may end on a conciliatory note, offering the opportunity for reaffirmation of the oath despite the Kassite's willful violation of it.)

Within the confines of the land of [Assyria   ] he imposed an
    ordinance, lest any secret [of the land?] go out.
They came [   ] very much ...
Those who bore the in[signia?]* of the king of the Kassites,
    merchants were captured at night(?),*   (5′)
They brought [them] before Tukulti-Ninurta,

lord of all peoples, bound together.*
The king gathered(?) [them] in the place of Shamash,
    he perpetrated no infamy,
(But) he sustained them,
    he did a good deed for the lord of Babylon:
He released the merchants ..., bearers of money bags,
He had them stand before Shamash and anointed
    their heads with oil.[1]   (10′)
The tablets(?) of the king of the Kassites, the seal
    impression which he had made official,[2]
He reconfirmed(?), before Shamash he [   ], his utterance
    he presented in measured words to the god,*
"O Shamash, [   ] lord, I respected(?) your oath,
    I feared your greatness.
"He who does not [   ] transgressed before your [   ],
    but I observed your ordinance.
"When our fathers made a pact before your divinity,   (15′)
"They swore an oath between them
    and invoked your greatness.
"You are the hero, the valiant one, who from of old
    was unalterable judge of our fathers,
"And you are the god who sets aright,
    who sees now our loyalty.
"Why has the king of the Kassites from of old invalidated
    your plan and your ordinance?
"He had no fear of your oath, he transgressed your
    command, he schemed an act of malice.   (20′)
"He has made his crimes enormous before you,
    judge me, O Shamash!
"But he who committed no crime [against] the king
    of the Kassites, [act favorably towards him],

1. A ceremony of release (Veenhof, BiOr 23 [1966], 310f.; Machinist, diss., 229f.).

2. Probably refers to official letters given by the king to the merchants as bonafide commercial agents. If the men acted as spies, this was presumably a violation of "commercial immunity," but Tukulti-Ninurta is careful to protect them as merchants, despite their questionable status.

"By your great [   ] bestow the victory ...
    on the observer of oaths,
"[He who does not] your command,
    obliterate his people in the rout of battle!"
[The wi]se [shepherd], who knows what should be done,
    waxed wroth, [his frigh]tening brilliance
    became enraged.   (25')
He sent a message [to Kashtili]ash the wicked,
    the obstinate, the heedless,
"[Whereas] formerly you [forswore] what belonged
    to the time of our forefathers' hostilities,
"[Now] you face Shamash with false testimony about us.
"[Enlil-nera]ri, my forefather, king of all peoples, ... [   ]
"[Against? Kur]igalzu, (he) pursued the oath of the gods, []   (30')
"[Adad-n]erari, my grandfather, [   ]
"[   ] Nazimaruttash [   ] in battle [   ]
"[   ] Shalmaneser, perceiver of his princeship, [   ]
"[   ] the lives of their [   ] ...
"[   ] ...   (35')
"[   ] ... [   ]
"[   ] among all lands he is the unalterable judge,

(fragmentary lines, then gap)

ii (= F col "x")

(Fragment F [Lambert, AfO 18 (1957/8), 48-51 and pl. IV] the reverse(?) of an excerpt(?) tablet that preserves a section of this epic, may belong here. For placement and interpretation, I follow Machinist, diss., 15f., 31ff., who suggests that this piece deals with an affront by Kashtiliash to Tukulti-Ninurta. As read here, the Babylonian king replies insolently to Tukulti-Ninurta's letter, while preventing the Assyrian messenger from returning, a diplomatic snub of the time. After a gap of uncertain size, Fragment D may be placed [Machinist, diss., 11ff.]. In 1-6 Kashtiliash is threatening Tukulti-Ninurta, and, beginning in 7, Tukulti-Ninurta replies in righteous wrath.)

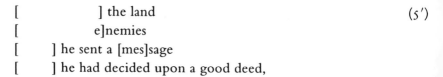

[   ] the land   (5')
[e]nemies
[   ] he sent a [mes]sage
[   ] he had decided upon a good deed,

[   ] he affirmed the compact.
[Kashtiliash said, "..."] your good deed!
    Detain the messenger (here)! (10′)
"[   ] don't let the [merchan]ts cross!
"[   ] take away!

(fragmentary lines, then gap)

ii (= D)

"[Against] your camp ... like a thunderstorm [   ] (1)
"[   ] like a flood that spares no [   ]
"[   ] your valiant warriors like [   ]
"[   ] the mighty onslaught of the Kas[site] army
"[   ] every stratagem in the onslaught of battle [], (5)
"[   ] your warriors on an [ill-fated] day [   ]!"
[The king], the wise shepherd,
    [who knows] what should be done, [ ],
[To Kashtilia]sh, the wicked, the obstinate,
    king of the Kassites [   ],
"[The ...], Kashtiliash, of your forefathers you [   ],
"[   ] in the unp[lundered?] sanctuaries, (10)
"[   ] my [ ], to set straight [   ]
"[   ] your warriors who [   ] combat
"[   ] of my land which you plundered [   ],
"[   ] the troops that you made off with [   ],

(fragmentary lines, including a reference to Shamash)

iii (= A obv)

(Tukulti-Ninurta exchanges letters with Kashtiliash and indicts him for his misdeeds. Tukulti-Ninurta calls upon Shamash to resolve their differences and to vindicate his adherence to the treaty by making him victorious in trial by battle. Kashtiliash is paralyzed with fear at the prospect and offers a soliloquy on his impending doom. After a gap in the text, Tukulti-Ninurta invades Babylonia and the doomed and desperate Kassite goes berserk [Fragment C].)

"And the borders of your territories [   ],
"Why did you retreat and [   ] the road from which there
    is no escape?

"And why are you turning afraid,
    and ... without engagement [   ]?
"You have plundered my whole land, [   ] pillage,   (5')
"You have made away with the armies of Assur,
    before hostilities even, you have [   ].
"The [   ] have steadily cast down in untimely death,
"Their [wives] are become widows in undue season.
"I raise aloft, therefore, the tablet of oath between us, and
    call upon the Lord of Heaven [   ]!
"You have showed forth a crime that [   ] us both to
    the battlefield,   (10')
"Saying: 'I released your father(?),* I took no revenge.'
"That you have plundered my unarmed people
    is an offense[1] to us forever!
"When we face one another in battle, let the judgment
    between us be ... [   ].
"We shall meet* that day just as a righteous man plunders
    the [   ] of a thief.
"Reconciliation cannot be made without conflict [   ],   (15')
"Nor can there be good relations without a battle,
    so long as you do not [   ].
"(And) until I expose your hair fluttering behind you[2] and
    you have [disappeared] to an untimely death,
"Until my eyes, in the battle with you, shall see ...,
    slaughter, and ...,
"So come to me in the battle of servants (of the gods?),
    let us get to the bottom of the matter together!
"From this festival of battle may the transgressor of oath not
    away, may they cast away(?)* his corpse!"   (20')
Tukulti-Ninurta, having put his trust in his observance
    of the oath, was planning for battle,
While Kashtiliash, insofar as he had trespassed the command
    of the gods, was altered within himself,
He was appalled on account of the appeal to Shamash

---

1. "Us" may refer to Tukulti-Ninurta and the Assyrian people.
2. That is, in flight.

and became fearful and anxious
    about what was laid before the gods.
The mighty king's utterance constricted his body
    like a demonic presence.
So Kashtiliash deliberated with himself, "I did not listen to
    what the Assyrian (said),
    I made light of the messenger.[1]   (25′)
"I did not conciliate him, I did not accept his favorable
    intention before.
"Now I understand how grievous the crimes of my land are
    become, how numerous its sins.
"Mortal punishments have smitten me down,
    death has me in its grip!
"The oath of Shamash sets upon(?) me,
    it catches me by the hem,
"You have entered in evidence against me an unalterable
    tablet with the seal impression of m[y forefather]s,   (30′)
"They too have intro[duced evidence] before me,
    a [   ] whose wording cannot be changed!
"My forefathers' treaty, which was not violated, [   ]
"Thus did the just judge, the unalterable, the valiant one,
    [Shamash] establish the case against me!
"As for the plundering which my forefathers did,
    I [have made it worse]!
"For it is I, indeed, who have put my people into a pitiless
    hand, a grasp [from which there is no escape].   (35′)
"Into a narrow strait with no way out
    I have gathered [my land].
"Many are my wrong-doings before Shamash,
    [great are] my misdeeds,
"Who is the god that will spare my people from [catastrophe]?
"The Assyrian is ever heedful of all the gods [   ]
"He ... the lords of our oath,
    ... of heaven and netherworld,   (40′)

---

1. Compare F 10′, where the messenger is delayed before returning to his sender, a diplomatic insult.

"I shall not examine in the extispicy
    (the signs for) "fa[ll of the regime],"⋆
"The omens for well-being of my army are [gone] from my land,
"The signs within the [   ] are ...
"The security of my house's foundation [ ] was never firm.
"Whatever my dream(s), they are terrifying [   ]   (45′)
"Omnipotent Assur glowers at me [   ]!"
This too: "Quickly, let me cast: [   ]
"To what shall I [   ] my omen?"⋆
This too: "Let me know: For ba[ttle   ]
"How long [   ]?   (50′)
"... [   ]
"Let me learn the secret [   ]
"Will he overcome me and [   ]?
"Like an inferno or a cyclone [   ]?
"He has closed in on me and [   ],   (55′)
"So death [   ]!"
He was exhausted [   ]

(fragmentary lines, the gap)

iii (= C)

[   ] he entered, and the city Akka[d]
And like a thunderstorm against the creatures of [... he ...]
[As for] Kashtiliash, king of the Kassites,
    who had yearned [for battle],   (5′)
And whose fondest hopes were ecstatic at comb[at   ],
He jumped from his chair and [ ] his table.
He twitched, he flung away the meat, he [   ],
He discarded his royal adornment in [   ].
He could not swallow a bite [   ].   (10′)
The dining tray was not ... where he arose [   ],
The seats of his palace, which used to be firm(?) [   ].
He mounted his chariot and harangued the hor[de?   ],
He said to his army, "I fought with [   ]!"
The king of the Kassites rushed hither and yon like a [   ],   (15′)
He sought all over the groves [for a place to hide   ],
He went away then turned back, with [   ].

He fled as if he were quarry, like a [   ].
No fervor raised he, with the [   ],
Nor could he [   ] his victory(?) against Annunitu.   (20')
He did not look behind him, [nor] over his soldiers [did he ...]
[Nor] over his own offspring, the creation of [   ]
Kashtiliash, like one in [   ]
The dust of death [   ]

iv (= C rev)

(Despite his doom, the obstinate Kashtiliash refuses to yield, and seeks to evade Tukulti-Ninurta's advance. Kashtiliash prefers guerilla tactics to a direct confrontation. Tukulti-Ninurta challenges him to a fight, but Kashtiliash stalls, hoping for a change of fortune. An indecisive battle is fought, apparently when Kashtiliash tries to surprise the Assyrians [A rev].)

[   ] with the point of his ar[row   ]
Which he sent off [   ]
The king of the Kassites did not trust ... [   ]
He summoned against him [   ]   (5')
He rained down upon him [   ]
Kashtiliash went out [   ]
"Surely our lord's treaty ... [   ]
"He will not leave the innermost [   ]
"Until he catches him alive [   ]."   (10')
They carried off the king [   ]
And the hero of his warriors [   ]
He would not submit(?) to Tukulti-Ninurta [   ]
Nor before his warriors did he [   ]
Where the weapon of Assur joins [battle   ]   (15')
The river banks were trampled, the cities [   ]
The king overcame the city [   ]
He turned to Annunitu [   ]
He became lord of the distant city which [   ] had never [   ]
He reckoned the land for devas[tation   ]   (20')
The king set to [   ]
He established for many a distant league [   ]

He dammed up the conflu[ence   ]
He repaired the paths [   ]
He overcame the city(?) [   ]   (25′)

(gap)

iv (= A rev)

Another time he ... [   ]   (5′)
But he did not submit before Tukulti-Ninurta [   ]
Nor would he face him [in battle   ]
Another time he ... [   ]
He was drawn up in [   ]
He decided(?) [   ]   (10′)
Tukulti-Ninurta ordered [   ]
A messenger to Kashtiliash to [   ]
"How much longer is [your army] to flee?
"You keep changing your army around by command [   ]."
Saying, "For what day are you keeping
    the [weapons] of combat [ ]?   (15′)
"And which of your weapons stands by for which day?"
Saying, "I am stationed in your land, [I   ] cult center,
"I plundered all the cities you had and [   ] your people!"
Saying, "When will your usual insolence [provoke you] to battle?
"The fury and slaughter you wanted so much we will soon show!   (20′)
"Surely now you have courage, for the month of the spring
    flood, the water will be your ally.
"And you have pitched your camp in remote places,
    trusting in G[irra],[1]
"But in the dry season, when the peak flood ends,
    and the god ... with fire,
"In what remote place will you trust to save your people?
"My army is camped not many leagues from you,   (25′)
"And as for you, all your chariotry is in readiness and
    your army is massed.
"Attack me, then, like a brave man,
    fight the battle that you strive so hard to attain!

---

1. The heat?

"Show your weapon, find release in the battle
    that your fondest hopes burned for!"
Kashtiliash gave the command for battle,
    but was anxious and agitated,
Saying, "Tukulti-Ninurta, your army should stand fast
    until the appointed time of Shamash arrives.   (30')
"Do not begin your fighting until the right season to fight me!"
Saying, "This is the day your people's blood will soak the
    the pastures and meadows,
"And, like a thunderstorm, I will make the levelling flood
    pass over your camp."
He dragged out the message-sending as a ruse
    until he could draw up his warriors,
And until he had made ready his battle plan,
    the chariotry was held back.   (35')
Then he despatched his army,
    but Girra held it back like a serious mutiny.
He brought his army across secret hideouts,
    blocking the crossing.
The valiant warriors of [Assur] espied the Kassite king's
    preparations,
They did not have their armor on, but sprang forward like lions,
Assur's unrivalled weapon met the onslaught of [his] ar[my?]*   (40')
And Tukulti-Ninurta, the raging, pitiless storm,
    made [their blood] flow.
The warriors of Assur [struck] the king of the Kassites
    like a serpent,
A mighty attack, an irresistible onslaught [   ] upon them.
Kashtiliash turned his [face] to save himself.
The weapon of Enlil, lord of the world,
    which hems in enemies, shattered [his troops],   (45')
The ... of battle, his allies were slaughtered like cattle,
    [his] nobles [   ]
Governors perished, warriors [   ]
[   ] the forefinger of the lord of the world.

    (fragmentary lines, then gap)

v (= A rev)

(After Kashtiliash's flight, the Assyrian troops urge their king to a decisive encounter, no matter what the cost to them. In 31'ff. the major battle is fought at last. Kashtiliash is defeated, but any account of his fate is lost in a gap in the text. According to an inscription of Tukulti-Ninurta, Kashtiliash was captured and brought to Assur: "(I) trod with my feet upon his lordly neck," see Grayson, ARI 1, 108 [No. 5].)

> The k[in]g ... [   ]
> His warriors ... [   ]   (10')
> "My lord, since the beginning of your reign [   ],
> "Battle and hardship have been our holiday and plea[sure].
> "You urge us to prepare for the melee [   ],
> "With the propitious sign of your lordship
>   let us proceed like men!
> "In your royal reign no king has stood equal to you,   (15')
> "Your exalted power has been set over the whole world,
>   the seas, and the mountains.
> "With the wrath of your scepter you have made to submit
>   all regions, in all quarters,
> "You spread the might of your land to territories
>   beyond count, you established (their) boundaries.
> "Kings know your valor and live in fear of battle with you.
> "They bear your frightfulness like slander and falsehood
>   homing in on the source.[1]   (20')
> "Now plan against the king of the Kassites,
>   destroy his forces before the season!
> "Rout the ranks he has set up, burn(?) his chariotry!
> "For how much longer in the future
>   is he to plot this evil against us?
> "Plotting basely against us, he plans murder by wont.
> "Daily he hopes to destroy the land of Assur, his threatening
>   finger is stretched out towards it.   (25')
> "He strives constantly to take control of the Assyrians' kingship.
> "Let us join battle, let him live to draw breath who advances,

1. I take this line to mean that just as lies come home to roost on the liar, so too the king's frightfulness cannot be avoided by those lesser kings; in fact, it sticks to them like some evil that they richly deserve. (For discussion of the passage, see Machinist, diss., 341ff.).

let him die who turns back! (You say),
"'While I was at peace he ended our friendly relations(?),'★
    so proceed with the battle!
"[ ], when they encouraged you before on the battlefield.
"And you will gain, our Lord, by command of Shamash,
    a victorious name over the king of the Kassites!"   (30′)
The lines of battle were drawn up,
    combat was joined on the battlefield.
There was a great commotion,
    the servants were quivering among them.
Assur went first, the conflagration of defeat burst out
    upon the enemy,
Enlil was whirling(?) in the midst of the foe, fanning the blaze,
Anu set the pitiless mace to the opponent,   (35′)
Sin, the luminary, laid upon them the tension of battle.
Adad, the hero, made wind and flood pour down
    over their fighting,
Shamash, lord of judgment, blinded the eyesight of the army
    of Sumer and Akkad,
Valiant Ninurta, vanguard of the gods,
    smashed their weapons,
Ishtar flailed her jump rope, driving their warriors berserk!   (40′)
Behind the gods, his allies, the king at the head of the army
    sets to battle,
He let fly an arrow, the fierce, overwhelming,
    crushing weapon of Assur, he felled one slain.
The warriors of Assur cried, "To battle!"
    as they went to face death,
They gave the battle cry, "O Ishtar, spare (me)!"
    and praise the mistress in the fray,
They are furious, raging, taking forms strange as Anzu.   (45′)
They charge forward furiously to the fray without any armor,
They had stripped off their breastplates, discarded their clothing,
They tied up their hair and polished(?) their ... weapons,★
The fierce, heroic men danced with sharpened weapons.
They blasted at one another like struggling lions,
    with eyes aflash(?),★   (50′)

While the fray, particles drawn in a whirlwind,
    swirled around in combat.
Death, as if on a day of thirsting,
    slakes itself at the sight of the warrior.*
[   ] furiously he attacked and turned north,

(fragmentary lines, then gap)

vi (= A rev)

(The victorious Assyrians plunder Babylonia. The first fragment mentions prisoners and treasures. In B rev Tukulti-Ninurta plunders collections of cuneiform tablets and brings them back to Assyria. He lavishly adorns temples there and in his royal city, Kar-Tukulti-Ninurta. In the concluding lines the poet praises the king.)

[   ] the population of the cities.
[   ] his [off]spring, the offspring of [   ]
[   ] the throne, the boundary stone [   ]
[   ] daughters of princes, dwelling in [   ]
[   ] their infants, sons and daughters.   (20′)
[   ] the enclosure of which ... for leagues,
[   ] the treasure of [ ] he plundered.[1]
[   ] innumerable subjects
[he di]d seven times in excess
[   ] he took special care for their lives   (25′)
[   ] who could pile up their [ ]?
[   ] a trustworthy house.
[so]ldiers, number of chariots,
[   ] the treasure of(?) the king of the Kassites,
[fr]om report of(?) the battle   (30′)
[   ] scepter
[   ] of the land
[   ] war vehicles

(traces, gap)

---

1. A late Babylonian chronicle (Chronicle P, Grayson, ARI 1, 134, 47*) states that Tukulti-Ninurta took booty from Esagila, carried off the cult statue of Marduk, installed a governor, and ruled as king in Babylon for seven years. For a booty list from this period, see Weidner, AfO 13 (1939/41), 119-123; compare Freydank, AOF 1 (1974), 55-73; Grayson, ARI 1, 132, 41.

vi (= B rev)

Treasure [   ],
Tablets of [   ],
Scribal lore [   ],
Exorcistic texts [   ],   (5')
Prayers to appease the gods [   ],
Divination texts ... the ominous marks(?) of heaven and earth,
Medical texts, procedure for bandaging [   ],
The muster lists of his ancestors [   ],
Records of(?) ... slaves(?), overseers(?), and soldiers [   ]:   (10')
Not one was left in the land of Sumer and Akkad![1]
The rich haul of the Kassite king's treasure [   ]
He filled boats with the yields for Assur [   ]
And the glory of his power was seen [   ]
[To] his victorious power the gods, lords [of   ]   (15')
[To] the great gods he bestowed fine [   ]
Gold and silver were [not] precious in his sight,*
He dedicated [   ] to the gods of his land.
He decorated [E-hur]sag-kurkurra[2] with [   ],
[He   E-kurm]esharra,[3] dwelling of Enlil of the Assyrians,   (20')
[   ] of the city Baltil[4] with pure red gold,
[He the san]ctuary of the Igigi-gods,
[   ] jewelry of fine [gold].
[   ] he praises his god As[sur   ],
Assur, who established him [for king]ship of his land [   ].   (25')
Adad [   ] the [   ] of his weapons,
[   ] which he rendered him [   ] greatly,
[   ] the weapons which he ... [   ]

1. A clay copy of an inscription on a seal taken by Tukulti-Ninurta in Babylonia is treated by Grayson, ARI 1, 127-128, 29. For discussion of the Babylonian tablets taken to Assyria at this time, see Weidner, AfO 16 (1952/3), 199-201; 206-211.

2. The cella of the Assur temple in Assur (G. van Driel, *The Cult of Assur* [Assen, 1969], 34-37).

3. The Assur temple in Kar-Tukulti-Ninurta, Tukulti-Ninurta's newly built royal city south of Assur.

4. Another name for Assur, apparently, the oldest part of the city (Tadmor, OAC 17 [1981], 27; Poebel, JNES 1 [1942], 263-267; J. Lewy, *Hebrew Union College Annual* 19 [1945/6], 467-472).

[the oa]th which Tukulti-Ninurta [sw]ore after Shamash [   ].
Let me [   ] the designs of the gods,   (30')
[   ] let me set the [   ] of the gods in the mouth
     of the people!
[   ] to the lyre bearer let me [   ]
[   ] ... of the gods, the people who [   ]
Let me proclaim his companion [   ]
[ ] established like heaven and earth till [remotest] days.   (35')
[The gods?] of Sumer and Akkad whose ...* he praised,
[   ] whom he praised, he became lord [   ].
[   ] the oath of the gods [   ]
[   ] the snare[1] of Shamash his reign [   ]
[   ] of the oath of the gods, observer of [   ]   (40')
He established [the   of the lands of Sumer] and Akkad.
[ ] of Nabu, sage, wise, of vast u[nderstanding],
[who in the land of Sumer] and Akkad has no rival, who ...
[   ] the depth of his understanding [   ]
[   ] the ultimate praise, his inscription [   ]
[Tu]kulti-Ninurta, the ... which he took [   ] he [   ]
[   ] you who have no riva[l   ]

(small gap)

Text: Middle Assyrian manuscript(s) from Nineveh, A–C = Campbell Thompson, *Archaeologia* 79 (1929), pl. xlvii–lii no. 122A + *Annals of Archaeology and Anthropology, University of Liverpool* 20 (1933), pl. ci–civ no. 107; W. G. Lambert, AfO 18 (1957/8), pl. I–III. These are fragments of one six-columned tablet. Middle Assyrian manuscript from Assur, D = Ebeling, KAR 303 + Weidner, AfO 7 (1931/2), 280–281. E, another Middle Assyrian manuscript from Assur(?), is published in transliteration only by Ebeling, MAOG 12/2 (1938), 42. F, a Neo-Assyrian manuscript from Nineveh (Rm 142), = W. G. Lambert, AfO 18 (1957/8), pl. IV. D and E rev are omitted in this translation. K 6007 = H. Winckler, *Sammlung von Keilschrifttexten* II (Leipzig, 1893/4) 76 is treated here as the opening lines of the poem, following a suggestion of W. G. Lambert.
Edition: P. Machinist, *The Epic of Tukulti-Ninurta I, A Study in Middle Assyrian Literature* (Yale University dissertation, 1978), with detailed commentary. I owe to him numerous readings and interpretations. Rather than document them all here, I refer to his treatment of the text. K 6007 is edited by Borger, EAK 1, 73f.
Literature: Ebeling, MAOG 12/2; W. G. Lambert, AfO 18 (1957/8), 38–51; P. Machinist, "Literature as Politics: The Tukulti-Ninurta Epic and the Bible," CBQ 38 (1976), 455–482.
*Notes to Text: (i 7) Collation Machinist. (i 12') *šá-aḫ!-ṭú* (WGL). (i 16') *mi-na-su* for *minassu?*

1. The punishment reserved for violators of oaths; compare Etana (III.21c) Tablet II lines 16ff.

(i 21′) Obscure. WGL suggests *lì-me-šu* "his clan." (i 23′) *iz-zi-za-am-ma* (WGL, unpublished fragment). (i 24′) *sarti* (WGL, ibid) (i 25′) [ ] *x šá la-a-aḫ-tu kab-tu* (WGL, ibid). (ii 5′) *š[i-kin-ti]* (WGL); *li-la-a-at?* (WGL). (ii 6′) See Machinist, diss., 226. (ii 12′) DINGIR.MEŠ is here construed as singular, referring to Shamash; for the usage, see W. G. Lambert, BWL, 67 and OrNS 36 (1967), 132. (iii 11′) *um-ma um-de-šèr-ma a-bu-uk*: obscure. (iii 14′) According to Machinist's suggestion that *ni-il-mar* is an apocopated N present of *amāru*, diss., 414. (iii 20′) *li-it-ta[q!-ta]?* (WGL). (iii 41′) *ni-[di kussê]*, Machinist, diss., 288. (iii 48′) For a suggestion that the following obscure word refers to an organ examined in divination, see AHw, 884a. (Frag C, obv iii′) WGL: *ka-r[a?]* 'camp'. (v 28′) Text: *ina salimija uqetti i-si-ta-ni*: obscure. The speaker is the warrior(s), urging Tukulti-Ninurta on to the fight. (v 48′) For suggestions about this line, see Landsberger, WdO 1 (1950), 373 note 74; von Soden, AHw, 1003b, 1367a. (v 50′) WGL. (v 51′) Reading [u] at the beginning of both 50′ and 51′. (v 52′) AHw, 1536a. (B rev vi 17′) W. G. Lambert, AfO 18 (1957/8), 44. (B rev vi 36′) AHw, 1345b.

III.2 PSALM TO ASSUR FOR TUKULTI-NINURTA I

The author of the Tukulti-Ninurta Epic (III.1) may also have composed this bilingual prayer in dialectal Sumerian and in Akkadian,[1] as suggested by their common style, turns of phrase, and subject matter. One imagines some imprint of the royal personality in the paranoiac tone, fondness for complex rhetoric, and in the bitter complaint, common to tyrants, that the benefits of their dominion are not appreciated. The subject of the text seems to be the hatred that the king feels on all sides, despite or perhaps because of his achievements; he seems to believe that Assur is angry and withholds support in the king's hour of need.

The text opens with an invocation of the god Assur and with a refrain. Line 7 may allude to the birth of Tukulti-Ninurta. Line 14' may refer to the exploits of Ninurta as avenger of his father Enlil (see III.22), to whom Tukulti-Ninurta is implicitly compared.

> [O   who has] no rival among [al]l [the gods],
> [The prince who sustains you makes] plentiful(?)
> [your offering],   *(= refrain)*   (1)
> [O   ] of Enlil,   *[refrain]*
> [O   s]on of Nunamnir,[2]   *[refrain]*
> [O one] created of [   ], lofty one, lord of Ekur,   *[refrain]*
> [   ] who is filled with [   ],   *[refrain]*   (5)
> [   ] who was begotten by Enlil,   *[refrain]*
> [Pure seed?] set in a maiden, a male she bore for you.   *[refrain]*
> [l]ord surveyed your awesomeness,   *[refrain]*
> [   ] made your lordship resplendent on high,   *[refrain]*
> He pronounced your name foremost among all the
>   gods, [   ] who are surpassing in your valor.   *[refrain]*   (10)
> He pro[nounced] your name to be told of in heaven,
>   ...   *[refrain]*
> Examining your [   ], your fame is surpassing
>   in the universe,   *[refrain]*

---

1. This translation follows the Akkadian where possible; restorations on the basis of the Sumerian are generally not indicated. Another bilingual text with historical information has been edited by W. G. Lambert, "Tukulti-Ninurta I and the Assyrian King List," *Iraq* 38 (1976), 85-94.
2. Another name for Enlil.

[   ] ... the great gods [established] order in the land, *[refrain]*
Who smo[te?] the evil gods insubmissive to your father, *[refrain]*
Who [established?] his name ... with all the gods, *[refrain]* (15)
Who [ ] with the weapon in your fury
      the irreverent(?). *[refrain]*
Your father Enlil [established?] your kingship in
      heaven and netherworld, *[refrain]*
You set the straight pathway for the gods, *[refrain]*
You are holy, you [ ] justice ... *[refrain]*
God [   ] in innermost heaven, *[refrain]*
You ever exercise your lordship over all the gods *[refrain]*

(fragmentary lines, then gap)

Oppressing* in [your] strength in all lands, *[refrain]*
You have instructed your country not to transgress
      the "net" and to observe the ordinances,[1] *[refrain]* (10′)
They do not go beyond the limits you drew,
      they heed your judgment, *[refrain]*
They heed the firm decision of your supreme godhead
      with abiding awe, *[refrain]*
They have put their trust in your benevolent judgment,
      they have constantly sought after your divinity, *[refrain]*
You are their broad security, their great good protection, *[refrain]*
They trust in your lordship, they learn from innermost
      heaven your resolve.[2] *[refrain]* (15′)
The lands of one accord have surrounded your city
      Assur with a noose of evil, *[refrain]*
All [of them] have come to hate the shepherd whom
      you named, who administers your peoples, *[refrain]*
All regions of the earth, for which you had produced
      benevolent assistance, held you in contempt, *[refrain]*
And though you extended your protection to them,
      they rebuffed (you) [and   ] your land. *[refrain]*

1. That is, an oath of fealty?
2. Presumably a reference to divination (Seux, *Hymnes*, 494 note 6).

The king for whom you held goodwill[1] made	
sure to disobey you,	[refrain] (20')
And even those whom you treated well unsheathed	
[their] weapons (against you),	[refrain]
The battlefield's task is ever in full readiness	
against your city Assur,	[refrain]
All the onrushings of a flood are mustered against it,	[refrain]
Your enemies and foes are glowering at [your	
standing?] place,	[refrain]
They have concerted to plunder your country,	
O Assur, they ... for treachery.	[refrain] (25')
The lands crave night and day for the destruction of	
your wondrous sights,	[refrain]
Everywhere they seek to overthrow your cities,	[refrain]
And they yearn to inflict a defeat upon(?) the spirits	
(of) his (ancestors?),[2]	[refrain]
All the evildoers await a dark day without sunshine,	[refrain]
Their threatening fingers[3] are stretched out to	
scatter the armies of Assur,	[refrain] (30')
Vilely they plot evil against their benefactor,	[refrain]
They trespass the ordinance of the lord of the world,	
they muster(?) both kings and auxiliaries.	[refrain]
(As) you are the lord of your land, O Assur, may you	
be its mighty one, its noble champion,*	[refrain]
For the future may your supremacy be its protection,	
as it raises high its head.	[refrain]
O Lord, do not neglect any favor	
for your land Assyria!	(= new refrain) (35')
O Assur, great lord, king of the Anunna-gods,	
the land of Assyria is yours!	[refrain]
O Assyrian Enlil, lord of the world, the land of Assyria	
is yours!	[refrain]
May Adad, hero of the gods, who inspires terror,	

1. Possibly a reference to the Babylonian king.
2. Obscure line; I take the ghosts to refer to the ancestors of the king, whose tombs might be violated by an enemy attack.
3. Compare III.1 v 25'.

come at your side,   [*refrain*]
May Shamash, who follows the paths of heaven and
    earth, come at your side.   [*refrain*]
Your land, Assur, which nooses of evil are surrounding, [*refrain*] (40′)
(And) Tukulti-Ninurta, whom you called by
    name ... Have mercy!   (= *new refrain*)
They glower at him to find [   ]   [*refrain*]

(gap)

(It is?) your people against whom all the world in its
    entirety plots evil,   [*refrain*]
None of the lands has regard for your city.   [*refrain*]
They put their trust in their own strength, they have
    not heeded your divinity,   [*refrain*] (45′)
They treat lightly your terrible oath, they wipe out
    your guidelines,   [*refrain*]
Did they honor your great word?
    Who keeps the ordinance of your supremacy?   [*refrain*]
They do not heed your lordly decision,
    nor do they seek your consideration.   [*refrain*]
They take courage on account of their own strength, ... [*refrain*]
Dwelling in peaceful abode, they have [confidence?] in
    the mass of their troops.   [*refrain*] (50′)
O my trust in heaven, my judge in the netherworld,
    [... your divine supremacy]   (= *new refrain*)
O Assur, great lord, king of all the gods [   ] in heaven, [*refrain*]
O Great mountain,[1] Enlil, who ordains⋆
    the destinies of heaven and netherworld,   [*refrain*]
You are my sweet security, my broad protection ...
    in heaven   [*refrain*]
I am he who ensures your rites, who keeps your
    ablutions pure.   [*refrain*] (55′)
My prayers are continuous before you, every[where],   [*refrain*]
With pure offerings and numerous sanctified food
    portions ...   [*refrain*]

---

1. Epithet of Enlil.

I have not neglected to give you "display" offerings,
     I [   ] eternally(?),   *[refrain]*

I never ceased* to offer sheep and I [   ]
     "kneeling offerings."   *[refrain]*

O Lord, in ... may your tense heart be calmed ...   *(=new refrain)* (60')

O Assur, great lord, mountain of the Igigi-gods,
     [may] your inner feelings [be calmed]!   *[refrain]*

O Enlil, mighty leader of the gods, warrior, [   ]   *[refrain]*

May Shamash, your radiance, light of heaven and earth,
     calm [you]!   *[refrain]*

May Addu, voice of your divine supremacy, lord of
     all living things, calm [you]!   *[refrain]*

May Ninurta, valiant weapon bearer, your splendid son,
     whom you love, calm [you]!   *[refrain]* (65')

May Nusku, your beloved sublime vizier on high(?),
     calm [you]!   *[refrain]*

May Amurru, lord of the uplands, calm you!   *[refrain]*

May Ninlil, great spouse, your beloved, calm you!   *[refrain]*

May Sherua, your pure creation, goddess of dawn,
     calm you!   *[refrain]*

May Tashmetu, sublime sovereign, protective goddess
     of the land, calm you!   *[refrain]* (70')

May the goddesses of heaven, the destinies of the entire
     netherworld, ca[lm you]!   *[refrain]*

Above, may Anu ... at your right ca[lm you]!   *[refrain]*

Below, may your lower part(?), Ea, lord of the entire
     netherworld, ca[lm you]!   *[refrain]*

(fragmentary lines, then gap)

[Pronounce] a good destiny [   ] forever,
[   ] ... the land and its people [   ]
[   ] you cause the people to dwell ..., you [   ]
[   ] may its allies(?) dwell(?) ... [   ]
[   ] ... [   ]
Let him praise your divinity to the land [   ]
That he may deliver the sustenance of [   ]
Let him [   ] your power!

Text: Ebeling, KAR 128 (+) 129/1, 2. I am grateful to H. Neumann for detailed information about the relationship of the fragments.
Edition: Ebeling, *Quellen* I, 62-70.
Translation: Seux, *Hymnes*, 493-497 (partial).

Notes to Text: (9') ⌜di⌝-*e-šú* (collation WGL). (33') From Sumerian (šu-gar = *gamālu*); Akkadian has "great" rather than "noble." (53') Reading *mu-šim!* for "who ordains." (59') Reading *ul ap-per-ku.*

III.3 HYMN TO TIGLATH-PILESER I

Tiglath-pileser I (1115-1077 B.C.), considered by one modern historian to be "an admirable oriental despot of the best kind,"[1] appears in his own inscriptions as a successful warrior king.[2] In the early years of his reign, he embarked on a series of campaigns against the Phrygians, and for about twenty years pursued a dogged war with the Arameans on the upper Euphrates. This suggests that he was not at the head of a great empire, as some historians would assert, but was rather under considerable pressure from that quarter; in fact, the wars may have been defensive.[3] Eventually the Arameans may have broken through Assyrian defenses, even occupying Nineveh. Tiglath-pileser's reign may have ended in disaster and obscurity. Much the same fate may have befallen his Babylonian contemporaries.[4]

Tiglath-pileser I enjoys greater fame today for his non-military interests. These included a taste for hunting on a grand scale, collection of exotic plants, a royal zoo, and possibly the establishment of a library of literary and scholarly tablets at Assur.[5] To judge from tablets discovered at Assur, his reign saw considerable literary and scholarly activity, including study and copying of Babylonian texts.

This poem commemorates campaigns by the king in the mountains north and west of Assyria, in lands called Qumanu, Musru, and Habhu. Its style and subject matter are comparable to those of the Tukulti-Ninurta epic (III.1) and Shalmaneser in Ararat (IV.1a).

(gap)

> The dwellers in the [   ] plotted battle,
> They prepared for w[ar], they whetted their weaponry,
> The foe launched their war.
> All the mountain men mustered by clans,   (10′)
> Qumani launched his attack,

---

1. Sidney Smith, *Cambridge Ancient History* (Cambridge, 1924), 2:251.

2. For English translations of the inscriptions and other relevant documents of the period, see Grayson, ARI 2, 1-45.

3. Grayson, ARI 2, 1 "reaffirmation of empire," "Assyrian splendour shines forth in all its glory." I follow H. Tadmor (1970 lectures at Yale University).

4. For the Arameans at this period, see Brinkman, PHPKB, 281ff.

5. E. F. Weidner, "Die Bibliothek Tiglatpilesers I.," AfO 16 (1952/3), 197-213. For a critique of Weidner's idea, see W. G. Lambert, *Iraq* 38 (1976), 85.

Musrian stood by him for the fray,
Their combined forces stood forth as comrades.
The Gutian raged, afire with awe-inspiring splendor,
All the hordes of the mountains, the Habhi-federation,
Formed a unity to help each other,   (15′)
[   ] their help [   ] before t[he]m.
They were raging like a tempest, fomenting disorder,
They were plotting [   ], seeking sedition.

Their talk of war [   ]
The Lord regally [   ] their destruction ...   (20′)
[   ] Enlil,
"[   ] I have heeded(?) the god of Ekur,
"[   ] ... their people,"
(So) the god made pride of the slaughter of the foe.
All the gods heard his utterance,   (25′)
Assur said, "Slaughter the enemy!"
"Destroy the foe!" came forth from [his] lips.
His heart resolved on slaughter,
His mouth com[manded] the scattering of the wicked.
In order to diminish their troops, he made war,   (30′)
He drew up battle, caused mutiny (among them).
He girded himself with awe-inspiring weapons,
He commanded his favorite to the battlefield's task,
He made proud the weaponry of Tukulti-apil-Eshara![1]   (35′)
Before him Enlil leads him into battle,
Ishtar, mistress of turmoil, aroused him to strife,
Ninurta, foremost of the gods, positioned himself at his front,
Nusku was slaughtering all enemies at his right,
Addu overwhelmed foes at his left,   (40′)
Stationed behind them, he was raining down weaponry.
Daily he set devastation upon them.
The king turned against the far-away(?)* Qumani.[2]
He conquers every one of their sanctuaries,

1. Tiglath-Pileser.
2. Qumanu was a mountainous region between the upper Zab and the Tigris (RGTC 5, 222-223).

Their lofty cities, all there are, he demolishes.   (45′)
He tears up the grain from the fields that sustain them,
He cuts down the fruit trees, he destroys the gardens,
He made a deluge pass over their mountains.
He cast terror(?) upon them,
All enemies were frightened,   (50′)
Fierce radiance covered their features,
The mountains(?) submitted fully to Assur,

(five fragmentary lines, then breaks off)

Text: Ebeling-Köcher-Rost, LKA 63.
Edition: V. Hurowitz, J. G. Westenholz, "LKA 63: A Heroic Poem in Honor of Tiglath-Pileser I's Muṣru-Qumanu Campaign," JCS 42 (1990), 1-49, with collations.
★Notes to Text: (43′) WGL: [*is*]-*saḫ?-ḫur? šarru a-na Qu-ma-né-e ru?-qu?-te*.

III.4 PSALMS TO ISHTAR FOR ASSURNASIRPAL I

(a) ON OCCASION OF ILLNESS

The Assyrian king Assurnasirpal I (1050-1032 B.C.) speaks here of his rise to power. He credits Ishtar of Nineveh with the divine favor that led to his success, and reminds her of various compensatory achievements, including restoration of images and construction of a magnificent bed for her. In view of their past relationship, the king asks the goddess for remission of his illness. The mood and message of this text recall the righteous sufferer tradition in Mesopotamian literature (compare II.5, III.14). This and the following text demonstrate fine poetic composition during this otherwise little-known period. W. G. Lambert, AnSt 11 (1961), 157 associates this output with "a tradition of writing poetry among the priests of Ishtar of Nineveh."[1] For another work in this tradition, see below, IV.1b and for reference to Ishtar of Nineveh as the "Mistress of Poetry," see IV.4d.

i

I will tell of [ ] that befell me:	(1)

To the creatress of wis[dom], the praiseworthy ... [goddess],
To her, who dwells in E-mashmash,
    [   ] I shall tell of myself,[2]
To the queen of the gods, into whose hands [all]*
    responsibilities are bestowed,
To the lady of Nineveh, the lofty [of the gods], (5)
To the daughter of Sin, twin sister of Shamash
        — she exercises all kingship* —
To her, who renders verdicts, the goddess of all there is,
To the mistress of heaven and netherworld,
    who accedes to entreaties,
To her, who hears prayers, who accepts lamentations,
To the merciful goddess, who loves justice, (10)

1. Lambert (AnSt 11 [1961], 157) considered (a) i-iv separate texts, of which (i) was a dedicatory inscription, but the pieces can be read, as by Brünnow, Seux, and von Soden, as a continuous discourse divided into sections by a scribe; compare III.4b.

2. E-mashmash was the temple of Ishtar at Nineveh; "tell of myself" stands for Akkadian "make manifest my name."

Ishtar, whose portion it is to keep alive(?):*
I set forth* before you all the anxieties that I undergo,
May your ear turn to my weary utterance,
May your feelings take pity on my ailing speech!
Look upon me, Mistress, may your heart be pained
      as I turn to you.   (15)

ii

I am Assurnasirpal, your ailing servant,
Humble, revering your divinity, responsible, your beloved,
Who ensures your divine sustenance,
      who unfailingly supplies your food offerings,
Who looks forward to your festivals,
      who provides for your shrine,
Who provides generously the beer that you want and enjoy,   (20)
Son of Shamshi-Adad, a king who revered the great gods.
I was formed in mountains unknown to you, lady.*
I was not mindful of your dominion,
      my prayers were not continual,
The people of Assyria did not know me nor did they
      confront your divine presence.
Yet it was you, Ishtar, terrifying dragon of the gods,   (25)
That appointed me by your desire and wished that I should rule.
You took me from the mountains and named me to be
      shepherd of the peoples,[1]
You established for me a just scepter until the world grows old.
It was you, Ishtar, who made glorious my name!
It was you who granted me the power to save and requite
      those who were loyal.   (30)
From your mouth came (the command) to repair the divine
      (images) that were stored away,
It was I who repaired the ruined sanctuaries,
I rebuilt the damaged divine images
      and restored them to their places,

---

1. According to some scholars, this is an oblique reference to an irregularity in the royal succession (Labat, *Réligions*, 250; Seux, *Hymnes*, 498).

I ensured their divine allotments and sustenance forever.
It was I who had made a couch of boxwood,
    a well-appointed bed for your divine repose,   (35)
The interior of which I overlaid
    with the finest gold cunningly wrought,
Which I adorned with the choicest precious stones from
    the mountain(s) like a [   ].¹
I consecrated it, I filled it with splendor to behold,⋆
I made it shine like the sun's brilliance, a seemly sight.
I provided it a place in the E-mashmash,
    your favorite abode⋆ that you love,   (40)
In what way have I neglected you
    that I should draw upon myself [such hardship]?
You have blanketed me with disease,
    why⋆ am I at my last gasp,
[   ] ... my sinews, in form a wreck.
[Panic], phobia, [   ] choked off(?) my life⋆

          (fragmentary lines)

          iii

Constantly [   ] I pray to your ladyship,
I sob⋆ before your divinity [   ] ...
[   ] who does not fear your divinity,
    who commits abominations,   (60)
How have I incurred no sins or misdeeds (before) that I
    should draw upon myself [punishment (now)]?²
I am constantly in a state of anxiety, [I abide] in darkness,
I am cut off and shall not see [offspring],⋆
I forsook(?) my royal throne and [   ]
I do not go near the meal I am to eat, [   ]   (65)
Beer, the support of life, [is become] disgusting [to me],
I loathe the sennet and sounding of strings, [kingship's] due,
Thus am I deprived of the joys of living! [   ]

1. The old tablet from which the existing manuscript was copied was evidently damaged here, as well as in lines 41 and 59-70.
2. That is, perhaps, he was never blameless; what unusual behavior justifies the goddess's anger?

My eyes (once) sharp-hued can perceive nothing,
I do not hold [my head] high, [but gaze at]
    the surface of the ground.   (70)
For how long, Mistress, have you afflicted me with this
    interminable illness?

iv

I am Assurnasirpal, in despair, who reveres you,
Who grasps your divine hem, who beseeches your ladyship:
Look upon me, let me pray to your divine ladyship(?),*
You who were angry, take pity on me,
    may your feelings be eased!   (75)
May your ever benevolent heart grow pained on my account,
Drive out my illness, remove my debility!
From your mouth, Mistress, may the command
    for mitigation fall!
Have pity on your (once) favored viceroy[1] who never changes,*
Banish his despair!   (80)
Take his part with your beloved Assur, the [warr]ior,
    father of the gods!
I will praise your divinity forever,
I will magnify the [nob]le one among the gods of heaven
    and netherworld!

Text: Brünnow, ZA 5 (1890), 79-80; photo AfO 25 (1974/7), 40-41.
Edition: von Soden, AfO 25 (1974/7), 37-45.
Translation: Labat, *Religions*, 250-252; Seux, *Hymnes*, 497-501. An earlier translation by von Soden appears in SAHG, 264-268 no. 14.
Literature: W. von Soden, *Herrscher im alten Orient* (Berlin, 1954), 77-78; W. G. Lambert, AfO 27 (1980), 71.
Notes to Text: (4) WGL. (6) Lambert, AfO 27 (1980), 71. (11) Tablet: *bullulu*, see von Soden, AfO 25 (1974/7), 11. (12) WGL: *a-pa?-šar*. (22) WGL. (38) Lambert, AfO 27 (1980), 72. (39) ms. accidentally repeats "favorite." (42) -[*ma*]? (44) WGL: *ú-nap-paq*. (59) WGL: *ut-ta-ḫa-as*. (63) WGL. (74) Text: NIN DINGIR.RA.KI; see Seux, *Hymnes*, 501 note 42 "ta divinite"?; von Soden, AfO 25 (1974/7), 45. (79) Differently Seux, *Hymnes*, 501 and von Soden, AfO 25 (1974/7), 44. CAD K, 39a, if I understand it correctly, applies the immutability to the suppliant, as here. The point of the line, as in 61, is that he has been consistent; why should he be punished now?

    1. A title of the Assyrian kings expressing their subservience to Assur, the national god and deified city.

(b) ON OCCASION OF AN OFFERING

This hymn was evidently commissioned for the celebration of the reinstallation of cult objects belonging to Ishtar of Nineveh(?) by Assurnasirpal I. The text opens with a song about the goddess's dominion and the special favor shown to Assurnasirpal. He asks her to bless him (i, ii). In iii is described the installation of the objects and their refitting in gold, just as the goddess wanted. In iv and v men and gods rejoice at the occasion, and in vi a blessing is asked on the king for his deed.

i

(large gap)

... who performs your rites that you lo[ve],
[   ] ... [   ]
[   ] your face
[   ] the [four world] regions.
[The bla]ck-headed folk [   ].[1]   (10)
 Lo[rds] and princes bear [your   ]
 You turned your eyes [upon   ]

ii

At your (favorable) glance, O Princess,
The pure priest, whom you n[ominated],
[Assur]nasirpal, pr[aiseworthy king],*   (15)
Son of Shamshi–Adad [   ],*
The one whom among all kings you have [   ],
By(?) your divinity [you   ] his prowess,
By your ladyship you made him great,*
By your faithful heart, you made him glorious.   (20)
You bestowed on him shepherdship of your land,
Grant him a hearing and (time) to grow old.
Let him always walk in your sweet protection.

1. The Mesopotamians.

iii

[You] have had made for him rites for your celebration:
[In] Assur, the city of all the gods,
[In Ekur?], in the holy place, the residence of Enlil,   (25)
[In the cel]la of your joyful divinity,
He has administered the [pur]e rites.
    [   ] five(?) pure [pearls?] of the seas,
    [   ] the sacred [ ] that you required,
    [   ] choice gold from the bowels of the earth,[1]   (30)

(two lines fragmentary)

[   ] he has administered splendidly.

iv

All lands are rejoicing
At your pure, worthy rites.   (35)
The mountains bring hither their yield.
Single out your favorite, he is always invoking you,*
The prince who reveres you, he is pure and sanctified,
He brings you the rites that you desired.   (40)
Look hither, mistress,* with your (favoring) glance,
Let your heart rejoice and be glad.

Rejoice, O Mistress of Heaven,
May Enlil, father of the gods, be happy,
May Assur rejoice in E-hursag-gula,[2]   (45)
May Anu, king of heaven, be glad,
May all the gods of heaven rejoice,
May Ea rejoice in the Apsu,
May the gods of the depths beam,
May the Fates, goddesses of the land, be glad,
May all the officiants in (these) rites[3] dance,   (50)
May their hearts be glad at (this) celebration.

---

1. Literally: "choice gold of Arallu," a poetic term for the netherworld.
2. "House of the Great Mountain," temple in Assur.
3. I take this (with Seux, *Hymnes,* 100) to refer to the officiants at the installation ceremony, though it could mean "the other gods who are interested parties" (or the like).

May the performer of the rites rejoice [   ],
[   ] the shepherd, the viceroy [   ]
Raise high Assurnasir[pal's head],   (55)
Make glo[rious his   ]

(fragmentary lines, breaks off)

Text: Ebeling, KAR 107, 358; Schroeder, KAH II 139.
Edition: Ebeling, *Quellen* I, 58–62; see also *Quellen* II, 76.
Translation: von Soden, SAHG, 268–269 no. 15; Seux, *Hymnes,* 98–100.
Notes to Text: (ii 15) Restoration Seux, *Hymnes,* 98 note 5. (ii 16) Variant omits. (ii 19) Reading
tu-šar-[bi-šu]. (ii 38) Seux, *Hymnes,* 99 note 17. (ii 41) Seux, *Hymnes,* 99 note 19.

III.5 PRAYERS FOR KINGS OF ASSYRIA

(a) CORONATION PRAYER

Three tablets dating sometime after the reign of Tukulti-Ninurta I preserve a new year's coronation ritual[1] of the kings of Assyria dating to the latter half of the second millennium B.C. When the text begins, the king is being hailed and carried into the Assur temple. He distributes gifts of silver and gold which are received by the priests. The king makes an offering to Assur and various other gods. The royal diadem is then set before the altar. After a procedure with a garment that is not clear, the ritual continues with the placing of a gold ring. The priest crowns the king with a turban-like headdress, here rendered "diadem," and speaks the prayer translated below. This sums up Assyrian imperial doctrine, with its religious and territorial emphasis.

> May Assur and Ninlil, owners of your diadem,   (1)
> Let you wear the diadem on your head for a century.
> May your foot go fair in Ekur and so too your hands in prayer
>   to Assur your god.
> May your priesthood and the priesthood of your sons go fair
>   before Assur your god.
> With your just scepter, enlarge your country.   (5)
> May Assur grant you commanding, hearing, and obedience,
>   truth and peace.

Text: Ebeling, KAR 135 (+ KAR 216, 137).
Edition: Müller, MVAeG 41/3 (1937), 12-13 lines 34-40.
Translation: Seux, *Hymnes,* 112-113.

1. For further information on Assyrian ritual, see K. F. Müller, *Das Assyrische Ritual*, MVAeG 41/3 (1937). It is not clear whether this coronation was an annual or a once-in-a-reign ceremony; see R. Frankena, *Tākultu, De sacrale maaltijd ...* (Leiden, 1954), 63; Tadmor, JCS 12 (1958), 28 note 52; Grayson, UF 3 (1971), 319 note 50; Garelli, *Nouvelle Clio 2 bis* (Paris, 1974), 309.

(b) PRAYER AT THE GODS' REPAST

This prayer was said in honor of the Assyrian king when the gods were served a cultic repast. One manuscript names a late Assyrian king, Assur-etil-ilani (ca. 626-623 B.C.), but the prayer dates earlier than his time.

He who made this repast, who provided food and drink to the gods, grant that he administer far and wide forever more. May he exercise the high priesthood (of Assur), kingship, and universal dominion. May he attain a ripe old age. To him who heeds these words be barley, silver, oil, wool; salt of Bariku[1] for their food, and oil for their lamps. Live, prosper, and enjoy good fortune! May the rites of the repast for the Mighty Ones in the land of Assyria be eternal. May Assur bless the one who provided this repast, Assur-etil-ilani.

Text: Ebeling, KAR 214, iv 7-27; see also Smith, III R 66, x 18-38.
Edition: Ebeling, OrNS 23 (1954), 120-121, 124-125.
Literature: R. Frankena, *Tākultu, de sacrale maaltijd* ... (Leiden, 1954), 8; Ebeling, OrNS 24 (1955), 1-15.

1. An esteemed variety of imported salt. For a general study of salt in ancient Mesopotamia, see D. Potts, "On Salt and Salt Gathering in Ancient Mesopotamia," JESHO 27 (1984), 225-271.

III.6 THE HUNTER

A student's tablet from Assur preserves a short, epic-style poem about a campaign of an Assyrian king against mountain peoples, cast in a metaphor of a hunter stalking wild game. Ebeling suggested that Tiglath-Pileser I is intended, and this has been argued convincingly by Hurowitz and Westenholz, JCS 42 (1990), 46-49. The text uses various strange words and peculiar spellings, either owing to scribal errors or to an attempt to make the language look archaic.

[Who curbs] foes, trampler of his enemies,	(1)
[Who hunts] mountain donkeys,	
flushes the creatures of the steppe,	
[The Hunter]: Assur is his ally, Adad is his help,	
Ninurta, vanguard of the gods, [go]es before him.	
The Hunter plans battle against the donkeys,	(5)
He sharpens(?) his dagger to cut short their lives.	
The donkeys listened, they gamboled alert,*	
The Hunter's terror had not come down upon them.	
They were bewildered, "Who is it that stalks us?	
"Who is it, not having seen who we are, who	
tries to frighten us all?	(10)
"Our ... will cut off* the high mountains,	
"Our dwelling place lies in the ... of the mountain.	
"Let the wind send flying the hunter's snare!*	
"May the shootings(?) of his bow	
not rise high enough to reach(?) (us) assembled!"	
The Hunter heard the chatter of the mountain beasts —	(15)
Their speech was anxious, their words troubled,	
"Mouth or muscles, men are what they're born!"[1]—	
To the warriors who will make the breaches(?)	
over the mountain he says,	
"Let us go and bring massacre upon the mountain beasts,	
"With our sharpened(?) weapons we will shed their blood."	(20)
He performed an extispicy for his appointed time,	

---

1. Obscure, translation doubtful. Perhaps this is a proverbial expression, "a man's a man for a' that." Lines 15-18 may be out of sequence.

He raged like a thunderstorm,
(like the) sun he was hitching up his chariotry.
A journey of three days he marched [in one].
Even without sunshine a fiery heat was among them,
He slashed the wombs of the pregnant, blinded the babies,   (25)
He cut the throats of the strong ones among them,
Their troops saw(?) the smoke of the (burning) land.
Whatever land is disloyal to Assur will turn into a ruin.
Let me sing of the victory of Assur, the mighty,
      who goes out to c[ombat],
Who triumphs over the cohorts of the earth!   (30)
Let the first one hear and te[ll it] to the later ones!

Text: Ebeling-Köcher-Rost, LKA 62.
Edition: Ebeling, OrNS 18 (1949), 30-39.
Literature: Borger, EAK 1, 112. The date of the text is discussed by Ebeling, OrNS 18 (1949), 30; cited in AHw as a late Babylonian or Neo-Assyrian text in archaizing style (e.g., 1124); not in Grayson, ARI for this king.
*Notes to Text: (7) *ina rēši*: perhaps "ahead," but taken here in parallelism to "listening," describing the wary unease of the herd. (11) WGL: *ina-ki-is?* (13) CAD B, 34a; CAD K, 399b. (14) AHw, 1237a.

B. BABYLONIAN POETRY AND PROSE

III.7 LEGENDS OF SARGONIC KINGS

(a) SARGON, KING OF BATTLE

This epic poem about Sargon of Akkad (see Chapter I, Introduction) opens with Sargon fretful for battle (compare IV.16 Tablet I).[1] He convenes his warriors to tell them that he plans a campaign to a distant place, the name of which is lost, and speaks of a rebellion against his suzerainty there. In 8ff. a soldier attempts to dissuade him, arguing that the journey is arduous and life is comfortable where they are in Agade.

In the meantime Nur-daggal, king of Burushhanda, a city in Anatolia, taunts Mesopotamian merchants resident in his kingdom because, as he believes, Sargon could never come to help them. The merchants, upset, send a delegation to Sargon, offering him rich booty in return for his campaign. Sargon's soldiers are disinclined to accept, but this is the opportunity that Sargon has been yearning for, so he launches a campaign.

The army traverses a wondrous forest. Nur-daggal, unaware of the advance, is confident that the Euphrates(?), not to mention the forest, will prove an impassable barrier, and his troops echo his confidence. No sooner has Nur-daggal spoken than Sargon bursts into the city, smites down his finest warriors, and demands his submission.

Nur-daggal's fabulous court is the scene of his humiliation. Sargon takes his seat and jeeringly parrots Nur-daggal's boasts. Nur-daggal, incredulous, confesses that some divine agency must have brought Sargon, then asks to be restored to his kingdom as a vassal. Sargon accepts and Nur-daggal offers tribute of exotic fruits never before seen in Mesopotamia. After three years in Burushhanda, Sargon departs.

Two Akkadian versions of this story are preserved (see also II.12a). (a) is known from a Middle Babylonian school tablet that was probably copied out at Hattusha, the Hittite capital in Anatolia, and sent from there to El-Amarna in Egypt to train Egyptians to read and write Akkadian. The manuscript is heavily damaged and full of mistakes and obscurities. The interest to the Hit-

---

1. A different interpretation is offered by Liverani (see below, Literature), whereby Sargon is encouraged in a dream by Ishtar. Although this element is not present in the preserved Akkadian text, Liverani offers arguments in favor of its importance in the story's archetype.

tites no doubt lay both in the exploits of Sargon himself, reports of which were known to them, and in the association with Anatolia.

A small fragment (b), dating to the seventh century B.C., from Assurbanipal's library, preserves what may be an expanded or parallel version of the merchants' delegation to Sargon. The epic may have circulated in Mesopotamia in a fuller form than is known from the Hattusha-Amarna edition (as was the case with the Nergal-Ereshkigal story, III.19). A Hittite version is also known, but not translated here.

While there are points in common between Sargon, King of Battle and the Sargon epic of the Classical period (II.12a), the text of the Mature period is not a lineal descendant from the older text. The deeds of Sargon were a topic for various writers using similar historical traditions. The historicity of the events portrayed here is a matter of debate. Since there is no mention of merchants in the Classical version of Sargon's invasion of Anatolia (II.12a), this part of the tale may have been a later second millennium interpolation. At the beginning of the second millennium, colonies of Mesopotamian merchants lived in Anatolia (see I.6 and Introduction to Chapter I, last paragraph). Recent archaeological discoveries in Anatolia, including the tentative identification of Burushhanda with Acemhöyük, point to cultural connections between Mesopotamia and Anatolia in the third millennium, so evidence may turn up to provide historical background to this story.

1. Middle Babylonian Version

[The king of battle, emiss]ary(?) of Ishtar,★ [who made firm?]
    the foundations(?)★ of the city Agade [   ],   (1)
[Might]y one in battle, king of the campaign(?) [ ],
[Sargon   ] speaks of war!
Sargon, [mighty in battle], [   ] his fierce weapons.
The palace of Sargon [assembles], he says this wo[rd to them],
"O my warriors! The land of [   ]   (5)
"[   ] thinks of war, (though) I made it submit [   ]."

[ ] brought [   ], Sargon was held in contempt [by   ].
"[O lord of a]ll daises, the road that ... [you wish] to travel
    [is a most difficult path], grievous to go.
"The Burushhanda road [that you wish to travel],

is a road I worry about,
"Did we ever [undertake such a] mission?   (10)
"(Here) we sit on chairs and have plenty of rest,
"Of a sudden [we set forth and] our arms have given out,
    and our knees become exhausted from traversing the road."

[Nur-daggal made] ready to speak,
    saying to the messenger of the merchants,
"[So where is Zababa], the campaigner who makes straight
    the way and spies out the regions of the earth?
"[So where is the lord of a]ll daises,
    who [   ] from sunrise to sunset?"   (15)
[   ] the merchants vomited up (what was in)
    their stomachs, mixed with bile,
"In a storm [   ] ... and pluck the Kishite from Agade!
"We have invoked [Sargo]n, king of the universe:

    'Come down to us that we may receive strength,[1]
        for we are no warriors.
    'Let us be responsible equally for the [   ] ...
        of the king's journey,
    'Let the king be responsible for those who stand
        in battle with him,
    'Let the king [   ] impose (tribute) of gold, let Sargon's
        warriors give him a silver mine.'"   (20)

"[O] our [lord], we must go, outrages are being committed
    in the ... of your god, Zababa."
[After the] merchants assembled, they entered the palace.
After they entered [the palace], the warriors would not
    accept the [   ] of the merchants.
Sargon made ready to speak and said,
"[I am the] king of battle! The city Burushhanda which arose,
    let us(?) see its troops in campaign!
"[What is] its direction? Which is its mountain?
    What is the road?
    Which one is it that goes (there)?"   (25)

---

1. Word play on *kiššati* "universe" and *kiššūti* "strength, vigor."

"[The road th]at you wish to travel is a most difficult path,
　　grievous to go,
"[The road to Burushha]nda that you want to go,
　　the road that I worry about, is a mission of seven(?) leagues."

[Sargon entered] the massive mountains,
　　in which are chunks of lapis and gold,
[　a]pricot tree, fig tree, boxwood, sycamore,
　　evergreen(?) trees with seven cones,★
[　] let them strike★ *urtu*-plants — search
　　for its crown seven leagues!★ — bramble,　　　　　　　　(30)
[　　] all the [fruits?] which for seven leagues the trees cast down,
The border of the [　] of the trees, sixty cubits, in all,
　　seven leagues,
[　　　　　] elevation, sixty cubits.

(fragmentary lines, then gap)

"[　　　　　　] troops [　　　　]."

[　these were] the words that they said.
Nur-da[ggal] made ready to speak
　　and spoke to [his] war[riors], saying,
"[Sargo]n will not come as far as we are.
"Riverbank and high water will surely prevent him,
"The massive mountain will surely make a reed thicket,
　　forest, grove(?), and woods hung about with tangles."　　(5′)
His warriors answered him, to Nur-daggal they said,
"Which are the kings, past or future, which king is he
　　who has come here and will have seen our lands?"
Nur-daggal had not spoken when Sargon surrounded his city
　　and widened the gate two acres!
He cut through ... his ramparts and smote
　　the most outstanding of the general's★ men!
[Sar]gon set up★ his throne in front of the city gate,
Sargon made ready to speak, [sa]ying to his warriors these words, (10′)
"Now then! Nur-daggal, favored of Enlil,
"[Let them br]ing him in, let me see him submit!"

[With] the gem-studded [crown?] on his head,
>and lapis footstool at his feet,
With fifty-five attendants [he] sat before him.
Since he was seated on a throne of gold,
>the king was enthroned like a god.[1]
[Wh]o is ... like the king?
Nur-daggal was made to sit before Sargon.
Sargon made ready to speak, saying to Nur-daggal,   (15′)
"Come, Nur-daggal, favored of Enlil, you said,

>'Sargon will not come as far as we are!
>'Riverbank and high water will surely prevent him.
>'The massive mountain will surely make a reed thicket,
>>forest, it will surely produce a grove(?),
>>and a woods of tangles!'"

Nur-daggal made ready to speak, saying to Sargon,
"My lord, no doubt your gods lifted up(?)
>and brought your soldiers across.*
"[   ] to cross the river.
"What lands could rival Agade? What king could rival you?   (20′)
"You have no adversary, you are their mighty opponent.
"Your opponents' hearts are seared,*
"They are terrified, and left paralyzed with fear.
"Restore (to) them* [city], field, and lea,
>the lord (to be your) ally in charge of it."

"[We have ...] to his place and come around to it,
"Its fruit* let him render: apricot, fig, medlar, grape,
"[   ], pistachio, olive, as never before.
"Never need we come around to it again,
>let him render [its fruit].   (25′)
"May the city be at peace, may I fetch fine things."
In going [the path] and staying, who (ever) followed Sargon?
He withdraws from the city,
Three years [in the city] he has stayed.

(The End)

---

1. Grammatically it is not clear whether Sargon or Nur-daggal is being described here.

2. Late Assyrian Version

"[   ] let your messenger bear his tribute. If ... [   ]
[   ] when he had heard the merchants' words,
      he became sick at he[art   ]
[   ] when [Sar]gon had heard the merchants' words,
      he became sick at h[eart   ]
[   ] weapons, axes, ... [   ]   (5')
[   ] on his own legs[1] he went and enter[ed   ]
[   ] Ishtar, queen of E-ulmash,[2] [   ]
[   ] Ishtar, who [   ]
[Ishtar, qu]een of E-ulmash, who [   ]
[   ] ... [   ]   (10')
[   ] world regions [   ]

(fragmentary line, then breaks off)

Text: (1) a = Schroeder, VAS 12 193 (photo MDOG 55 plates 6 and 7 after p. 42); b = a small, illegible piece from El-Amarna published by Gordon in OrNS 16 (1947), 21 (*375) could be an excerpt from the same story or a similar one. c = Schroeder, KAV 138, a piece from Assur that contains a text similar, so far as preserved, to the El-Amarna edition. (2) W. G. Lambert, AfO 20 (1963), 161-162.

Edition: (1) Weidner, *Boghazköy Studien* 6 (1922), 62-75 (treats a and KAV 138), with collations; Rainey, AOAT 8 (1976), 6-11 (a and c only); see pp. 47-48 there for *375. (2) W. G. Lambert, AfO 20 (1963), 161-162.

Translation: Albright, JSOR 7 (1923), 1-20.

Literature: Borger, HKL 1, 478; Güterbock, ZA 42 (1934), 21f. and 86-91; JCS 18 (1964), 1-6; MDOG 101 (1969), 14-26 (edition of Hittite version); M. Liverani, "Naram-Sin e i presagi difficili," in F. M. Fales, ed., *Soprannaturale e potere nel mondo antico e nelle società tradizionali* (Milan, 1985), 34-37.

Notes to Text: (1) Sargon was referred to in his own inscriptions as MAŠKIM.GI INANNA, "emissary of Ishtar," the Akkadian reading of which is uncertain; read here perhaps [mašk]im!? The meaning of *a-su-ri* is unknown. I connect with *asurrû* "foundation," though this particular word is not attested in such a metaphorical usage. Did the Babylonian original have SUḪUŠ, here read with the wrong word? (28) Reading GIŠ.TASKARIN.BÀNDA 7 *šú-um-bi-ra-šu*, where *sumbir* = *snbr* "pineseed." (29) *li!-im-taḫ-ṣu-ni* (WGL). (30) Text apparently corrupt. I read *ur-du-u ši-te-a ri-ši-šu* and take it to be an exclamation over the height of the tree. (9') *ša* GEŠTIN

---

1. That is, he was so agitated that he was not borne on the royal sedan chair but rushed off to the temple on foot?

2. The Ishtar temple in Agade.

šu-pu-u eṭ-lu-tu-šu. I take GEŠTIN to stand here for GAL.GEŠTIN, a high military rank among the Hittites, but this would be itself, even if correct in terms of this edition, a misunderstanding of the Mesopotamian original, which could scarcely have contained such a word. Perhaps the original had ANŠE "equids," a sign similar in appearance to GEŠTIN. (10′) *it-ta-di*. (18′) Güterbock, JCS 18 (1964), 5 note 62. (20′) KAV 138.8. (20′+4) Very doubtful. According to Weidner, 69, the tablet has *du-te-er-šu-nu-ti*, but he offers no note on the emendation, as is his wont, so his transliteration may be here mistaken. (20′+6) Reading *innipša* as *inibša*; otherwise: "it was done."

(b) THE CUTHAEAN LEGEND OF NARAM-SIN

The Cuthaean Legend of Naram-Sin is a pseudonymous[1] poetic narrative in which Naram-Sin, grandson of Sargon of Akkad, relates how a supernatural host devastated his armies and land. While the story is based on a series of battles Naram-Sin of Akkad fought against coalitions of foreign and Mesopotamian enemies, the events are fictionalized and presented as a divine judgment against Naram-Sin, an arrogant and impetuous king who fails to heed unfavorable omens. "Cuthaean" refers to the city Cutha, in northern Babylonia, where, according to the late version of the poem (below, 3), Naram-Sin left this account inscribed on a stela.

1. Old Babylonian Version

The Old Babylonian version of this story, on a large tablet of 300 lines or more, is included because of the close correspondence of column iii with lines 85-93 of the later version. Column ii, in which the king dispatches a messenger, is too fragmentary for translation. The messenger episode may correspond to 63ff. of the later version. Column iv contains a lament on the destruction that was not used in the later version.

(Naram-Sin describes his moves against the enemy host.)

a') [The first time, I sent out against it 180,000 troops],

iii

It defeated them, it lef[t no one]!	(1)
A second time I sent out against it 120,000 troops,	
It defeated them and filled the plains (with their corpses)!	
A third time I sent out against it 60,000 troops,	
That (host) made a greater (slaughter) than before!	(5)

---

1. A study of this genre, though outdated in details, is H. G. Güterbock, "Die historische Tradition und ihre literarische Gestaltung bei Babyloniern und Hethitern bis 1200," ZA 42 (1934), 1-91. For more recent discussion of specific aspects of the pseudo-autobiographical genre, see Finkelstein in H. D. Lasswell *et al.*, eds., *Propaganda and Communication in World History* I: *The Symbolic Instrument in Early Times* (Honolulu, 1979), 74ff.; H. Galter, "Probleme historisch-lehr-hafter Dichtung in Mesopotamien," CRRAI 32 (1985), 71-79. For a detailed, up-to-date study of the entire genre, see T. Longman III, *Fictional Akkadian Autobiography* (Winona Lake, IN, 1991), this text discussed 103-117.

Having killed 360,000 troops,
>   it made a greater slaughter than ever before!
As for me, I was confounded, bewildered,
I was at a loss, exhausted, anxious, and reduced to naught.
I said, "What has the god brought upon my reign?   (10)
"I am a king who brings no well-being to his land,
"And a shepherd who brings no well-being to his people.
"What has my reign brought me?
"How shall I place myself that
"I may proceed effectively?*   (15)
"He has mobilized against me a mighty foe
>   to lay low the plains of Akkad.
"[He has ta]ken* battles as far as Malgium![1]
"[How shall I ...   ] ...
"[   ] the plains of Akkad, to lay low [   ]
"[He has   ]

(gap)

iv

Sanctuaries [   ]
The land was [utterly] devastated [   ]
The [   ] which Adad called out over the la[nd],
It has stamped out its hubbub and scattered its reason.   (5)
It laid low cities, hamlets, and holy places,
It has levelled everything completely!
Like a deluge of water that has arisen,
Among the people [   ] ...
It has levelled the land of [Akk]ad,   (10)
It has laid the land low,
It has so diminished* (the land) as if it had never been,
The land is [des]troyed, all of it transformed!
Because of the anger of the gods, agony [   ],
Cities are laid waste, hamlets are laid low,   (15)
The hubbub of the [land it has bro]ught low and stamped out.

---

1. A Transtigridian city.

Like a [   ] deluge, it has levelled the land,
[It has utterly destr]oyed [   ]

(gap)
(The last column consists only of fragmentary lines.)

2. Middle Babylonian Version

The Middle Babylonian version of this story was an extensive composition, to judge from the remains of the hexagonal prism from Hattusha in Anatolia that preserves portions of the text. It deals with some of the same episodes as the later version (below, 3) but contains, like the Old Babylonian one, additional episodes and a different arrangement of them. To column B 2'-4' compare the later version, line 29; 5'-6' compare to the later version, lines 31 and 33; 7'-8' correspond to the later version, line 37. For 10'ff. compare the later version, line 94. The preserved text opens by condemning a king (Enmerkar?) who left no commemorative stela. It then describes the supernatural host. The gods decree that the host have no permanent dwelling and should not partake of civilized life. The episode preserved in column c has no parallel in the later version.

Naram-Sin [   ]   (1)

(gap)

b'

[   ] a stele, nor did he write for me a stele,
[   ] he is not my brother,* I did not [   ] my hand,
[   ] nor did I bless him before Shamash.

In the face of them, humankind entered caves,[1]   (5')
City, in the face of them, was no city,
Ground, in the face of them, was no ground.
Six were their kings, glorious allies,
Their troops were 360,000(?).
Ea, lord of [the city], sent them against the city,
He created them with his own hand.
[He   ] ... them, and [gave them] the awesomeness of lions,   (10')
Death, plague, mourning* ... [   ]
Hunger, want, [high] prices [   ].
The Great One sent off with them [   ].

---

1. This line is corrupted in the later version, line 31, to read "humans with raven faces" (see below, Late Assyrian Version).

Ea made ready to speak, saying to the gods his brethren,
"I made this host, do you pronounce its fate,   (15′)
"Lest humankind be utterly destroyed.
"Let its name be spoken of for all time.
"Let them reverence the wall and the bricks of the wall,
"Let it be a god, let them worship it.[1]
"Let it not seize the city of Shamash the warrior,   (20′)
"Let it not do any plundering, nor let it thrive within,
"Let it not eat food to sustain it,
"Let it smell no [ar]oma of beer,
"Let it drink water!
"I cut off the clay (to fashion it), for all days it is c[ut off],
"Let it not pinch off its (own) clay."[2]   (25′)

[Six] were their kings, glorious allies,
[360],000(?) were their troops.
The mountains [bore them],
[The   ] reared them [   ]
[   ] to the edge [ ] the land [   ]
[   ] plunder [   ]   (30′)
[   ] they saw [   ]

(gap)

c′

They penetrated Akkad, to the land of [   ]
They penetrated to the gate of Agade [   ]
To Naram-Sin thus [they] cried,   (10′)
Saying, "We are six kings, allies, glorious, ..."

(Rest of speech too fragmentary for translation. Naram-Sin gives a brief reply,
also lost, then the narrative may resume.)

---

1. These lines may mean that the enemy is supposed to worship Naram-Sin's capital, Agade,
as a god (so argued by the translator, RA 73 [1979], 179, but this has not found wide acceptance).
2. That is, regenerate itself.

3. Late Assyrian Version

Known from eighth and seventh century manuscripts, the late version of the Cuthaean legend is about 80% preserved. Like the Old Babylonian version (above, 1), this text takes the form of a fictitious stela, beginning with a self-introduction of the king, turning to autobiographical narrative, and concluding with blessings on the reader who heeds its words.

The mood and style of this version are sombre and convoluted. Gloomy soliloquy is conveyed by long, complicated sentences (for example, 23-30, in which subject and verb are separated by six lines of parenthetic observations; or 132-134a, a double appositional sentence); as well as by abrupt changes of subject (22-23, 30-31); unanswered rhetorical questions (53-54); leaden repetition (56-58); piling up of near synonyms (67, 88), and the concluding sober counsels. The abrupt change of person in lines 169-172 may indicate that they are conventional wisdom quoted here from another, unknown source (so Landsberger, see below, Literature).

The principal message of this text is that kings who carry out projects in the face of unfavorable omens are doomed to catastrophe. This renders more specific the general caution of Mesopotamian proverbs, prophecies, and oracles that deal with self-preservation of the king, and stresses the importance of divination, especially extispicy, for important decisions.[1] This text combines the cautious, even pessimistic approach of wisdom literature with a theme more common in poetry: affirmation that man's highest duty is to transmit knowledge and experience to the future.

> [Open the foundation box]* and read well the stela   (1)
> [That I, Naram-Sin], son of Sargon,
> [Have written for] all time.
> [Enmerkar? ruled the land],* then passed away,
> [My father ruled the land], then passed away,   (5)
> [I became r]uler of the land.
> [When the years   ] passed,
> [When the   ] came,

---

1. For general cautions, compare, for example, this version, lines 170f. to III.16a, lines 42ff. For a literary analysis of this text from the perspective of the king's reaction to unfavorable omens, see the study of Liverani, cited below, Literature. Grayson (AfO 27 [1980], 171) suggests that the text promotes extispicy over other means of divination such as astrology.

[Ishtar chan]ged her mind,

[Against ... she ...-ed] and rode. (10)

[I inquired of the] great [gods]:

[Ishtar, Ilaba?], Zababa, Annunitum,

[Shullat, Hanish, Shamash] the warrior.

[I summoned] and charged [the diviners].

[Seven upon seven extispicies I] made, (15)

[I set up ho]ly reed altars.

[The diviners spoke to me thus]:

"[   ] the 'thread' [   ]

"[   ] the 'mark' [   ]

"[   ] (20)

"[   ] you [   ] ... yourself,

"Until [the host?   ] of the great gods."

Enmerkar [the king?]¹ the judgment ... which Shamash
    [gave him] —

The judgment for him, the decision (binding on) his ghost,
    the ghosts of [his children],

The ghosts of his family, the ghosts of his descendants —
    (the judgment of) Shamash [the warrior] — (25)

The Lord of Above and Below, the lord of the Anunna-gods,
    lord of the ghosts (of the dead),

Who drink muddy water and drink no clear water —

(Enmerkar) whose wisdom and weaponry captured,
    defeated, and killed that host,

Did not write (that judgment) upon a stela, nor leave (it) for me,

Nor did he publish his name, so I did not bless him. (30)

Troops with bodies of "cave birds," humans with raven faces

Did the great gods create.

In the earth which the gods made was its ...,*

---

1. Enmerkar, a Sumerian ruler of the first dynasty of Uruk (early third millennium B.C.), was the subject of several Sumerian epic poems. For further discussion of these, see G. Komoróczy, "Zur Ätiologie der Schrifterfindung im Enmerkar Epos," AOF 3 (1975), 19-24; "Zum sumerischen Epos 'Enmerkar und der Herr von Aratta'," AASH 16 (1968), 15-20. Why Naram-Sin cites Enmerkar is unclear, nor is any story now known wherein he triumphs over an enemy host. For another allusion to Enmerkar, see below, III.20b.

Tiamat suckled them,[1]

Belet-ili their mother made (them) fair.   (35)

Inside the mountain(s) they grew up, became adults,
> got their stature.

Seven kings they were, allies, glorious in form,

360,000 were their troops.

Anu-banini[2] their father was king; their mother wa named Melili,

Their eldest brother, their vanguard, was named Memandah,   (40)

Their second brother was named Midudu,

Their third brother was named [   ]pish,

Their fourth brother was named Tartadada,

Their fifth brother was named Baldahdah,

Their sixth brother was named Ahubandih,   (45)

Their seventh brother was named Harzishakidu.

They rode against the shining mountains,

A soldier seized them, they smote their thighs (in frustration).

At the beginning of their incursion,
> when they invaded Burushandar,[3]*

The entire region of Burushandar was destroyed,   (50)

Pulu was destroyed,

Puramu was destroyed.

"Should I go out beyond Nashhuhuhhu [   ]?[4]

"Should I strike out(?)* into the midst of that host

---

1. Compare Tiamat's role as creatress of monsters in the Creation Epic, III.17, and Belet-ili's role as creatress of an enemy host in the Old Babylonian fragment edited by Römer, WdO 4 (1967), 12–28.

2. This is the name of a historical personage who may have lived about the time of Naram-Sin of Agade; see D. O. Edzard, "Zwei Inschriften am Felsen von Sar-i-Pul-i-Zohab: Anubanini 1 und 2," AfO 24 (1973), 73–77. The other names are unknown and presumably imaginary.

3. An echo of Burushhanda, a wealthy commercial city in south central Anatolia; see above, III.19a.

4. All unknown, and presumably fabulous or corrupted toponyms. I take these to be rhetorical oracular inquiries of a type well-known especially from later Assyrian history; see I. Starr, Questions to the Sungod, Divination and Politics in Sargonid Assyria (Helsinki, 1990), xvi. These are often connected with specific military maneuvers. For further discussion of this list of places, see Landsberger, State Archives of Assyria, Bulletin 3/1 (1989), 44.

whose camp is Shubat-Enlil?"[1]

Then they s[ettled down]* inside Subartu,[2] (55)

They destroyed the (upper?) Sealands[3] and invaded Gutium,[4]

They destroyed Gutium and invaded Elam,[5]

They destroyed Elam and arrived at the seacoast,

They killed the people of the (sea) crossing,[6]

    they were thrown to [   ],

Dilmun, Magan, Meluhha,

    whatever is in the midst of the sea they killed.[7] (60)

Seventeen kings with 90,000 troops

Came with them to support them!

I summoned a soldier and charged him,

"I [give you a lance] and a pin,

"Touch them with the lance, [prick them] with the pin. (65)

"If [blood] comes out, they are human like us.

"If no blood comes out, then they are spirits, ill fate,

"Phantoms, evil demons, handiwork of Enlil."

The soldier brought back his report [to me],

1. Shubat-Enlil, modern Tell Leilan in the Habur region, was an important city at the end of the third millennium B.C. and became the capital of the empire of Shamshi-Adad in the eighteenth century B.C. Abandoned before the middle of the second millennium B.C., the place could only have been a remote historical name to an eighth-century scholar.

2. Subartu, as used here, was a traditional name for northern Mesopotamia; see P. Michalowski, "Mental Maps and Ideology: Reflections on Subartu," in H. Weiss, ed., *The Origin of Cities in Dry-farming Syria and Mesopotamia in the Third Millennium* B.C. (Guilford, CT, 1986), 129-156.

3. I take this to refer to the "Upper Sea," a vague term that at different times may refer to the Mediterranean, the Black Sea, and perhaps Lake Van.

4. As used here, a traditional term for the mountainous regions east and northeast of Mesopotamia; see W. W. Hallo, "Gutium," RLA 3, 708-720; Oppenheim, *Cambridge History of Iran* 2:547 note 2.

5. May refer to peoples whose abodes could only be reached by a sea voyage, that is, the lands mentioned in line 60.

6. Southwest Iran.

7. In the third millennium, Bahrain, Oman/Makran, and the Indus Valley respectively; perhaps by the time of this text traditional literary names for far-off lands reached by sea. See J.-J. Glassner, "Mesopotamian Textual Evidence on Magan/Makan in the Late Third Millennium B.C.," in P. M. Costa and M. Tosi, eds., *Oman Studies, Serie Orientale Roma* 63 (Rome, 1989), 181-191; D. T. Potts, ed., *Dilmun, New Studies in the Archaeology and Early History of Bahrein* (Berlin, 1983). For Meluhha, a bibliography has been assembled by S. and A. Parpola and R. Brunswig, Jr., JESHO 20 (1977), 129 note 1.

"I touched them with [the lance], (70)
"I pricked them with [the pin], and blood came out."
I summoned the diviners and charged them,
[Seven] upon seven extispicies I performed,
[I set up] holy reed altars,
I inquired of the great gods (75)
Ishtar, Ilaba(?), Zababa, Annunitum,
Sh[ullat, Hanish],* Shamash the warrior.
The breath of the great gods,* the spirit did not allow me to go.*
Speaking to myself, thus I said,
"What lion observed divination? (80)
"What wolf consulted a dream interpreter?
"I will go, as I like, like a brigand,
"And the (very) lance of Ninurta I will grasp!"[1]
When the following year had come,
I sent out 120,000 troops against them, not one returned alive. (85)
When the second year arrived, I sent out 90,000 troops
        against them, not one returned alive.
When the third year arrived, I sent out 60,700 troops against
        them, not one returned alive.
I was confounded, bewildered, at a loss, anxious, in despair.
Speaking to myself, thus I said,
"What have I left for a reign? (90)
"I am a king who brings no well-being to his land,
"A shepherd who brings no well-being to his flock.
"How shall I place myself that I may proceed effectively?

    'Fear of lions,* death, plague, spasms,*
    'Panic, ague, economic collapse, starvation, (95)
    'Want, anxiety of every kind came down upon them.
    'Above, in [the earth?], there was a deluge,
    'Below, in [the netherworld?], there was [an earthquake?].'"

Ea, lord of the city [of that host?],*
Spoke to the [gods his brethren] and said, (100)

---

1. Compare the Sumerian poem "The Curse of Agade," 92ff. (J. S. Cooper, *The Curse of Agade* [Baltimore, 1983], 128ff.), in which Naram-Sin finally gives up waiting for a favorable oracle. The significance of the "lance of Ninurta" is unclear; perhaps a term for "taking the bull by the horns."

"O great gods [   ],
"You told me [to make this host],
"And the dirt¹ [of my finger nails?] you [spat on?]."
When New Year of the fourth year arrived,
At the prayer to Ea, [sage] of the great gods,   (105)
[When I offered] the holy offerings of New Year,
I [received] the holy instructions.
I summoned the diviners and [charged them],
Seven upon seven extispicies I performed.
I set up holy reed altars,   (110)
I inquired of the great gods
Ishtar, Ilaba(?), Zababa, Annunitum,
[Shullat and Hanish, Shamash the warrior].
The [diviners spoke to m]e [thus],
"[   ] will bear [   ]   (115)
"[   ] will be [   ]
"[   ] you have [   ]
"[   ] sent down ... [   ]
"[   ] blood [   ]."
From their midst twelve troops flew off from me,   (120)
I went after them in haste and hurry [   ],
I overcame those troops,
I brought those troops back [   ].
Speaking to myself, [thus I said],
"Without divination (of liver), flesh, and entr[ails],*
    [I will not] lay [hand on them to kill?]."   (125)
[I performed] an extispicy concerning them:
The breath of the great gods [ordered] mercy for them.
The shining Morning Star spoke from heaven thus,
"To Naram-Sin, son of Sargon:
"Cease, you shall not destroy the perditious seed!*   (130)
"In future days Enlil will raise them up for evil.
"It (the host) awaits the angry heart of Enlil,
"O city! Those troops will be killed,

1. If read correctly, this recalls the creation of Saltu from the dirt under Ea's nails, Agushaya Poem (II.6) I v 24.

"They will burn and besiege dwelling places!

"O city! They will pour out their blood!

"The earth will diminish its harvests, the date palms their yield,

"O city! Those troops will die!   (135)

"City against city, house against house will turn.

"Father to father, brother to brother,

"Man to man, companion to friend,

"None will tell the truth to each other.

"People will teach untruth, strange things [will they learn].   (140)

"This hostile city they will kill,

"That hostile city (another) hostile city will capture.

"Ten quarts of barley will cost a mina of silver,

"No strong king ... will have been in the land."

To the great gods I brought (the captives) as tribute,   (145)

I did not lay hand on them to kill.

Whoever you may be, governor, prince, or anyone else,

Whom the gods shall name to exercise kingship,

I have made a foundation box for you,

     I have written you a stela,

In Cutha in the E-meslam,   (150)

In the cella of Nergal have I left it for you.

Behold this stele,

Listen to the wording of this stela:

You should not be confounded, you should not be bewildered,

You should not be afraid, you should not tremble,   (155)

Your stance should be firm.

You should do your task in your wife's embrace.

Make your walls trustworthy,

Fill your moats with water.

Your coffers, your grain, your silver, your goods and chattels   (160)

[ ] bring into your fortified city.

Gird on your weapons, (but) stay out of sight,

Restrain your valor, take care of your person.

Though he raids your land, go not out against him,

Though he carries off(?) your livestock, go not nigh him,   (165)

Though he eats the flesh of your soldiery(?),

Though he murders [   ],

Be moderate, control yourself,

Answer them, "Yes, my lord!"
To their wickedness, repay kindness, (170)
To kindness (add) gifts and gratifications.
You should not trespass against them.

Let expert scholars tell you my stela.
You who have read the stela and placed yourself that you
      can proceed effectively,
You (who?) have blessed me, so may a future one bless you. (175)

Text: (1) Finkelstein, JCS 11 (1957), 84-85, photo pl. III-IV. (2) Otten, KBo 19 98. (3) King, CT 13 39-41, 44; Campbell Thompson, GETh pl. 34 (K. 8582); Gurney, STT 30; OECT 11 103. For minor variants, see *Notes to Text.
Edition: (1) Finkelstein, JCS 11 (1957), 83-88. (2) None. (3) Gurney, AnSt 5 (1955), 93-106.
Literature: Walker, JCS 33 (1981), 191-194; M. Liverani, "Naram-Sin e i presagi difficili" in F. M. Fales, ed., *Soprannaturale e potere nel mondo antico e nelle società tradizionali* (Milan, 1985), 31-45; Landsberger, *State Archives of Assyria, Bulletin* 3/1 (1989), 42-44.
*Notes to Text: (OB iii 15) *pagram u ramānam šuṣû* (compare Late Assyrian Version 30, 93, 174, which has *pagram u pūtam šuṣû*). The expression means literally "cause body and face to go forth." It is generally taken to mean "save oneself" or "publish oneself," but the proposal of Landsberger, *State Archives of Assyria, Bulletin* 3/1 (1989), 42f. is adopted here. (iii 17) [*iš*]-*ši-a?*, compare Atrahasis (II.39a) Tablet I line 58. (iv 12) "Diminished" by suggestion of WGL. (MB b' 3') WGL. (11') *giḫlu* (WGL). (LAssyr 1) For this restoration, see Walker, JCS 33 (1981), 191-195. (4) The restoration of this and the succeeding lines is guesswork. (33) Text: *a-lu-šu*, meaning unknown. (49) AHw, 1025a (*ittaspaḫ*). (54) *lul-pu-ut! lib!-bu-u*. (55) *it-[taš-bu]*, WGL. (77) Restoration here (whence lines 13 and 113) courtesy von Soden. (78) Variant omits; 78 bis. WGL. (94) Variant adds "(at?) night"; (94 bis) Or: "famine." (99) The mss. seem to differ here on the alignment of this and the following lines; I have followed Gurney's reconstruction, 104. (125) Reading courtesy von Soden: *bi-ri ṣe-ri ta-kal!-[ti]*. (130) For *ḫalqāte*, see Cogan and Tadmor, OrNS 46 (1977), 80 note 26, who suggest "ruinous." (144) Variant(?): "[who] has [rea]son"(?).

III.8 SHULGI PROPHECY

This enigmatic text, like III.13, alludes in vague terms to future events in Babylonia, in this case through the mouth of Shulgi. Shulgi was a Sumerian king of the Third Dynasty of Ur from the end of the third millennium B.C., here considered a god and founder of the city Nippur. From the condition of the text, it is not clear whether it conveys prophecy in retrospect, referring to events that had already happened, or represents a wishful program for royal benefactions cast as an ancient prophecy. This text was paired in later scribal editions with the Marduk prophecy (III.13). References to Nippur and Babylon point to a date for its composition in the latter half of the second millennium B.C. or the first part of the first millennium B.C. The text is badly broken and written in an arcane style, so that for much of it one can only guess at its general tenor rather than translate it.

(i 1) I (am) Shulgi, beloved of Enlil and Ninlil: the noble one, Shamash, has told me, Ishtar my lady has revealed (this) to [me]. Father and mother, (personal) god [and (personal) goddess], whatever my fathers heard from the mouth of the [great] gods [   ], may Ur always s[ing], may Larsa [   ]! [When] he came down from his rooftop,[1] when from the roof of his gate [he   ], wild bulls and wild donkeys ... of my lordly city N[ippur] ... may [   ] sixfold, may [   ]. *(large gap)*

(ii 2') I was lord of the four world regions, from the rising of the sun to the setting of the sun. I founded Nippur, Bond of Heaven and Earth. When I spoke, the gods would listen to me. At my own expense, I built that wall and made it firm. Enlil ordered me, "Build ..." Enlil gave me the order, and I annihilated Baldaha.[2] Enlil ordered me, "Make war!" and I annihilated Baldaha. I ... from his family over the four world regions. Ninlil ordered me, "Put Humba in order(?)!"[3] The [   ] of the king of Susa(?) ... *(large gap)*

1. Suitable place for prayer, especially to Shamash.
2. Meaning unknown, reference obscure. One may compare the Baldahdah of the Cuthaean Legend (III.7b 3 line 44). The "wall" referred to here may be a recollection of a wall built by the kings of Ur to resist Amorite invaders from the north and west, or it may be a tradition, not otherwise documented, that Shulgi built the walls of Nippur.
3. Elamite deity.

(iii 3′) Babylon ... the citizens of Nippur [and?] Babylon. [The god/dess] will not stand ..., nor will (s)he give him [scepter], nor will (s)he give him reign. [A king of the] four world regions [... who?] neglects the citizenry of Nippur [and Babylon] and renders no righteous judgment, [   ] that prince will proceed with "woe!" and "alas!" The lands are given as one to the king of Babylon and Nippur. Whichever king shall arise after me, on account of(?) Balda[ha] (and) the land of Elam to the east, he will be [thrown into] complete [disorder]. The Hittites will [conquer] Babylon [   ]. *(large gap)*

(iv 1′) [   ] will be built. In the region of Babylon, the builder of that palace will come to grief, that prince will experience misery, and will have no satisfaction. So long as he is king, fighting and warfare will not cease. In that reign brother will devour his brother, people will barter their children for silver, the lands will be thrown into complete disorder. Man will forsake maid, maid will forsake man. Mother will bar her door against daughter. The possessions of Babylon will go to Subartu[1] and the land of Assyria. The king of Babylon will send out the possessions of his palace to the prince of Assur in [Baltil]. For all time Baltil[2] [   ].

(v) [   ] ... will take place, friend will slay his friend with a weapon, companion will destroy companion with a weapon, [the lands] will be totally destroyed. [The (great?) people] will become small; Nippur will be cast down. That prince's head will be held high, (because of?) the city which is established [for him?] on the bank of the Tigris and the Euphrates. By the command of E[nlil] the reign of the king of Babylon will come to an end. A certain one [   ] will arise ... he will restore Bad-Tibira, he will renew Girsu and Lagash, the [sanc]tuary of the gods will be (re)built. He will maintain [the offerings of the great gods]. He will restore the [   ] and shrines. The [sanctuar]y of Nippur [and] Isin [   ] will be (re)built, [   ] will be cast down. *(large gap)*

---

1. Assyria is meant.
2. Assur (restored from variant); see p. 227 note 4.

Text: col i 1-17 = Borger, BiOr 28 (1971), 20; 1'-18' = Strong, *The Babylonian and Oriental Record* 6 (1892/3), 4ff. = H. Winckler, *Sammlung von Keilschrifttexten* II (Leipzig, 1893/4) 73. cols ii–iii = Strong-Winckler, op. cit. + Borger, BiOr 28 (1971), 13 (right-hand piece). col iv = King, CT 13 49. col v = King, CT 13 49 + Lambert, JCS 18 (1964), 26 "ii." col vi = Lambert, JCS 15 (1964), 26 "i."

Edition: Borger, BiOr 28 (1971), 14-15, 20-21; Güterbock, ZA 42 (1934), 83-86.

III.9 AGUM-KAKRIME AND THE RETURN OF MARDUK

This document, known only from mid-first millennium manuscripts, purports to be a first-person account by a certain Agum, an early Kassite king (mid-second millennium B.C.?) of how he restored the cult image of Marduk in Babylon. No one knows whether this inscription was actually composed in the time of the king named, or whether it is later and pseudonymous.

On the one hand, pseudonymity is well known in Mesopotamian literature (see III.7b). No early copies of this text are known, nor is the king known outside of this text. Another certainly pseudonymous text deals with the story of Marduk's statue (III.13).

On the other hand, without consideration of the text's genre, there is no good reason to doubt its genuineness on either linguistic or historical grounds. Even if pseudonymous, it may be based on an actual inscription. It is hard to understand why this particular king would have been chosen for a putative "author" since, unlike other pseudonymous authors in Mesopotamian tradition, he is not well known. In sum, the genuineness of the text can neither be established nor disproved.

Genuine or not, the text deals with an important event in second-millennium Babylonian history: recovery of the cult statues of Marduk and his consort, Sarpanitum, from the Hittites. The Hittites had taken the precious statues as booty from the sack of Babylon in the mid-sixteenth century. Their recovery was essential for Babylonian pride and perception of their divine favor. Compare Marduk and the Elamites (III.11c) and the Return of Marduk from Elam (III.12d).

After an introduction praising himself, Agum explains that Marduk and the other gods had at last resolved that Marduk should return to his temple in Babylon, Esagila. He does not explain how the Hittites or their allies were persuaded to relinquish the image. Agum takes omens to determine how the image is to be treated while it and its sanctuary are repaired (see also Erra and Ishum [IV.16]). The images are lavishly refurbished and the sanctuary restored with a set of magnificent doors. In addition, Agum dedicates the craftsmen who repaired the images to the temple by exempting them from taxes and service. He concludes by asking a blessing upon himself for his works. A scribal "afterword" enjoins that the text be considered privileged lore, presumably because it has to do with the fortunes of Marduk.

(i 1) [Agum]-kakrime, son of Tashshigurumash, pure offspring of (the god) Shuqamunu,[1] whom Anu and Enlil, Ea and Marduk, Sin and Shamash nominated (for kingship), the mighty man of Ishtar, the most warlike of goddesses, am I!

(i 11) Intelligent and understanding king, obedient and conciliatory king, son of Tashshigurumash, descendant of Abirattash, the valorous [man] among his [brethren?], lawful heir of Agum the elder, pure offspring, royal offspring, who holds firm the leadrope of mankind(?),* shepherd, lordly one am I! Shepherd of numerous mankind, warrior, shepherd who makes secure his ancestral house am I!

(i 31) King of the Kassites and the Akkadians, king of the wide land of Babylonia, he who made the numerous peoples of Eshnunna to settle down; king of Padan and Alman, king of Gutium, a stupid people, king who caused the four world regions to submit,* favorite of the great gods am I!

(i 44) When Marduk, lord of Esagila and Babylon, (and) the great gods ordered with their holy command his [ret]urn to Babylon, (and?) Marduk had set his face towards Babylon, [I prayed to?] Marduk, [   ] my prayers. I carefully planned to fetch Marduk, and towards Babylon did I set his face. I went to the assistance of Marduk, who loves my reign.

(ii 8) I asked of king Shamash by divination(?),[2] I sent to a far-off land, to the land of the Haneans,[3] and Marduk and Sarpanitum did they conduct to me. Marduk and Sarpanitum, who love my reign, did I return to Esagila and Babylon. In the chamber which Shamash had confirmed to me in my inquiry (by divination) did I return them. I settled various craftsmen there, metal worker, gold smith, engraver did I [   ] ... did I [   ]. Four talents of [red gold] did I grant for the attire of Marduk and Sarpanitum; in magnificent

---

1. Patron deity of the Kassite dynasty.

2. Perhaps by pouring oil over water and studying the resulting pattern; see G. Pettinato, *Die Ölwahrsagung bei den Babyloniern, Studi Semitici* 21-22 (Rome, 1966). It is tempting to emend the sign to read the more common word "extispicy" rather than the unusual "oil divination."

3. Possibly here a literary term for the Hittites (Landsberger, JCS 8 [1954], 65 note 160 and 238), or to be taken literally to mean that the statue was left in Hana, a land on the Middle Euphrates, by the Hittites.

attire, attire of red gold did I attire Marduk and Sarpanitum. Genuine lapis,[1] green chlorite(?),* chalcedony(?), ...-gems, agate,* ...-agate, Meluhha-beads, alabaster, yellow *shilu*-stones, *sikillu*-stones, whatever is choice(st) in its mountains, for the sanctuary of Marduk and Sarpanitum did I grant. The surface of the attire of their great divinity did I embellish. Tiaras with magnificent horns, lordly tiaras, symbolic of divinity, full of splendor, of lapis and gold did I set upon (their) heads.* On the top of his crown a *mushsharu*-gem and choice stones did I set. The surface of his crown with chalcedony(?), *mushsharu*, chlorite(?), lapis, and agate did I embellish.

(iii 13) A dragon, an eagle, [symbolic?] of their divinity [   ], gold (*gap here of thirteen lines*) did I surround and dress [   ]. The storehouse [   ] ... did I set. ... Chalcedony(?) [   ] for the second large chamber

(iii 39) ... did I add to [   ], a gold necklace, obsidian, ..., on (his?) neck did I s[et]. Jewelry [   ], jewelry [   ], eye-stones, ... beads, imported copper (*gap of four lines*) did I overlay. Upon his seat, the cedar seat, did I install him until I moved them into their magnificent godly sanctuaries.

(iv 9) [For what? the] various craftsmen used: [   ] cedar, juniper, [ ], to the holy mountain [for? its] pleasing s[cent? did] I send. Silver, (*gap of twenty lines*) ... great matching doors of cedar did I have fashioned, in the cult chamber of Marduk and Sarpanitum did I set (them) up. The ... with ... of bronze did I ... . Their doorposts with bands of refined copper did I hold fast. With serpent, hairy hero-man, bull man, lion monster, lion man, fish man, [   ], [fish] goat[2] of lapis, yellow agate(?), carnelian, and alabaster did I inlay them. Their purification did I carry out, the sanctified doors in the sanctuary of Marduk and Sarpanitum did I set up.

(v 14) Finally, I purified Esagila throughout (with) snake charmers. After the purification of the temple throughout (*gap of seventeen lines*)... the "Door of Awe-Inspiring Brilliance," the

---

1. Literally: "lapis of the mountain," as opposed to artificial lapis, well known in Mesopotamia from an early date.

2. For these monsters, see Creation Epic (III.17), Tablet I lines 141ff. and p. 359 note 1.

sanctuaries of Marduk did I bring them (the gods) in, and their magnificent festivals of rejoicing did I perform. The E-edadihegal did I cause to be cared for(?).* Their gift(?) to my lord and lady did I grant. (*gap of four lines*).

(vi 5) A chalice of gold ... [   ], a chalice of lapis, a great service(?) of silver did I create for Marduk. Gifts of silver and gold for the gods of Esagila did I grant. Afterwards(?) I appointed (what was) fine and fair for Esagila.*

(vi 17) For the des[tinies?] for Marduk [and Sarpanitum] (*gap of twenty-one lines*] did I [   ].

(vi 33) Umman-[   ], together with his household, his fields, and [his orchards]; Qishti-[   ], the exorcist, together with [his household], his fields, and his orchards; Marduk-muballit, the carpenter, together with his household, his fields, and his orchards:

(vi 42) I,* the king, Agum, who constructed the sanctuary of Marduk, who restored Esagila, who brought Marduk into his dwelling (with?) gifts,* exempted those craftsmen (from service and taxes), as well as the houses, fields, and orchards, in honor of Marduk and Sarpanitum.

(vii 11) May King Agum's days be long, may his years be prolonged, may his reign be awash(?) in prosperity. May the bosom of the vast heavens be opened for him and the clouds [   ] rain. [   ] Marduk ... orchard [   ] forever [   ] fa[ir] fruit let it produce for good king Agum, who constructed the sanctuaries of Marduk, who exempted the craftsmen.

(vii 34) May Anu and Antu bless him in heaven, may Enlil and Ninlil in Ekur ordain him a destiny of (long) life, may Ea and Damkina, who dwell in the great depths, grant him a life of long days! May Dingir-mah, Lady of the "Great Mountains," perfect for him pure offspring.* May Sin, luminary of heaven, grant him royal descent for all time! May the young (hero) Shamash, young (hero) of heaven and netherworld, make firm the foundations of his royal throne for all time! May Ea, lord of the deep, perfect him in wisdom! May Marduk, who loves his reign, lord of the deep, perfect him with respect to his prosperity!

(viii 24) Thus says Agum: The one who understands should reveal (this only) to one who understands; the one who does [not] understand should not see (this). That would be an abomination to Shullat and Hanish, Shamash and Adad, the lords of divination.

Text: Pinches, V R 33; Campbell Thompson, GETh pl. 36 Rm 505.
Edition: Jensen, KB III/1, 134-153.
Literature: J. Brinkman, *Materials and Studies for Kassite History* I (Chicago, 1976), 97; Borger, HKL 1, 406.
Notes to Text: (i 21) Reading ṣir-re-ti ni!-i-ši. (i 40) muštaškin, see Heidel, JNES 4 (1945), 252 (šukēnu); von Soden, ZA 49 (1949), 332 (šakānu); the latter seems preferable for the parallelism. (ii 36) Steinkeller, ZA 72 (1982), 251. (ii 38) Sollberger, *Studies Reiner*, 379ff. (iii 2) Text: "his" head, either a mistake for -šunu or intended as a distributive. (v 1) [suḫur].máš-ku₆ (WGL). (v 44) von Soden, AHw, 826b. (vi 16) Lines apparently corrupt. (vi 42) Reading a-na-<ku>. (vii 4) Obscure, perhaps referring to the craftsmen as "gifts." (vii 11) Differently Livingstone, *Nabu* 1990/86. (viii 1) [zē]ra el-la! li-šak-lil-šu (WGL).

III.10 KURIGALZU, KING OF THE KASSITES

There were several Kassite kings name Kurigalzu in Babylonian history, so there can be no certainty that the two texts translated below refer to the same person.

(a) KURIGALZU AND THE ISHTAR TEMPLE

This inscription, like the preceding, is known only from variant copies on clay tablets. Its authenticity is also open to question, since the lands and emoluments bestowed so generously could have been reason for a later forgery, which then could have been "rediscovered" and presented as a precedent to the ruling authority. Indeed, "The Donation of Kurigalzu" might be an appropriate nickname for this document.

> (i 1) Kurigalzu, great king, mighty king, king of the universe, favorite of Anu and Enlil, nominated (for kingship) by the lord of the gods am I! King who has no equal among all kings his ancestors, son of [Kadash]man-Harbe,[1] unrivalled king, who completed the fortifications of ..., who [fin]ished the Ekur, who [prov]ides for Ur and Uruk, who [guar]antees the rites of Eridu, who constructed the temples of Anu and Ishtar, who [guarantees] the regular offerings of the great gods,
>
> (i 16) I caused Anu, father of the great gods, to dwell in his exalted sanctuary. To Ishtar, the most great lady, who goes at my side, who maintains my army, shepherds my people, subdues those disobedient to me:
>
> (i 24) From the town Adatti, on the bank of the Euphrates, as far as the town Mangissi, bordering on the field Duranki, beloved of Enlil. From the town of my lady, Bit-Gashan-ama-kalla,* as far as the border of the city Girsu,[2] an area of 216,000 kor using a ratio per surface unit of 30 quarts of seed barley, measured by the large

---

1. Brinkman, *Materials* (below, Literature), 209.
2. Variant: Girri. Not to be confused with the well-known Girsu of Lagash; this locality is unknown otherwise.

cubit,[1] to Ishtar I granted.

(ii 5) 3 kor of bread, 3 kor of fine wine, 2 (large measures)[2] of date cakes, 30 quarts of imported dates, 30 quarts of fine(?) oil, 3 sheep per day did I establish as the regular offering for all time.

(ii 11) I set up boundary stones in all directions[3] and guaranteed the borders. The towns, fields, watercourses, and unirrigated land, and their rural settlements[4] did I grant to Ishtar, my lady.

(ii 16) Whosoever shall arise afterward and shall alter my deeds and change the command which I spoke, shall take out my boundary stones, shift my boundary lines, take away the towns, fields, watercourses, and unirrigated lands, or the rural settlements in the neighborhood of Uruk, or cause (another) to take (them) away, or who shall attempt to convert them to state lands, may Ishtar, the most great lady, not go at his side in battle and combat, but inflict defeat and heavy losses upon his army and scatter his forces!

Text: Gadd, CT 36 6, 7; Keiser, BIN 2 33 (collated).
Edition: Ungnad, *Archiv für Keilschriftforschung* I (1923), 29-36.
Literature: Borger, HKL I, 136 (considers to be genuine); J. Brinkman, *Materials and Studies for Kassite History* I (Chicago, 1976), 209: "there are at present no compelling reasons for doubting its authenticity"; see also Sommerfeld, AOAT 213 (1982), 172 note 4.
Notes to Text: (i 29) What is combined in CT 36 6-7 as AMA is construed in BIN 2 36 as É.DINGIR, while the following traces, which I cannot decipher, have no parallel in the other manuscript.

---

1. The tract is measured, as was customary in this period, by expressing surface area in terms of the capacity of the dry measure of seed used to sow it, based on a schematic ratio of 30 quarts = 1 surface unit, the last expressed in linear measurements using the "large cubit." For the figures involved, see Ungnad, *Archiv für Keilschriftforschung* I (1923), 23. He reckons the area at about 524.88 square kilometers, or, if the sides of the tract were equal in length, a square about twenty kilometers on a side, a princely gift.

2. Variant: 2 (ordinary) measures.

3. Literally: "above and below." This may be a reference to the "upper" and "lower" sides of the tract (long sides), but is taken here to mean "all."

4. Variant: "fields, watercourses, unirrigated land, and rural settlements of the town"(?).

(b) THE FAVOR OF KURIGALZU

This fragmentary poem opens with Kurigalzu's election to kingship by the assembled gods, then refers to his installation in Dur-Kurigalzu and Babylon. He grants a charter of privileges and exemptions to Babylon. After a gap of over a hundred lines, the text concludes with a plea, perhaps by a courtier, for royal favor and largesse, and a curse on anyone who changes the name of the petitioner in the document. The recondite style is comparable to that of the Poem of the Righteous Sufferer (III.14), and may have been typical of that cultivated at the Kassite court.

> The creator gods [   ]   (1)
> The Igigi-gods ... were assembled,
>   made the king greater than all ... .
> The great gods, one after another,
>   nominated him in the land of Karduniash,[1]
>   Dur-Kurigalzu,[2] the city [   ]
> In Babylon, seat of the Kassite king,
>   city from ancient times, founded ... .
> In the temple of Shumaliya and Shuqamuna,[3]
>   the great gods, they made great his responsibilities,
>   bedizened him with awe-inspiring radiance,
>   perfected his flawless readiness for kingship.   (5)
> Kurigalzu, king of the universe, wise king,
>   who heeds mighty Shamash,
> Anu, Enlil, and Ea heed him!
> His kingship is magnificent, it has no rival,
> Weapon that overwhelms enemies, captor of his foes,
>   beloved of Marduk,
> Relentless storm, huge flood that wrecks watercraft,
>   lofty one, Anu's trust,   (10)
> Judge who finds out the truth like Shamash, who restores
>   well-being to the oppressed among all peoples,
> Grantor of a charter to the people of Babylon,

1. Kassite name for Babylonia.
2. Important Kassite city.
3. Kassite gods.

Who exempted its people from service,
> for the sake of Marduk, who loves his reign,

You removed from them recruiter, foreman, inspector, governor,

(You) who made the joyful people of Babylon lie down
> in green pastures,

[   ] of his land, who gathered in the scattered peoples [   ],

[   ] king Kurigalzu

(large gap)

I, like a (drifting) raft, have none to put confidence in me,
> like a sunken vessel, I was not deemed useful,
>> the shore gave me up,

O Marduk, for the sake of Kurigalzu, your favored one,
> blot out my evil, shatter the consequences of my neglect!

Let me be called to mind in my lord's palace, let me find favor,
> let me see relief,

Let my frustration quit me, my misery forsake me,
> let me put my evil out of my mind!

May my lord bestow upon me favor and wealth,

Grain, oil, wool, cattle, sheep and goats, arable land,
> a settlement, garden, a gift of the king, my lord,

For his servant, who made (this) praise of the king.[1]

Whosoever shall erase my name written (here) and shall write his
own name on this tablet, may the gods invoked herein curse him!

[ ], may he want for bread and water, like a wicked man who

[   ] his god, [   ] may the (whole) land learn of his case!

Text: Sommerfeld, AfO 32 (1985), 2, 4, 6-8.
Edition: Sommerfeld, AfO 32 (1985), 1-22.
Literature: W. G. Lambert in W. S. McCollough, ed., *The Seed of Wisdom, Essays in Honour of T. J. Meek* (Toronto, 1964), 8.

1. Reference to author of text; compare Agushaya Poem (II.6) vii lines 24ff.

III.11 KUDUR-NAHHUNTE AND HIS TIMES

Elam, or the land in the southwest corner of Iran, was a traditional enemy of Babylonia in historical times. The texts grouped in III.11 and III.12 deal with warfare and hostility between Elam and Babylonia towards the end of the second millennium B.C.

The three documents of III.11 are sometimes referred to as the "Kedor-Laomer Texts" because of the supposed affinity between the name of the Elamite king, Kudur-nahhunte, and Kedor-Laomer of Genesis 14.[1] The three tablets, which date to the Persian period (6th to 4th centuries B.C.), refer to an Elamite invasion of Babylonia, destruction at Nippur and Babylon, and the sacking of Esagila. Although damaged and often unintelligible, these documents are included because of their connection with the texts about Nebuchadnezzar I (III.12). Their interest to a Babylonian scholar of the Achaemenid period may have lain in analogies between the Elamites and the rapacious post-Darius Persian monarchs, in addition to their historical interest as pertaining to a turning-point in Babylonian history. While the precise time of the texts is uncertain, they may refer to events in Babylonia and Elam during the twelfth century B.C.

III.11a consists of correspondence between Kudur-nahhunte and the Babylonians. In the part preserved, the Elamite king presses his claim to the vacant throne of Babylon. This claim was based on his descent from a Kassite king through the female line. Kudur-nahhunte holds out hopes for peace and reconciliation between the two lands, traditional enemies. The Babylonians answer that his claim is unfounded; they hope for the coming of a legitimate king. They predict a defeat of Elam to occur in the hot season, such as was actually inflicted by Nebuchadnezzar I (see III.12d). For another, related letter, see van Dijk, OrNS 55 (1986), 159-170.

In (b), his claim spurned, the Elamite king invades Sumer and Babylonia, destroying holy places and incurring the wrath of the gods.

---

1. W. F. Albright, "The Historical Background of Genesis XIV," *Journal of the Society of Oriental Research* 1926, 231-269; "A Fixed Date in Hebrew History," BASOR 88 (1942), 33-36; E. A. Speiser, *Genesis* (Anchor Bible, New York, 1964), 106-109; M. Astour, "Political and Cosmic Symbolism in Genesis 14 and in Its Babylonian Sources," in Alexander Altmann, ed., *Biblical Motifs: Origins and Transformation* (Cambridge, MA, 1966), 65-112. For a skeptical view of the question, see L. W. King, *The Letters and Inscriptions of Hammurabi, King of Babylon ...* 1 (London, 1898), l - lvi.

In (c) destruction and warfare continue. At last Marduk is moved to anger against the invader. The text concludes with a plea for Marduk's return.

(a) KUDUR-NAHHUNTE AND THE BABYLONIANS

(obverse mostly lost, save for a ruling and the superscription
"Letter of Kudur-[nahhunte ...]")

(rev)

(3) "[   ] the bond of heaven which [   ] to the four winds.
He (Marduk) decreed for them the punishment which [   ] in
Babylon, pr[aise]worthy* city. He decreed for them the property
of the Babylonians, young and o[ld ...]. With their firm counsel,
they established the [   ] of Kudur-nahhunte, king of Elam. Now,
one who is pleasing* to them [   ] will exercise kingship in
Babylon, the city of Babylonia [   ]. In Babylon, city of the king
of the gods, Marduk, they have set up [his? thr]one. (10) Shall
livestock and ravening wolf come to terms? Shall firm-rooted thorn
and soaring raven love one another? Shall raven and venomous
snake come to terms? [   ] Shall bone-gnawing dog come to terms
with mongoose? Shall dragon come to terms with blood-letting
bandit? (15) What king of Elam is there who provided for Esagila
and ...?"

The Babylonians ... and [   ] their message: "(As for) [the wo]rds
that you wrote: 'I am a king, son of a king, of [royal seed e]ternal,*
[indeed] the son of a king's daughter who sat upon the royal
throne.[1] [As for] Durmah-DINGIR.ME(?), son of Arad-Etusha,[2]
who [carried off] plunder of [ ], (20) he sat on the royal throne ...
[   ].' [As for] us, let a king come whose [lineage is] fi[rmly
founded] from ancient days. He should be called lord of Babylon,
... It will be done in June and July [   ] ... the Goat (star?) ...
(which portends) one overthrowing all lands, (25) [ ] in their firm
counsel [ ] ... [ ] the [king of the?] gods among the booty which
they will bring out."

(traces, then breaks off)

---

1. Kudur-nahhunte evidently claimed the throne on the basis of his descent from the daughter
of a Kassite king; see van Dijk, OrNS 55 (1986), 166f.

2. The name of a usurper king; one expects here a reference to Tukulti-ninurta I, who ruled
in Babylon, but it is hard to see this in the name; for a proposal, see Astour, "Symbolism" (p.
284 note 1), 82f. See also (c), line 9.

(b) THE ELAMITE ATTACK ON NIPPUR

The obverse consists of a fragmentary poetic narrative describing the Elamite attack on the cult center at Nippur; the reverse describes the aftermath, then continues with an attack on Borsippa and Babylon.

(obv)

(several lines gone)

[E]kur[1]
[   ] Elam
[   ] his possessions
[   ] their features   (5)
He [   ] to reveal it to Shamash.
He examined the [   ] to the great gate,
He chose and tore out the gate of Ishtar and threw it aside.*
Like merciless Erra he entered Durmah,[2]
He stood in Durmah and gazed at Ekur.   (10)
He made ready to speak and cried to his followers,
To all of his warriors he sped the blasphemy on,
"Plunder Ekur, take its possessions!
"Obliterate its design, cut off its rites!"
He examined the [   ] for an acre,   (15)
He destroyed its design* which [   ]
[   ] Esharra,[3]
[   ] its protective spirit was frightened off.
He obliterated [Esharra] and carried off its cult objects,
He entered the E-adgigi[4] and tore out the screen,   (20)
The enemy approached with evil intent Ennun-dagalla.[5]
Before him the god was clad in light,
He flashed like lightning, he shook in the dwelling!
The enemy became afraid, betook himself off.

1. Temple of Enlil at Nippur.
2. Nippur.
3. Temple in Nippur.
4. "The House of Counsel," a sanctuary at Nippur.
5. A name for part of the sanctuary of Enlil in Ekur?

His priest was frightened off, he said to him,   (25)
"[   ]." The god was clad in light,
He flashed like lightning, he shook in the dwelling!
[The enemy   ] Ennun-dagalla: "Take away(?) his diadems!
"You must lead him [... from] his dwelling."
[The priest?] had no fear and was not mindful of (his own) life,   (30)
[   ] Ennun-dagalla, he did not take away(?) his diadems.
[   ] the Elamite said ...
[   ] the Elamite, a vile man, said ...
[   ] ... guarantor, he repeats the answer
"[   ] ... let them take to Ekur,   (35)
"[   ] ... let him dwell in Durmah, I obligate(?) the priest."
[the one whom?] the guarantor stood for(?)
[   ] the priest

(fragmentary lines, then gap)

(rev)

(several lines gone)

[   ] ... the table of [   ]   (1)

When the guardian of well-being cries [   ],
The protective spirit of Esharra, [   ] was frightened away.
The Elamite hastened to evil deeds,
For the Lord devised evil for Babylon.   (5)

When the protective genius of justice stood aside,
The protective spirit of Esharra was frightened away.
The Elamite enemy took away his possessions,
Enlil, who lived upon it, had become furious!

When mighty ones(?)* redoubled their evil deeds,   (10)
The fiery glare and ill wind obliterated their faces.*
Their gods were frightened off, they went down to the depths.
Whirlwinds, ill wind engulfed the heavens.
Anu (the gods') creator had become furious!

He weakened their (the gods') features,[1]
    he laid waste(?) his (own) abode,   (15)
With a flash he obliterated(?) the designs of Eanna,
The foundations of Esharra fell to pieces [   ].

[   ] he commanded total destruction.
[The god   had] become furious:
The bar[barian hor]de [took] the road to Sumer,
    ... the land of En[lil].   (20)
Which one is Kudur-nahhunte, the evil-doer?
He called up the barbarian horde, [it level]led the land of Enlil,
He laid waste(?) [   ] at their side.

When the [   ] of Ezida
And Nabu, trustee of all [   ] hastened to [   ] ...*   (25)
He set [out] below, towards the ocean,
Ibbi-Tutu of the Sea(land) hastened, a storm monster(?),[2]
He (Nabu) crossed the sea
    and occupied a dwelling not his own,
The rites of Ezida, the sure house, were deathly still.

The Elamite [enemy] sent forth his chariotry,   (30)
He headed north towards Borsippa,
He came down the dark way, the road towards the land,*
The vile Elamite torched its sanctuary.
He slew the noble one [   ] with weapons,
He [plun]dered all the temples.*   (35)
He took their possessions and carried them off to Elam.
He destroyed his enclosures,*
He filled the land [with weeping ...]

---

1. That is, he caused their images to be taken off?
2. Ud-ulu was a name for Ninurta, perhaps used here as descriptive of the actions of Ibbi-Tutu?

(c) MARDUK AND THE ELAMITES

(obv)

(top half of tablet lost; two fragmentary lines)

[   ] his un[just](?) deeds [   ]
[   ] ... [   ]
[   ] ... the gods, creation of A[nu?]   (5)
[   ] ... [   ] Shamash, illuminator [   ]
[   ] lord of lords, Marduk, in the steadfastness of his heart,
[   ] ... of everything, an improvident sovereign
[   ] he felled with weapons Dur-mah-DINGIR.ME,
    son of Arad-[E]atush,
He plundered [   ] and [   ] water over Babylon and Esagila,   (10)
He slaughtered its [   ] with his own weapon like sheep,
[   ] he burned with fire, old and young,
    he [   ] with weapons,
[   ] he cut down young and old.
Tudhula son of Gazza[   ],[1] plundered
    the [... (and) ...] water over Babylon and Esagila,
[   ] his son smote his pate with his own weapon.   (15)
[   ] his lordship to the [rites] of Annunit[u   ]

(rev)

[king of] Elam, [   ] the city Ah[   ],
    plundered the great ...,   (1)
[   ] he sent like the deluge, all the cult centers
    of Akkad and their sanctuaries he burned [with fi]re.
Kudur-nahhunte his son c[ut?] his middle
    and his heart with an iron dagger,
[   ] his enemy he took and sought out(?).
The wicked kings, criminals, [   ] captured.
The king of the gods, Marduk, became angry at them,   (5)
[   ] were ill, their breast ..., [their] plans [   ],
[   ] to the desert, all of them ... to the king our lord.

---

1. Unknown. The name is written to suggest an etymology "Evil-of-Birth" son of "Slaughterer ..." Various scholars have compared the Hittite royal name Tudhaliyas.

[Shazu],[1] who knows the heart of the gods,
The merciful one, Marduk, at the invocation of his name,
[... Babylon] and Esagila, let him(?) return to his place!
Let the king my lord put this [in] your [heart?], (10)
[The doer] of evil to him [   ] his heart ...
[   ] the doer of sin must not [   ]

Text: (a) BM 35404 (collated) = Pinches, JTVI 29 (1897), 84-85. (b) BM 34062 (collated) = Pinches, JTVI 29 (1897), 86-89. (c) BM 35496 (collated) = Pinches, JTVI 29 (1897), 92-83.
Edition: (a) Jeremias, MVAeG 21 (1917), 92-94. (b) Jeremias, MVAeG 21 (1917), 84-90. (c) Jeremias, MVAeG 21 (1917), 80-84.
Literature: Landsberger apud Güterbock, ZA 42 (1934), 21; van Dijk, OrNS 55 (1986), 167.
Notes to Text: (a 4) *tanda[dāti]*, WGL. (a 7) Brinkman, PHKB, 80. Previous editors read "not pleasing," but the tablet should be read *ša eli-šú-nu ṭá-a-bi x*. (a 17) CAD D, 117a. (b obv 8) *ṣe-le-niš* "sideways" (WGL); see AHw, 1089b (vs. CAD N/1, 74). (b obv 17) GIŠ.ḪUR-*šú* (collated). (b rev 10) Collation excludes the reading *a!-bu-ru-u* (as in AHw, 1121a, and, already, Pinches, 89 note 2). I read *šá-<ga>-pu-ru-<tú>(?) iš-ta-nu* HU[L.M]EŠ-*šú-un*. (b rev 11) Reading *ú-pa-as-si-ʾsuʾ ʾpaʾ-ni-šú-un*. (b rev 25) UR clear by collation. (b rev 32) KASKAL.MEŠ KI-*iš* (collation). (b rev 35) WGL: *šá ekurrāti kalašin [iš]lul*. (b rev 37) WGL: *pit-qí-šú*.

1. A name for Marduk, "He Who Knows the Heart," compare Creation Epic (III.17) Tablet VII lines 35ff.

III.12 NEBUCHADNEZZAR I AND HIS TIMES

Nebuchadnezzar I (1124-1103 B.C.) was a successful and energetic monarch whose name became a by-word in later Babylonian historical and literary tradition.[1] He ascended the throne of Babylon (or Isin?) when Babylonian fortunes were at an ebb. The Kassite dynasty had been deposed after nearly half a millennium. Assyrians and Elamites had successively invaded. The Elamite king had deported one of Nebuchadnezzar's predecessors and removed the statue of Marduk from his temple at Babylon.[2]

Nebuchadnezzar marched against the Elamites in a series of campaigns. At first turned back by an outbreak of plague among his soldiery (III.12b), he later mounted a surprise attack during the summer hot season, routed his foe, and recovered the statue of Marduk (III.12c; III.11, A.23). The return of the statue (III.12d) occasioned a burst of patriotic literary activity.[3]

Nebuchadnezzar's dynasty, known as the Second Dynasty of Isin, was evidently fascinated by the Sumerian background of Babylonian culture. This is suggested by the following poem that asserts the antediluvian, Sumerian origin of Nebuchadnezzar's kingship (III.12a).

(a) THE SEED OF KINGSHIP

This composition alludes to the remote descent of Nebuchadnezzar I, king of Babylon, from Enmeduranki, an antediluvian cultural figure, sage, and king of Sippar. This extraordinary claim may be interpreted in various ways.[4] During the Mature and Late periods, Babylonian scholars interested themselves in the remote ancestry of individuals, texts, and institutions for antiquarian, political, social, heuristic, and perhaps even patriotic reasons.[5] In particular, Nebuchad-

---

1. For a historical survey of his reign, see Brinkman, PHPKB, 104-116.

2. J. J. M. Roberts, "Nebuchadnezzar I's Elamite Crisis in Theological Perspective," *Studies Finkelstein*, 183-187.

3. A. Boissier, "Nebukadnezzar Ier," *Revue Sémitique* 2 (1894), 78, refers to "*une renaissance de la littérature babylonienne.*" W. G. Lambert ascribes this to the emergence of Marduk at this period as supreme god of Mesopotamia, "The Reign of Nebuchadnezzar I: A Turning Point in the History of Ancient Mesopotamian Religion," in W. S. McCollough, ed., *The Seed of Wisdom, Essays in Honour of T. J. Meek* (Toronto, 1964), 3-13. See below, III.12c and III.17; Sommerfeld, AOAT 213 (1982), 174-181; W. G. Lambert, BSOAS 47 (1984), 4.

4. W. G. Lambert, JCS 21 (1967), 134-138; CRRAI 19 (1971), 439-440.

5. W. G. Lambert, "Ancestors, Authors, and Canonicity," JCS 11 (1957), 1-14, 112.

nezzar I asserts that his claim to the throne antedated that of the Kassites and that of the Amorite kings of Babylon (most of the second millennium) and could be anchored in remotest known Babylonian tradition at Sippar (the only city still important at his time that was believed to have antedated the flood). Perhaps some connection was posited between this personage and the king's lineage in order to assert a revival of native Babylonian tradition. In any case, the text was composed in both Sumerian and Akkadian, an unusual undertaking at such a late date (see also III.12d).

Praise is [for him w]hose mig[ht is] over the universe for eternity, (1)
Whose anger [is grievous but whose re]lenting is sweet,
     glorious to praise![1]
In his power are casting down and setting up, he reveals
     to future peoples how to watch for his sign.
Nebu[chadnezzar], king of [Babylon], who sets in order all
     cult centers, who maintains regular offerings,
He (Marduk) exalted his [wisdom] and made him foremost, (5)
He (Marduk) made great [his might], he exalted his great destiny.[2]
[Nebuchadnezzar], king of Babylon, who sets [in order a]ll
     cult centers, who maintains regular offerings,
Scion of royalty remote (in time), seed which has been
     watched for[3] since before the deluge,
Descendant of Enmedura[nki], king of Sippar, who instituted
     the sacred diviner's bowl, who held the cedar,[4]
(And) who took his place before Shamash and Adad,
     the divine judges,[5] (10)
Foremost son of [Ninurta-nadin]-shumi, just king, faithful
     shepherd who makes firm the foundations of the land,

1. Compare Poem of the Righteous Sufferer (III.14) Tablet I lines 1ff. and Creation Epic (III.17) Tablet VII lines 153ff.

2. That is, Marduk chose Nebuchadnezzar to be the agent of his return to Babylon (so Akkadian; Sumerian slightly different in sense so far as preserved).

3. Compare line 3 above, where "watching for" is also alluded to. The poet may have had a specific omen in mind, to judge from the astrological omen(?) alluded to in III.11a.

4. Enmeduranki, an antediluvian king of Sippar, is here credited with being an early practitioner of oil divination.

5. A reference to divination, particularly hepatoscopy (Lambert, JCS 21 [1967], 133).

Superb offspring(?) of Adad and Gula, the great gods,
    of Nippurian descent and eternal lineage,
Foremost attendant of Shuzianna,[1] twin sister of Anshar,
Nominated by Anu and Dagan,
    chosen by the steadfast hearts of the great gods am I!
It came to pass that in the reign of a previous king
    the signs changed: (15)
Good vanished and evil was prevailing,
The Lord became angry and waxed furious.
He commanded that the gods of the land forsake it, its people
    went out of their minds, they were incited to falsehood.
The guardian of well-being became furious and went up to
    heaven, the protective genius of justice stood aside,
[ ], the guardian of living creatures, over[threw] the people,
    and they all became as if they had no god!   (20)
Malignant demons filled the land,
    remorseless plague penetrated the cult centers,
The land was diminished, its counsel changed.
The vile Elamite, who did not hold precious [the gods],
    whose battle was swift, whose onslaught was quick to come,
Laid waste the habitations, ravaged the gods,
    turned the sanctuaries into ruins!
Marduk, king of the gods, who ordains the destinies
    of the lands, observed all —   (25)
When the Lord is angry,
    the Igigi-gods in [heaven] can[not] bear his fury,
His frightfulness is terrifying,
    no man can withstand his glowering —
The hardest ground sustained not his tread,
    oceans trembled [at] his rage,
No rock withstood his footstep,
    the gods of the universe knelt before him!
All existence(?) is entrusted to his power, when he grew angry,
    who could appease him?   (30)
[ ] who learned [   ] him and sees his artfulness,

---

1. A healing deity known as "The Lady of Babylon."

[ ] himself [   ] the capable Enlil of the gods,
[ ] the I[gigi-gods   ], solicitous prince,
[ ] who in [ ] adorned with splendor,
    enthroned in terrifying radiance,
The powerful one [   ], whose leadership excels

(breaks off)

(For a possible continuation of the text, see III.12d)

Text: W. G. Lambert, JCS 21 (1967), 134-138; CRRAI 19 (1971), 439-440.
Edition: W. G. Lambert, JCS 21 (1967), 126-131; CRRAI 19 (1971), 434-438.

(b) THE WAR WITH ELAM

This fragment of a first-person narrative deals with a conflict between Babylon and Elam; the speaker may be Nebuchadnezzar I. The war was prolonged and bitter, so the avenging of their humiliation must have occasioned great joy to the Babylonians. More than half the tablet is broken away; moreover it is difficult to follow the course of events across the lacunae, so the restorations, which follow in the main Tadmor's proposals, are tentative.

(large gap)

[Shutruk-nahhunte][1] drove away(?) Zababa-shum-iddina[2]
    and ousted his royal authority,
He be[stowed royal authority] upon his eldest son,
    Kudur-nahhunte.
[K.?], whose crime exceeded those of his forefathers, whose
    monstrous sin was the greatest of them all,
Plotted [wick]edness [   ] against the land of Akkad[3] and
    perpetrated villainy.   (5′)
[The Babylonians? elevated] Enlil-nadin-ahi,[4] my predecessor,
[K.?] set to hostility,[5] vowing destruction(?).
[K.?] over[ran] all the people of Akkad like the deluge,
He turned all the sublime [hol]y places into [ruin heaps],
He made the great [lo]rd [Marduk] rise from his [royal] dwelling.   (10′)
He carried off the [possessions] of Sumer and Akkad [to Elam].
He took Enlil-nadin-ahi [to Elam],
[Overthrew] his [kingship], ousted his royal authority.
[   ] not of Babylonian descent, hostile [to Marduk],

(two broken lines, then gap)

---

1. An Elamite king, ca. 1165 B.C. See M. Stolper in E. Carter and M. Stolper, *Elam, Surveys of Political History and Archaeology* (Berkeley, 1984), 39-43.

2. Penultimate king of the Kassite dynasty, ca. 1160 B.C., here replaced by the Elamite king with an Elamite prince as viceroy.

3. That is, Babylonia.

4. Final king of the Kassite dynasty, ca. 1159-1157 B.C. One can also read the name as Enlil-shum-usur.

5. It is not clear whether the subject is the Elamites or Enlil-nadin-ahi.

(rev)

(about three lines gone)

[... perduring ter]ror befalling him, he took to the mountains,
[   ] ... harried the enemy.
His [sign?] they saw,
    and besought the decision of Mar[duk].★   (5′)
[   ], bitter, harassed, and in despair, I said to myself,
"[Unlike] my [predecessor] who flourished(?)★ in Elam,
    let me die this very day!
"[   ] battle with him, let me turn not back!"
[   ] I awaited him at the 'head(?)' of the Uqnu river[1]
    with the rest of the army,
[I did not tu]rn back, but, against the will of the gods,   (10′)
Erra, mightiest of the gods, decimated my [war]riors,[2]
The enfeebling [   ] bound(?)★ my horse teams,
[   ] a demon was killing my fine steeds.★
I became afraid of death, did not advance to battle,
    but turned back.
With heavy [   ] I camped, stupefied,
    at the city Kar-Dur-Apil-Sin.   (15′)
[Then] the Elamite [advanced] and I withdrew before him.
[I lay on a] bed of misery and sighs,
"[   ] me, that I ... before him,
"[   ] you must not untie the ... of the doors,
"[   ] let his enemy enter,   (20′)
"[   ] perpetrator of wickedness,
"[   ] the words of my lips,
"[   ] may Enlil's heart be appeased,
"[   ] his feelings eased."
[   ] rebellion   (25′)
[   ] my vow

(breaks off)

---

1. Kerkha river.
2. Probably a reference to a plague.

Text: G. Smith, III R 38 No. 2 (collated).
Edition: Tadmor, JNES 17 (1958), 137-139.
Literature: Brinkman, PHPKB, 79f., 88ff. and 106; Hallo, IEJ 16 (1966), 238.
*Notes to Text: (rev 5′) PHPKB, 106 note 575 (collation). (rev 7′) Text: *uššubu*. Tadmor seems to derive from *wašābu* (form?); WGL suggests *uššubu* (*ešēbu*). (rev 12′) WGL (compare *ubburu*). (rev 13′) CAD K, 307b.

(c) NEBUCHADNEZZAR IN ELAM

A carved stone monument commemorating a grant of land and exemptions by Nebuchadnezzar I to one of his officers in the Elamite campaign, Sitti-Marduk, opens with a literary description of the campaign, the work of the scribe Enlil-tabni-bullit.

(1) When Nebuchadnezzar, pious and pre-eminent prince, of Babylonian birth, aristocrat of kings, valiant governor and viceroy of Babylon,[1] sun god of his land, who makes his people flourish, guardian of boundaries, establisher of measuring lines(?),* righteous king who renders a just verdict; valiant male whose strength is concentrated on warfare, who wields a terrible bow, who fears no battle, who felled the mighty Lullubi[2] with weaponry, conqueror of the Amorites,[3] plunderer of the Kassites,[4] pre-eminent among kings, prince beloved of Marduk, was sent forth by Marduk, king of the gods, he raised his weapon to avenge Akkad.

(14) From Der, sanctuary of Anu, he made an incursion for a distance of thirty leagues. He undertook the campaign in July. With the heat glare scorching like fire,* the very roadways were burning like open flames! There was no water in the bottoms, and drinking places were cut off. The finest of the great horses gave out, the legs of the strong man faltered. On goes the pre-eminent king with the gods for his support, Nebuchadnezzar presses on, nor has he a rival. He does not fear the difficult terrain, he stretches the daily march!

(25) Sitti-Marduk, head of the house of Bit-Karziabku,[5] whose chariot did not lag behind the king his lord's right flank, held his chariot back.

---

1. The city name is written Eridu, an ancient place sacred to Ea/Enki in southern Sumer. The scribe wishes thereby to equate Babylon with the sacred city of the god of wisdom (see Brinkman, PHPKB, 116 note 653).

2. Literary term for "mountain people" (RGTC 2, 112).

3. Literary term for "(uncivilized, nomadic) West Semites," perhaps here a reference to inhabitants of the Trans-Tigridian region (as suggested by Weidner, AfO 16 [1952/3], 18 note 134).

4. Perhaps used here as a literary term for mountain peoples in the East.

5. A Kassite eponymous tribal domain. Sitti-Marduk was thereby a member of the Kassite nobility.

(28) So hastened the mighty king, and reached the bank of the Ula river.[1] Both kings met there and made battle. Between them a conflagration burst out, the face of the sun was darkened by their dust, whirlwinds were blowing, raging was the storm! In the storm of their battle the warrior in the chariot cannot see the other at his side.

(35) Sitti-Marduk, head of the house of Bit-Karziabku, whose chariot did not lag behind the king's right flank, and who held his chariot back, he feared no battle (but) went down to the enemy and went furthest in against the enemy of his lord. By the command of Ishtar and Adad, gods who are the lords of battle, Hulteludish, king of Elam, retreated and disappeared. Thus king Nebuchadnezzar triumphed, seized Elam, and plundered its possessions.

(Text continues with record of the exemptions made to Sitti-Marduk's ancestral lands.)

Text: King, BBST 6 Plates 84–86.
Edition: King, BBST, 31–33.
Literature: Borger, HKL 1, 220; HKL 2, 122.
Notes to Text: (5) For a different view, see Seux, RA 64 (1970), 188. Perhaps read *èš-le-e*? (17f.) von Soden, RA 82 (1987), 190; George, BiOr 46 (1989), 383. (25) For the name, see Borger, AfO 23 (1970), 8.

---

1. Karun river.

(d) THE RETURN OF MARDUK FROM ELAM

This fragmentary poem is a bilingual Sumero-Akkadian commemoration of the return of the statue of Marduk from Elam. In all probability, the two versions were composed simultaneously, rather than one being intended as a translation of the other. The Sumerian seems heavily influenced by the non-Sumerian speech habits of its author. Since the text begins with unexpected abruptness, other tablets may have preceded it. Lambert has suggested that III.12a is in fact the lost beginning (JCS 21 [1967], 127). Nebuchadnezzar I is no doubt the subject.

(gap)

[ ] the arms of whomsoever the weapon touched turned
    stiff of their own accord, as if dying of cold,
    and their corpses were spread far and wide,   (1-2)
He (Marduk) made (it) pass over above and below,*
    right and left, front and rear, like the deluge;
    what was inside the city, outside the city,
    in the steppe, in the open country,
    he filled with deathly stillness and turned into a desert.
[?] the servant who revered him, who was assiduous in prayer,
    obedient, and constantly awaiting his[1] revelation,
    ceased not from praying until he (Marduk) would
    fulfill his heart's desire,   (5-6)
[?] "until I behold his lofty figure, dejection of heart will
    never depart from my person, even for a day,
    nor can I have full term of sleep in night's sweet lap!"
[On account of] my most distressing lamentations, my ardent
    prayers, my entreaties, and the prostration that I
    performed in lamentation before him daily,
    his profound(?) heart(?) took pity, and he relented,
    [Marduk it was?] who resolved to go to the "New City."
He, having set forth from the evils of Elam, having taken the
    road of jubilation, the path of gladness, and the way
    (that signified his) hearing and acceptance of their prayers,

---

1. Surely Marduk's (though CAD K, 93a understands the moon's).

The people of the land looked upon his lofty, suitable,
    noble form, as they acclaimed his brilliance,
        all of them paying heed to him.   (15-16)
The lord entered and took up his comfortable abode,
Ka-sushi(?),[1] his lordly cella, beamed for joy.   (19-20)
The heavens bore him their abundance, earth its yield,
    sea its catch, and mountains their tribute:
Their gifts beyond compare, or that tongue could tell,
Their massive tribute to the lord of lords!   (25-26)
Many sheep were slaughtered, grown bulls were provided
    in abundance, food offerings were magnificent,
        incense was heaped up,
Aromatics gave off sweet fragrance,
[   ] offerings were [   ], full of gladness.   (30-31)
[   ], there was rejoicing,
[Gods of hea]ven and netherworld exult
    as they [lo]ok upon valiant Marduk,
[   ] a song of praise of his valor,
[   ] who makes the kettle and snare drums glow(?).

(end of text)

Text: (a) K 3317 + 3319 (+) 8319 = Pinches, IV R² 20 No. 1; (b) BM 99067 + K 3444 = Meek, AJSL 35 (1918/19), 139 (bilingual).
Edition: Hehn, BA 5 (1905), 339-344; H. Winckler, *Altorientalische Forschungen* I (Leipzig, 1897), 538ff. (a only).
Literature: Jestin, RA 52 (1958), 193-202 (edition of Sumerian of a only); W. G. Lambert, JCS 21 (1967), 126-127 and in W. S. McCollough, ed., *The Seed of Wisdom, Essays in Honour of T. J. Meek* (Toronto, 1964), 9 note 19.
Notes to Text: (2-3) Restored from K 5191, cited CAD A/1, 76f.

---

1. A temple in Babylon, sometimes read as ka-sulim.

(e) NEBUCHADNEZZAR AND MARDUK

This epic-style poem recounts in summary fashion the events dealt with in more detail in III.15b–d.

When Nebuchadnezzar [the king] dwelt in Babylon,	(1)
He would roar like a lion, would rum[ble] like thunder,	
His illustrious great men would roar like lions.	
[His] prayers went up to Marduk, lord of Babylon,	
"Have mercy on me, in despair and pros[trate],*	(5)
"Have mercy on my land, which weeps and mourns,	
"Have mercy on my people, who wail and weep!	
"How long, O lord of Babylon,	
will you dwell in the land of the enemy?	
"May beautiful Babylon pass through your heart,	
"Turn your face towards Esagila which you love!"	(10)
[The lord of Babylon] heeded Nebuchadnezzar['s prayer],	
[ ] befell him from heaven,	
"I command you with my own lips,	
"[A word of] good fortune do I send you:	
"[With] my [help?] you will attack the Westland.	(15)
"Heed your instructions, [ ]	
"Take me [from El]am to Babylon.	
"I, [lord of Bab]ylon, will surely give you Elam,	
"[I will exalt] your [kingship] everywhere."	
[ ] the land of [ ] and seized [ ] of? his gods	(20)

(breaks off)

Text: King, CT 13 48 (collated).
Edition: H. Winckler, *Altorientalische Forschungen* I (Leipzig, 1897), 542f.
Literature: W. G. Lambert, "The Reign of Nebuchadnezzar I: A Turning Point in the History of Ancient Mesopotamian Religion," in W. S. McCollough, ed., *The Seed of Wisdom, Essays in Honour of T. J. Meek* (Toronto, 1964), 3–13.
Notes to Text: (5) WGL: *ú-tu-[lu]*, confirmed by collation.

(f) NEBUCHADNEZZAR TO THE BABYLONIANS

A fragmentary manuscript from the Late period preserves a letter, evidently addressed by Nebuchadnezzar to the Babylonians, telling them of his victory in Elam and recovery of Marduk's statue.

> [To the citizenry of Babylon], of protected status, leaders learned and wise, [   ], men of business and commerce, great and small, [thus says Nebuchadnezzar, v]iceroy of Enlil, native of Babylon, the king, your lord, [   ] on a stele: [   ] you should know [that the great lord Marduk, who] was angry at all the holy places for a long time, took [pity] on Babylon. He gave me in his majesty the [sublime] command, [in?] the awe-inspiring sanctuary [Esagila] he ordered me to take the road of march to [the land of] Elam.
>
> I gave reverent heed [to the command of the great lord] Marduk, assembled the army of Enlil, Shamash, and Marduk, and set forth towards [the land of] Elam. On I went, traversing distant [ways], waterless roads, night and d[ay.   At the] Ulaya River, the enemy, the vile Elamite, [blocked] the watering place in the gr[oves   ] the troops [ ] traversed. I could give no water, nor could I relieve their fatigue.
>
> He advanced, hurtling his arrows, weapons [brandished] in battle. Through the might of Enlil, [Shamash, and Marduk, which] has no [equ]al, I overwhelmed(?) the king of Elam, defeating him … His army scattered, his forces dispersed, [   ] deathly still, he(?) ravaged his (own) land, abandoned his strongholds, and disappeared.
>
> I hastened on [ ] I beheld the [great lord] Marduk, lofty warrior of the gods, and the gods of the land [of Babylonia whom?] he commanded to convene with him. I raised [   ] … and set up a wailing, I brought the great lord [Marduk] in procession and set out on the road to his homeland.

(Rest fragmentary. The king commands the restoration of Marduk and his treasures to Esagila.)

Text: van Dijk, VAS 24 87.
Edition: None.
Literature: George, BiOr 46 (1989), 382-383, whence several restorations used here.

(g) PRAYER IN THE NAME OF NEBUCHADNEZZAR

The following short prayer is engraved on a bronze axehead inscribed with Nebuchadnezzar's name.

O Marduk, you can save the prayerful who frequents your shrines and make him stand (in triumph) over his enemies. Your breeze wafted upon me, I could overcome my enemies. Strengthen my weapon that I may slay my foe!

Text: Dossin, *Iranica Antiqua* 2 (1962), 158 no. 14 = pl. xxiv.
Edition: Sommerfeld, AOAT 213 (1982), 184.
Literature: Borger, HKL 2, 47.

III.13 MARDUK PROPHECY

This text purports to be a speech of the god Marduk in which he relates his history prior to the time of Nebuchadnezzar I. He explains that he is wont to traverse the universe; implicitly one is not to be surprised then at his peregrinations. He dwelt for a while among the Hittites (the image was captured by a Hittite king in 1594), and then returned to Babylonia. Unlike the Agum text (III.9), which does not explain how he was brought back from Hatti, this account asserts that Marduk was brought back by military means. Marduk then speaks of a stay in Assyria (Baltil, image captured by Tukulti-Ninurta I, see III.1). He blessed Assyria during his residence there. No such blessing is in store for Elam, whose attack on Babylon in the time of Kudur-nahhunte (III.12) resulted in the transport of the statue of Marduk to Elam. In fact, a terrible fate is foretold for Elam. Marduk speaks warmly of a prince who is to arise and restore the land, who will bring him home again, and through whose good offices he will be reconciled to Babylon once more. Babylon will then flourish as never before.

The Marduk Prophecy may have been composed to glorify Nebuchadnezzar I and perhaps suggest to him specific benefactions (last column). The "future" there revealed included detailed recommendations about some otherwise unknown cult centers. As Borger suggests,[1] the text may well have achieved its desired effect, for at least three manuscripts exist that are more than half a millennium later than the time of Nebuchadnezzar I.

> (i 1) O Haharnum, Hayyashum,[2] Anu, Enlil, Nudimmud, Ea, …, Nabium, great gods who are learned in my mysteries! Now that I am ready for a journey, I will tell you my name.
>
> (i 7) I am Marduk, great lord, the most lofty one, he who inspects, who goes back and forth through the mountains, the lofty one, inspector, who smites(?)* lands, he who goes constantly back and forth in the lands from sunrise to sunset, am I!
>
> (i 13) I gave the command that I go to Hatti, I put Hatti to the test, there I set up the throne of my supreme godhead. For twenty-four years I dwelt there. I made it possible for Babylonians to send

---

1. BiOr 28 (1971), 21.

2. Two little-known primeval deities, presumably cited here so as not to give primacy to the better-known and younger deities in the list.

(commercial) expeditions there, and they marketed(?)* its [   ] goods and property [in] Sippar, Nippur, [and Babylo]n.

(i 23) A king of Babylon arose [and] led [me in procession to] ... Babylon, ..., fair was the processional way of Babylon! The crown of my [supreme godhead] and the image of [   ] workmanship [   ]. Water and [propitious] winds [   ]. Three days [   ] the crown of my supreme godhead [   ], and the image of [   ] workmanship to my body did I [   ]. I returned, [and for Babylon I said], "Bring [your tribute, ye] lands [to Babylon!]." *(gap)*

(i 3′) [The king? of] Baltil was pleasing [to me], the temple of Baltil was [.... to me]. His [temple]s [shone] like gems, I bestowed [   ] and abundance [upon him] ... [Month, day, and y]ear [I blessed him]. Having drawn up with him troops of Enlil, I set upon him wings like a bird and I delivered all [lands] (into his power), I blessed the land of Assur. I gave him the [tablet?] of destinies, I granted him stability. [   ] ... [I retur]ned, and for Babylon I said, "Bring your tribute, ye lands! ..."

(i 18′) I am Marduk, great lord, lord of destinies and decision am I! Who (but me) made this journey? I have returned from whence I have gone, it was I who ordered it. I went to the land of Elam, and that all the gods went, it was I who ordered it. I cut off the offerings to the temples, I caused gods of cattle and grain to go away to heaven. The goddess of fermentation sickened the land, the people's corpses choked the gates. Brother consumed brother, comrade slew his comrade with a weapon, free citizens spread out their hands (to beg of) the poor! Authority was restricted, injustice afflicted the land, rebellious kings diminished the land, lions cut off travel, dogs [went mad] and bit people. As many as they bit did not live but perished! I fulfilled my days, I fulfilled my years. I resolved to return to my city Babylon and to Ekur-sagila. I spoke to all the ...* It was I who ordered it, "Bring your tribute, ye lands, to Babylon! ..."

(iii 9) A king of Babylon will arise, he will renew the marvelous temple, the Ekur-sagila. He will create the plans of heaven and earth in Ekur-sagila, he will double(?)* its height. He will establish exemptions for my city Babylon. He will lead me in procession to my city Babylon and bring me into eternal Ekur-sagila. He will restore my (processional) boat, he will inlay its rudder with precious metal, he will [cover] its [com]ing with gold leaf. The boatmen who serve [it] he will bring aboard. They will be divided to [right] and left. The king will [ ] from(?) the dock(?) of Esagila (*gap, then some following fragmentary lines which deal with the restoration of another processional ship.*)

(Assur iii 7′) ... [this prince] will see the benevolence of the god. [The years of] his reign will be long.

(Assur iii 9′) He will make [Ekur]-Ekishnugal shine [like] a gem, the sanctuary of Ningal, the sanctuary of Sin, to[gether] with their treasures, possessions, and properties ... (*fragmentary lines, gap*)

(Assur iv 5) ... He will provide for the city and gather in the scattered ones. Ekur-Egalmah and the other sanctuaries he will make shine like gems. Ningal, Gula, and Kurnunitum ... he will bring back to their favorite temples. This prince will cause his land to browse on the splendor of his pastures, and his days will be long ... [ ] He will make the sanctuaries shine like gems. He will bring back all their gods. He will gather in the scattered land and make firm its foundations.

(iii) The gate of heaven will be open,[1] [ ] ... will get [ ] forever. Ningirsu will prevail. The watercourses will bring fish. Field and acreage will be full of yield. The winter crop will last till the summer harvest, the summer crop till the winter. The harvest of the land will be bountiful, market prices will be favorable. Wickedness will be rectified. Obscurities will be brought to light. Clouds will always be visible.[2] Brother will have consideration for brother, son will revere father like a god. Mother will [ ] daughter, bride will be mar[ried] and r[evere her husband]. There will always be consideration among the people. The young man will [always bear] his burden(?). This prince will [ru]le [all] lands.

(iii 21) Finally, I and all the gods will be reconciled with him. He will smash Elam, he will smash its cities, he will dismantle its fortresses. He will lift the great king of Der from his unsuitable position, change his desolation, [ ] his bad situation, take him by

1. A reference to rainfall?
2. Favorable prognosis.

the hand, and bring him into Der and (its temple) Ekur-Dimgal-kalamma forever.

(iv B′) 40 quarts of [ ], 40 quarts of [ ], 10 quarts of flour, 1 quart of [ ], 1 quart of honey, 1 quart of butterfat, 1 quart of figs(?), 1 quart of raisins, 1 quart of alabastron [oil], 1 quart of finest [ ] without alkali(?), 1 regular sheep, a fatted calf will be burned for this spirit. Month, day, and year I will bless him!

Text: Borger, BiOr 28 (1971), 5-13 (Kuyunjik); W. G. Lambert, JCS 18 (1964), 27-28 (Assur).
Edition: Borger, BiOr 28 (1971), 5-20.
Translation: Hecker, TUAT II/1, 65-68.
Literature: Sommerfeld, AOAT 213 (1982), 188-189.
*Notes to Text: (i 9) Doubtful, see AHw, 1585b; perhaps, with Borger, "who traverses." (i 22) Hecker, TUAT II/1, 66. (ii 15′) On the basis of the parallel lines (i 15′), one expects a place; read perhaps ÈŠ *da-ra-a-ti?* Otherwise, perhaps, "goddesses." (iii 24) WLM.

III.14 THE POEM OF THE RIGHTEOUS SUFFERER

The Poem of the Righteous Sufferer is a poetic monologue, opening and concluding with hymns, that tells how a certain noble gentleman, once important and prosperous, for no apparent reason was driven to disgrace and disease by the god Marduk. His story is set forth as exemplary of the two sides to divine character, anger and forgiveness, and as exemplary of the unfathomable will of the gods.

The poem opens with a hymn setting forth contrasts of Marduk's nature and then proceeds to the narrative (Tablet I line 41). The speaker loses his luck and his personal defenses are lowered, exposing him to misfortune. He consults experts (line 52), to no avail. He loses favor at court (line 55) and paints a vivid picture of seven base conspirators excitedly clamoring over the advantages they plan to take of his downfall (lines 59-64). Physical disintegration sets in (lines 70ff.), followed by social ostracism. He is reviled everywhere and suffers financial setbacks (lines 99ff.). He loses his post and a long period of depression and foreboding ensues (lines 103ff.). He still hopes for deliverance (lines 119-120).

As Tablet II opens, a year has elapsed, longer than such suffering is usually visited upon a man. Prayer and consultation are to no avail. One would think he was godless (Tablet II lines 12-22), but he was always scrupulous in his observances of god and sovereign. Does that matter (lines 33ff.)? Can anyone hope to understand the will of the gods? People's fortunes rise and fall — what is the lesson in that?

The speaker has no further opportunity for reflection as he comes down with a textbook of illnesses (Tablet II lines 49ff.). Pains, agony, malfunction, disability crush him. He can neither eat nor drink (Tablet II lines 86ff.). He falls bedridden (Tablet II lines 95ff.) and writhes helplessly in filth and torment. Continued consultations with experts yield nothing. He is given up for lost, his tomb is made ready, grave goods set out, his wretched obituary written (Tablet II lines 114ff.; compare also Tablet I line 13). Gloom settles over his loved ones.

As he lapses into the coma of death, the sufferer, whose name is now revealed to be Shubshi-meshre-Shakkan, sees a dream visitant: a young man in fine clothes (perhaps a personification of the speaker's own self in better days?). The apparition promises him relief and dries up his sores. The ministrant speaks on behalf of a lady, who, as Bottéro has suggested (see below, Literature), may be Sarpanitum, Marduk's wife (see Tablet IV fragment C, lines 10'-11'). She may have interceded with her husband on behalf of the sufferer, a common motif in Mesopotamian literature (compare Against Enlil's Anger [III.38c] line 8'). In Tablet III lines 16-18 the sufferer tries vainly to convince his skeptical family of the truth of what he saw. In a second vision, a man washes him off with water and massages him. In a third, a female figure intercedes for him in oblique terms; thereupon a scholar appears with a written text that contains the wording for his release (Tablet III line 41). Signs are sent so the people will believe; Marduk forgives him his misdeeds. The sufferer's illnesses are thereupon cured, he begins to eat and drink, gets out of bed, and testifies to his health.

Tablet IV opens with Shubshi-meshre-Shakkan's testimony that it was Marduk who saved him. He goes through a river ordeal to prove himself guiltless, then goes to the temple of Marduk. His progress through the city echoes the note of encouragement for the human race sounded by the name of each gate and quarter and fulfills the implications of the names. In Tablet IV lines 51ff. he makes lavish thank offerings; finally, in Tablet IV lines 97-98, he gives a banquet for the citizenry at the site of his intended entombment. In a closing hymn, the Babylonians proclaim the wondrous healing power of Marduk to rescue mankind. So great is this healing power that it can heal even the most terrible of afflictions — those sent by Marduk himself.

The language of the poem is rich in rare words. The author was steeped in the scholarly lore of his age, including medical texts; some of the pathological terms used are otherwise attested only in diagnostic treatises. The author makes use of every poetic device in the Akkadian repertory. He is fond of word plays, alliteration, rhyme, intricate parallelism, inclusion by opposites. He develops various elaborate over-arching symbolic frames of reference in his text, among them darkness and light, day and night.[1] He displays his humility throughout his text by various ingenious devices.[2] An ancient commentary and numerous manuscripts from different localities attest to the esteem this composition enjoyed among the educated.

The text sets forth a Mesopotamian notion of guilt and divine power. The modern term "righteous sufferer" is a misnomer when applied to this and comparable texts; at least, Shubshi-meshre-Shakkan was not so confident of his righteousness as Job. The author of Job makes clear that Job's suffering had

1. Moran, JAOS 103 (1983), 257f.; in general, see W. von Soden, "Licht und Finsternis in der sumerischen und babylonisch-assyrischen Religion," *Studium Generale* 13 (1960), 647-653.
2. Foster, JAOS 103 (1983), 123ff.

nothing to do with his righteousness, but was a test of faith. Here the speaker says that, so far as he knows, he has been righteous, and whatever his fault may have been (who can know?), he is sorry for it and begs forgiveness. There is none of the defiance and bitterness of Job. In short, this text sees suffering and redemption as signs of divine power, while Job sees them as tests of human strength. Despite these differences, the two documents belong to a common Near Eastern literary tradition. Each works out its version of the problem of divinely inflicted human suffering in an original manner.

The reader is left to conclude that Marduk can redeem anyone, no matter how lost to the human race. This sounds a note of optimism that for the author outweighs his despair and agnosticism. In expatiating this theme, the poet drew freely on a vast store of knowledge to lend his text richness and broad scholarly appeal. The product is one of the finest literary monuments of Mesopotamian antiquity.

Tablet I

I will praise the lord of wisdom, solicitous god,	(1)
[Fur]ious in the night, calming in the daylight:*	
Marduk! lord of wisdom, solicitous god,	
[Fur]ious in the night, calming in the daylight:	
Whose anger engulfs(?) like a tempest,	(5)
Whose breeze is sweet as the breath of morn,	
In his fury not to be withstood, his rage the deluge,	
Merciful in his feelings, his emotions relenting.	
The skies cannot sustain the weight of his hand,	
His gentle palm rescues the moribund.	(10)
Marduk! The skies cannot sustain the weight of his hand,	
His gentle palm rescues the moribund.	
When he is angry, graves are dug,	
His mercy raised the fallen from disaster.	
When he glowers, protective spirits take flight,	(15)
He has regard for and turns to the one whose god*	
has forsaken (him).	
Harsh is his punishment, he ... in battles(?),	
When moved to mercy,	
he quickly feels pain like a mother in labor.	

He is bull-headed in his love of mercy,[1]
Like a cow with a calf, he keeps turning around watchfully.[2]   (20)
His scourge is barbed and punctures the body,
His bandages are soothing, they heal the doomed.
He speaks and makes one incur many sins,
On the day of his justice sin and guilt are dispelled.
He is the one who makes shivering and trembling,   (25)
Through his sacral spell chills and shivering are relieved.★
Who raises the flood of Adad, the blow of Erra,
Who reconciles the wrathful god [and god]dess,
The Lord divines the gods' inmost th[oughts],★
(But) no [god] understands his behavior.   (30)
Marduk divines the gods' inmost thoughts,
(But) no god understands his behavior!
As heavy his hand, so compassionate his heart,
As brutal his weapons, so life-sustaining his feelings.
Without his consent, who could cure his blow?   (35)
Against his will, who could sin and [escape]?★
I will proclaim his anger, which [runs deep?], like a fish.
He punished(?) me abruptly, then gran[ted?] life.
I will teach the people, [I will instruct the land] to [fear],★
To be mindful of him is propitious for [   ].   (40)
After the Lord [changed] day [into night],
And the warrior Marduk [became furious with me],
My own god threw me over(?) and disap[peared],
My goddess broke rank and vanis[hed].
He cut off the benevolent angel who (walked) beside [me],   (45)
My protecting spirit was frightened off, to seek out someone else.
My vigor was taken away, my manly appearance became gloomy,
My dignity flew off, my cover leaped away.
Terrifying signs beset me:

---

1. Literally: "Pointed (of horns), he cherished his mercy, like a cow ..." There is a wordplay on "mercy/bull." "Pointed" seems to imply impetuous action; "bull-headed" of the translation attempts to maintain the parallelism. Other wordplays in the preceding line, built on "suckling/ battles" and "mother giving birth" remain obscure.

2. The image, well known in Near Eastern art, appears to be that of the maternal cow turning to lick the newborn calf.

I was forced out of my house, I wandered outside.   (50)
My omens were confused, they were abnormal(?) every day,
The prognostication of diviner and dream interpreter could
      not explain what I was undergoing.
What was said in the street portended ill for me,
When I lay down at night, my dream was terrifying.
The king, incarnation of the gods, sun of his peoples,   (55)
His heart was enraged with me and appeasing him was impossible.*
Courtiers were plotting hostile action against me,
They gathered themselves to instigate base deeds:
If the first "I will make him end his life"
Says the second "I ousted (him) from his command!"   (60)
So likewise the third "I will get my hands on his post!"
"I'll force his house!" vows the fourth
As the fifth pants (to speak)
Sixth and seventh follow in his train![1]
The clique of seven have massed their forces,   (65)
Merciless as fiends, equal to demons.*
So one is their body, united in purpose,
Their hearts fulminate against me, ablaze like fire.
Slander and lies they try to lend credence against me.
My mouth, once proud, was muzzled like a ...,   (70)
My lips, which used to discourse, became those of a deaf man.
My resounding call struck dumb,
My proud head bent earthward,
My stout heart turned feeble for terror,
My broad breast brushed aside by a novice,   (75)
My far-reaching arms pinned by (flimsy) matting(?),
I, who walked proudly, learned slinking,
I, so grand, became servile.
To my vast family I became a loner,
As I went through the streets, ears(?) were pricked up(?) at me,   (80)
I would enter the palace, eyes would squint at me,
My city was glowering at me like an enemy,
Belligerent and hostile would seem my land!

---

1. Literally: "in his protective spirit."

My brother became my foe,
My friend became a malignant demon,   (85)
My comrade would denounce me savagely,
My colleague was constantly keeping the taint to his weapons,
My best friend would pinch off my life.
My slave cursed me openly in the assembly (of gentlefolk),
My slavegirl defamed me before the rabble.   (90)
An acquaintance would see me and make himself scarce,
My family disowned me.
A pit awaited anyone speaking well of me,
While he who was uttering defamation of me forged ahead.
One who relayed base things about me had a god for his help,   (95)
For the one who said "What a pity about him!" death came early,
The one of no help, his life became charmed,★
I had no one to go at my side, nor saw I a champion.
They parceled my possessions among the riffraff,
The sources of my watercourses they blocked with muck,   (100)
They chased the harvest song from my fields,
They left my community deathly still, like that of a (ravaged) foe.
They let another assume my duties,
They appointed an outsider to my prerogatives.
By day sighing, by night lamentation,   (105)
Monthly, trepidation, despair the year.
I moaned like a dove all my days,
I let out groans as my song.
My eyes are forced to look(?) through constant crying,
My eyelids are smarting(?) through [ ] of tears.   (110)
My face is darkened from the apprehensions of my heart,
Terror and panic have jaundiced my face.
[The ... of] my heart is quaking for unremitting fright!
[   ] like a burning fire,
[Like the burs]ting of a flame falsehood beset me,   (115)
[   ] lamentation, my imploring!
[The speech of] my lips was senseless, like a moron's,
When I tried to talk, my conversation was gibberish.
I watch,★ that in daylight good will come upon me!
The moon will change,★ the sun will shine!   (120)

Tablet II

One whole year to the next! The (normal) time passed.   (1)
As I turned around, it was more and more terrible.
My ill luck was on the increase, I could find no good fortune.
I called to my god, he did not show his face,
I prayed to my goddess, she did not raise her head.   (5)
The diviner with his inspection did not get to the bottom of it,
Nor did the dream interpreter with his incense clear up my case.
I beseeched a dream spirit, but it did not enlighten me,
The exorcist with his ritual did not appease divine wrath.
What bizarre actions everywhere!   (10)
I looked behind: persecution, harassment!
Like one who had not made libations to his god,
Nor invoked his goddess with a food offering,
Who was not wont to prostrate, nor seen to bow down,
From whose mouth supplication and prayer were wanting,   (15)
Who skipped holy days, despised festivals,
Who was neglectful, omitted the gods' rites,
Who had not taught his people reverence and worship,
Who did not invoke his god, but ate his food offering,
Who snubbed his goddess, brought (her) no flour offering,   (20)
Like one possessed(?), who forgot his lord,
Who casually swore a solemn oath by his god:
      I, indeed, seemed (such a one)!
I, for my part, was mindful of supplication and prayer,
Prayer to me was the natural recourse, sacrifice my rule.
The day for reverencing the gods was a source
      of satisfaction to me,   (25)
The goddess's procession day was my profit and return.
Praying for the king, that was my joy,
His sennet was as if for (my own) good omen.
I instructed my land to observe the god's rites,
The goddess's name did I drill my people to esteem.   (30)
I made my praises of the king like a god's,
And taught the populace reverence for the palace.
I wish I knew that these things were pleasing to a god!
What seems good to one's self could be an offense to a god,

What in one's own heart seems abominable
    could be good to one's god! (35)
Who could learn the reasoning of the gods in heaven?
Who could grasp the intentions of the gods of the depths?
Where might human beings have learned the way of a god?
He who lived by (his) brawn died in confinement.
Suddenly one is downcast, in a trice full of cheer, (40)
One moment he sings in exaltation,
In a trice he groans like a professional mourner.
People's motivations change in a twinkling!
Starving, they become like corpses,
Full, they would rival their gods. (45)
In good times, they speak of scaling heaven,
When it goes badly, they complain of going down to hell.
I have ponde[red]* these things;
    I have made no sense of them.
But as for me, in despair, a whirlwind is driving(?) me!
Debilitating disease is let loose upon me: (50)
An evil vapor has blown against me [from the] ends
    of the earth,
Head pain has surged up upon me from the breast of hell,
A malignant spectre has come forth from its hidden depth,
A relentless [ghost] came out of its dwelling place.
[A she-demon came] down from the mountain, (55)
Ague set forth [with the] flood [and sea?],
Debility broke through the ground with the plants.
[They assembled] their host, together they came upon me:
[They struck my he]ad, they closed around my pate,
[My features] were gloomy, my eyes ran a flood, (60)
They wrenched my muscles, made my neck limp,
They thwacked [my chest], pounded(?) my breast,
They affected my flesh, threw (me) into convulsions,
They kindled a fire in my epigastrium,
They churned up my bowels, they tw[isted] my entrails(?), (65)
Coughing and hacking* infected my lungs,
They infected(?) my limbs, made my flesh pasty,
My lofty stature they toppled like a wall,

My robust figure they flattened like a bulrush,
I was dropped like a dried fig, I was tossed on my face.   (70)
A demon has clothed himself in my body for a garment,
Drowsiness smothers me like a net,
My eyes stare, they cannot see,
My ears prick up, they cannot hear.
Numbness has spread over my whole body,   (75)
Paralysis has fallen upon my flesh.
Stiffness has seized my arms,
Debility has fallen upon my loins,
My feet forgot how to move.
[A stroke] has overcome me, I choke like one fallen,   (80)
Signs of death★ have shrouded my face!
[If someone th]inks of me, I can't respond to the inquirer,
"[Ala]s!" they weep, I have lost consciousness.
A snare is laid on my mouth,
And a bolt bars my lips.   (85)
My way in is barred, my point of slaking blocked,
My hunger is chronic, my gullet is constricted.
If it be of grain, I choke it down like stinkweed,
Beer, the sustenance of mankind, is sickening to me.
Indeed, the malady drags on!   (90)
For lack of food my features are unrecognizable,
My flesh is waste, my blood has run dry,
My bones are loose, covered (only) with skin,
My tissues are inflamed, afflicted with gangrene(?).
I took to bed, confined, going out was exhaustion,   (95)
My house turned into my prison.
My flesh was a shackle, my arms being useless,
My person was a fetter, my feet having given way.
My afflictions were grievous, the blow was severe!
A scourge full of barbs thrashed me,   (100)
A crop lacerated me, cruel with thorns.
All day long tormentor would torment [me],
Nor at night would he let me breathe freely a moment.
From writhing, my joints were separated,
My limbs were splayed and thrust apart.   (105)

I spent the night in my dung like an ox,
I wallowed in my excrement like a sheep.
The exorcist recoiled from my symptoms,
While my omens have perplexed the diviner.
The exorcist did not clarify the nature of my complaint,   (110)
While the diviner put no time limit on my illness.
No god came to the rescue, nor lent me a hand,
No goddess took pity on me, nor went at my side.
My grave was open, my funerary goods ready,
Before I had died, lamentation for me was done.   (115)
All my country said, "How wretched he was!"
When my ill-wisher heard, his face lit up,
When the tidings reached her, my ill-wisher,
      her mood became radiant.
The day grew dim for my whole family,
For those who knew me, their sun grew dark.*   (120)

Tablet III

Heavy was his hand upon me, I could not bear it!   (1)
Dread of him was oppressive, it [me].
His fierce [pun]ishment* [   ], the deluge,
His stride was ..., it ... [   ]
[Ha]rsh, severe illness does not ... [ ] my person,   (5)
I lost sight of [aler]tness,* [ ] make my mind stray.
I gro[an] day and night alike,
Dreaming and waking [I am] equally wretched.
A remarkable young man of extraordinary physique,
Magnificent in body, clothed in new garments,   (10)
Because I was only half awake, his features lacked form.
He was clad in splendor, robed in dread —
He came in upon me, he stood over me.
[When I saw him, my] flesh grew numb.
[   ] "The Lady(?) has sent [me],   (15)
"[   ].""

[   ] I tried to tell [my people],[1]
"[   ] sent [for me]."
They were silent and did not [speak],
They heard me [in silence and did not answer].   (20)
A second time [I saw a dream].
In the dream I saw [at night],
A remarkable purifier [   ],
Holding in his hand a tamarisk rod of purification,
"Laluralimma,[2] resident of Nippur,   (25)
"Has sent me to cleanse you."
He was carrying water, he po[ured it] over me,
He pronounced the resuscitating incantation,
          he massaged [my] bo[dy].
A third time I saw a dream.
In my dream I saw at night: (30)
A remarkable young woman of shining countenance,
Clothed like a person(?), being li[ke] a god,
A queen among peoples [   ],
She entered upon me and [sat down] ... [   ]
She ordered my deliverance [   ]
"Fear not!" she said, "I [will   ]   (35)
"Whatever one sees(?) of a dream [   ]."
She ordered my deliverance, "Most wre[tched] indeed is he,
"Whoever he might be, the one who saw the vision at night."[3]
In the dream (was) Ur-Nindinugga, a Babylonian(?) ...
A bearded young man wearing a tiara,   (40)
He was an exorcist, carrying a tablet,
"Marduk has sent me!
"To Shubshi-meshre-Sakkan[4] I have brought a sw[athe],
"From his pure hands I have brought a sw[athe]."

---

1. These three lines may mean that when the sufferer told of his dream to his family, no one believed him. For the restoration, see line 47 below, where they need a sign to be convinced.

2. An academic Sumerian name, typical of Babylonia of the second half of the second millennium B.C. Compare Why Do You Curse Me? (IV.24).

3. These are oblique references to the sufferer, perhaps meaning something like "whoever has seen this vision should have pity taken upon him."

4. The name of the sufferer. This time the object of mercy is more specific than the preceding. Note that Marduk is named here for the first time since the opening of the poem.

He has entru[sted] me into the hands of my ministrant.   (45)
[In] waking hours he sent a message,
He reve[aled] his favorable sign to my people.
I was awake in my sickness, a (healing) serpent slithered by.[1]*
My illness was quickly over, [my fetters] were broken.
After my lord's heart had quiet[ed],   (50)
(And) the feelings of merciful Marduk were ap[peased],
[And he had] accepted my prayers [   ],
His sweet [relen]ting   [   ],
[He ordered] my deliverance!: "He is g[reatly trie]d!"
[   ] to extol [   ]   (55)
[   ] to worship and [   ]
[   ] my guilt [   ]
[   ] my iniquity [   ]
[   ] my transgression [   ]
He made the wind bear away my offenses.   (60)

(The exact placement of the following lines is unknown.)

[He applied] to me his spell
        which binds [debilitating disease],[2]
[He drove] back the evil vapor to the ends of the earth,
He bore off [the head pain] to the breast of hell,   (5′)
[He sent] down the malignant spectre to its hidden depth,
The relentless ghost he returned [to] its dwelling,
He overthrew the she-demon, sending if off to a mountain,
He replaced the ague in flood and sea.
He eradicated debility like a plant,   (10′)
Uneasy sleep, excessive drowsiness,
He dissipated like smoke filling the sky.
The turning towards people(?) with "Woe!" and "Alas!"*
        he drove away like a cloud, earth ... [   ].
The tenacious disease in the head,
        which was [heavy] as a [mill]stone,

---

1. The serpent, like the serpents of Aesculapius, was sometimes associated with the goddess of healing.
2. See Tablet II lines 5off.

He raised like dew of night, he removed it from me.   (15′)
My beclouded eyes,
    which were wrapped in the shroud of death,
He drove (the cloud) a thousand leagues away,
    he brightened [my] vision.
My ears, which were stopped
    and clogged like a deaf man's,
He removed their blockage, he opened my hearing.
My nose, whose bre[athing] was choked
    by symptoms of fever,   (20′)
He soothed its affliction so I could breathe [freely].
My babbling lips, which had taken on a h[ard crust?],
He wiped away their distress(?)
    and und[id] their deformation.
My mouth, which was muffled,
    so that proper speech was diffi[cult],
He scoured like copper and r[emoved] its filth.   (25′)
My teeth, which were clenched
    and locked together firmly,
[He op]ened their fastening, fre[ed?] the jaws(?).*
My tongue, which was tied and [could] not converse,
[He] wiped off its coating
    and [its] speech became fluent(?).
My windpipe, which was tight and choking,
    as though on a gobbet,   (30′)
He made well and let it si[ng] its songs like a flute.
My [gul]let, which was swollen so it could not take [food],
Its swelling went down and he opened its blockage.
My [   ], which [   ]
[   ] above [   ]   (35′)
[which] was darkened like [   ]

      (three damaged lines, then gap)

(The following lines are known only from the ancient commentary, but must go in the gap here, in sequence but not necessarily seriatim.)

a. My intestine, which was ever empty for want,
     and was coiled (tight) like basketry,
b. Accepts nourishment, holds drink.
c. My neck, which was limp and twisted at the base,
d. He shored up,* a hillock,[1] he planted upright like a tree(?).
e. He made my body that of a perfect athlete.[2]
f. He pared my nails as if to drive out a "vengeance."[3]
g. He drove out their illness and made their upper parts well.
h. My knees, which were tied and b[ound] like a ... bird's
i. The shape of my bo[d]y [he made] remarkable(?)
j. He wiped off the grime, he cleansed its filth
k. My gloomy mien began to glow (=120?)*

1. The image may be of piling up around the bottom of something to make it strong (differently CAD A/2, 1b).
2. Literally: "perfect in strength."
3. Obscure word (*naqqimtu*). The frame of reference may be witchcraft and countermeasures; one pares the nails well lest "vengeance" (= black magic?) come to fester under them to assault the body? "Vengeance" is either male or female (as here). See also III.31 line 77.

Tablet IV[1]

(Episode A)

The Lord [ ] me,	(1')
The Lord took hold of me,	
The Lord set me on my feet,	
The Lord revived me,	
He rescued me [from the p]it,	(5')
He summoned me [from destruc]tion,	
[ ] he pulled me from the river of death.	
[ ] he took my hand.	
[He who] smote me,	
Marduk, he restored me!	(10')
He smote the hand of my smiter,	
It was Marduk who made him drop his weapon.	
[He] the attack of my foe,	
It was Marduk who [ ]	

*(Two fragmentary lines, then gap. Insert here, perhaps, two lines known only
from the ancient commentary.)*

l.   At the place of the river ordeal, where people's fates are decided,
m.   I was struck on the forehead, my slavemark removed.

(Fragment B)

[   ] which in my prayers [   ]
[With] prostration and supplication [   ] to Esagila [   ]
[I who went] down to the grave
           have returned to the "Gate of [Sunrise]."[2]
[In the] "Gate of Prosperity" prosperity was [given me].

---

1. The assignment of texts to this tablet remains uncertain. Various arrangements have been proposed by Lambert, BWL, 24-25; OrNS 57 (1988), 88; Borger, JCS 18 (1964), 51; von Soden, MDOG 94 (1979), 51 note 5; Vogelzang, RA 73 (1979), 180; Reiner, *Poetry*, 118. Von Soden and Reiner place Fragment A at the end rather than the beginning of the tablet (Fragment A = Lambert, BWL, 1-15; Fragment B = Lambert, BWL, 76-101; Fragment C = Lambert, BWL, 24-50).
2. This and the following are gates in Babylon.

[In the] "Gateway of the Guardian Spirit" a guardian spirit
    [drew nigh to me]. (40′)
[In the] "Gate of Well-being" I beheld well-being.
In the "Gate of Life" I was granted life.
In the "Gate of Sunrise" I was reckoned among the living.
In the "Gate of Splendid Wonderment"
    my signs were plain to see.
In the "Gate of Release from Guilt"
    I was released from my bond. (45′)
In the "Gate of Petition"(?) my mouth made inquiry.
In the "Gate of Release from Sighing" my sighs were released.
In the "Gate of Pure Water"
    I was sprinkled with purifying water.
In the "Gate of Conciliation" I appeared with Marduk,
In the "Gate of Joy" I kissed the foot* of Sarpanitum. (50′)
I was consistent in supplication and prayer before them,
I placed fragrant incense before them,
An offering, a gift, sundry donations I presented,
Many fatted oxen I slaughtered, butchered many …,
Honey-sweet beer and pure wine I repeatedly libated. (55′)
The protecting genius, the guardian spirit,
    divine attendants of the fabric of Esagila,
I made their feelings glow with libation,
I made them exultant [with] lavish [meals].
[To the threshold, the bolt] socket, the bolt, the doors
[I offered] oil, butterfat, and choicest grain. (60′)
[   ] the rites of the temple.

(large gap)

(insert here?)

o. I proceeded along Kunush-kadru Street in a state of redemption.
p. He who has done wrong by Esagila, let him learn from me.
q. It was Marduk who put a muzzle on the mouth of the lion
    that was devouring me.
r. Marduk took away the sling of my pursuer
    and deflected his slingstone.

(Fragment C)

[ ] golden grain [   ]   (1')
[He?] anointed himself with sweet cedar perfume, upon him [ ]¹
A feast for the Babylonian(s?) [   ]
His tomb he(?) had made [was set up] for a feast!
The Babylonians saw how [Marduk] can restore to life,   (5')
And all mouths proclaimed [his] greatness,
"Who (would have) said he would see his sun?
"Who (would have) imagined
        that he would pass through his street?
"Who but Marduk revived him as he was dying?
"Besides Sarpanitum, which goddess
        bestowed his breath of life?   (10')
"Marduk can restore to life from the grave,
"Sarpanitum knows how to rescue from annihilation.
"Wherever earth is founded, heavens are stretched wide,
"Wherever sun shines, fire blazes,
"Wherever water runs, wind blows,   (15')
"Those whose bits of clay Aruru pinched off (to form them),
"Those endowed with life, who walk upright,
"[Tee]ming mankind, as many as they be,
        give praise to Marduk!
"[   ] those who can speak,
"[   ] may he rule all the peoples   (20')
"[   ] shepherd of all habi[tations]
"[   ] floods from the deep
"[   ] the gods [   ]
"[   ] the extent of heaven and netherworld,
"[   ]   (25')
"[   ] was getting darker and darker for him."*

1. Unlike other translators, I read these lines throughout in the third person (*elišu/bit qeberišu,*
ēpušu = Assyrianism?). This distancing is the result of attention now focusing on the Babylonians'
view of the sufferer and culminates in the Babylonians singing a hymn of praise to Marduk.

Text: (Tablet I) W. G. Lambert, BWL Plates 1-4, 74; Ebeling-Köcher-Rost, LKA 24; Leichty, *Studies Finkelstein*, 145; Wiseman, AnSt 30 (1980), 102-104. (Tablet II) Lambert, BWL, Plates 4-11, 74. (Tablet III) Lambert, BWL, Plates 12-13, 74. (Tablet IV) Lambert, BWL, Plate 18. Source u = 1-15; t = 36-61, 94-116; w = 101-112; v = 107-120. See also Gurney, OECT 11 48 (not used). (Commentary) Lambert, BWL, Plates 15-17.

Edition: Lambert, BWL, 21-62, 343-345; Wiseman, AnSt 30 (1980), 104-107.

Translation: Biggs, ANET³, 596-600; Labat, *Religions*, 328-341; Bottéro, *Recherches et Documents du Centre Thomas More*, Document 77/7, 11-24; von Soden, TUAT III/1, 110-135 (with new readings and interpretations adopted here).

Literature: (in general) W. von Soden, "Das Fragen nach der Gerechtigkeit Gottes im alten Orient," MDOG 96 (1965), 41-59; J. Bottéro, "Le Problème du Mal en Mésopotamie ancienne, Prologue à une Étude du 'Juste Souffrant'," *Recherches et Documents du Centre Thomas More*, Document 77/7 (1977), 1-43. (To specific aspects of the poem) Foster, JAOS 103 (1983), 123-130; Moran, JAOS 103 (1983), 255-260 (with proposals for the opening of Tablet I adopted here); Groneberg, JAOS 107 (1987), 323-324 (to opening of Tablet I); Vogelzang, RA 73 (1979), 180 (basic arrangement of Tablet IV adopted here); Reiner, *Poetry*, 101-118 (translation and literary study of Tablet II, to which I owe insights); Borger, HKL 1, 266; HKL 2, 159.

*Notes to Text: (I 2) Moran, JAOS 103 (1983), 257. (I 9) von Soden, TUAT III/1, 115. (I 16) DINGIR-*šú(?)*, so apparently, w.105; otherwise, "whom sunlight has forsaken" (so copy). (I 26) For 25-26, Foster, RA 75 (1981), 189. Differently, with unconvincing arguments against this proposal, Moran, JAOS 103 (1983), 260. Moran posits a logographic writing for the verb unparalleled in the manuscript, as well as an omitted sign, all in the same line! (I 27) von Soden, TUAT III/1, 116. (I 37) WGL. (I 39) WGL. (I 56) AHw, 1571a. (I 66) WLM: *ú-tuk!-kiš*(?). So also Freydank, communicated by WGL. (I 97) Doubtful; Moran, JAOS 103 (1983), 258. (I 119) von Soden, TUAT III/1, 121; compare Moran, JAOS 103 (1983), 217 note 20 (suggests another logographic verb here!); Reiner, *Poetry*, 103. (I 120) von Soden, TUAT III/1, 121. (II 48) AHw, 703a. (II 66) *su-ú-lu ḫa-aḫ-ḫu* (WGL, from unpublished text); for *ḫaḫḫu*, see Adams, JRAS 1979, 4. (II 81) von Soden, TUAT III/1, 124. (II 120) For this oft-debated crux, see B. Landsberger, *Brief eines Bischofs von Esagila an König Asarhaddon*, MKNAW NR 28/VI (1965), 72 note 134 (which I follow in essentials); Cooper, JCS 27 (1975), 248-249; Moran, JAOS 103 (1983), 257 note 11; differently Lambert, 46 and 295. (III 3) Moran, JAOS 103 (1983), 259 note 18. (III 6) [*e*]-*ru-ti*, AHw, 248a. (III 11) CAD M, 200a reads *ruš-šu-qat*, seemingly without basis. I follow von Soden, TUAT III/1, 127. (III 13') Note that the copy shows ina *'ù-ú-a*. (III 27') Bottéro, "Juste Souffrant," 20. (III 48) von Soden, TUAT III/1, 128. (III 14') von Soden, TUAT III/1, 129. (k) Moran, JAOS 103 (1983), 257. (IV B 50') Or, with CAD A/1, 9: "fell at the feet of." (IV C 26') Moran, JAOS 103 (1983), 257 note 5.

III.15 A SUFFERER'S SALVATION

This composition, which has expressions in common with III.14, is known from a fourteenth(?)-century manuscript from Ugarit in Syria. Nougayrol has considered the possibility that the Poem of the Righteous Sufferer (III.14) and this text derive from a common ancestor of the Classical period.[1] However, both texts may simply be drawing on stock motifs. As preserved, the text does not deal with the causes of the sufferer's punishment, but portrays his privations and afflictions before glorifying Marduk, his redeemer.

(gap of about fifteen lines)

Evil [portents?] were continually set against me [   ]   (1')
My omens were obscure, they became like [   ]
The diviner could not reach a ruling concerning me,
The "Judge"[2] would give no sign.
The omens were confused, the oracles mixed up.   (5')
Dream interpreters used up the incense, diviners the lambs,
Learned men debated the tablets (about my case),⋆
They could not say when my affliction would run its course.
My family gathered round to bend over me before my time,
My next of kin stood by ready for the wake.   (10')
My brothers were bathed in blood like men possessed,
My sisters sprinkled me with fine(?) oil from the press.
Until the Lord raised my head,
And brought me back to life from the dead,
Until Marduk raised my head,   (15')
And brought me back to life from the dead,
I could eat scant bread,
[I took for my] drink bilge(?) and salt pools.⋆
[When I lay down], sleep would not overcome me,
[I would lie aw]ake my whole night through.   (20')
My heart [   ] me, my(!) mind ...,
I was wasting away(?) from the sickness I suffered.

---

1. So Nougayrol, *Ugaritica* 5, 266-267; see also von Soden, TUAT III/1, 140-141.
2. Shamash?

[I] was made most anxious [   ]
My [te]ars [had to serve] as my sustenance.
[Lest] Marduk be forgotten,   (25')
That Marduk be praised:
Were it not for Marduk, breath had gone from me,
  ... would have cried out 'Alas for him!'
I praise, I praise, what the lord Marduk has done I praise!
[I praise, I praise], what the angry (personal) god [has done]
        I praise!   (30')
[I praise, I praise], what the (personal) goddess [has done]
        I praise!
Praise, praise, do not be bashful, but praise!
[He it] is, Marduk, I entreat(?) him, I entreat(?) him,
[He it] was who smote me, then was merciful to me,
He scuttled(?) me, then moored me,   (35')
He dashed me down, then grabbed me (as I fell),
He scattered me wide, then garnered me,
He thrust me away, then gathered me in,
He threw me down, then lifted me high.
He snatched me from the maw of death,   (40')
He raised me up from hell.
He smashed my smiter's weapon,
He wrested the shovel from the digger of my grave.
He opened my shrouded eyes,
He made my [sp]eech intelligible,   (45')
He [   ] my ears.

(breaks off)

Text: Nougayrol, *Ugaritica* 5 162 (p. 435).
Edition: Nougayrol, *Ugaritica* 5, 265-273.
Translation: von Soden, TUAT III/1, 140-143, whence some readings used here.
Literature: von Soden, UF 1 (1969), 191; W. G. Lambert, *Ugaritica* 5, 272-273.
Notes to Text: (7') von Soden, TUAT III/1, 141. (17') Butz, JESHO 27 (1984), 309. The
restoration proposed there for 19' is implausible.

III.16 WORDS OF THE WISE

Numerous Akkadian and Sumerian texts are known that retail conventional wisdom in the form of apodictic sayings and advice. The timelessness of the wisdom they convey makes dating of any particular collection impossible. I include as well a selection of proverbial sayings known from letters and other contexts.

(a) COUNSELS OF WISDOM

A learned man [   ]   (1?)
From [his] wisdom [   ]:
"Come, my son,
"[Pay heed to] the instruction which [I give you],
"Master the counsels [   ] ..."

Don't stop to talk with a frivolous person,   (21)
Nor go consult with a [   ] who has nothing to do.
With good intentions you will do their thinking for them,
You will diminish your own accomplishment,
        abandon your own course,

You will play false to your own, wiser, thinking.
Hold your tongue, watch what you say.   (26)
A man's pride: the great value on your lips.
Insolence and insult should be abhorrent to you.
Speak nothing slanderous, no untrue report.
The frivolous person is of no account.

Don't go stand where there's a crowd,   (31)
Do not linger where there is a dispute.
They will bring evil upon you in the dispute,*
Then you will be made their witness,
They will bring you to bolster a case not your own.   (35)
When confronted with a dispute, avoid it, pay no heed.
If it is a dispute with you, put out the flame,
A dispute is a wide-open ambush,
        a wall of sticks that smothers its opponents,[1]

It brings to mind what a man forgot and charges him.
Do no evil to the man who disputes with you,   (42)
Requite with good the one who does evil to you.
Be fair to your enemy,
Let your mood be cheerful to your opponent.
Be it your ill wisher, tre[at him generous]ly.*
Make up your mind to no evil,
Suc[h is not] acceptable [to the] gods,
Evil [ ] is abhorrent to [   ] Marduk.

[ ] the lowly, take pity on him.   (56)
Do not despise the miserable and [   ],
Do not wrinkle up your nose haughtily at them.
One's god will be angry with him for that,
It is displeasing to Shamash, he will requite him with evil.

Give food to eat, beer to drink,   (61)
Present what is asked for, provide for and honor.
One's god will be happy with him for that,
It is pleasing to Shamash, he will requite him with favor.
Do good deeds and be helpful all the days of your life.

You must not make a slave girl important in your house,   (66)
She must not rule your bedroom like a wife
...
Let your people have this to tell you:
"The household that a slave girl rules, she will break up."

Don't marry a prostitute, whose husbands are legion,   (72)
Nor a temple harlot, who is dedicated to a goddess,
Nor a courtesan, whose intimates are numerous.
She will not sustain you in your time of trouble,

---

1. Literally: "a brushwood defense that overwhelms its foes" (restored on the basis of an unpublished duplicate cited CAD A/1, 63a). "Brush" or "tinder" (*abu*) was used in similes for quick consumption by fire. A dispute is broad enough for anyone to fall into and containing and inflammable enough that both parties will be consumed in the conflagration. Hence the initial exhortation to "put out the fire" acquires special significance.

She will snigger at you when you are embroiled in controversy.
She has neither respect nor obedience in her nature.
Even if she has the run of your house, get rid of her,
She has her ears attuned for another's footfall.
Variant: As to the household she enters, she will break (it) up.
The man who married her will not have a stable home life.

My son, should it be the prince's will that you serve him,   (81)
His closely guarded seal should hang (around your neck).
Open his vault and go in, for there is none but you
    (should do so).
You may find countless treasures therein,
You must not covet any of it,
You must not set your mind on stealth.
Later the matter will be [brought out],*
And the stealth you attempted will be ex[posed].
When the prince hears, he will [   ],
His beaming countenance will [darken].
As for you, you will have an explanation [to devise] ...

(gap)

Do not backbite, speak fair words.   (127)
Do not speak of evil things,
Think of something good to say.
As for the backbiter and the speaker of evil,
They will be forced to settle their accounts with Shamash.

Do not speak lightly, guard your speech.   (131)
Do not speak your innermost thoughts, (even) when alone.
What you say on the spur of the moment
    you will still have with you later,
So set your mind on restraining your speech.

Bless your god every day,   (135)
Sacrifice and prayer are meet with incense.
You should give freewill offerings to your god,
For this is meet for a deity.

Prayer, supplication, and genuflection:
For every grain you render,* your profit will be a talent,[1]
So you will proceed at a premium with your god.

Since you are accomplished, read this text: (142)
"Reverence begets benevolence,
"Sacrifice prolongs life,
"And prayer atones for guilt.
"He who reverences the gods is despised by [no one],
"He who favors the Anunna-gods prolongs [his days]."

(fragmentary lines, then gap)

Text: W. G. Lambert, BWL, Plates 27-29; Gurney, OECT 11 50 and 88 (not used), 51.
Edition: W. G. Lambert, BWL, 96-107.
Translation: Biggs, ANET³, 595-596; von Soden, TUAT III/1, 163-168.
**Notes to Text:* (33) von Soden, TUAT III/1, 165. (45) von Soden, TUAT III/1, 165.
(88) von Soden, TUAT III/1, 167. (140) von Soden, ZA 71 (1981), 108.

1. A large sum of money, approximately fifty pounds of silver.

(b) WISDOM OF UGARIT

1. The Instructions of Shube-Awilim

A tablet from Ugarit in Syria contains teachings of a certain Shube-Awilim(?),[1] addressed to his son. These deal with the necessity of making one's own way in life, trust, self-reliance, decent behavior, discretion, and other virtues. The text is damaged and difficult to understand, so this version contains much guesswork. A similar text, quoted here as "B," is known from Hattusha, the capital of the Hittites in Anatolia.

i

Hear the counsel of Shube-awilim,   (1)
    Whose wisdom is l[ik]e that of Enlil-banda,[2]
The wise counsel of Shube-awilim,
    Whose wisdom En[lil-ban]da gave him!
From his mouth have come t[imeles]s rules
    for lesser(?) mankind,   (5)
[For Z]uranku(?),[3] his son, has his wisdom come forth.
He has spoken well-considered words(?) [and] entreaties:

"My son, your time has come(?),
"The wayfarer forsakes his house,   (10)
"(So too) have you made yourself ready to go.
"You have taken on the threat of the wilderness
    and must be careful(?).*
"(Who) among(?) the shades of the dead(?)
    can go in green pastures?[4]
"But [make?] your [journey?] with a f[rien]d(?),

---

1. Though presented as a Sumerian sage, apparently of Uruk, the name as read is unknown in Mesopotamian tradition. It may be a corruption of Shuruppak or Utnapishtim. Nougayrol (*Ugaritica* 5, 283) suggests that Shube-awilim means "Submerge man!", but this is implausible.
2. Another name for Enki/Ea.
3. This may be a corruption of Ziusudra, the Sumerian flood hero (so Nougayrol, *Ugaritica* 5, 284); other possibilities include a name (S)ur-Enki "Servant of Enki" or a corruption of Duranki "Bond of Heaven and Earth," a term usually used of Nippur, Enlil, and his temple (see Anzu [III.22a] Old Babylonian Version, Tablet II line 21).
4. As construed here: one should proceed with life's adventures when opportunity allows.

"He who goes with a friend is watched out for(?), (15)
"He who goes with a troop goes in safety.

"Son, do not frequent public houses,
"[Excessive drinking, gluttony] bloat the body.
"Son, it is not [meet] to chit-chat with menials,
"You should ... your hunger,
        you should take your pleasure in the beer.[1] (20)

"Hold your tongue as you pass through the bustling(?) street,
"Say nothing derogatory of people.
"A friend has nothing to say of one not his friend.[2]

"You would garner a harvest?
"The over-hasty harvest is ..., treachery(?), and
        unbreakable enmity. (25)

"Do not covet the [treasures] of the ruler,
"[   ] the most grievous [   ] of Uruk.
"[   ] accumulated possessions are lost.
"[   ] of the road, ... it is a capital [crime]. (30)
"Whether they catch him or let him go free, he knows,
        and turns himself in.
"[   ] he shall receive his punishment:
"A vision(?) [will haunt?] him ... [   ]

(gap)

ii

(five lines too fragmentary for translation)

"My son, break no bread with(?)* insolent young men,
        be not frivolous with oldsters.
"Do not address ... god without thinking(?).
"Let your strength match your plan(?),

---

1. That is, in public places eat only what you need, keep quiet, and leave.
2. That is, not speaking to strangers is a sign of respect and not hostility? (For discussion of the line, see von Soden, UF 1 [1969], 193).

"Do not pit yourself against a man of strength,   (10)
"Do not (try to) jump too wide a canal:
"You will hurt yourself and do yourself injury.
"[Your?] physician will ...,
            you will have to slaughter a sheep to feed him.

(two lines damaged)

"Do not open your heart (too much) to the woman you love,
"Seal it up, however much she importune.
"You should k[eep?] your wealth in your strong room,
"Do not let your wife learn what is in your purse.

"Our forebears established this of old,   (20)
"Our fathers divided ...:
"They drove in a peg, and, making firm a ring,
            they daubed it with clay.[1]
"Keep your seal[2] safe on (its) ring.
"Surround the (door) bolt with a ring: (so) [gu]ard your house!
"Let your seal (be the only) access to [your capi]tal(?),   (25)
"Whatever you see, leave it there,
"For you will need something, and then you can [bu]y(?).[3]

(five lines unintelligible)

iii

"Do [not] dig a well at the head of your [field].   (5')
"If you dig a well at the head of your [field],
"You will [   ] footmarks[4] of strangers in your field,
"Your field will be destroyed(?) ...

1. Refers to sealing a strong room with a peg and ring covered with clay and then sealed so no one can enter without breaking the seal. See Zettler, JCS 39 (1987), 211ff., with other literature cited there 197 note 1.

2. That is, the cylinder seal that is needed to reseal the storeroom.

3. As interpreted here, with hesitation, an injunction not to touch the principal except in time of need. The principal is what is in the storeroom; one's investments or ready cash are the "purse." Line 26 apparently refers to the capital.

4. According to B; A has "your feet."

"And as for you, they will draw (your water) with a curse.[1]
"Do not buy [an ox? in the springtime], (10')
"Do not choose a girl to marry on a h[oliday].
"(Even) a bad ox will look good in (that) season,
"A ba[d] girl [just wears] g[oo]d [clothe]s for the occasion ..."

(rest too fragmentary for translation)

2. Akkado-Hurrian Bilingual

Deposit money for an oath, you can take it (back) from a god. (1)
Respect an oath and keep yourself safe.
One who swears (falsely) is fully answerable(?)
    to the river ordeal for his life(?),
His wife will never have a son.[2]

One unconscious of guilt hastens to his god, (10)
Without thinking, he hurriedly prays to god.
His guilt is much(?) ...
He is simply unaware of it, so (that) man hastens to his god.

Text: (1) (A) = Nougayrol, *Ugaritica* 5 163 (pp. 436-437); (B) = Weidner, KUB 4 3. A is unilingual Akkadian, B Akkadian-Hittite bilingual. (2) Nougayrol, in *Le Palais royale d'Ugarit* (Paris, 1955) III/2, CVI.
Edition: (1) Nougayrol, *Ugaritica* 5, 273-290 (A); Laroche, *Ugaritica* 5, 779-784 (B). (2) Nougayrol and Laroche, in *Le Palais royale d'Ugarit* (Paris, 1955), III/1, 311-324; W. G. Lambert, BWL, 116.
Literature: (1) von Soden, UF 1 (1969), 193-194.
Notes to Text: (1 i 12) *ta-<na>?-[a]h̬-h̬i-<id>*? (ii 107) Doubtful. The parallelism suggests that *tamlula* is to be connected with *mēlulu* "play," but this is problematic.

1. Guessing from B, which, however, implies: "they will throw you out (of your field)," A incomprehensible.
2. Compare, however, Kussulu to the Moon God (II.36), where this consequence did not occur.

(c) WISDOM OF HATTI

Akkado(-Sumerian?) wisdom from Hatti is known from various poorly understood fragments, a selection from one of which follows.

> My well is not exhausted, so my thirst is not too great.
> The net is loosed, the fet[ter] unnoosed.[1]   (5)
> I pledged myself as guarantor, the losses never end.
> You went — so what? You stayed — so what?
> You stood where you were — so what?
>   You came back — so what?

Text: Weidner, KUB 4 40.
Edition: W. G. Lambert, BWL, 278.
Translation: Pfeiffer, ANET[3], 425.

---

1. Literally: "do not remain" (AHw, 1221b). Wordplay on "net" and "remain" in the original.

(d) SUMERO-AKKADIAN WISDOM AND PROVERBS

Sumerian proverbs and wisdom were closely studied by Akkadian-speaking scholars of the second and first millennium B.C. These were often provided with Akkadian translations or equivalents. Since proverbs and epigrams were regarded as common speech, relatively few native Akkadian proverbs have come down to us. The Sumerian material may have been studied because of its antiquity and linguistic value as well as its content. Proverbs, as opposed to epigrams or incidental pieces of wisdom, are hard to identify with certainty, nor is it always clear where a unit of text begins or ends. Furthermore, sayings of this type are often unfathomable to those without living cultural competence. The selections that follow are mostly made from the edition by Lambert in BWL; the reader interested in the problems presented by these texts should consult his treatment. I have arbitrarily titled the various manuscripts treated here. In a few cases I have placed in parentheses an interpretation. This is simply a guess as to what the saying refers to, without direct authority from the texts.

1. The Assyrian Collection

This group opens with a curious prologue, in which a "blockhead" (or, possibly, an Amorite), invites his wife to switch roles with him. This is usually understood to refer to sexual activity, but could be interpreted as a school exercise in grammar.

col i

A [b]lockhead says [to] his wife, "[Yo]u be the young man, [I] will be the girl. [When] I turn to being the young man, [let ... be] feminine, [let ...] be masculine."

col ii

(The Dumbfounded Fool)

He tried to snare birds without a trap: there weren't any! (4)

(A Marriage Ditty)

(He)

My face is a lion's, my figure a guardian angel's,
    my thighs(?) absolute delight!
Who will be the wife for me to adore?

(She)

My heart is discretion, my(!) inmost self is good counsel,
    my emotions are restrained,
    my lips speak delightful words!
Who will be the groom of my choice?   (13)

(Marrying for Money)

Who is wealthy? Who is rich?
For whom shall I reserve my intimacy?   (19)

That you fall in love (means) that you bear a yoke.   (21)
Plan ahead, you will succeed,
Make no plan ahead, you will not succeed.

("No tickee, no shirtee")

"Let me lie with you!" "Give god the due!"[1]   (27)

(The Lord helps them ...)

[Gi]rd yourself, your god shall be your help.   (29)
[Draw?] your sword! A god shall be your ally.

When you are down, let a friend help.   (33)
You did evil to your well-wisher —
    what will you do to your enemy?
Wealth is not your help, but god.
(Be you) great or small, god is your help.

---

1. Lambert, BWL, 231, suggests that this refers to temple prostitution: pay the temple its due and then take the prostitute's services.

col iii

The wise man is clad in finery,
    the fool is dressed in a gory rag.*   (13)
May the land be destroyed over our enemies' heads,
May the tottering wall collapse on our opponents,
May the land of the foe be wholly awash.

col iv

Shamash (=Divine Justice and Truth) will sustain your
    government, even if your king is an ignoramus.   (9)
If the plow has turned up evil,
    Shamash could not be the cause(?).
People without a king are (like) sheep without a shepherd.
People without a foreman are (like) a canal without a regulator.
Workers without a supervisor are
    (like) a field without a cultivator.
A household without a master is
    (like) a woman without a husband.

(Fear the Nearest?)

Have a lord, have a king, (but) respect a governor.   (22)

When you have seen for yourself the profit
    of reverencing god,   (27)
You will praise god and bless the king.
Refuse a boy's wish, he will make a fuss(?),
Throw a sop to a puppy, he will fawn over you.

2. The Power of Government

The command of the palace is like the command of Anu,
    it cannot be repudiated.   (1)
The king's command is sure as that of Shamash,
    His command cannot be rivalled nor his utterance altered.
The command of the palace is sure as that of Anu.
    Like Shamash, (the king) loves justice and hates evil.

3. Practical Wisdom

She looked at you, how far will she go with you?   (13)
To go, or not to go, to god your lord?
Would you hand a clod to him who throws?

4. Domestic Wisdom

col i

I shall drink thin beer, but I shall sit in the seat of honor.   (1)
Linen is laid for fleas, the meat basket(?) is woven for flies,
    the storehouse is constructed for lizards.*   (8)
The duck not eaten at the right time.[1]
He accumulated much but he slaughtered his pig.*   (17)
He accumulated much but he used up his firewood.

col ii

(A Woman's Lot)

The wife of the tongue-tied talker is a slave girl.   (3)
My mouth can make me the rival of men.
My mouth has made me renowned among men.

col iii

He left the city for the amazement of the land.   (9)

5. Life and Labor

col ii

Eat no fat, void no blood.   (9)
Do no falsehood, fear of [god] will not consume you.
Speak no evil, woe will not work its way into you,
Do no evil, you will undergo no lasting [mis]fortune.
A scorpion stung a man, what did it gain?   (21)
An informer caused a man's death, [wh]at did he profit?

---

1. Alster, RA 72 (1978), 109 suggests that this means "strike while the iron is hot."

The scorpion [   ], informing [   ] ...
[Win]ter is malignant, summer reasonable.
As they say, is she pregnant without intercourse?   (40)
    Fat without eating?[1]
Intercourse hinders lactation.*
Let me store up, they will rob (me),   (45)
Let me squander, who will pay then?
He dug a well which had no water,
He tanned a hide which did not ...

(The Unthanked Good Advisor)[2]

As its(?) gods returned to its ruins,   (50)
Woe has entered the ruined house,
Where the evil man was tenant
(And) the heedful man was not to grow old.
The wise vizier, whose wisdom his master has heeded not,
And anyone valuable whom his master has forgotten,
When the need arises, he will be reinstated.

col iii

The shadow which catches me is caught (too).   (1)
As they say: did the canebrake turn a profit on its reeds,
    the meadow on its grass?
The strong man lives by the profit of his arm,   (7)
The weak by the profit on his children.
My vagina is fine, (though) some of my folks consider
    me a has-been;   (14)
It's all fine, and I still (need to) wear a tampon.
Would you slap a moving ox in the face with a pin?
My knees are always on the go, my legs are never tired,   (21)
A simpleton dogs me with adversity.
I am a riding steed, yoked to an ass,

---

1. This is noted by Mark Bryant, *Riddles Ancient and Modern* (New York, 1984), 11, as a riddle, the answer being "clouds," but I know of no textual basis for this. I take the meaning to be something like "is there smoke without fire?"

2. Reiner, OrNS 30 (1961), 8-9. I understand the first part of the saying to refer to the consequences of not following good advice (differently Reiner).

I pull the wagon, I bear the lash!
My source of warmth is (only) the garment draped on me,   (45)
My carrying basket rests on my neck.*
I dwell in a house of brick and mortar, yet a lump of dirt
    falls on my head.   (50)
Last year I ate garlic; this year I have heartburn.

col iv

The life of yesterday was repeated today.[1]   (5)
Like winter's chair: you decorate it and put it beside me.
Like a chair for a man whose god is Shahan:
You regret it: burn its leather, and set it on fire.[2]

When you are on the river, the water is putrid,   (19)
When you are in a garden, your dates are gall.[3]

If I instruct him, he is only what I begot,   (25)
If I polish him, he is only a blockhead.

May the furrow bear no stalk, may the seed not produce.[4]   (27)

As they say, the early grain will flourish, how can we know?   (34)
The late grain will flourish: how can we know?
Suppose I die, let me consume; suppose I live,
    let me store up.   (42)

They capsized me and I almost died,   (46)
I caught no fish and ruined my clothes.

Where the high ground comes down(?), the canal is opened,   (51)
The enemy quits not the gate of the city
    where defenses are weak.

---

1. Nothing new under the sun.
2. The chair in winter is set by the fire for warmth, the chair of a man with a communicable disease(?) is thrown into the fire (perhaps: "cast off like an old shoe"?).
3. "Things is tough all over"?
4. "Stop it before it multiplies"?

col v

It is as hard to change you as an old oven.	(10)

You went and plundered the enemy territory,	(14)
The enemy came and plundered your territory.	

Never too late to spread out dried malt.	(23)

Would you lay out money [for] a pig's squeal?	(39)
I make the rounds for an ass's foal.	(43)

6. Prolixity

While the backside was breaking wind,
    the mouth brought forth babble(?).

7. Who is My Keeper?

The hired boat sank at Zabala.[1] O Shamash of Larsa,	
whose was the loss?	(1)
I would go to my brother, (but) my brother lives like me.	(6)
I would go to my sister, (but) my sister lives like me.	

8. Wellsprings of Contentment

Long life begets a feeling of satisfaction;	(19)
Concealing a matter, sleepless anxiety;	
Wealth, respect.	

9. Reflections on Power

When you commit a crime (out of weakness),	(1)
The Tigris will bear (it) away.	
When you commit a crime (from a position of power),*	
Heaven itself will forsake you.	

---

1. A small town, port and cult center, in Sumer. Compare Jacobsen in E. Gordon, *Sumerian Proverbs* (Philadelphia, 1959), 462: who is to pay for the boat, hirer or lessor?

When you get away, you are a wild bull.   (5)
When they catch you, you fawn like a dog.

You can't jump a ditch when you're lame.

10. Every Man for Himself

When fire consumes the one in front,   (2)
The one behind doesn't ask, "Where's the one in front?"

11. Fat Men and Forked Tongues

Fat is he who, when he goes in the fields,
    his pouch dangles down.   (4)

The scoundrel chases after women's intimacy,   (7)
The rogue has two sickles.[1]

One who has not supported a wife,   (11)
One who has not supported a son,
Is irresponsible and will not support himself.⋆

12. Management

I am a manager: hand-picked and brawny of arm.   (8)

The foreigner's ox forages, while his own lies hungry.

13. Candle under a Bushel

When oil is poured inside a stick, no one knows.   (1)

Giving is for the king, giving pleasure for the cupbearer.
Giving is for the king, doing a favor for the manager.   (7)

---

1. That is, one sickle is enough for an honest man.

Friendship is for a day, association forever.

There is quarreling among associates,   (12)
Backbiting among priests.
A resident alien in another city is a slave.   (16)

You need not watch a millstone.

The scribal art is mother of the eloquent and father of the erudite. (19)

14. Tempest in a Teapot

Something that has never happened from time out of mind: (5)
A young girl broke wind in her husband's embrace.

15. Blind Leading the Blind

The unskilled is the cart, the ignorant his road.   (6)

Bride, you have made a mother-in-law,   (10)
They'll do that to you too (someday).[1]

16. Favors

May kindness be requited to one who does it,   (12)
May Humma[2] grant favor to one well spoken of.

(rev)

As the potter looks at the rain (that might ruin his pots),   (4)
May Enlil look at the city whose fate is accursed.

The farmer is one who watches, what (else) can he do?   (9)
The day turned dark, but it did not [rain],
It rained but he did not (need) to take off his sandals.

---

1. That is, by marrying a son, she makes a mother-in-law; she is doomed, in her day, to the same fate.
2. Possibly an early Sumerian ruler, why cited here is unknown.

The (very) Tigris by its ... command did not irrigate fields.

17. The Puniness of Mankind

Can strong warriors withstand a flood?   (8)
Or mighty men quiet a conflagration?

(rev)

The will of god cannot be understood,   (7)
The way of god cannot be known:
Anything divine is [impossible] to find out.

18. Gain and Loss

You find something, it gets lost.   (12)
You discard something, it is preserved forever.

19. The Odds

col iii

Who will go out against mighty warriors who are one of purpose? (5)

Do the wish of the one present,
Slander the one not present!

20. One's Deserts

(a)

You took out a loan, but will spend it on a trifle.   (5)
The mash is bitter, how can the beer be sweet?

The bucket floats on the river.[1]

Since there is no malt, let him consume,   (10)

---

1. That is, the empty vessel only floats on the surface, the filled one brings good?

Since there is no malt, let him squander.

(b)

Flesh is flesh, blood is blood.   (16)
Alien is alien, foreigner is foreigner.

21. Bestiary

The ass of Anshan, the bear of Parahshe,   (5)
The cat of Meluhha, the elephant of the east:
These bite off a poplar tree like a leek.[1]

22. Bon Voyage

A young man said, "Alas!" and his boat sank. He said, "Hurrah!"
and his rudder broke. He said "Alas!" and "...!" and his boat got
to shore.[2]

23. A Riddle

It came in, (but) is not right,[3]
It goes out, (but) is not used up: The king's property.

24. From a Cylinder Seal

I have sought after and turned towards what pertains to god.
A man whose god chooses him shall lack for nothing.

---

1. Anshan: city in southwestern Iran; Parahshe: southeastern Iran; Meluhha: Indus Valley, (see p. 265 note 7).
2. Unfortunately the meaning of the last exclamation, essential for the "punch line," is unknown. It is most likely an expression of hope. In the first case the man was overly pessimistic, in the second overly optimistic, while in the third he tempered his expectations and so was not disappointed.
3. Either "not just" or perhaps in the sense "won't do."

Text: (1) W. G. Lambert, BWL, pl. 58, 59. (2) BWL, pl. 60 (K 4160+). (3) BWL, pl. 61 (K 4207).
(4) BWL, pl. 60 (K 4327+). (5) BWL, pl. 61-63 (K 4347+). (6) BWL, pl. 60 (K 5688). (7) BWL,
plate 60 (K 7654). (8) BWL, pl. 64 (K 7674+). (9) BWL, pl. 63 (K 8216). (10) BWL, pl. 64 (K
8315). (11) BWL, pl. 64 (K 8338). (12) BWL, pl. 65 (K 15227+). (13) BWL, pl. 65 (Sm 6). (14)
BWL, pl. 65 (BM 98743). (15) BWL, pl. 67-68 (VAT 10810). (16) BWL, pl. 66 (BM 38283). (17)
BWL, pl. 66 (BM 38486). (18) BWL, pl. 67 (BM 38539). (19) BWL, pl. 69 (BM 38596). (20)
BWL, pl. 70 (BM 56607). (21) BWL, pl. 71 (N.3395). (22) BWL, 274 (transliteration only). (23)
BWL, 275; CAD E, 259. (24) C. Gordon, *Iraq* 6 (1939), p. v 31 (photo).

Edition: (1) W. G. Lambert, BWL, 225-233. (2) BWL, 233-234. (3) BWL, 234-235. (4) BWL,
235-238. (5) BWL, 239-250. (6) BWL, 251. (7) BWL, 251. (8) BWL, 252-253. (9) BWL, 253-
254. (10) BWL, 254-255. (11) BWL, 255. (12) BWL, 257-258. (13) BWL, 258-259. (14) BWL,
260. (15) BWL, 260-262. (16) BWL, 262-264. (17) BWL, 264-266. (18) BWL, 266-267. (19)
BWL, 267-269. (20) BWL, 270-271. (21) BWL, 272-273. (22) BWL, 274. (23) BWL, 275. (24)
W. G. Lambert, BiOr 32 (1975), 223.

Literature: (4) Alster, RA 72 (1978), 103-112. (21) Collation, CAD M/1, 278a.

Notes to Text: (1 iii 13) For restoration of Sumerian, see CAD E, 314. (4 i 18) For restoration
of Sumerian, see CAD L, 68b; Alster, RA 72 (1978), 108-109. (4 i 17) See E. Gordon, *Drevnij
Mir* (= *Studies Struve*) (Moscow, 1962), 243 and note 86; I follow CAD L, 101; Alster, RA 72
(1978), 109. (5 ii 44) CAD E, 165a. (5 iii 46) For the second part of the saying, see Civil, JAOS
88 (1968), 10 (ba-ab-ri-ri). (9 3) Translation a guess based on *ḫbt* i/i "prevail" (or the like),
admittedly a rare poetic word(?), see Kraus, RA 69 (1975), 33. (11 11) Following the interpretation of E. Gordon, *Sumerian Proverbs* (Philadelphia, 1959), 121 note 3. The Akkadian text may
be corrupt.

(e) PROVERBS FROM LETTERS

1. The Hasty Bitch

The bitch in her haste gave birth to blind whelps.

2. Making an Example

When fire consumes a rush, its companions will pay attention.

3a. A Dog's Thanks

When the potter's dog enters the kiln,
    it (still) will bark at the potter.

3b. An Adulteress's Word

In court what the (accused) adulteress says carries more weight
    than the words of her husband.[1]

4. Brains over Brawn

The man who seized the lion's tail sank in the river.
He who seized the fox's tail escaped.

5. Servitude

Man is the shadow of god, and slave the shadow of man.

6. No Hiding Place

Where can the fox go to escape the sun?

---

1. Apparently adultery could be proven in court only if the husband caught the wife *in flagrante delicto*, as suggested by Roth, JESHO 31 (1988), 195. The different interpretation of Livingstone, AOAT 220 (1988), 185-186, is not convincing.

7. The Valorous Ant

When an ant is struck, does it not fight back
and bite the hand of the man that strikes it?

8. Silenced Protest

He who has been struck on the back, his mouth may still speak.
He who has been struck on the mouth, how shall he speak from it?

9. The Dangerous Fool

The ignoramus worries the [jud]ge,
the inept makes the powerful nervous.

Text: (1) Dossin, ARMT 1 5, 11-13. (2) Dossin, ARMT 10 150, 9-11. (3) Harper, ABL 403, obv 4-7, 13-15. (4) Harper, ABL 555, rev 3-6. (5) Harper, ABL 652, rev 9-13. (6) R. Campbell Thompson, *The Prisms of Esarhaddon and Assurbanipal Found at Nineveh*, 1927-8 (London, 1931), p. 24 line 25. (7) C. Bezold, E. A. W. Budge, *The Tell el-Amarna Tablets in the British Museum* (London, 1892) 61, 16-19. (8) Harper, ABL 1285, rev 11-13; photo Parpola, *Studies Reiner*, 266-267. (9) Harper, ABL 37, rev 3-6.
Edition: (1) Dossin, ARM 1 5, 11-13. (2) Dossin, ARM 10 150, 9-11. (3) W. G. Lambert, BWL, 281. (4) BWL, 281. (5) BWL, 281-282. (6) BWL, 282. (7) BWL, 282. (8) Parpola, *Studies Reiner*, 257-278. (9) Parpola, LAS 12.
Literature: (1) Moran, *Eretz-Israel* 14 (1978), 32-37; *Harvard Studies in Classical Philology* 82 (1978), 17-19; Alster, WO 10 (1979), 1-5; Avishur, WO 12 (1981), 37-38. (2) A. Marzal, *Gleanings from the Wisdom of Mari* (Rome, 1976), 23-27. (3) W. G. Lambert, BWL, 281. (4) Alster, JCS 41 (1989), 187-193. (5) W. G. Lambert, BWL, 281-282. (6) W. G. Lambert, BWL, 282.
Translation: (7) W. L. Moran, *Les Lettres d'El Amarna* (Paris, 1987), 479.

C. MYTHOLOGOCAL POETRY

III.17 EPIC OF CREATION

The Epic of Creation celebrates the exaltation of the Babylonian god Marduk to supreme deity of the Mesopotamian pantheon after he had saved the gods from attack by Tiamat, the ocean. The poem ascribes to Marduk reorganization of the universe, with Babylon at the center of it, and inspiration for the creation of mankind in order to sustain the gods. It offers an explanation of various names it assigns to Marduk. This poem should not be considered "the" Mesopotamian creation story; rather, it is the individual work of a poet who viewed Babylon as the center of the universe, and Marduk, god of Babylon, as head of the pantheon. This message was not lost on contemporary readers, for, in some Assyrian versions of the poem, Assur was substituted for Marduk. Therefore this poem can be read as a document of Babylonian nationalism. It may be a product of Babylonian nationalistic revival at the time of Nebuchadnezzar I (see III.12), though there is no firm evidence for its date of composition. To judge from its language and content, the poem dates to the latter part of the second millennium B.C.[1]

Some modern scholars have used this text as a Babylonian explanation for the necessity of absolute rule. According to them, it portrays an evolution of political authority from an assembly of equals working out policy to an absolute monarch proclaiming policy. In their view, the text can be read as a metaphor for the evolution of Mesopotamian political institutions from a reconstructed local assembly of elders to absolute kingship claiming divine sanction on a regional or international scale. The catalyst for this change is portrayed as outside threat calling for a resolute war leader. The leader demanded, as his terms for leadership, absolute obedience, even when the threat of war was removed.[2]

As the poet portrays this, the gods willingly surrender their power in return for perpetual safety and maintenance. For the latter purpose mankind is created.

---

1. See Lambert, "A New Look" (below, Literature).

2. T. Jacobsen, "Primitive Democracy in Ancient Mesopotamia," JNES 2 (1943), 159-172; similar ideas were developed independently by I. M. Diakonoff, *Obščestvennyj i gosurdarstvennyj stroj drevnego Dvurec'ja: Šumer* (Moscow, 1956), 120 note 1. Information on assemblies found in other literary contexts, such as omens, does not support such a hypothesis, although it can suggest the possibility of opposition between assembly and king; see Oppenheim, OrNS 5 (1936), 224-228.

The rebellious human spirit, as seen in Atrahasis (II.39), has no place in this poem, where the highest good for man is to discover and understand his place in the divinely ordered universe.

The poem is a work of great complexity and abounds with conceptual and philological problems. There are still many obscure passages and words. A predilection for certain types of words and constructions, together with the over-arching scheme of the poem, suggests the work of a single author. Though naturally there are variants in the manuscript tradition, there is no reason to suppose that the fundamental content of the work has been altered by successive generations, as has sometimes been suggested, just as there is no reason to elevate this composition to a greater authority than it deserves. It was esteemed highly in the first half of the first millennium B.C, as witnessed by the numerous copies that have turned up in both Assyria and Babylonia, by the preparation of an ancient commentary to the names of Marduk (Tablet VII), and by the ritual use of the composition in the Babylonian new year's festival as stated in late sources.[1] It was quoted or referred to in other texts about Marduk; see General Introduction, D.3.

The least accessible part of the text for the modern reader will be the passage dealing with the names of Marduk, as it exemplifies techniques of Mesopotamian explanatory philology. The names are explained or translated, where their etymology seemed transparent, and then expounded in other ways through assigning further significance to elements within the name. For some names an ancient commentary is preserved; this is excerpted below in the notes to each name. There is no proof that the commentary reflects the original author's intent in every instance, but it stands as an example of how a learned Mesopotamian reader approached this document.

The poem begins and ends with concepts of naming. The poet evidently considers naming both an act of creation and an explanation of something already brought into being. For the poet, the name, properly understood, discloses the significance of the created thing. Semantic and phonological analysis of names could lead to understanding of the things named. Names, for this poet, are a text to be read by the informed, and bear the same intimate and revealing relationship to what they signify as this text does to the events it narrates. In a remarkable passage at the end, the poet presents his text as the capstone of creation in that it was bearer of creation's significance to mankind.

---

1. A. Heidel, *The Babylonian Genesis*[2] (Chicago, 1951), 16-17.

The poetry of the Creation Epic shows command of a wide range of traditional poetic techniques and profound learning. A contrast between speech and action is drawn in the first four tablets, in that speech, characteristic of the old order of the gods, can run to considerable length and repetition. A hint of circularity is provided by the concentrically arranged rehearsals of the narrative; by the climax of Tablet III speech occurs within speech within speech within speech. This device is favored in traditional tale-telling as a narrative frame and as a demonstration of virtuosity, but it is seldom developed to such an extent in Akkadian literature (though compare the Anzu poem, III.22, on which the Creation Epic may have been modeled). By contrast, the speech and action characteristic of the new order of the gods under Marduk are narrated rapidly, with a minimum of repetition. The last part of the poem is one continuing speech, explaining and celebrating Marduk's fifty names.

Tablet I

*(Before anything was, mother ocean [Tiamat] and fresh water(?) [Apsu] mingled to pro-
duce the first of a series of pairs of gods. The descendants, with their boisterous behavior,
stir Tiamat and Apsu. Although Tiamat bears it in good part, Apsu wishes to kill the
offspring. The father is urged on by his counsellor. Apsu's intentions are foiled by Ea,
who kills him and restrains his counsellor. He founds his home in Apsu, the watery
domain represented by the slain primeval father, and dwells there with his wife.)*

When on high no name was given to heaven,	(1)
Nor below was the netherworld* called by name,	
Primeval Apsu, their progenitor,	
And matrix-Tiamat,[1] who bore them all,	
Were mingling their waters together,	(5)
No cane brake was intertwined nor thicket matted close.[2]*	
When no gods at all had been brought forth,	
None called by names, none destinies ordained,	
Then were the gods formed within the(se two).	
Lahmu and Lahamu[3] were brought forth,	
were called by name.	(10)
When they had waxed great, had grown up tall,	
Anshar and Kishar[4] were formed, greater than they,	
They grew lengthy of days, added years to years.	
Anu their firstborn was like his forebears,	
Anshar made Anu, his offspring, his equal.	(15)
Then Anu begot in his image Nudimmud,[5]	
Nudimmud was he who dominated(?) his forebears:	
Profound in wisdom, acute of sense, he was massively strong,	
Much mightier than his grandfather Anshar,	

1. Tiamat is the name of the ocean; Apsu is generally taken to refer to fresh water. The word rendered here "matrix" (after Jacobsen) is *mummu*, meaning "wisdom" or "skill," according to W. G. Lambert, JSS 14 (1969), 250; hence "creator" or "craftsman" (CAD M/2, 197). *Mummu* can also mean "noise"; see Michalowski, *Studies Moran*, 386.

2. That is, nothing divided or covered the waters.

3. For Lahmu and Lahamu, see W. G. Lambert, "The Pair Lahmu-Lahamu in Cosmology," OrNS 54 (1985), 189-202. Anshar and Kishar are the circle or horizon of heaven and earth.

4. Anshar was later used by Assyrian scholars as a way of referring to Assur, thus giving him primacy over Marduk; see p. 715 note 1.

5. Another name for Ea, god of wisdom.

No rival had he among the gods his brethren.   (20)
The divine brethren banded together,
Confusing Tiamat as they moved about in their stir,
Roiling the vitals of Tiamat,
By their uproar distressing the interior of the Divine Abode.[1]
Apsu could not reduce their clamor,   (25)
But Tiamat was silent before them.
Their actions were noisome to her,
Their behavior was offensive, (but) she was indulgent.
Thereupon Apsu, begetter of the great gods,
Summoned Mummu[2] his vizier, saying to him,   (30)
"Mummu, vizier who contents me,
"Come, let us go to Tiamat."
They went, took their places facing Tiamat,
They took counsel concerning the gods their offspring.
Apsu made ready to speak,   (35)
Saying to her, Tiamat, in a loud voice,
"Their behavior is noisome to me!
"By day I have no rest, at night I do not sleep!
"I wish to put an end to their behavior, to do away with it!
"Let silence reign that we may sleep."   (40)
When Tiamat had heard this,
She grew angry and cried out to her spouse,
She cried out bitterly, outraged that she stood alone,
(For) he had urged evil upon her,
"What? Shall we put an end to what we formed?   (45)
"Their behavior may be most noisome,
        but we should bear it in good part."
It was Mummu who answered, counselling Apsu,
The vizier was not receptive to the counsel of his creatrix,[3]
"Put an end here and now, father, to their troublesome ways!
"By day you should have rest, at night you should sleep."   (50)
Apsu was delighted with him, he beamed.

1. Andurna, a cosmic locality, perhaps an abode of the gods.
2. The same word, *mummu*, translated above as "matrix," here the personal name of Apsu's advisor; see p. 354 note 1.
3. Play on words between Mummu-Tiamat and Mummu the vizier.

On account of the evils
> he plotted against the gods his children,
He embraced Mummu, around his neck,
He sat on his knees so he could kiss him.[1]
Whatever they plotted between them,   (55)
Was repeated to the gods their offspring.
The gods heard it as they stirred about,
They were stunned, they sat down in silence.
Surpassing in wisdom, ingenious, resourceful,
Ea was aware of all, recognized their stratagem.   (60)
He fashioned it, he established it, a master plan,
He made it artful, his superb magic spell.
He recited it and brought (him) to rest in[2] the waters,
He put him in deep slumber, he was fast asleep,
He made Apsu sleep, he was drenched with slumber,   (65)
Mummu the advisor was drowsy with languor.
He untied his sash, he stripped off his tiara,
He took away his aura, he himself put it on.
He tied up Apsu, he killed him,
Mummu he bound, he locked him securely.   (70)
He founded his dwelling upon Apsu,
He secured Mummu, held (him) firm by a leadrope.
After Ea had captured and vanquished his foes,
Had won the victory over his opponents,
In his chamber, in profound quiet, he rested.   (75)
He called it "Apsu," which he assigned sanctuaries.
He established therein his chamber,
Ea and Damkina his wife dwelt there in splendor.

(Birth and childhood of the hero Marduk, who is born with full strength. He is
given the four winds by his grandfather.)

In the cella of destinies, the abode of designs,
The most capable, the sage of the gods, the Lord was begotten,   (80)

---

1. As interpreted here, Apsu bends down to kiss Mummu, so is presumably taller; Bottéro, "Création," 33 suggests that Mummu is sitting on Apsu's knees.
   2. Variant: "on the waters."

In the midst of Apsu Marduk was formed,
In the midst of holy Apsu was Marduk formed!
Ea his father begot him,
Damkina his mother was confined with him.
He suckled at the breasts of goddesses, (85)
The attendant who raised him endowed him well with glories.
His body was magnificent, fiery his glance,
He was a hero at birth,
  he was a mighty one from the beginning!
When Anu his grandfather saw him,
He was happy, he beamed, his heart was filled with joy. (90)
He perfected him, so that his divinity was strange,
He was much greater, he surpassed them in every way.
His members were fashioned with cunning
  beyond comprehension,
Impossible to conceive, too difficult to visualize:
Fourfold his vision, fourfold his hearing, (95)
When he moved his lips a fire broke out.
Formidable[1] his fourfold perception,
And his eyes, in like number, saw in every direction.
He was tallest of the gods, surpassing in form,
His limbs enormous, he was surpassing at birth. (100)
"The son Utu, the son Utu,[2]
"The son, the sun, the sunlight of the gods!"
He wore (on his body) the auras of ten gods,
  had (them) wrapped around his head too,
Fifty glories[3] were heaped upon him.
Anu formed and produced the four winds, (105)
He put them in his hand, "Let my son play!"[4]
He fashioned dust, he made a storm bear it up,

---

1. "Formidable" is an attempt to render a pun in the original between *rabû* "great" and *erbu* "four."

2. A series of interlingual puns on son and sun, only one level of which can be rendered in English. The cuneiform signs used to write the name Marduk, AMAR.UD, are here construed as *māru* "son" and Utu "sun."

3. Marduk has fifty names in this text. In a Late period god list, Marduk was assigned the number 50. Perhaps this was done so that Marduk could replace Enlil (also number 50) as head of the pantheon; see W. G. Lambert, BSOAS 47 (1984), 3 and below, p. 400 note 4.

4. Or: "My son, let them whirl."

He caused a wave and it roiled Tiamat,
Tiamat was roiled, churning day and night,
The gods, finding no rest, bore the brunt of each wind.*   (110)

(Tiamat is stirred to action by the angry gods.)

They plotted evil in their hearts,
They said to Tiamat their mother,
"When he killed Apsu your husband,
"You did nothing to save him but sat by, silent.
"Now he has made four terrible winds,   (115)
"They are roiling your vitals so we cannot sleep.
"You had no care for Apsu your husband,
"As for Mummu, who was captured, you remained aloof.
"You are [no mo]ther, you churn back and forth, confused.
"As for us, who cannot lie down to rest,
          you do not love us!   (120)
"Our ... [   ], our eyes are pinched,
"Lift this unremitting yoke, let us sleep!
"[Rai]se a [storm], give them what they deserve,
"[Ma]ke a [tempest], turn them into nothingness."
When Tiamat [heard] these words, they pleased her,   (125)
"[As y]ou have counselled, we will make a tempest,[1]
"[We will   ] the gods within it,
"(For) they have been adopting [wicked ways]
          against the gods [thei]r parents."
[They clo]sed ranks and drew up at Tiamat's side,
Angry, scheming, never lying down night and day,   (130)
[Ma]king warfare, rumbling, raging,
Convening in assembly, that they might start hostilities.

Mother Hubur[2] who can form everything,

---

1. Or: "monsters," but this would leave the reference in line 127 unclear.
2. Another epithet of Mummu-Tiamat, as a proper name suggesting a creative force (so Speiser, JAOS 68 [1948], 12), more commonly (as in IV.17 line 17), a name of the netherworld river, construed here as "Mother Noise" by Michalowski, *Studies Moran*, 385 (see General Introduction, E.3); see also Conti, RA 82 (1988), 128.

Added countless invincible weapons,
>   gave birth to monster snakes,
Pointed of fang, with merciless incisors(?),   (135)
She filled their bodies with venom for blood.
Fierce dragons she clad with glories,
Causing them to bear auras like gods, (saying)
"Whoever sees them shall collapse from weakness!
"Wherever their bodies make onslaught,
>   they shall not turn back!"   (140)
She deployed serpents, dragons, and hairy hero-men,
Lion monsters, lion men, scorpion men,
Mighty demons, fish men, bull men,
Bearing unsparing arms, fearing no battle.[1]
Her commands were absolute, no one opposed them,   (145)
Eleven indeed on this wise she crea[ted].[2]
From among the gods her offspring,
>   who composed her assembly,
She raised up Qingu[3] from among them,
>   it was he she made greatest!
Leadership of the army, command of the assembly,
Arming, contact, advance of the melee,   (150)
Wardenship of the (spoils?) of battle,
(All) she entrusted to him, made him sit on the dais.

---

1. For the appearance and names of the demons in this list, see W. G. Lambert, "The History of the muš-ḫuš in Ancient Mesopotamia," *Les Cahiers du CEPOA, Actes du Colloque de Cartigny 1981* (Geneva, 1985), 87-94; A. Green, "A Note on the 'Scorpion-Man' and Pazuzu," *Iraq* 47 (1985), 75-82; "A Note on Assyrian 'Goat-Fish', 'Fish-man' and 'Fish-woman'," *Iraq* 48 (1986), 25-30; "Neo-Assyrian Apotropaic Figures," *Iraq* 45 (1983), 87-96; R. S. Ellis, "'Lion-Men' in Assyria," *Studies Finkelstein*, 67-78; F. Wiggermann, "Exit Talim! Studies in Babylonian Demonology I," JEOL 27 (1981/2), 90-105. For discussion of the list as a whole, see W. G. Lambert, CRRAI 32 (1985), 56-57; F. Wiggermann, *Babylonian Prophylactic Figurines: The Ritual Texts* (Amsterdam, 1986), 268-323.

2. This number was reached by adding the "monster serpents" of 134, the "fierce dragons" of 137, and the nine creatures of 141-143. As shown by W. G. Lambert, CRRAI 32 (1985), 56-57, this is an expansion of a traditional list of eight in order to incorporate the heroic deeds of Ninurta into Marduk's *res gestae*.

3. A male deity about whom little otherwise is known. Jacobsen, SANE 2/3, 16 has proposed to derive his name from the Sumerian word for "work," and hence, he infers, Qingu's blood used to create man gave him his working capacity.

"I cast your spell.
    I make you the greatest in the assembly of the gods,
"Kingship of all the gods I put in your power.
"You are the greatest, my husband, you are illustrious,   (155)
"Your command shall always be greatest,
    over all the Anunna-gods."
She gave him the tablet of destinies,[1]
    had him hold it to his chest, (saying)
"As for you, your command will not be changed,
    your utterance will be eternal.
"Now that Qingu is the highest and has taken [supremacy],
"And has [ordained] destinies for his divine children,   (160)
"Whatever you (gods) say shall cause fire to [subside],[2]
"Your concentrated venom shall make
    the mighty one yield."

---

1. The tablet of destinies, though not a clearly defined concept in Mesopotamian tradition (see W. G. Lambert, OrNS 39 [1970], 174ff.), was sometimes considered to be in the netherworld and was presumably inscribed with a person's destiny and day of death. In the Anzu story (III.22), on which this episode is based, the tablet gave the power to control divine spheres of responsibility and thus universal authority. For further comparative discussion, see S. Paul, "Heavenly Tablets and the Book of Life," JANES 5 (1973), 345-353.
2. Contrast Tablet I line 96.

Tablet II

(Tiamat's preparations are known to Ea, who, in apparent despair, goes to Anshar, king of the gods. The relevant passages of Tablet I are repeated verbatim. Anshar is horror-stricken; he blames Ea for what has occurred. Since Ea started the trouble, he must find a solution to it. This accords well with Ea's plans for his son.)

Tiamat assembled her creatures,	(1)
Drew up for battle against the gods her brood.	
Thereafter Tiamat, more than(?) Apsu,	
was become an evildoer.[1]	
She informed Ea that she was ready for battle.	
When Ea heard this,	(5)
He was struck dumb with horror and sat stock still.	
After he had thought and his distress had grown calm,	
He made straight his way to Anshar his grandfather.	
He came in before his grandfather, Anshar,	
All that Tiamat plotted he recounted to him,	(10)
"My father, Tiamat our mother has grown angry with us,	
"She has convened an assembly, furious with rage.	
"All the gods rallied around her,	
"Even those you created are going over to her side,	
"They are massing around her, ready at Tiamat's side.	(15)
"Angry, scheming, never lying down night and day,	
"Making warfare, rumbling, raging,	
"Convening in assembly, that they might start hostilities.	
"Mother Hubur, who can form everything,	
"Added countless invincible weapons,	
gave birth to monster serpents,	(20)
"Pointed of fang, with merciless incisors(?),	
"She filled their bodies with venom for blood.	
"Fierce dragons she clad with glories,	
"Causing them to bear auras like gods, (saying)	
'Whoever sees them shall collapse from weakness!	(25)
'Wherever their bodies make onslaught,	

---

1. With Bottéro, "Création," 36. One could also understand "on account of Apsu" or "against Apsu" (= in that case the domain of Ea).

they shall not turn back!'

"She deployed serpents, dragons, and hairy hero-men,

"Lion monsters, lion men, scorpion men,

"Mighty demons, fish men, bull men,

"Bearing unsparing arms, fearing no battle. (30)

"Her commands were absolute, no one opposed them,

"Eleven indeed on this wise she created.

"From among the gods her offspring,
> who composed her assembly,

"She raised up Qingu from among them,
> it was he she made greatest!

"Leadership of the army, command of the assembly, (35)

"Arming, contact, advance of the melee,

"Wardenship of the (spoils?) of battle,

"(All) she entrusted to him, made him sit on the dais.

> 'I cast your spell. I make you the greatest in the assembly
> > of the gods,
> 'Kingship of all the gods I put in your power. (40)
> 'You are the greatest, my husband, you are illustrious.
> 'Your command shall always be greatest,
> > over all the Anunna-gods.'

"She gave him the tablet of destinies,
> had him hold it to his chest, (saying)

> 'As for you, your command will not be changed, your
> > utterance will be eternal.
> 'Now that Qingu is the highest
> > and has taken [supremacy], (45)
> 'And has [ordained] destinies for his divine children,
> 'Whatever you (gods) say shall cause fire to [subside],
> 'Your concentrated venom shall make the mighty one yield.'"

(Anshar flies into a passion at Ea, blaming him for what has transpired. Ea defends himself by pointing out the necessity of Apsu's murder. Anshar thereupon orders Ea to subdue Tiamat. Ea is unable to do so, so Anshar sends out Anu, who is likewise unable. This situation was no doubt anticipated by Ea, who is waiting to produce his favorite son from the wings. This provides the opportunity for Marduk to take his place and to make his great demand.)

[When Anshar heard] the speech, he was deeply distressed,*

He cried out "Woe!"; he bit his lips, (50)

His spirits were angry, his mind was uneasy,

His cries to Ea his offspring grew choked,

"My son, you yourself were instigator of battle!

"Do you bear the consequences of your own handiwork!

"You went forth and killed Apsu, (55)

"So Tiamat, whom you have enraged,

  where is one who can face her?"

The sage counsellor, wise prince,

Producer of wisdom, divine Nudimmud,

Answered his father Anshar gently,

With soothing words, calming speech, (60)

"My father, inscrutable, ordainer of destinies,

"Who has power to create and destroy,

"O Anshar, inscrutable, ordainer of destinies,

"Who has power to create and destroy,

"I will declare my thoughts to you, relent for a moment, (65)

"Recall in your heart that I made a good plan.

"Before I undertook to kill Apsu,

"Who had foreseen what is happening now?

"Ere I was the one who moved quickly to snuff out his life,

"I indeed, for it was I who destroyed him,

  [wh]at was there?[1] (70)

When Anshar heard this, it pleased him,

He calmed down, saying to Ea,

"Your deeds are worthy of a god,

"You can(?) [ ] a fierce, irresistible stroke,

"Ea, your deeds are worthy of a god, (75)

1. Following al-Rawi and George, *Iraq* 52 (1990), 151.

"You can(?) [   ] a fierce, irresistible stroke,
"Go then to Tiamat, sub[due] her onslaught,
"May her anger [be pacified] by [your] magic spell."
When he heard the command [of his father] A[nshar],
He set off, making straight his way,   (80)
Ea went to seek out Tiamat's stratagem.
He stopped, horror-stricken, then turned back.
He came before Anshar the sovereign,
He beseeched him with entreaties, saying,
"[My father], Tiamat has carried her actions beyond me,   (85)
"I sought out her course, but my spell cannot counter it.
"Her strength is enormous, she is utterly terrifying,
"She is reinforced with a host, none can come out against her.
"Her challenge was in no way reduced but overwhelmed me,
"I became afraid at her clamor, I turned back.   (90)
"My father, do not despair, send another to her,
"A woman's force may be very great, but it cannot match a man's.
"Do you scatter her ranks, thwart her intentions,
"Before she lays her hands on all of us."
Anshar was shouting, in a passion,   (95)
To Anu his son he said these words,
"Stalwart son, valiant warrior,
"Whose strength is enormous, whose onslaught is irresistible,
"Hurry, take a stand before Tiamat,
"Soothe her feelings, let her heart be eased.   (100)
"If she will not listen to what you say,
"Say something by way of entreaty to her, so that she be pacified."
When he heard what his father Anshar said,
He set off, [made str]aight his way,
Anu went to seek out Tiamat's stratagem.   (105)
He stopped, horror-stricken, then turned back.
He came before [Ansha]r, [his father who begot him],
He beseeched him with entreaties, s[aying],
"My father, Tiamat has carried her actions beyond me,
"I sought out her course, but my s[pell cannot counter it].   (110)
"Her strength is enormous, she is utterly terrifying,
"She is reinforced with a host, none can [come out against] her.

"Her challenge was in no way reduced, but overwhelmed me.

"I became afraid at her clamor, I turned back.

"My father, do not despair, send another to her, (115)

"A woman's strength may be very great,
    but it cannot match a man's.

"Do you scatter her ranks, thwart her intentions,

"Before she lays her hands on all of us."

Anshar fell silent, gazing at the ground,

Nodding towards Ea, he shook his head. (120)

The Igigi-gods and Anunna-gods were all assembled,

With lips closed tight, they sat in silence.

Would no god go out [at his] command?*

Against Tiamat would none go as [he] ordered?

Then Anshar, father of the great gods, (125)

His heart was angry, he [would not summon] anyone!*

(Ea summons Marduk privately and informs him that his hour is now come. He enjoins him to present himself respectfully before his great-grandfather as a volunteer in time of crisis. Ea does not explicitly advise Marduk what price to set on his services, as the poet makes that come from the heart of Marduk himself. Marduk is warmly received by the elder gods and his offer to be champion is willingly accepted. Now Marduk offers his terms: if he is to save all the gods, he is to become their supreme, unquestioned leader, always.)

The mighty firstborn, champion of his father,

Hastener to battle, the warrior Marduk

Did Ea summon to his secret place,

Told him his secret words,[1] (130)

"O Marduk, think, heed your father,

"You are my son who can relieve his heart!

"Draw nigh, approach Anshar,

"Make ready to speak. He was angry,
    seeing you he will be calm."* (135)

The Lord was delighted at his father's words,

He drew near and waited upon Anshar.

1. Uncertain. While this could be a reference to magic words (CAD K, 36a; AHw, 420a ["wish"]), it could as well refer to Marduk's demand, 122-129.

When Anshar saw him, his heart was filled with joyful feelings,
He kissed his lips, he banished his gloom.
"My father, let not your lips be silent but speak,   (140)
"Let me go, let me accomplish your heart's desire.
"[O Anshar], let not your lips be silent but speak,
"Let me go, let me accomplish your heart's desire!
"What man is it who has sent forth his battle against you?"
"[My son], Tiamat, a woman,
        comes out against you to arms."   (145)
"[My father], creator, rejoice and be glad,
"Soon you will trample the neck of Tiamat.
"[Anshar], creator, rejoice and be glad,
"Soon you will trample [the neck] of Tiamat!"
"[Go], son, knower of all wisdom,   (150)
"Bring Tiamat to rest with your sacral spell.
"Make straight, quickly, with the storm chariot,
"Let it not veer from its [course], turn (it) back!"*
The Lord was delighted at his grandfather's words,
His heart was overjoyed as he said to his grandfather,   (155)
"Lord of the gods, of the destiny of the great gods,
"If indeed I am to champion you,
"Subdue Tiamat and save your lives,
"Convene the assembly, nominate me for supreme destiny!
"Take your places in the Assembly Place of the Gods,[1]
        all of you, in joyful mood.   (160)
"When I speak, let me ordain destinies instead of you.
"Let nothing that I shall bring about be altered,
"Nor what I say be revoked or changed."

1. Ubshu-ukkenna, a cosmic locality, called "abode of counsel" in IV.37d line 28.

Tablet III

(Anshar convokes the gods for this purpose, commissioning his vizier, Gaga, to wait upon Lahmu and Lahamu to tell them the story of Tiamat's threat and Marduk's offer. Lahmu and Lahamu are terrified. They and the other gods convene, eat and drink liberally, and in the festive mood of a reunion, they surrender their authority to Marduk.)

Anshar made ready to speak,   (1)
Saying to Gaga his vizier these words,
"Gaga, vizier who contents me,
"Let it be you that I send off towards Lahmu and Lahamu.
"You know how [to find a way] you can make a fine speech.   (5)
"Send over to my presence the gods my ancestors,
"Let them bring all the gods before me.
"Let them converse, sit down at a feast,
"On produce of the field let them feed, imbibe of the vine.
"Let them ordain destiny for Marduk, their champion.   (10)
"Be off, Gaga, wait upon them,
"All that I tell you, repeat to them:

'It is Anshar your son who has ordered me to come,
'He has bade me speak in full the command of his heart,
'To wit:

"Tiamat our mother has grown angry with us,   (15)
"She has convened an assembly, furious with rage.
"All the gods rallied around her,
"Even those you created are going over to her side.
"They are massing around her, ready at Tiamat's side.
"Angry, scheming, never lying down night and day,   (20)
"Making warfare, rumbling, raging,
"Convening in assembly, that they might start hostilities.
"Mother Hubur, who can form everything,
"Added countless invincible weapons,
        gave birth to monster serpents,
"Pointed of fang, with merciless incisors(?),   (25)
"She filled their bodies with venom for blood.
"Fierce dragons she clad with glories,
"Causing them to bear auras like gods, (saying)

'Whoever sees them shall collapse from weakness!
'Wherever their bodies make onslaught,
    they shall not turn back.'   (30)

"She deployed serpents, dragons, and hairy hero-men,
"Lion monsters, lion men, scorpion men,
"Mighty demons, fish men, bull men,
"Bearing unsparing arms, fearing no battle.
"Her commands were absolute, no one opposed them.   (35)
"Eleven indeed on this wise she created.
"From among the gods her offspring,
    who composed her assembly,
"She raised up Qingu from among them,
    it was he she made greatest!
"Leadership of the army, command of the assembly,
"Arming, contact, advance of the melee,   (40)
"Wardenship of the (spoils?) of battle:
"All she entrusted to him, made him sit on the dais.

    'I cast your spell, I make you the greatest
        in the assembly of the gods,
    'Kingship of all the gods I put in your power.
    'You are greatest, my husband, you are illustrious,   (45)
    'Your command shall always be greatest,
        over all the Anunna-gods.'

"She gave him the tablet of destinies,
    had him hold it to his chest, (saying)

    'As for you, your command will not be changed,
        your utterance will be eternal.
    'Now that Qingu is the highest and has
        taken over [supremacy],
    'And has [ordained] destinies for his divine children,   (50)
    'Whatever you (gods) say shall cause fire to [subside],
    'Your concentrated venom shall make
        the mighty one yield.'

"I sent Anu, he could not confront her,
"Nudimmud was afraid and turned back.
"Marduk came forward,

> the sage of the gods, your son,   (55)
"He has resolved to go against Tiamat.
"When he spoke, he said to me,

> > 'If indeed I am to champion you,
> > 'Subdue Tiamat and save your lives,
> > 'Convene the assembly,
> > > nominate me for supreme destiny!   (60)
> > 'Take your places in the Assembly Place
> > of the Gods, all of you, in joyful mood,
> > 'When I speak, let me ordain destinies instead of you.
> > 'Let nothing that I shall bring about be altered,
> > 'Nor what I say be revoked or changed.'

> "Come quickly to me,
> > straightaway ordain him your destinies,   (65)
> "Let him go and confront your powerful enemy."

Gaga went and made straight his way
Towards Lahmu and Lahamu the gods his ancestors.
He prostrated, kissed the ground before them.
He stood up straight and said to them,   (70)
"It is Anshar your son who has ordered me to come,
"He has bade me speak in full the command of his heart:

> 'Tiamat our mother has grown angry with us,
> 'She has convened an assembly, furious with rage.
> 'All the gods rallied around her,   (75)
> 'Even those you created are going over to her side.
> 'They are massing around her, ready at Tiamat's side.
> 'Angry, scheming, never lying down night and day,
> 'Making warfare, rumbling, raging,
> 'Convening in assembly, that they might begin hostilities.   (80)
> 'Mother Hubur, who can form everything,
> 'Added countless invincible weapons,
> > gave birth to monster serpents,
> 'Pointed of fang, with merciless incisors(?),
> 'She filled their bodies with venom for blood.
> 'Fierce dragons she clad with glories,   (85)
> 'Causing them to bear auras like gods, (saying)

"Whoever sees them shall collapse from weakness!
"Wherever their bodies make onslaught
    they shall not turn back!"

'She deployed serpents, dragons, and hairy hero-men,
'Lion monsters, lion men, scorpion men,   (90)
'Mighty demons, fish men, bull men,
'Bearing unsparing arms, fearing no battle.
'Her commands were absolute, no one opposed them.
'Eleven indeed on this wise she created!
'From among the gods her offspring
    who composed her assembly,   (95)
'She raised up Qingu from among them,
    it was he she made greatest!
'Leadership of the army, command of the assembly,
'Arming, contact, advance of the melee,
'Division of the (spoils?) of battle:
'(All) she entrusted to him, made him sit on the dais.   (100)

    "I cast your spell and make you the greatest
      in the assembly of the gods,
    "Kingship of all the gods I put in your power.
    "You shall be the greatest, you are my only spouse,
    "Your name shall always be greatest,
      over all the Anunna-gods."

'She gave him the tablet of destinies, had him
    hold it to his chest, (saying)   (105)

    "As for you, your command will not be changed,
      your utterance will be eternal.
    "Now that Qingu is the highest
      and has taken over [supremacy],
    "And has [ordained] destinies for his divine children,
    "Whatever you (gods) say shall cause fire to [subside],
    "Your concentrated venom will make
      the mighty one yield."   (110)

'I sent Anu, he could not confront her,
'Nudimmud was afraid and turned back.
'Marduk came forward, the sage of the gods, your son,

'He has resolved to go against Tiamat.
'When he spoke, he said to me,   (115)

    "If indeed I am to champion you,
    "Subdue Tiamat and save your lives,
    "Convene the assembly,
        nominate me for supreme destiny!
    "In the Assembly Place of the Gods
        take your places, all of you, in joyful mood.
    "When I speak,
        let me ordain destinies instead of you.   (120)
    "Let nothing that I shall bring about be altered,
    "Nor what I say be revoked nor changed."

   'Hurry to me,
      straightaway ordain him your destinies,
   'Let him go and confront your powerful enemy.'"

When Lahmu and Lahamu heard, they cried aloud,   (125)
All of the Igigi-gods wailed bitterly,
"What (is our) hostility,
    that she has taken a[ct]ion (against) us?[1]
"We scarcely know what Tiamat might do!"
They swarmed together and came.
All the great gods, ordainers of [destinies],   (130)
Came before Anshar and were filled with [joy].
One kissed the other in the assembly [ ],
They conversed, sat down at a feast,
On produce of the field they fed, imbibed of the vine,
With sweet liquor they made their gullets run,   (135)
They felt good from drinking the beer.
Most carefree, their spirits rose,
To Marduk their champion they ordained destiny.

---

1. Or, "Why be opposed?" The second half of the line is problematic.

Tablet IV

(Marduk takes the throne and is hailed by all the gods in a coronation ceremony. Proof is administered of his supremacy. He is hailed as king, is given the trappings of royalty, chooses his weapons, and sets forth on his quest.)

They set out for him a princely dais,   (1)
He took his place before his fathers for sovereignty.
"You are the most important among the great gods,
"Your destiny is unrivalled, your command is supreme.
"O Marduk, you are the most important among the great gods,   (5)
"Your destiny is unrivalled, your command is supreme!
"Henceforth your command cannot be changed,
"To raise high, to bring low, this shall be your power.
"Your command shall be truth, your word shall not be wrong.
"Not one of the gods shall go beyond the limits you set.   (10)
"Support is wanted for the gods' sanctuaries,*
"Wherever their shrines shall be, your own shall be established.*
"O Marduk, you are our champion,
"We bestow upon you kingship of all and everything.
"Take your place in the assembly, your word shall be supreme. (15)
"May your weapon never strike wide but dispatch your foes.
"O Lord, spare his life who trusts in you,
"But the god who has taken up evil, snuff out his life!"
They set up among them a certain constellation,
To Marduk their first born said they (these words),   (20)
"Your destiny, O Lord, shall be foremost of the gods',
"Command destruction or creation, they shall take place.
"At your word the constellation shall be destroyed,
"Command again, the constellation shall be intact."
He commanded and at his word the constellation was destroyed, (25)
He commanded again and the constellation was created anew.
When the gods his fathers saw what he had commanded,
Joyfully they hailed, "Marduk is king!"
They bestowed in full measure scepter, throne, and staff,
They gave him unopposable weaponry that vanquishes enemies.   (30)
"Go, cut off the life of Tiamat,

"Let the winds bear her blood away as glad tidings!"
The gods, his fathers, ordained the Lord's destiny,
On the path to success and authority did they set him marching.
He made the bow, appointed it his weapon, (35)
He mounted the arrow, set it on the string.
He took up the mace, held it in his right hand,
Bow and quiver he slung on his arm.
Thunderbolts he set before his face,
With raging fire he covered his body. (40)
Then he made a net to enclose Tiamat within,
He deployed the four winds that none of her might escape:
South Wind, North Wind, East Wind, West Wind,
Gift of his grandfather Anu;[1] he fastened the net at his side.
He made ill wind, whirlwind, cyclone, (45)
Four-ways wind, seven-ways wind, destructive wind,
 irresistible wind:
He released the winds which he had made, the seven of them,
Mounting in readiness behind him to roil inside Tiamat.
Then the Lord raised the Deluge, his great weapon.
He mounted the terrible chariot,[2]
 the unopposable Storm Demon, (50)
He hitched to it the four-steed team, he tied them at his side:[3]

"Slaughterer," "Merciless," "Overwhelmer," "Soaring."
Their lips are curled back, their teeth bear venom,
They know not fatigue, they are trained to trample down.
He stationed at his right gruesome battle and strife, (55)
At his left the fray that overthrows all formations.

---

1. The gift refers to the four winds (see Tablet I lines 105-106), not the net. The original has an elaborate poetic structure that cannot be reproduced clearly in translation. "At his side" could also mean "on his arm" (Landsberger, JCS 21 [1967], 150 note 62).

2. Literally: "the storm chariot ..., the terrible one." A late bilingual fragment may preserve part of a hymn(?) to Marduk's chariot; see W. G. Lambert, "The Chariot of Marduk," *Studies Böhl*, 275-280.

3. Apparently the ends of the reins, normally held by an attendant, are here strapped to him, to keep both hands free for fighting. Balancing in a chariot with weapons in both hands and guiding a four-steed team by the belt is, of course, a heroic feat of the first order.

He was garbed in a ghastly armored garment,[1]
On his head he was covered with terrifying auras.
The Lord made straight and pursued his way,
Toward raging Tiamat he set his face.   (60)
He was holding a spell ready upon his lips,
A plant, antidote to venom, he was grasping in his hand.
At that moment the gods were stirring, stirring about him,
The gods his fathers were stirring about him,
        the gods stirring about him.

(Marduk approaches for battle while the gods hover fearfully near him. He is temporarily discomfited by the sight of the enemy. Tiamat intimates that Marduk's support is disloyal. Ignoring Qingu, he challenges her to single combat and indicts her for the contemplated murder of her own children. Stung to a fury, Tiamat herself advances for battle. Marduk kills her, destroys her forces, takes the tablet of destinies, and puts it on himself.)

The Lord drew near, to find out the intent(?) of Tiamat,   (65)
He was looking for the stratagem of Qingu her spouse.
As he looked, his tactic turned to confusion,[2]
His reason was overthrown, his actions panicky,
And as for the gods his allies, who went at his side,
When they saw the valiant vanguard, their sight failed them.   (70)
Tiamat cast her spell pointblank,
Falsehood, lies she held ready on her lips.*
"... lord, the gods rise against you,
"They assembled [where] they are, (but) are they on your side?"[3]
The Lord [raised] the Deluge, his great weapon,   (75)
To Tiamat, who acted conciliatory,[4] sent he (this word),
"Why outwardly do you assume a friendly attitude,
"While your heart is plotting to open attack?

1. This line is a remarkable example of alliteration, a device esteemed by this poet: *naḫlapti apluḫti pulḫāti ḫalipma.*

2. Marduk is temporarily discomfited by the sight of his enemy.

3. Uncertain. Tiamat evidently tells Marduk that the gods he is championing are actually disloyal to him. For a discussion of the battle between Marduk and Tiamat, see Jacobsen, JAOS 88 (1968), 104-108; Jacobsen interprets these lines quite differently, *The Treasures of Darkness* (New Haven, 1976), 177.

4. Or: "who was furious" (so CAD K 109a etc.); I follow Bottéro, "Creation," 46.

"Children cried out as their parents were deceitful,
"And you, their own mother, spurned all natural feeling.[1]   (80)
"You named Qingu to be spouse for you,
"Though he had no right to be, you set him up for chief god.
"You attempted wicked deeds against Anshar,
        sovereign of the gods,
"And you have perpetrated your evil against the gods my fathers.
"Though main force is drawn up,
        though these your weapons are in array,   (85)
"Come within range, let us duel, you and I!"
When Tiamat heard this,
She was beside herself, she turned into a maniac.
Tiamat shrieked loud, in a passion,
Her frame shook all over, down to the ground.   (90)
He was reciting the incantation, casting his spell,
While the gods of battle were whetting their blades.
Tiamat and Marduk, sage of the gods, drew close for battle,
They locked in single combat, joining for the fray.
The Lord spread out his net, encircled her,   (95)
The ill wind he had held behind him he released in her face.
Tiamat opened her mouth to swallow,
He thrust in the ill wind so she could not close her lips.
The raging winds bloated her belly,
Her insides were stopped up, she gaped her mouth wide.   (100)
He shot off the arrow, it broke open her belly,
It cut to her innards, it pierced the heart.
He subdued her and snuffed out her life,
He flung down her carcass, he took his stand upon it.
After the vanguard had slain Tiamat,   (105)
He scattered her forces, he dispersed her host.
As for the gods her allies, who had come to her aid,
They trembled, terrified, they ran in all directions,
They tried to make a way out(?) to save their[2] lives,

---

1. The precise significance of Marduk's remarks is not clear. While he may refer to Tiamat's natural goodwill towards her children (Tablet I lines 28, 46), it seems more likely that he refers to her insinuation that he had best beware the loyalty of those he championed.
2. Text has "his life."

There was no escaping the grasp that held (them)!   (110)
He drew them in and smashed their weapons.
They were cast in the net and sat in a heap,
They were heaped up in the corners, full of woe,
They were bearing his punishment, to prison confined.
As for the eleven creatures, the ones adorned with glories,   (115)
And the demonic horde(?), which all went at her side,
He put on lead ropes, he bound their arms.
He trampled them under, together with their belligerence.
As for Qingu, who was trying to be great among them,
He captured him and reckoned him among the doomed.   (120)
He took away from him the tablet of destinies
          that he had no right to,
He sealed it with a seal and affixed it to his chest.

(Splitting Tiamat's corpse in half, Marduk uses one piece to create the heavens. Her blood is borne off by the wind as evidence of her death. Marduk makes Esharra, an abode in heaven, as a counterpart of Apsu.)

Having captured his enemies and triumphed,
Having shown the mighty(?) foe subservient(?),[1]
Having fully achieved Anshar's victory over his enemies,   (125)
Valiant Marduk having attained what Nudimmud desired,
He made firm his hold over the captured gods,
Then turned back to Tiamat whom he had captured.
The Lord trampled upon the frame of Tiamat,
With his merciless mace he crushed her skull.   (130)
He cut open the arteries of her blood,
He let the North Wind bear (it) away as glad tidings.
When his fathers saw, they rejoiced and were glad,
They brought him gifts and presents.
He calmed down. Then the Lord was inspecting her carcass,   (135)
That he might divide(?) the monstrous lump
          and fashion artful things.
He split her in two, like a fish for drying,

---

1. This may refer to a triumphal parade.

Half of her he set up and made as a cover, (like) heaven.[1]
He stretched out the hide* and assigned watchmen,
And ordered them not to let her waters escape.   (140)
He crossed heaven and inspected (its) sacred places,[2]
He made a counterpart of Apsu,
      the dwelling of Nudimmud.
The Lord measured the construction of Apsu,
The Great Sanctuary, its likeness, he founded, Esharra.[3]
The Great Sanctuary, Esharra, which he built, (is) heaven,[4]
He made Ea, Enlil, and Anu dwell in their holy places.

1. That is, he made a cover to the watery deep that served as a "sky" for it.

2. For discussion of this line, see Moran, *Eretz Israel* 14 (1978), 35. Marduk models his new home after the domain of Ea, Apsu. "Sacred places" (*ašrātu*) is a difficult word; Lambert suggests it might mean something like "covering" (AfO 23 [1975], 43 and Tablet V line 121).

3. Esharra means "The House of Totality," the domain of Enlil. See Tablet IV line 145, V line 120, VI line 66 and Moran, AnBi 12 (1959), 264 note 2. For discussion of this passage and its cosmological implications, see W. G. Lambert in C. Blacker and M. Loewe, ed., *Ancient Cosmologies* (London, 1975), 55-58; Livingstone, *Explanatory Works*, 79-81.

4. Or, perhaps, "(is in) heaven."

Tablet V

(Marduk organizes the stars and planets and marks off years. He establishes his own planet, called Nebiru, as a marker for all the others in their motion. He regulates the moon, sun, weather, and subterranean waters. He links the various parts of the cosmos.)

He made the position(s) for the great gods,	(1)

He established (in) constellations the stars, their counterparts.[1]
He marked the year, described its boundaries,[2]
He set up twelve months of three stars each.[3]
After he had patterned the days of the year,   (5)
He fixed the position of Nebiru to mark the (stars') relationships.[4]
Lest any make an error or go astray,
He established the position(s) of Enlil and Ea in relation to it.[5]
He opened up gates on both (sides of her) ribs,*
He made strong bolts to left and right.   (10)
In her liver he established the zenith.
He made the moon appear, entrusted (to him) the night.
He assigned to him the crown jewel of nighttime
        to mark the day (of the month):
"Every month, without ceasing, start off with the (crescent) disk.
"At the beginning of the month, waxing over the land,   (15)
"You shine with horns to mark six days,
"At the seventh day, the disk as [ha]lf.

---

1. These lines and the following, especially 24, parallel a passage from the astrological omen series Enuma Anu Enlil, where the same proceedings are assigned to Anu, Enlil, and Ea. See Weidner, AfO 17 (1954/6), 89; Landsberger and Kinnier Wilson, JNES 20 (1961), 172; Rochberg-Halton, AfO Beiheft 22 (1988), 270-271. For translations of similar texts, see Bottéro, Mythologie, 491-496.

2. That is, laid out the ecliptic?

3. Babylonian astrolabes assign three stars to each month; here Marduk is portrayed as creating this pattern.

4. Refers to the daily rotation of the stars. For Nebiru, see J. Koch, "Der Mardukstern Nēberu," WdO 22 (1991) 48-72. The planet Mercury best fits the astronomical data, though Nebiru, in another tradition, could also have referred to Jupiter or the central area in the sky where Jupiter was to be found.

5. "It" refers to Nebiru, apparently in relation to the equator, rather than to the ecliptic. I am grateful to J. Britton for advice on astronomical matters. Variant substitutes Anu for Ea.

"At the fifteenth day, you shall be in opposition,
    at the midpoint of each [month].[1]
"When the sun f[ac]es you from the horizon of heaven,
"Wane at the same pace and form in reverse. (20)
"At the day of di[sappeara]nce, approach the sun's course,
"On the [   ] of the thirtieth day, you shall be in conjunction
    with the sun a second time.
"I d[efined?] the celestial signs, proceed on their path,
"[   ] approach each other and render (oracular) judgment.
"The sun shall [   ] ..., killing, oppression (25)
"[   ] me."
W[hen he   ]
The val[iant   ]
The sun [   ]
In [   ] (30)
"Let [   ]
"[   ]
"Let there arise no [   ]
"Let there be [   ]
"In [   ] (35)
"Da[ily   ]."
After [he had   ]
[   ]
He ma[de   ]
One year [   ] (40)
At New Year [   ]
(Another) year [   ]
"Let [   ]
"The doorbolt of sunrise [ ]."
After he had as[signed   ], (45)
[And fixed] the watches of night and day,
[   ] the foam of Tiamat,
Marduk created [   ]
He compacted (the foam) into c[louds] and made (them) billow.

---

1. For discussion, see Vanstiphout, JCS 33 (1981), 196-198; Livingstone, *Explanatory Works*, 39-40.

To raise the wind, to cause rainfall,   (50)
To make mists steam, to pile up her spittle (as snow?),
He assigned to himself, put under his control.
He set down her head and piled [   ]¹ upon it,
He opened underground springs, a flood was let flow(?).*
From her eyes he undammed the Euphr[ates] and Tigris,   (55)
He stopped up her nostrils, he left ...
He heaped up high-peaked mo[unt]ains from(?) her dugs.
He drilled through her waterholes to carry off the catchwater.
He coiled up her tail and tied it as(?) "The Great Bond."²
[   ] Apsu beneath, at his feet.   (60)
He set her crotch as the brace of heaven,
He set [half of] her as a roof, he established the netherworld.
[t]ask, he caused the oceans to surge within her.
[He spre]ad his net, let all (within) escape,
He formed the ... [   ] of heaven and netherworld,   (65)
Tightening their bond [   ] ...

*(Marduk distributes trophies, parades his defeated enemies, and is celebrated as
a returning hero.)*

After he had designed his prerogatives
        and devised his responsibilities,
He founded (their) [sanc]tuaries,* entrusted (those) to Ea.
[The tablet] of destinies, which he took from Qingu
        and brought away,
As the foremost gift he took away, he presented (it) to Anu.   (70)
The [   ] of battle, which dangled and fluttered about
        (in the net),
[   ] he led before his fathers.
[And as for] the eleven creatures which Tiamat created ...
He smashed their [wea]pons, he tied them to his feet.
He made images [of them] and set them up
        at the [Gate of] Apsu: (75)
"Lest ever after they be forgotten, let this be the sign."

---

1. On the basis of Tablet VII line 71 one may restore "mountain" here, but this is not assured.
2. That is, the link that holds heaven and the world below together.

When [the gods] saw, they rejoiced and were glad,
Lahmu, Lahamu, and all his fathers.
Anshar [embra]ced him,
     proclaimed (his) salutation (to be) "king."*
[A]nu, Enlil, and Ea gave him gifts, (80)
[   ] Damkina his mother made cries of joy over him,
She(?) made his face glow with (cries of) "Good …!"[1]
To Usmu,[2] who brought (Damkina's) gift at the glad tidings,
[He en]trusted the ministry of Apsu and care of the sanctuaries.
All the Igigi-gods together prostrated before him, (85)
[And] the Anunna-gods, all there are, were doing him homage,
The whole of them joined together to pay him reverence,
[Before him] they stood, they prostrated, "This is the king!"

*(Marduk cleans himself and dons his insignia. The gods swear allegiance to
him; he undertakes to maintain them.)*

[After] his fathers had celebrated him in due measure,
[   ] covered with the dust of battle. (90)
[   ] …
With cedar [oil] and [ ] he anoi[nted] his body,
He clothed himself in [his] princely [gar]ment,
The kingly aura, the awe-inspiring tiara.
He picked up the mace, he held it in his right hand, (95)
[   ] he held in his left hand.
[   ]
[   ] he made firm at his feet.
He set over [   ]
The staff of success and authority [he hung] at his side. (100)
After he [had put on] the aura of [his kingship],
His netted sack, the Apsu [ ] awesomeness.
He was seated like [   ]
In [his] throne room [   ]

1. This is evidently a congratulatory exclamation, with a play on Damkina and *dumqu* ("good").

2. Advisor or messenger god to Ea, a Janus-like figure with a double head; see R. M. Boehmer and W. G. Lambert, "Isimu," RLA 5, 178-181.

In his cella [   ]   (105)
The gods, all there are, [   ]
Lahmu and Lahamu [   ]
Made ready to speak and [said to] the Igigi-gods,
"Formerly [Mar]duk was 'our beloved son',
"Now he is your king, pay heed to his command."   (110)
Next all of them spoke and said,
"'Lugaldimmerankia' is his name, trust in him!"
When they had given kingship over to Marduk,
They said to him expressions of good will and obedience,
"Henceforth you shall be provider for our sanctuaries,   (115)
"Whatever you shall command, we will do."

(Marduk creates Babylon as the terrestrial counterpart of Esharra, abode of the gods in heaven. The gods are to repose there during their earthly sojourns.)

Marduk made ready to speak and said
(These) words to the gods his fathers,
"Above Apsu, the azure dwelling,
"Opposite Esharra, which I built above you,   (120)
"Below the sacred places, whose grounding I made firm,
"A house I shall build, my favorite abode.[1]
"Within it I shall establish its holy place,
"I shall appoint my (holy) chambers,
        I shall establish my kingship.
"When you go up from Apsu to assembly,   (125)
"Let your stopping places be there to receive you.[2]
"When you come down from heaven to [assembly],
"Let your stopping places be there to receive all of you.
"I shall call [its] name [Babylon], Abode of the Great Gods,
"We shall all hold fe[stival]s with[in] it."   (130)
When the gods his fathers heard what he commanded,
They ... [   ]

1. For discussion of this passage, see Livingstone, *Explanatory Works*, 80-81; W. G. Lambert, "Himmel," RLA 4, 411-412.

2. That is, when the gods or their cult images travel in Babylonia, they can find accommodation in specific chambers of the Babylonian temples.

"Over all things which your hands have created,
"Who has [authority, save for you]?
"Over the earth that you have created,   (135)
"Who has [authority, save for] you?*
"Babylon, to which you have given name,
"Make our [stopping place] there forever.
"Let them¹ bring us our daily portions,
"[   ] our [   ]."   (140)
"Whosoever shall [ ] our task which we [ ],
"In his place [ ] his toil [   ]."
[Marduk] rejoiced [   ]
The gods [   ] ... them.
... [   ] them li[ght].   (145)
He opened [   ] ... [   ]

(two lines fragmentary)

The gods prostrated before him, saying,
To Lugaldimmeran[ki]a, their lord, they [said],   (150)
"Formerly [we called you] 'The Lord, [our beloved] son,'
"Now 'Our King' ... [shall be your name],
"He whose [sacral] sp[ell] saved [our lives],
"[au]ra, ma[ce], and ne[t],
"[Ea?   ev]ery [sk]ill.   (155)
"Let him make the plans, we ... [   ]."

---

1. Who "they" refers to is disputed. It may refer to the defeated gods (Landsberger and Kinnier Wilson, JNES 20 [1961], 178-179); it may be impersonal, or it may refer proleptically to the Babylonians.

Tablet VI

(The rebellious gods are offered a general pardon if they will produce their leader. They produce Qingu, claiming that he started the war. He is sacrificed, and his blood is used to make a human being; compare Atrahasis [II.39] Tablet I lines 225ff.)

When [Mar]duk heard the speech of the gods,	(1)
He was resolving to make artful things:	
He would tell his idea[1] to Ea,	
What he thought of in his heart he proposes,	
"I shall compact blood, I shall cause bones to be,	(5)
"I shall make stand a human being, let "Man" be its name.	
"I shall create humankind,	
"They shall bear the gods' burden that those may rest.[2]	
"I shall artfully double the ways of the gods:	
"Let them be honored as one but divided in twain."[3]	(10)
Ea answered him, saying these words,	
He told him a plan to let the gods rest,[4]	
"Let one, their brother, be given to me,	
"Let him be destroyed so that people can be fashioned.	
"Let the great gods convene in assembly,	(15)
"Let the guilty one be given up that they may abide."	
Marduk convened the great gods in assembly,	
He spoke to them magnanimously as he gave the command,	
The gods heeded his utterance,	
As the king spoke to the Anunna-gods (these) words,	(20)
"Let your first reply be the truth!	
"Do you speak with me truthful words!	
"Who was it that made war,	
"Suborned Tiamat and drew up for battle?	

1. Literally: "his utterance," but to judge from the context, the utterance is so far purely internal.

2. From the necessity of providing for themselves; see Atrahasis (II.39 Tablet I lines 39ff.).

3. A reference to two main divisions of the Mesopotamian pantheon, Anunna-gods and Igigi-gods, or to the supernal and infernal deities (compare Tablet VI lines 39ff.).

4. The text assigns Marduk primacy in the creation of man by giving him the "idea," since Mesopotamian tradition, established centuries before this text was written, agreed that Ea/Enki had been the actual creator, along with the Mother Goddess.

"Let him be given over to me, the one who made war, (25)
"I shall make him bear his punishment, you shall be released."
The Igigi, the great gods answered him,
To Lugaldimmerankia, sovereign of all the gods, their lord,
"It was Qingu who made war,
"Suborned Tiamat and drew up for battle." (30)
They bound and held him before Ea,
They imposed the punishment on him and shed his blood.
From his blood he made mankind,
He imposed the burden of the gods and exempted the gods.
After Ea the wise had made mankind, (35)
They imposed the burden of the gods on them!
That deed is beyond comprehension,
By the artifices of Marduk did Nudimmud create!

(Marduk divides the gods of heaven and netherworld. The gods build Esagila,
Marduk's temple in Babylon.)

Marduk the king divided the gods,
The Anunna-gods, all of them, above and below, (40)
He assigned to Anu for duty at his command.
He set three hundred in heaven for (their) duty,
A like number he designated for the ways of the netherworld:
He made six hundred dwell in heaven and netherworld.
After he had given all the commands, (45)
And had divided the shares of the Anunna-gods
        of heaven and netherworld,
The Anunna-gods made ready to speak,
To Marduk their lord they said,
"Now, Lord, you who have liberated us,
"What courtesy may we do you? (50)
"We will make a shrine, which is to be called by name
"'Chamber that shall be Our Stopping Place,'
        we shall find rest therein.
"We shall lay out the shrine, let us set up its emplacement,
"When we come thither (to visit you), we shall find rest therein."
When Marduk heard this, (55)

His features glowed brightly, like the day,
"Then make Babylon the task that you requested,
"Let its brickwork be formed, build high the shrine."
The Anunna-gods set to with hoes,
One (full) year they made its bricks.   (60)
When the second year came,
They raised up Esagila, the counterpart of Apsu,
They built the high ziggurat of (counterpart-)Apsu,
For Anu-Enlil-Ea[1] they founded his house and dwelling.
Majestically he took his seat before them,   (65)
Its pinnacles were facing toward the base of Esharra.
After they had done the work of Esagila,
All the Anunna-gods devised their own shrines.

(The gods come to the new temple for a celebration. After a feast, they take their places to ordain destinies.)

The three hundred Igigi-gods of heaven
        and the six hundred of Apsu all convened.
The Lord, in the Highest Shrine,
        which they built as his dwelling,   (70)
Seated the gods his fathers for a banquet,
"This is Babylon, your place of dwelling.
"Take your pleasure there, seat yourselves in its delights!"*
The great gods sat down,
They set out cups, they sat down at the feast.   (75)
After they had taken their enjoyment inside it,
And in awe-inspiring Esagila had conducted the offering,
All the orders and designs had been made permanent,
All the gods had divided the stations
        of heaven and netherworld,
The fifty great gods took their thrones,   (80)
The seven gods of destinies were confirmed forever
        for rendering judgment.

---

1. The three divine names together may here be taken as a syncretism for Marduk; compare Tablet VII lines 136, 140, and below, p. 390 note 3. For discussion of this passage, see Moran, AnBi 12 (1959), 262.

(Marduk's bow becomes a constellation.)

The Lord took the bow, his weapon, and set it before them,
The gods his fathers looked upon the net he had made.
They saw how artfully the bow was fashioned,
His fathers were praising what he had brought to pass. (85)
Anu raised (it), speaking to the assembly of the gods,
He kissed the bow, "This be my daughter!"
He named the bow, these are its names:
"'Longwood' shall be the first,
    'Conqueror' shall be the second."
The third name, 'Bow Star', he made visible in heaven, (90)
He established its position
    with respect to the gods his brethren.

(Marduk is made supreme god. Anshar gives him a second name, Asalluhi. Anshar explains Marduk's role among gods and men with respect to this second name.)

After Anu had ordained the destinies of the bow,
He set out the royal throne
    which stood highest among the gods,
Anu had him sit there, in the assembly of the gods.
Then the great gods convened, (95)
They made Marduk's destiny highest, they prostrated themselves.
They laid upon themselves a curse (if they broke the oath),
With water and oil they swore, they touched their throats.[1]
They granted him exercise of kingship over the gods,
They established him forever for
    lordship of heaven and netherworld. (100)
Anshar gave him an additional name, Asalluhi,
"When he speaks, we shall all do obeisance,
"At his command the gods shall pay heed.
"His word shall be supreme above and below,
"The son, our champion, shall be the highest. (105)
"His lordship shall be supreme, he shall have no rival,

---

1. A symbolic slashing gesture meaning that they may die if they break the oath.

"He shall be the shepherd of the black-headed folk,[1]
> his creatures.
"They shall tell of his ways, without forgetting, in the future.
"He shall establish for his fathers great food offerings,
"He shall provide for them,
> he shall take care of their sanctuaries.   (110)
"He shall cause incense burners to be savored,
> he shall make their chambers rejoice.
"He shall make on earth the counterpart
> of what he brought to pass in heaven,
"He shall appoint the black-headed folk to serve him.
"Let the subject peoples be mindful
> that their gods should be invoked,
"At his command let them heed their goddess(es).   (115)
"Let their gods, their goddesses be brought food offerings,
"Let (these) not be forgotten, let them sustain their gods.
"Let their holy places be apparent(?),
> let them build their sanctuaries.[2]
"Let the black-headed folk be divided as to gods,
"(But) by whatever name we call him, let him be our god.[3]   (120)

(Beginning of the explanation of Marduk's fifty names. Names 1–9 are those borne by Marduk prior to this point in the narrative. Each of them is correlated with crucial points in the narrative as follows: (1) his birth, (2–3) his creation of the human race to provide for the gods, (4) his terrible anger but his willingness to spare the rebellious gods, (5) his proclamation by the gods as supreme among them, (6) his organization of the cosmos, (7) his saving the gods from danger, (8) his sparing the gods who fought on the side of Tiamat, but his killing of Tiamat and Qingu, and (9) his enabling the gods to proceed with the rest of what is narrated.)

---

1. The Mesopotamians.

2. The holy places show forth their own qualities of holiness so that mankind builds shrines there.

3. That is, Marduk is to be the one god of all the gods, no matter how many gods mankind may serve.

"Let us pronounce his fifty names,

"That his ways shall be (thereby) manifest, his deeds likewise(?):*

> (1) MARDUK!

"Who, from his birth, was named by his forefather Anu,

"Establisher of pasture and watering place,
> who enriches (their) stables,

"Who by his Deluge weapon subdued the stealthy ones,   (125)

"Who saved the gods his forefathers from danger.

"He is indeed the Son, the Sun,[1]
> the most radiant of the gods,

"They shall walk in his brilliant light forever.

"On the people whom he made,
> creatures with the breath of life,

"He imposed the gods' burden, that those be released.   (130)

"Creation, destruction, absolution, punishment:

"Each shall be at his command, these shall gaze upon him.

"(2) MARUKKA shall he be,
> the god who created them (mankind),

"Who granted (thereby) the Anunna-gods contentment,
> who let the Igigi-gods rest.

"(3) MARUTUKKU shall be the trust of his land,
> city, and people,   (135)

"The people shall praise him forever.

"(4) MERSHAKUSHU, angry but deliberative,
> furious but relenting,[2]

"Deep is his heart, all encompassing his feelings.

"(5) LUGALDIMMERANKIA is his name
> which we all pronounced,

"Whose commands we exalted above those
> of the gods his fathers.   (140)

---

1. See above, Tablet I lines 101f. and p. 357 note 2. For the name Marduk, see Sommerfeld, AOAT 213 (1982), 7ff.

2. The text construes MER = "angry," SHAKUSHU = "be appeased, calm." This contrast is developed more fully in the hymn to Marduk that opens the Poem of the Righteous Sufferer; see III.14 Tablet I lines 1ff.; III.12a lines 1ff.

"He shall be 'Lord of All the Gods
of Heaven and Netherworld',[1]
The king at whose revelations the gods above and below
stand in dread.
"(6) NADE-LUGALDIMMERANKIA
is the name we invoked, instructor of all the gods,[2]
"Who founded for us dwellings out of danger
in heaven and netherworld,
"And who divided the stations for the Igigi and Anunna-gods.   (145)
"At his name the gods shall tremble and quake
in (their) dwellings.
"(7) ASALLUHI is that name of his which Anu,[3]
his father, pronounced.
"He is the light of the gods, the mighty leader,
"Who, according to his name,
is protective spirit of god and land,
"And who in mighty single combat
saved our dwellings from harm.[4]   (150)
"Asalluhi they named secondly (8) NAMTILA,
god who maintains life,[5]
"Who, according to his nature, repaired the shattered gods,
"The lord who revived the moribund gods by his sacral spell,[6]
"Let us praise the destroyer of the wayward foes!
"Asalluhi, whose name was called thirdly (9) NAMRU,   (155)
"The pure god[7] who purifies our ways."
Anshar, Lahmu, and Lahamu named three each of his names,
They said to the gods their sons,

1. See Tablet V line 112, translation of Sumerian name.
2. Translation of Sumerian name.
3. One expects Anshar on the basis of Tablet VI lines 101 and 159. The substitution may have been intentional if the poet was trying to include the triad Anu-Enlil-Ea (see Tablet VII lines 136, 140).
4. Etymologizing elements in the name.
5. Interpretation of Sumerian name. It is unclear whether or not DINGIR should be construed as part of the proper name; variant has Namtilaku.
6. That is, saved the gods whom Tiamat would have killed (see p. 393 note 4).
7. Interpretation of NAMRU as Akkadian *namru* "shining," hence "pure" (see General Introduction, E.4).

"We have named three each of his names,
"Do you, as we have, invoke his names." (160)
Joyfully the gods heeded their command,
As they took counsel in the Assembly Place of the Gods,
"The valiant son, our champion,
"Our provider, we will exalt his name!"
They sat down in their assembly to name (his) destinies, (165)
In all their rites they invoked of him a name.

Tablet VII

(Deals with Marduk's three Asaru-names [10-12], his five Tutu-names [13-17], his six Shazu-names [18-23], his four Enbilulu-names [24-27], his two Sirsir-names [28-29]. Some of these reflect Marduk's role as a vegetation deity.)

"(10) ASARI, bestower of cultivation, who established surveys,   (1)
"Creator of grain and fibrous plants,
    who causes vegetation to sprout.[1]
"(11) ASARALIM, who is honored in the house of counsel,
    whose counsel excels,
"Whom the gods heed, without fear,[2]
"(12) ASARALIMNUNNA, the honored one,
    light of the father who begot [him],   (5)
"Who implements the decrees of Anu, Enlil, Ea, and Ninshiku.
"He is their provider who assigns their portions,
"Who increases abundance of the field for the land.[3]
"(13) TUTU is [he] who effected their restoration,
"He shall purify their shrines that they may be at rest,   (10)
"He shall devise the spell that the gods may be calm.
"Should they rise in anger, they shall turn [back].
"He shall be supreme in the assembly of the gods his [fathers],
"No one among the gods shall [make himself equal] to him.[4]
"Tutu is (14) ZIUKKENNA, life of [his] masses,   (15)
"Who established the holy heavens for the gods,

1. Commentary: RI = "bestower," RU = "bestow," SAR = "cultivation," A = "border," RA = "establish," RU = "creation," SAR = "grain" and "herbs," SAR read MA as "cause to sprout," and SAR = "vegetation."

2. Commentary: SA = "house," SA = "counsel," ALIM = "honored," SA = "excelling," SA = "counsel," DINGIR = "god," SA = "heed," SA = "fear," SA = "learn" (*i.e.*, "has not learned to fear").

3. Commentary to this name broken. Line 6 is puzzling because Ninshiku is normally an epithet of Ea, but is here referred to (erroneously?) as if a separate god.

4. Commentary: TU = "effect," TU = "restore," DA (implied phonetic complement to TU) = "he," TU = "purify," DU (rhyming sound) = "shrine," DA = "he," [DA]= "should," DU$_6$.DU(?) = "relieve," TU = "devise," TU = "spell," DINGIR = "god," TI (like TU) = "be at rest," TU = "be angry," DA = "should," TU = "rise," TU+DU = "turn back," DA = "should," DA = "lofty," elative "supreme," TA = "in, from among," TU = "assembly," DINGIR = "[god, father]."

"Who took control of where they went,
    assigned their stations,
"He shall not be forgotten by teeming mankind,
    [let them hold fast to] his [deeds].[1]
"Tutu they called thirdly (15) ZIKU, who maintains purity,
"God of the fair breeze,[2]
    lord who hears and accedes (to prayers),   (20)
"Producer of riches and wealth, who establishes abundance,
"Who turned all our want to plenty,
"Whose fair breeze we caught whiff of in our great danger,
"Let them ever speak of his exaltation,
    let them sing his praises![3]
"Tutu let teeming mankind
    magnify fourthly as (16) AGAKU,   (25)
"Lord of the sacral spell, reviver of the moribund,
"Who had mercy on the vanquished gods,
"Who removed the yoke imposed on the gods, his enemies,
"Who, to free them, created mankind,
"The merciful, whose power is to revive.   (30)
"Word of him shall endure, not to be forgotten,
"In the mouth of the black-headed folk,
    whom his hands have created.*[4]
"Tutu, fifthly, is (17) TUKU,
    his sacral spell shall ever be on their lips,

---

1. "Life of his host" = translation of Sumerian name; "establish" = play on Sumerian ukkenna ("in the assembly") and Akkadian *ukinnu* "which he establishes." Commentary: ZI = "[go = way?]," ZI = "[hold?]," ZU (=ZI+U) "[determine]," NA = "sta[tion]," TA = "must not," TU/ZI = (forget?), TA = "by, from among," UKKIN = "tee[ming mankind]," TU = "deeds," DU = "hold."

2. Literally: "Propitious wind," "(holy) spirit."

3. Commentary: DU = "create, name," ZI = "maintain," KU = "pure, purity," DINGIR = "god," TU = "wind," DU (rhymes with TU) = "fair," DINGIR = "lord," ZI = "listen, agree, produce," KU = "riches, abundance," ZI = "establish." Commentary breaks off here.

4. "Sacral spell" (translation of Sumerian) means primarily an incantation to revive the ill, a special concern of Marduk's, but here refers as well to the protective spell used against Tiamat, as in Tablet V line 153. The "revival" includes saving the gods from Tiamat, sparing the rebellious gods who were doomed to death, and the creation of mankind. How the other explanations were construed in the commentary is unknown. "Black-headed folk" refers to the Mesopotamians.

"Who with his sacral spell uprooted all the evil ones.
"(18) SHAZU, who knows the heart[1] of the gods, who
      was examining the inside,   (35)
"Lest he allow evildoers to escape from him,
"Who established the assembly of the gods,
      who contented them,
"Who subdued the unsubmissive,
      their (the gods') broad [pro]tection,
"Who administers justice, uproots twisted testimony,
"In whose place falsehood and truth are distinguished.[2]   (40)
"Shazu they shall praise secondly as (19) ZISI,
      who silenced those who rose (against him),
"Who banished paralyzing fear from the body
      of the gods his fathers,[3]
"Shazu is, thirdly, (20) SUHRIM,
      who uprooted all enemies with the weapon,
"Who thwarted their plots, turned them into nothingness,
"Who snuffed out all wicked ones,
      as many as came against him.[4]   (45)
"The gods shall ever be joyful in the assembly!
"Shazu is, fourthly, (21) SUHGURIM,
      who ensured obedience for the gods his fathers,
"Who uprooted the enemy, destroyed their offspring,
"Who thwarted their maneuvers, excepting none of them.
"His name shall be invoked and spoken in the land!"[5]   (50)

---

1. Translation of Sumerian name. The following clause may be read either as a general statement or as a reference to Tablet IV lines 65f., 110ff.

2. Commentary preserved for lines 37-40, construing [ZI] (like ZU) = "[establish]," [ŠA = "assem]bly" (semantic extension from 'within' to 'corporate body' easily made in Akkadian); DINGIR = "god," [ŠA] = "[goo]d," ŠA ="heart," Z[I = "sub]due, one who assents," ZU = "[pro]tect, broad, falsehood," ZI = "true, di[sti]nguish, [pl]ace."

3. Commentary lost. The first element ZI = "rise up, banish," SI = "silence, paralyzing fear," SI (like SU) for "body" (so Böhl, AfO 11 [1936/7], 204); "silences the attacker," (translation uncertain, AHw, 1177b), is evidently a translation of ZI.SI; a word play may underlie it.

4. Translation uncertain. Commentary not preserved. SUH = "uproot, thwart, turn back, extinguish(?)," RIM = "all" (etc.).

5. Presumed explanations similar to preceding. Note the progression of each name's sphere of recognition: "place" (18), "body of the gods" (19), "assembly" (20), and "land" (21), the first name as locus for action, the others loci for praise.

"Shazu later generations shall tradite fifthly as (22) ZAHRIM,
"Who destroyed all adversaries, all the disobedient,
"Who brought all the fugitive gods into their sanctuaries.
"This his name shall be the truth![1]
"To Shazu, moreover, they shall render all honor sixthly as
      (23) ZAHGURIM,   (55)
"He it is who destroyed all foes in battle.[2]
"(24) ENBILULU, lord who made them flourish, is he,
"The mighty one named by them, who instituted offerings,
"Who established grazing and watering places for the land,
"Who opened channels, apportioned abundant waters.[3]   (60)
"Enbilulu they shall [invoke] secondly as (25) EPADUN,
    lord of open country and flood(?),*
"Irrigator of heaven and earth, former of furrows,
    who formed the sacred(?) plowland in the steppe,
"Who regulated dike and ditch,
    who delimited the plowed land.[4]
"Enbilulu they shall praise thirdly as
    (26) ENBILULU-GUGAL,
    irrigator of the watercourses of the gods,
"Lord of abundance, plenty, high yields,   (65)
"Producer of wealth, enricher of all the inhabited world,
"Bestower of grain,* who causes barley to appear.
"Enbilulu is (27) HEGAL,
    who heaps up abundance[5] for the ...* peoples,
"Who rains prosperity over the wide earth,
    who makes vegetation flourish.
"(28) SIRSIR,
    who heaped up the mountain(s) above Tiamat,   (70)
"Who ravaged the corpse of Ocean with [his] weapon,
"Ruler of the land, their faithful shepherd,

---

1. Presumed explanations similar to the preceding.
2. Presumed explanations similar to the preceding.
3. Commentary lost. The first epithet is intended as a translation of the Sumerian name.
4. Commentary lost.
5. Epithet = translation of Sumerian name; other explanations not preserved.

"To whom have been granted* the cultivated field,
　　the subsistence field, the furrow,
"Who crossed vast Tiamat back and forth in his wrath,
"Spanning her like a bridge at the place of single combat.[1]　　(75)
"Sirsir they named secondly (29) MALAH, let it remain so,
"Tiamat is his vessel and he the boatman.[2]

(The remaining names are treated singly or in groups, beginning with the defeat of Tiamat and ascending to his proclamation as lord of the universe. Whereas his earlier names referred to his innate nature, his later ones commemorate his roles, accomplishments, and their outcome. Names 30-50 ascend in scope from earth to heaven.)

"(30) GIL, who stores up grain in massive mounds,
"Who brings forth barley and flocks,
　　grantor of the land's seed.[3]
"(31) GILIMMA, who established the bond of the gods,
　　creator of enduring things,　　　　　　　　　　　(80)
"The bridle(?)* that curbed them,
　　provider of good things.[4]
"(32) AGILIMMA, the lofty one, uprooter of flood waves(?),
　　who controls the sn[ow],
"Creator of the earth above the waters,
　　establisher of things on high.[5]
"(33) ZULUM, who assigned fields,
　　measured off tracts(?) for the gods,

1. This passage may contain mythological material about a little-known deity, Sirsir, that is here worked into the Marduk story by association and syncretism. Sirsir, made into a name of Marduk, evidently figured in a tradition in which he slew the ocean in single combat. For discussion, see Landsberger, WO 1 (1950), 362-366.
2. Malah = Akkado-Sumerian word for "boatman."
3. Commentary lost.
4. The sign GIL(IM) is two crossed reeds, here explained as a (celestial) linkage and restraint. "Good things" and "enduring things" could also mean "excellence" and "truth."
5. Commentary: IL = "lofty," MA = "tear up," GIL = "crown, tiara" (taking *agû* as "crown" rather than "wave" as here, so also CAD N/2, 4. If correct, "crown" could refer to the royal pretensions of the enemy?); GIL = "guide," (hence "provide"), "snow," MA = "create," IM = "cloud(?)," read in the commentary erroneously or with a different text as "ea[rth]," DINGIR = "hi[gh?]," MU = "waters" (bilingual pun), GI = "end[ure]."

"Grantor of portions and food offerings,
     tender of sanctuaries.[1]   (85)
"(34) MUMMU, creator of heaven and netherworld,
     who administers (their) offices.
"Divine purifier of heaven and netherworld,[2]
     is, secondly, (35) ZULUMMU,
"To whom no other among the gods was equal in strength.[3]
"(35) GISHNUMUNAB, creator of all people,[4]
     who made the world regions,
"Destroyer of the gods of Tiamat,
     who made mankind from parts of them.[5]   (90)
"(36) LUGALABDUBUR, the king who thwarted
     the maneuvers of Tiamat, uprooted [her] weapons,
"Whose support was firm in front and rear.[6]
"(37) PAGALGUENNA, foremost of all lords,
     whose strength was supreme,
"Who was greatest of the gods his brethren, lord of them all.[7]
"(38) LUGALDURMAH, king of the juncture of the gods,
     lord of the great bond,   (95)
"Who was greatest in the abode of kingship,
     most exalted among the gods.[8]
"(39) ARANUNNA, counsellor of Ea,
     fairest of the gods [his] fathers,

---

1. Commentary: ZU = "[know]" (transitively as "designate"), UL = "[fields]," ZU = "[measure off]," UL = "[forms]" (here: "tracts"); further explanations not preserved.

2. Explanations broken in commentary; "creator" = translation of Sumerian.

3. Commentary lost.

4. Commentary lost. NUMUN means "seed" or "semen," see Böhl, AfO 11 (1936/7), 206.

5. That is, "from something of them" = "their substance" or the like.

6. Commentary: [LUGAL = "king"], B[IR? = "thwart"], DU = "ac[tions]" = "maneuvers," AB = "Tiamat" (by extension from AB.BA "ocean"), BU = "root out," DU = "weapon," LU = "[who]," (commentary breaks off; [DUBUR = "foundation"]).

7. Preserved explanations are [DINGIR] = "god," [PA] = "brethren(?)," [GAL] = "great, hero," [GU] = "totality."

8. "King" and "lord" = translations of Sumerian. Commentary: LUGAL = "king, lord," DUR = "bond," DINGIR = "god," LU = "who," DUR = "in, dwelling," LUGAL = "king(ship)," MAH = "great(est)," DUR = "among," DINGIR = "god," MAH = "most, exalted."

"Whose noble ways no god whatever could equal.[1]

"(40) DUMUDUKU,

    whose pure dwelling is renewed in holy hill,

"son of holy hill, without whom the lord of holy hill

    makes no decision.[2]   (100)

"(41) LUGALSHUANNA, king whose strength

    was outstanding among the gods,

"Lord, strength of Anu, who became supreme

    at(?) the nomination(?) of Anshar.[3]

"(42) IRUGGA, who ravaged all of them amidst Tiamat,

"Who gathered all wisdom to himself, profound in perception.[4]

"(43) IRQINGU, ravager of Qingu, ... of battle,[5]   (105)

"Who took charge of all commands, established lordship.[6]

"(44) KINMA, leader of all the gods, grantor of counsel,

"At whose name the gods quake like a whirlwind for fear.[7]

"(45) ESIZKUR shall dwell aloft in the house of prayer,[8]

"The gods shall bring in their presents before him,   (110)

"While they receive their due.[9]

"None besides him can create artful things,

"The four black-headed folk are his creatures,[10]

"No god but he knows how long they will live.

"(46) GIBIL, who maintained the ... of the weapon,   (115)

---

1. Commentary: A.RA = "counsel(lor)," NUN = "Ea," RU = "creator," DINGIR = "god," A = "father," RA = "who," A.RA = "way," N[UN] = "[pr]ince," NU = "no," RU = "[equal]," (breaks off).

2. "Holy Hill," part of the Marduk temple in Babylon. Commentary lost. Dumu-Duku means "Son of Holy Hill" and Lugal-Duku "King of Holy Hill" (the latter refers to Ea).

3. Commentary lost; perhaps LUGAL = "king," LU = "who," AN = "among," (etc.), SU = "strength(?)."

4. IR = "ravage," GU = "all," [IR] = "amidst(?)," [GU] = "all," [GI = "wisdom"], [UR = "gath]er," [GI = "perception, profound"].

5. Variant: "like an enemy"; Bottéro, "en plein combat." The passage remains uncertain.

6. Commentary lost; IR = "ravage."

7. Or perhaps "quake (as in a) whirlwind." Commentary lost.

8. "House of Prayer" = translation of Sumerian name. Commentary partially preserved, e.g., IL = "high," RA = "in," E = "house," SIZKUR = "prayer," RA = "dwell," DINGIR = "god," (rest fragmentary).

9. The gods bring gifts and receive their income, with chiastic word play on "before him/receive" and "bring in/income ('dues')."

10. That is, the people of the four points of the compass.

"Who because of the battle with Tiamat can create artful things,
"Profound of wisdom, ingenious in perception,
"Whose heart is so deep
      that none of the gods can comprehend it.[1]
"(47) ADDU shall be his name, the whole sky he shall cover,
"His beneficent roar shall thunder over the earth,   (120)
"As he rumbles, he shall reduce the burden of the clouds,
      Below, for the people, he shall grant sustenance.[2]
"(48) ASHARU, who, according to his name,
      mustered the gods of destinies,
"He has taken all peoples in his charge.[3]
"(49) NEBIRU shall hold the passage of heaven and earth,
"So they shall not cross above and below without heeding him, (125)
"Nebiru is his star which he made visible in the skies.
"It shall hold the point of turning around,
      they shall look upon him,
"Saying, 'He who crossed back and forth,
      without resting, in the midst of Tiamat,
'Nebiru ("Crossing") shall be his name,
      who holds the position in its midst.'
"He shall maintain the motions of the stars of heaven,   (130)
"He shall herd all the gods like sheep.
"He shall keep Tiamat subdued, he shall keep her life cut short,
"In the future of mankind, with the passing of time,

---

1. Commentary: GI = "[be permanent]" (factitively "establish"), ... [LU = "who"], RA = "[in]," IR = "[battle]," MA = "T[iamat]" (from mu, Akkadian word for water?), RU = "c[reate, do something artful]," GI = "p[rofound], wi[sdom]," RU = "[do]," GI = "p[erception]," I[R = "heart, remote]," RA = "[whose, not]," [IR? = "comprehend"] (breaks off). For line 115, Bottéro, 59 suggests "*l'issue de la guerre.*"

2. Commentary mostly lost.

3. Commentary mostly lost. "Muster" in the Akkadian is a word homophonous with the name.

"She shall always be far off, she shall be distant forever."[1]
Because he created "places" and fashioned the netherworld,   (135)
Father Enlil has pronounced his name (50) Lord of the World,[2]
The Igigi-gods pronounced all the names.
When Ea heard (them), he was joyful of heart,
He said, "He whose name his fathers have glorified,
"His name, like mine, shall be 'Ea.'[3]   (140)
"He shall provide the procedures for all my offices,
"He shall take charge of all my commands."
With the name "Fifty" the great gods
Pronounced his fifty names, they made his way supreme.[4]

(Composition and purpose of this text, its approval by Marduk.)

They must be grasped: the "first one"[5] should reveal (them),   (145)
The wise and knowledgeable should ponder (them) together,
The master should repeat, and make the pupil understand.
The "shepherd," the "herdsman" should pay attention,[6]
He must not neglect the Enlil of the gods, Marduk,
So his land may prosper and he himself be safe.   (150)
His word is truth, what he says is not changed,

---

1. The text etymologizes *nebiru* as *nebēru* "crossing, passage." Commentary: DINGIR = "star," RA = "which, in," DINGIR = "heaven," E = "visible, splendid," RA = "shall, hold," KUN.SAG.GA = "front-back," DINGIR = "front," RU = "back," RU = "look upon," MA = "saying, son," RA = "which, in," IR = "inside," MA = "ocean" (see above, p. 399 note 1), BU = "cross," RA = "not," BI = "resting, his name" (from Sumerian mu-bi "its name"), RA = "shall," NEBIRU = Nebiru; RA = "hold," IR = "within," RA = "which," DINGIR = "star, heaven," RA = "go, be permanent," IR "like," RI = "sheep, shepherd" (from Akkadian *rē'û*, shepherd?), DINGIR = "god," IR = "heart," ŠA = "heart, all (of them)," IR = "subdue," MA = "ocean, ..." ŠI = "li[fe]," RIM = "be sh[ort]" (life).

2. The commentary glosses "places" as "heaven"; RU = "create, fashion." For "lord of the world" (that is, "lands"), the commentary has MA = "name," A = "father." "Lord of the Lands" = "Enlil," meaning that Enlil has given Marduk his own name (as Ea does in the succeeding lines). The commentary continues through line 139 as if 137-139 were part of the explanation of "Lord of the World," or at least could be used for such an explanation.

3. Marduk is now made god of wisdom and magic.

4. Marduk is here assigned the number fifty. In Mesopotamian scribal practice, the number 50 was used to write the name of Enlil, so herewith Marduk has replaced Enlil as supreme deity; see p. 357 note 3.

5. See General Introduction, D.3.

6. Kings and other rulers.

Not one god has annulled his utterance.
If he frowns, he will not relent,
If he is angry, no god can face his rage.
His heart is deep, his feelings all encompassing,   (155)
He before whom crime and sin must appear for judgment.
The revelation (of the names) which the "first one"
        discoursed before him (Marduk),
He wrote down and preserved for the future to hear,
The [wo]rd of Marduk who created the Igigi-gods,
[His/Its   ] let them [   ], his name let them invoke.   (160)
Let them sound abroad* the song of Marduk,
How he defeated Tiamat and took kingship.

Text: W. G. Lambert and S. Parker, *Enuma Eliš, The Babylonian Epic of Creation* (Oxford, 1966).
I have used this standard text and have indicated only a few variants. Tablet II is based on
al-Rawi and George, *Iraq* 52 (1990), 150, 152. Additional fragments have been listed by Borger,
HKL 2, 151-152; see also Vanstiphout, *Nabu* 1987/70 and W. G. Lambert, *Nabu* 1987/100.
Edition: R. Labat, *Le Poème babylonien de la création* (Paris, 1935). Tablet II is edited by al-Rawi
and George, *Iraq* 52 (1990), 149-157; Tablet V by Landsberger and Kinnier Wilson, JNES 20
(1961), 154-179. I have benefited from Lambert's profound knowledge of this text, as well as
from detailed comments by Moran on an earlier version of this translation.
Translation: A. Heidel, *The Babylonian Genesis*[2] (Chicago, 1951); Speiser and Grayson, ANET[3],
60-72, 501-503; Labat, *Religions*, 36-70; Dalley, *Myths*, 228-277. I am particularly indebted to
the treatment by J. Bottéro, "L'Epopée de la Création," *Documents Centre Thomas More* 79/5, 29-
60, see also *Mythologie*, 602-679.
Literature: In general, see Borger, HKL 1, 259-260; HKL 2, 151-152; J. Bottéro, *Annuaire* 1975/
6, 70-126; D. O. Edzard, "Schöpfung," WdM, 121-124; T. Jacobsen, *The Treasures of Darkness*
(New Haven, 1976), Chapter 6; "The Battle Between Marduk and Tiamat," JAOS 88 (1968),
104-108; A. Kragerud, "The Concept of Creation in Enuma Elish," in *Ex Orbe Religionum,
Studia Geo. Widengren, Pars Prior* (Leiden, 1972), 39-49; R. Labat, "Les origines et la formation
de la Terre, dans le poème babylonien de la création," AnBi 12 (1959), 205-215; W. G. Lambert,
"A New Look at the Babylonian Background of Genesis," *The Journal of Theological Studies NS*
16 (1965), 287-300. For the names of Marduk, the following two studies have been used, but
will prove a challenge to the non-specialist reader: F. M. Th. de L. Böhl, "Die fünfzig Namen des
Marduk," AfO 11 (1936/7), 191-217; J. Bottéro, "Les Noms de Marduk," *Studies Finkelstein*, 5-28.
Notes to Text: (I 2) Hutter, RA 79 (1985), 187-188. (I 6) Held, AOAT 25 (1968), 233-237; for
the syntax of this and the first ten lines, Moran, *Nabu* 1988/21; Buccellati, *Studies Moran*, 125-
128. (I 110) Translation uncertain; I take *šariša* to stand for *šarišam*. (II 49) Reading *dal-pa*, though
one can also read *dal-ḫat* "the matter was confused." (II 123f., 126) al-Rawi and George, *Iraq* 52
(1990), 157. (IV 72) Borger, RA 72 (1980), 96. (IV 125) With AHw, 976a; see CAD M/2, 304.

(IV 139) Reading *mašku*. CAD M/1, 342a suggests *parku* "dividing line." (V 9) See Heimpel, JCS 38 (1986), 134. (V 54) Emending: *a-<gu>-ú*. The text of the second half of the line is obscure; see AHw, 1207b. (V 68) WLM: [*èš-r]e-ti*; for the plural of *uṣurtu* one would expect *uṣrāti*. (V 136) After Bottéro, "Création," 50. (VI 73) Reading *wšb* with WLM. Others read *šebû* "have a sufficiency of"; compare CAD N/1, 124a; Bottéro, "Création," 54. (VI 118) Unclear, for suggestions see CAD M/1, 419b and CAD A/2, 204b; AHw, 634b. (VI 122) I follow CAD A/1, 298a ("likewise"), Bottéro, "Création," 54. (VII 61) Translation uncertain, see CAD A/2, 518. (VII 67) So AHw, 1294b, but the parallel in Tablet VII 79 suggests that *šâ* "sheep" could here be meant. (VII 68) Word of uncertain meaning, see AHw, 987b. (VII 73) Translation uncertain, I follow CAD M/2, 24e rather than AHw, 1192a and Bottéro, "Création," 58. (VII 81) CAD L, 113a; others, "yoke" or "hoop." (VII 161) Collation by Lambert, CAD M/1, 367b.

III.18 DESCENT OF ISHTAR TO THE NETHERWORLD

In this poem, Ishtar decides to visit the netherworld and demands to be admitted. Her sister, Ereshkigal, queen of the netherworld, is suspicious and jealous, and instructs her gatekeepers to remove all of Ishtar's clothing as she enters. As she enters the netherworld naked, her sister sets upon her sixty disease demons and she dies. Sexual reproduction vanishes from the world; the gods need a way to bring Ishtar back to life. Ea, god of wisdom, sends a male prostitute to the netherworld, who so pleases Ereshkigal by adroit flattery that she grants him any wish. He asks for the body of Ishtar, as instructed by Ea. The enraged queen gives up the body, but dooms the prostitute to a squalid earthly existence. Ereshkigal orders the death god to bring someone else in Ishtar's stead and at the same time to get revenge on Ishtar. The death god finds Ishtar's lover, Tammuz, removes all signs of mourning for Ishtar's death from him, and gives him a ring and a flute to play on. The next part of the story is omitted in the Akkadian text, perhaps presumed as understood. When Ishtar returns from the netherworld to find her lover dallying with harlots and not in mourning, in a fit of jealous passion she offers him to the netherworld in her stead. In lines 131ff. the text switches abruptly to Tammuz's sister Belili, who, when she hears the wailing for her dead brother, institutes a ceremony for the dead.

This composition, known from two manuscripts from Assurbanipal's library, and an earlier, variant version from Assur, may have emerged from a Sumerian original. The present text is shorter than the Sumerian version of the same story, with large pieces omitted. The final episode of the text is so elliptical as to be incomprehensible to the modern reader. To him, the Akkadian text will seem poorly conceived in comparison to its Sumerian forerunner. In any event, the story is not without drama and narrative art.

For the Sumerian background of this composition, see S. N. Kramer, "Inanna's Descent to the Nether World: Continued and Revised," JCS 5 (1951), 1-17; *The Sacred Marriage Rite* (Bloomington, IN, 1969), 107-133; "The Third Tablet of the Ur Version of 'Inanna's Descent to the Nether World'," PAPS 124 (1980), 299-310. For a retelling of the Sumerian poem, see D. Wolkstein and S. N. Kramer, *Inanna, Queen of Heaven and Earth: Her Stories and Hymns from Sumer* (New York, 1983), 52-73.

To the netherworld, land of n[o return],[1]   (1)
Ishtar, daughter of Sin, [set] her mind.
Indeed, the daughter of Sin did set [her] mind
To the gloomy house, seat of the ne[therworld],
To the house which none leaves who enters,   (5)
To the road whose journey has no return,
To the house whose entrants are bereft of light,
Where dust is their sustenance and clay their food.
They see no light but dwell in darkness,
They are clothed like birds in wings for garments,   (10)
And dust has gathered on the door and bolt.
When Ishtar reached the gate of the netherworld,
She said (these) words to the gatekeeper,
"Gatekeeper! Open your gate for me!
"Open your gate for me that I may enter!   (15)
"If you will not open the gate that I may enter,
"I will break down the door, I will smash the bolt,
"I will break down the frame, I will topple the doors.[2]
"I will raise up the dead to devour the living,
"The dead shall outnumber[3] the living!"   (20)
The gatekeeper made ready to speak,
Saying to the great one,[4] Ishtar,
"Stay, my lady, do not cast it down.[5]
"Let me go announce your name to the queen E[resh]kigal."
The gatekeeper went in and said to Ereshkigal,   (25)
"Here is your sister Ishtar at [your gate],
"She who holds the great skip-rope,[6]
        who roils up the deep before Ea the [king?]."
When Ereshkigal heard this,
Her face went pallid as a cut-down tamarisk,
Her lips went dark as the lip of a vat.*   (30)

1. Translation of Sumerian word for netherworld. See also III.19b iii.
2. A adds: "I will smash the 'balance' and tear off the knob."
3. Variant: "I will make the dead outnumber ..."
4. Variant: "the lady."
5. Or: "Do not leave it."
6. Symbol of the warlike Ishtar (Landsberger, WZKM 56 [1960], 121ff.).

"What made her resolve on me?
    What has aroused bad feelings in her against me?*
"Here now, shall I drink water
    with the (netherworld) Anunna-gods,
"Shall I eat clay for bread, shall I drink dirty water for beer?
"Shall I weep for the young men who have left [their] helpmeets?
"Shall I then weep for the young women
    who are wrenched from lovers' loins?   (35)
"Shall I weep for the helpless infant
    who was taken before its time?[1]
"Go, gatekeeper, open [your] gate to her,
"Treat her according to the age-old rules."
Off went the gatekeeper and opened [the] gate to her,
"Enter, my lady, that Cutha[2] rejoice over you,   (40)
"That the palace of the netherworld be glad at your presence."
He brought her in the first gate,
    he ... and removed the great tiara of her head.
"Why, gatekeeper, did you remove the great tiara of my head?"
"Enter, my lady.
    Thus the rules of the mistress of the netherworld."
He brought her in the second gate, he ...
    and removed the earrings of her ears.   (45)
"Why, gatekeeper, did you remove the earrings of my ears?"
"Enter, my lady.
    Thus the rules of the mistress of the netherworld."
He brought her in the third gate,
    he ... and removed the beads of her neck.
"Why, gatekeeper, did you remove the beads of my neck?"
"Enter, my lady.
    Thus the rules of the mistress of the netherworld."   (50)
He brought her in the fourth gate,
    he ... and removed the pectorals of her breast.
"Why, gatekeeper, did you remove the pectorals of my breast?"

---

1. That is, if Ishtar succeeds in her plan, Ereshkigal will join the dead, instead of being their queen? Bottéro, *Mythologie*, suggests that lines 32-36 are Ishtar's thoughts, as imagined by Ereshkigal.
2. Cult center of Nergal, god of the netherworld.

"Enter, my lady.
    Thus the rules of the mistress of the netherworld."
He brought her in the fifth gate, he ... and removed
    the girdle of birth stones of her waist.
"Why, gatekeeper, did you remove the girdle of birth
    stones of my waist?"   (55)
"Enter, my lady.
    Thus the rules of the mistress of the netherworld."
He brought her in the sixth gate,
    he ... and removed her bracelets and anklets.
"Why, gatekeeper, did you remove my bracelets and anklets?"
"Enter, my lady.
    Thus the rules of the mistress of the netherworld."
He brought her in the seventh gate,
    he ... and removed the loincloth of her body.   (60)
"Why, gatekeeper, did you remove the loincloth of my body?"
"Enter, my lady.
    Thus the rules of the mistress of the netherworld."
As soon as Ishtar had entered the netherworld,
Ereshkigal saw her and trembled with fury at her.
Ishtar, without thinking, sat(?) (in the place of honor) above her.* (65)
Ereshkigal made ready to speak, and said
To Namtar her vizier these words,
"Go, Namtar, [take her from] my presence!
"Let loose against her sixty di[seases   ] Ishtar,
"Eye disease [against] her [eyes],   (70)
"Side disease a[gainst] her [sides],
"Foot disease a[gainst] her [feet],
"Heart disease a[gainst her heart],
"Head disease [against her head],
"I [let them loose?] against all of her!"   (75)
After the lady Ishtar [went down] to the netherworld,
The bull would not mount the cow,
    [the ass would not impregnate the jenny],
The [young man would not impregnate] the girl
    in the thoroughfare,
The young man slept in [his bedroom?],

The g[irl s]lept [by herself].   (80)

Papsukkal, vizier of the great gods,

       was downcast and his features [were gloomy].

He was dressed in mourning and [left] his hair unkempt.

Off went he in despair before Sin his father, weeping,

Before Ea the king[1] [his] tears flowed down.

"Ishtar has gone down to the netherworld, she has not come up. (85)

"As soon as Ishtar went down to the netherworld,

"The bull will not mount the cow,

       the ass will not impregnate the jenny,

"The young man will not impregnate the girl in the thoroughfare,

"The young man has slept in his [bedroom?],

"The girl has slept by herself."   (90)

Ea, in his wise heart, conceived (what was) called for,[2]

He created Asushunamnir, an impersonator.[3]

"Go, Asushunamnir, make your way to the netherworld,

"Let the seven gates of the netherworld be opened before you.

"Let Ereshkigal see you and feel well-disposed towards you.   (95)

"When she calms and her feelings are well disposed,

"Have her swear the oath of the great gods,[4]

"Look up and set your mind on the waterskin,

"'Oh, my lady, let them give me the waterskin,

       that I may drink water from it.'" [5]

When Ereshkigal heard this,   (100)

She smote her thigh, she bit her finger.

"You asked of me[6] the unaskable!

"Come, Asushunamnir, I will curse you a great curse,

---

1. A omits "king."

2. A: w[ord?]. The Akkadian word (*zikru*) is of disputed meaning in the sense used here. It may imply something commanded or required for a specific situation: Reiner, "stratagem," Bottéro, "*idée*."

3. Male prostitutes or transvestites were devotees of Ishtar. It is not clear how such a person could avoid being held by the netherworld. Perhaps a male in female costume "partook of both worlds" or could pass anywhere as an itinerant entertainer. The name means "He is resplendent as he comes forth." A has the name as Asnamir.

4. A adds a line here, too broken to read, which refers to a "midwife" and "creatress."

5. A section seems to have been omitted here by the scribe, consisting of the narrative recapitulation of lines 93-99.

6. A adds Asnamir.

"Let me ordain you a fate never to be forgotten.[1]
"May bread of the city bake-women* be your food,
"May the city crockery be your drink.   (105)
"The shadow of a wall be your station,
"The threshold be your dwelling.
"May drunk and sober slap your cheek!"
Ereshkigal made ready to speak,
Saying these words to Namtar her vizier,   (110)
"Go, Namtar, knock at the Egalgina,[2]
"Decorate the thresholds with cowrie shells.
"Bring out and seat the (netherworld) Anunna-gods
        on thrones of gold,
"Sprinkle Ishtar with water of life
        and take her from(?) my presence."
Namtar went and knocked at the Egalgina,   (115)
He decorated the thresholds with cowrie shells,
He brought out and seated the (netherworld) Anunna-gods
        on thrones of gold,
He sprinkled Ishtar with water of life and brought her away.[3]
He brought her out the first gate
        and returned to her the loin cloth of her body,
He brought her out the second gate and returned to her
        her bracelets and anklets,   (120)
He brought her out the third gate and returned to her
        the girdle of birth stones of her waist,
He brought her out the fourth gate
        and returned to her the pectorals of her breast,
He brought her out the fifth gate
        and returned to her the beads of her neck,
He brought her out the sixth gate
        and returned to her the earrings of her ears,
He brought her out the seventh gate
        and returned to her the great tiara of [her h]ead.   (125)

1. This clause in A only.

2. As construed in the Nineveh version, evidently a palace in the netherworld. A has DI.LI.GI.NA.

3. A adds three broken lines: (a) "Go, Namtar [ ] (the god) [ ]/ (b) "[I]f she does not pay [you] her ransom, bring her back." / (c) Namtar [ ] her [ ]. Compare below, line 126.

"If she does not pay you her ransom, bring [her] back here.
"Tammuz, her childhood lover,
"Bathe in a bath of pure water and a[noint with] fine oil,
"Dress him in a red garment,
      let him strike up a lapis flute [... a carnelian ring?],
"Let prostitutes turn [his] mood." [1]   (130)
[The lady] Belili was put[ting right?] her jewelry,
[   ] eyestones with which she filled her l[ap?].
When she heard the wailing for her brother,
      Belili smote the jewelry of her body,
The eyestones which filled the Wild Cow's face(?).*
"Do not rob me of my only brother!   (135)
"On the day Tammuz (says) "Hurrah!"*
      the lapis flute and carnelian ring (say) "Hurrah!"
"With him (say) "Hurrah!" the wailing men and wailing women,
"Let the dead come up and smell the incense."[2]

Text: (N)ineveh: King, CT 15 45-48; CT 34 18; (A)ssur: Ebeling, KAR 1, collated Borger, HKL 2, 55; (C) = Ebeling-Köcher-Rost, LKA 62, rev 10-20. Some variants, such as in formulae of direct speech, are not noted here, nor is text C.
Edition: Borger, BAL 2, 86-91.
Translation: Speiser, ANET[3], 106-109; Reiner, *Poetry*, 29-49, including Text C; Bottéro, *Mythologie*, 318-324; Dalley, *Myths*, 155-162.
Literature: Borger, HKL 1, 96, 227; G. Buccellati, "The Descent of Inanna as a Ritual Journey to Kutha?" *Syro-Mesopotamian Studies* 4/3 (1982), 3-7; A. Kilmer, "How Was Queen Ereshkigal Tricked? A New Interpretation of the Descent of Ishtar," UF 3 (1971), 299-309; Reiner, *Poetry*, 29-49 (literary analysis of the whole poem); Bottéro, *Annuaire* 1971/2, 79-97; *Mythologie*, 325-330.
Notes to Text: (30) Obscure. Perhaps *šapat* is a reinterpretation of *ṣbt* "strike," by attraction of *šaptu* "lip" in the same line. *kuninu* may refer to a brewing vat, or, as Reiner suggests, *Poetry*, 37, a plant (reed?). The original image may therefore be that of a bruised or smashed-down reed. (31) *uš-tam-ṭa-an-ni* (WGL); *uš-per-da-an-ni* (CAD K, 13b, Borger, etc.). (65) *uš-bi*. See, e.g., CAD E, 85a. The meaning of the word is unknown. (104) I follow Reiner, *Languages and Areas: Studies Presented to George V. Bobrinskoy on the Occasion of His Academic Retirement* (Chicago, 1967), 116-117; *Poetry*, 44-45. (134) von Soden, ZA 58 (1967), 194. (136) Differently other translations, e.g., CAD E, 122a; Reiner, *Poetry*, 47, which have "On the day Tammuz comes up to me, with him will come up ..." I follow a suggestion of Lambert's, who sees in *el-le-an-ni* a word for a shout or cry (for references, including its use in the Tammuz cult, see CAD E, 101b).

1. I assume here a gap in the narrative, including a narrative recapitulation of 127-130, Ishtar's catching sight of him, and Tammuz's removal to the netherworld by Namtar.
2. The meaning may be that when Tammuz emerges with a joyful shout from the netherworld, the dead will rise too. One has here, apparently, an aetiology for some cult festival. For further information, see Notes to Text to line 136.

III.19 NERGAL AND ERESHKIGAL

The poem of Nergal and Ereshkigal relates how Nergal became king of the netherworld. The story hinges on the isolation and sexual frustration of the queen of the netherworld, Ereshkigal. This aspect of the tale is related with warmth, even humor.

Whereas the outline of the story is fairly well known (see below), considerable portions of text are still missing. A short Middle Babylonian version (A+B) is known from a manuscript discovered at El-Amarna in Egypt. This text is not only badly damaged but was written by someone not familiar with Akkadian, so contains numerous aberrant spellings and obscure words.

A large eighth-century manuscript (C) from Sultantepe contributes the most to our understanding, but this too was heavily damaged and contains many obscurities. A Neo-Babylonian manuscript from Uruk (D), treated here with C, restores a few episodes and lines. C and D clearly belong to the same tradition, and A+B to a different one. Because of the complicated interrelationships of these versions, an interpretive outline by numbered episodes is provided below.

1. (= A+B 1-6, C i 6'-15'). The celestial gods give a banquet and send a messenger to Ereshkigal, queen of the netherworld, inviting her to send up a messenger to receive her share. In C i 16'-37' the messenger of Anu, Gaga, descends to the netherworld, greets Ereshkigal, and relates the message. In C i 38'-50' Ereshkigal and Gaga exchange civilities.

2. (= A+B 7, C i 51'-56'). Ereshkigal sends off Namtar, her messenger, up to heaven to get her food portion.

3. (= A+B 8-12). Namtar comes into the celestial court to collect the food. All the gods show him respect (A+B: stand up; C: kneel) in deference to his mistress — all except one, Nergal. The incident itself is not well preserved. One may hypothesize that Namtar did not accept the food under these conditions but returned to the netherworld empty-handed. Ereshkigal, in mortification, refuses to sit on her throne and exercise judgment over the netherworld. The gods are thrown into consternation. In C ii 1'-11', Ea is remonstrating with Nergal, demanding to know why he showed no respect despite his cues that Nergal pretended not to see. Nergal's reply, C ii 18'-20', is lost in a break. He evidently announces his intention to go the netherworld,

either as an act of defiance or to set things right again; in the earlier version he is being summoned for execution.

4. (= C ii 21'-35'). Ea resolves to take advantage of this for some purpose that is lost in a break. Perhaps he had decided that Nergal should be king. In any case, he gives instructions as to how to avoid execution at the hands of the angry goddess. He commissions Nergal to make a throne out of various kinds of wood that are painted to imitate precious materials.

5. (= C ii 36'-48'). Ea enjoins Nergal not to accept any of the norms of hospitality in the netherworld, and not to become aroused when he sees Ereshkigal strip for her bath.

6. (= C ii end - C iii 8'). Nergal descends to the netherworld. This part of the text uses the same language as the Descent of Ishtar (III.21) and is quotation of a stock motif.

7. (= C iii 9'-22'). The gatekeeper, in reply to Nergal's call, goes to his mistress and informs her that there is a visitor whose identity he does not know. Namtar volunteers to go identify the visitor. To his astonishment, he recognizes the very god who showed no respect when he came for the food.

8. (= C iii 23'-29'). Namtar tells Ereshkigal the story of her slight in heaven once again.

9. (= C iii 30'-37'). Ereshkigal orders Namtar to take her place as ruler of the netherworld, but not to attempt any heroics or usurpation; she will go up herself to get her food. Given the state of the text, the logic of her rejoinder is not readily apparent. One expects this exchange to have been the climax of Episode 3 above, and its presence here may be owing to a repetitive expansion of the text. Or does the queen believe that Nergal has been sentenced to die for his offense, and so sees a way out of her impasse?

10. (= C iii 38'-60'). Nergal is admitted to the netherworld, announces to Ereshkigal that the supernal deities have sent him to ask her to resume her offices, and declines all offer of hospitality. When she strips for her bath, he remains unmoved.

11. (= C iv 4'-20'). After a gap in the text, Ereshkigal is found stripping again for her bath. This time, however, Nergal is aroused; they embrace and become passionate lovers. After six days of love-making, Nergal arises early and urges Ereshkigal not to be concerned. She drifts back to sleep.

12. (= C iv 21′-32′). Nergal is released from the netherworld by tricking the gatekeeper, and reascends to heaven. The gods are astonished. Certain that a hue and cry will be raised, Ea disguises Nergal by deforming him.

13. (= C iv 33′-45′). Ereshkigal rises in a leisurely way, enjoys a bath, and calls that the rooms be freshened and breakfast served.

14. (= C iv 46′-59′). Namtar breaks the news to her that her lover has absconded. Sobbing, she laments bitterly that she wants him back. Namtar, touched, vows to go up to heaven, find him, and bring him back.

15. (= C v a-30′). Ereshkigal dispatches Namtar with a double plea. She asks pity first of all, for she has never had a lover, and, as queen of the dead, has never enjoyed the pleasures of childhood. She wants her lover back. Then her plea turns to threat: not only will she not exercise her offices, she will raise up the dead to devour the living. Namtar ascends to heaven with her message.

16. (= C v 31′-41′). Namtar examines the gods, all of whom, it seems, are careful to receive him respectfully this time. He sees no one unusual except the deformed Nergal, whom he fails to recognize. He returns empty-handed. Ereshkigal, however, sees through the ruse and sends him back to fetch down the deformed god.

17. (= C v 42′-54′). Namtar returns to heaven but is still unable to find Nergal, this time perhaps because he has resumed his normal shape?

18. (= C vi 1′-42′). After a gap in the text, Nergal is being told by Ea(?) that he can take over dominion of the netherworld if he proceeds as instructed. He is to take the throne he made, and, instead of yielding his clothing at each of the gates to the netherworld, he is to surrender a piece of it(?) to the gatekeeper so that he will not enter Ereshkigal's court naked (and hence dead?). Nergal uses this strategy to enter her court, apparently without forewarning. He yanks Ereshkigal from her throne and they become passionate lovers again, this time for seven full days and nights.

19. (= C vi 43′-51′). Anu sends Gaga to announce that Nergal is king of the netherworld forever.

Comparison of the two versions of the story is instructive for understanding the formation and expansion of Akkadian literary works (see also Reiner, *Poetry*, 55f.). A+B foreshortens episodes 4-16 such that the initial snub is treated as the cause of Ereshkigal's sending up Namtar to bring back the offending god that she may execute him. In A+B Ea arms Nergal with seven plagues that he stations by each of the seven gates to the netherworld. They hold the gates open while he makes a rush for Ereshkigal, yanks her from her throne, and makes ready to decapitate her. She submits and proposes marriage. They reign happily thereafter as king and queen.

One need not conclude that C is an expansion of A+B. Rather, A+B is perhaps a drastic shortening of some earlier version now lost, while C is perhaps an expansion of a different earlier version, also lost. One may suggest that the expansion and revision of the story developed its motif of sexuality, and in fact makes this the cause of Nergal's triumph, rather than his derring-do, as in A+B. This expansion worked in liberal quotations from the same material used in the Descent of Ishtar, though in each instance with an interesting reversal of their application. Furthermore, the exchanges of messengers are expanded to nearly the fullest potential of repetition of speech and action (see General Introduction, C.4 and E.3). Although in both versions the triumph of Nergal was engineered by Ea, who presumably had reasons of his own for wishing Nergal to be king in the netherworld, C omits the plagues given Nergal in A+B as his weapon, and uses instead the throne, though the implication of this episode eludes me. Does the gatekeeper think in each case that the imitations of precious substances are adornment of Nergal rather than pieces of a chair? In short, this is the same story, but told differently in different sources.

(a) MIDDLE BABYLONIAN VERSION

(A, B)

When the gods held a banquet,   (1)
They sent a messenger
To their sister, Ereshkigal,
"We cannot come down to you,
"Nor can you come up to us.   (5)
"Send here that they may take your food portion."
Ereshkigal send Namtar her messenger.
Up went N[amtar] to high heaven,
He entered [the place] the gods were [se]ated(?).
They inter[rupted their talk?, stood, re]cei[ved] Namtar,   (10)
The messenger of their great sister.
They set out [food and drink],
     "Let him t[ake] her [food por]tion."
The gods ... [   ]
[he   to] his mistress
[   ] she was weeping and sobbing

(fragmentary lines, then gap)

Ea [   ] ...
He to[ok   ] ...
"Go to [our great] sister [   ] ...   (25)
Saying, "Where is the [one who] did not stand
     [in the presence of] my [mes]senger?
"Bring him to m[e] that I may kill him."
Namtar came to speak to the gods,
They summoned him and the gods spoke with him, dea[th],
"Find the god who did not stand in your presence,   (30)
"Take him before your mistress."
Namtar counted them; a god in the back was bald.
"The god who did not stand in my presence is not here."
Namtar went to [give] his report,
[Saying, "   I counted] them,   (35)
"[A god] in back [was bald],

"[The god who did not stand in my presence] was not there."

[   ]

[   ] her [mess]enger

[   ]   (40)

Ea [   ] which he seized(?),

"... one [in]to the power of [Ereshkigal].

"Take (him) to Ereshkigal!"

We[eping, he went] before Ea his father,

"When she sees [me], she will not let me live."

"Do not fe[ar her ...],   (45)

"I will give you seven and seven wa[tchers?]*

"To go with you: [Id ..., ..., ..., Mutabriqu,[1]]

"Sharabdu, [Rabisu,[2] Tirid, Idibtu[3]],

"Ben[nu,[4] Sidanu,[5] Miqit,[6] Beluri],

"Umma, [Libu,[7] shall go] with you."   (50)

[Nergal went and, as he stood at the g]ateway
        of Ereshkigal, he called,

"G[atekeeper, open] your gate,

"Free the lock that I may enter,

"I am sent to the presence of your mistress Ereshkigal."

Off went the gatekeeper and said to Namtar,

"A certain god is standing at the gateway,   (55)

"Come and examine him that he may come in."

Out went Namtar, when he saw him ...
        he said [to his mis]tress,

"My lady, [it is the god who] month[s] a[go] disappeared

"And did not stand [in my pre]sence."

"Bring him in, [le]t him come here that I may kill [him]."   (60)

Out went Namtar, [saying], "Enter, [my] lord, [   ]

"Into your sister's house. Re[cei]ve your deserts [   ]."

---

1. "Lightning Flash."
2. "Lurker."
3. "Wind."
4. "Epilepsy."
5. "Vertigo."
6. "Collapse" (a disease).
7. A disease symptomized by spots on the skin and high fever.

[... said] Nergal, "May [you] be well-disposed
    towards me [   ]."

(gap)

He stationed Id[   ] at the first, [   ] at the second,
[   ] at the third, Mutabriqu at the fourth,
[Sha]rabdu at the fifth, Rabisu at the sixth,
Tirid at the seventh, Idibtu at the eighth,   (70)
Bennu at the ninth, Sidanu at the tenth,
Miqit at the eleventh, Beluri at the twelfth,
Umma at the thirteenth, Libu at the fourteenth gate ...
He cut down Namtar in the courtyard, ordering his troops:
"Let the gates stand open! Now I will run by you!"   (75)
In the palace he seized Ereshkigal by her hair,
He bent her down from the throne to the ground
    to cut off her head.
"Don't kill me, my brother! Let me say a word to you!"   (80)
When Nergal heard her, he released his grip.
She was weeping and sobbing,
"You be my husband, I will be your wife!
"Let me make you hold dominion
    over the vast netherworld,
"Let me set the tablet of wisdom in your hand,
"You be lord, I be lady!"   (85)
When Nergal heard this that she said, he seized her
    and kissed her, wiping away her tears,
"Whatever you have wished for from me
    for these months (past)!"
  ...*

(end of tablet)

(b) LATE VERSION

(C, D)

i

[Anu made ready to speak], (5′)
[Saying to Gaga his messenger],
"[Let me send you, Gaga, to the Land of No Return],
"[To the house of Ereshkigal who dwells in the netherworld],
"[Saying],

'[You are not able to come up],
'[Not (once) in a year can you come up before us]. (10′)
'[We cannot go down],
'[Nor (once) in a month can we descend before you].
'[Let your messenger come here],
'[Let him remove food from the table,
    let him receive your serving].
'[Whatever I give him, let him bring safely to] you.'" (15′)

[Gaga descended the long staircase] of heaven.
[When] he reac[hed the gate of Ereshkigal he said],
"[Gatekeeper], o[pen] the gate [to me]."
"[Enter, Gaga], may the gate ble[ss you]."
He brought [the god G]aga in [the first gate], (20′)
He brought [the god] Gaga [in the second] gate,
He brought [the god] Gaga [in the third] gate,
He brought the god Gaga in the fourth gate,
He brou[ght] the god Gaga in the fifth gate,
He br[ough]t the god Gaga in the sixth gate, (25′)
He br[ough]t the god Gaga in the seventh gate.
He entered her b[roa]d courtyard,
He knelt and k[issed] the ground before her.
He straightened, stood, and said to her,
"Anu [your] father has sent [me], (30′)
"Saying,

'You are not able to come up,
'Not (once) in a year can you come up before us.
'We cannot go down,
'Nor (once) in a month can we descend before you.
'Let your messenger come here,   (35')
'Let him remove food from the table,
        let him receive your serving,
'Whatever I give him, let him bring safely to you.'"

Ereshkigal made ready to speak, saying to G[aga] (these) words,
"Messenger of Anu our father, who has come to us,
"(I hope) all is well with Anu, Enlil, and Ea, the great gods?   (40')
"(I hope) all is well with Nammu and Nanshe,[1] the pure gods?
"(I hope) all is well with the husband of the Mistress of Heaven?
"(I hope) all is well with Nin[urta, mightiest] in the land?"
Gaga made ready to speak, saying to Ereshkigal these words,
"All is well with Anu, Enlil, and Ea, the great gods,   (45')
"All is well with [Namm]u and Nanshe, the pure (gods),
"All is wel[l with the husband of the M]istress of Heaven,
"All is we[ll] with Ni[nurt]a, the mightiest in the land."
[G]aga made ready to speak, saying to Ereshkigal these words,
"[   ] may all be well with you."   (50')
[Ereshkigal] made ready to speak, saying to Namtar,
        her messenger, these words,
"Nam[tar], my [messenger], let me send yo[u to] heaven
        to Anu our father.
"Namtar, go up the long [staircase of heaven],
"Take food from the table, [receive my serving].
"Whatever Anu shall give [you, you must bring safely to me]."   (55')
[Namtar went up the long staircase of heaven]

(gap)

ii

[Ea made ready to speak, saying to Nergal these words],
"[   ]   (1')

---

1. As Gurney suggests (AnSt 10 [1960], 111 note 16), the "Nash" of the text may be a form of Nanshe, a Sumerian goddess. Nammu was a Sumerian mother goddess.

"[When he a]rrived a[t   ]
"[   ] the path [   ]
"[The gods] all k[nelt before] him,
"[The great god]s, lords of destin[ies],   (5')
"[For he] bore the authority, the authority [of the gods],
"[The gods] who dwell in the netherworld.
"Why were you not [kneeling] before him?
"[   ] I kept winking at you,
"But you were [affe]cting not to be aware.   (10')
"[You were not ...], y[our] e[yes] were looking at the ground."

                              (gap)

[Nergal made ready to speak, saying to Ea these words],
"Let me proceed [   ]
"[   ] what you said.
"[   ] ... I will twine it double."   (20')
When Ea heard this, he said to himself,
"[Let me bring it] about that I entrust(?) ..."[1]
Ea made ready to speak, saying to Nergal these words:
"Wayfarer, do you wish to go on your mission with a ...
        thorn(?) in your hand?
"Go down to the forest of sissoo-trees(?),   (25')
"Cut down sissoo(?), whitewood(?), cedar(?),
"Cut off f[rankincense?] and staffs."
[He went down to the forest of sissoo-trees?],[2]
[He cut sissoo(?), whitewood(?),[3] and c]edar(?)
He cut off frankincense(?) and fruit trees,   (30')
He made [a work], a throne of Ea, the leader.[4]
[In imitation of] silver he colored with gypsum(?),
In imitation of lapis he colored with faience,
In imitation of gold he made multicolored
        with cobalt(?) and potash(?).*

---

1. Uncertain. Ea evidently wishes to ensure that Nergal will survive the journey to the netherworld.
2. D adds: "He lifted the axe in his hands, he [dr]ew the sword from his belt."
3. C: "Apple."
4. C: "[ ] and Ningizzida."

The work was complete, the throne done.   (35')
Then he (Ea) summoned him to give his instructions,
"Wayfarer, if you wish to go,
"[Take to] heart whatever instructions I [give you].[1]
"When you arrive there,
"When they bring you a chair,
"Do not proceed to sit upon it.   (40')
"When the baker brings you bread, do not proceed to eat.
"When the butcher brings you meat, do not proceed to eat.
"When the brewer brings you beer, do not proceed to drink.
"When someone brings water for your footbath,
        do not proceed to wash your [feet].
"When she goes in to bathe,   (45')
"And puts on her [   ] garment,
"She will let you see her body ...
"You must not [become arous]ed as man and woman."
Nergal [   ]

                        (gap)

[To the netherworld, Land of No Return],
[Nergal set his mind ...]
[To the gloomy house, seat of the netherworld],
[To the house which none leaves who enters],

                        iii

[To the road whose journey] has no return,   (1')
[To the house who entrants] are bereft of light,
[Where dust is their sustenance and] clay their food.
[They are clothed like bi]rds in wings for garments,
[They see no light] but dwell in darkness,   (5')
[   ] moaning,
[they moan] like [do]ves.
[   ] ...
[The gatekeeper made ready to speak],
        saying to Nergal these words,

---

1. Variant omits.

"I shall take back report [concerning the wayfarer
      standing] at the gate." (10′)
[The gatekeeper went in to Ereshkiga]l to say (these) words,
"[Mistress, a certai]n [wayfarer] has com[e to us],
"[Wh]o will [identify?] him?"

(gap)

(Namtar is speaking.)

"[let me] identify him.
"[I will look at] him outside the gate,
"I shall take back report [ ] to my mistress."[1]
Namtar went and looked at Erra [through the ...] of the gate, (20′)
Namtar's face went pallid as a cut-down tamarisk,
His lips went dark as the lip of a vat.[2]
Namtar went to [his] mis[tress] to say (these) words,
"Mistress, that time you sent me [to] your father,
"When I entered the court of [Anu], (25′)
"[All the gods   ] knelt humbly,
"[The gods of the land] knelt humbly ...
"The god who kept on st[anding] in my presence[3]
"Is now come down to the Land of No Return."
[Ereshkigal made ready to speak, saying]
      to [Namtar, her messenger, (these) words], (30′)
"Namtar, you must not strive for divine supremacy,
      nor let your spirit imagine deeds of valor.
"Go up and take your seat on the throne, the royal dais,
"Do you render the judgments of the vast netherworld.
"Let me go up to the heaven of Anu my father,
      that I may eat the food of Anu my father,
"And drink the beer of Anu my father. (35′)
"Go, Namtar, bring that god into my presence."
Namtar went and brought in the god Erra.
When he entered the first gate, Pituh,

1. Text: "Lord."
2. See Descent of Ishtar (III.18) lines 29f. with note to text.
3. 28′-29′ and 35′ff. from D iii 2′ff. and 5′ff.

When he entered the second gate, Enkishar,
When he entered the third gate, Endashurimma,   (40′)
When he entered the fourth gate, Nerulla,
When he entered the fifth gate, Nerubanda,
When he entered the sixth gate, Endukuga,
When he entered the seventh gate, Ennugigi,
He entered her spacious court,   (45′)
He knelt and kissed the ground before her,
He straightened, stood, and said to her,
"Anu your father sent me to your presence,

   'Do you (be the one to) sit on this throne
   'And render the judgments of the great gods,
   'The great gods who dwell in the netherworld.'"   (50′)

As soon as he came, they brought him a chair,
He did not proceed to sit upon it.
The baker brought him bread,
   he did not proceed to eat his bread,
The butcher brought him meat,
   he did not proceed to eat his meat,
The cupbearer[1] brought him beer, he did not
   proceed to drink his beer,   (55′)
They brought him water for his footbath,
   but he did not proceed to wash his feet.
Finally she went in to the bathing chamber,
She put on her [   ] garment,
She let him see [her body],
[He was not ar]oused as man for woman   (60′)

(gap)

iv

(gap)

Nergal ... [   ]
She [went] in to the ba[th]ing chamber,   (5′)
[She put on   ] garment,

---

1. So D; C presumably had "brewer" on the basis of ii 43′ above.

[She let him see her body].
He [became aroused as man for woman],
They embraced [one another],
Pa[ssionately they went] to bed.   (10′)
One day, a second day they lay,
        [Queen Ereshkigal and Erra],
A third day, a fourth day [they lay,
        Queen Ereshkigal and Erra],
[A fifth day], a sixth day [they lay,
        Queen Ereshkigal and Erra].
[When the seventh] day [came],
Nergal was [   ] for not being present [in heaven],   (15′)
He ... after him [   ]
"Release me, sister, [   ]
"[Do not] make a fuss [at my going   ],
"I must go from(?) the Land of No Return."
As for her, her [   ] turned dark.   (20′)
[Nergal went strai]ght to [   ]
[To   ] the gatekeeper (he said these words),
"[Ereshkigal] your [mis]tress [has sent me, saying],
"'[I would send you to the heaven] of Anu [our father].'
"Let me out that [I may deliver] the message."   (25′)
Nergal went [up the long staircase of heaven].
[When he reached] the gate of Anu, En[lil, and Ea],
Anu, Enlil, and [Ea saw him],
"The son of Ishtar [has come up to us]!
"[Ereshkigal] will look for [him to take him back].   (30′)
"[Let] Ea his father [sprinkle him] with spring water
        that he be bald,[1]
"Have a tic, be la[me, ... let him sit among all the gods]."
Ereshkigal [   ]
[Went into] the bath chamber [   ]
... [   ]   (35′)
[   ] her body
... [   ]

---

1. Or, possibly, "stunted."

She called out [   ]
"[Bring a] cha[ir   ]
"[Sprinkle the rooms with [   ] water,
"S[prinkle] the rooms with [   ] water,   (40')
"Sprin[kle] the rooms with [   ] water,
"[... the] two daughters of [   ] and Enmeshar,
"Sprinkle them with [water of] ...
"The messenger of Anu our father who came to us,
"Let him eat our bread, let him drink our beer."   (45')
Namtar made ready to speak,
Saying to Ereshkigal, his mistress, (these) words,
"[The messenger] of Anu your father, who came to us,
"Made off before daybreak."
[Eresh]kigal was crushed and let out a wail,   (49'+1)
She fell [fr]om her chair to the ground,
[She got] up [from] the ground, her eyes raining tears,
Her tears ran down the sides of her nose,
"Erra, my voluptuous lover!
"I had not had my fill of his charms, but he left me!
"Erra, my voluptuous lover!   (55')
"I had not had my fill of his charms, but he left me!"
Namtar made ready to speak, saying to Ereshkigal,
"Send me [to Anu] your [father], let me seize that god,
"[Let me fetch] him to you!"

v

[Ereshkigal made ready to speak],
        saying to Namtar (these) words,
"[to] Anu, Enlil, and Ea and say as follows,   (1')

    'Since I was a young girl,
    'I have not known the play of maidens,
    'Nor have I known the frolic of little girls.
    '[That god whom] you sent, he has had intercourse
        with me, so let him lie with me.   (5')
    'Send me [that go]d that he be my husband
        and spend the night with me.

'I am defiled, impure(?),
      I cannot render judgments for the great gods,
'The great gods who reside in the netherworld.
'If [you do not] send t[hat] god,
'Accor[ding to the authority of the netherworl]d
      and the great netherworld,   (10′)
'I shall raise up the dead to devour the living,
'I shall make the dead outnumber the living!'"

Up went Namtar the long staircase of heaven.
When he reached the gate of Anu, Enlil, and Ea,
[An]u, Enlil, and Ea saw him,   (15′)
"[Wh]y are you come, Namtar?"
"Your [daught]er sent me,
"Saying,

    'Since I was a young girl,
    'I have not known the play of maidens,
    'Nor have I known the frolic of little girls.   (20′)
    'That god whom you sent,
        he has had intercourse with me,
        so let him lie with me.
    'Send me that god that he be my husband
        and spend the night with me.
    'I am defiled, impure(?),
        I cannot render judgments for the great gods,
    'The great gods who reside in the netherworld.
    'If you do [not] send that god,   (25′)
    <'According to the authority of the netherworld
        and the great netherworld,>
    'I shall raise up the [dead to devour] the living,
    'I shall make the dead [outnum]ber the living.'"

Ea made ready to speak, [saying to Namtar] (these) words,
"Na[mtar, come into] the cour[t of Anu],
"[   ]."   (30′)
When he came into [the court of An]u,
All the gods kne[lt humbly   ],
[The god]s of the land k[nelt   ].

[He went straight to the] first one, but did not see that god,
He went straight [to a second, a thi]rd,
  but did not see that god.   (35′)
Namtar went to speak to his mistress,
"My lady, [in the heaven of] Anu, your father,
  where you sent me,
"My lady, [there was a certain god, b]ald, with a tic, lame,
  [   ], sitting among all the gods."
"Go, seize that god, f[etch] (him) t[o m]e!
"Ea his father has spri[nkled him] with spring water,   (40′)
"So he is bald, has a tic, is lame,
  [is sitting] among all the gods."
Up went Namtar the long staircase of heaven.
When he re[ached] the gate of Anu, Enlil, and Ea,
Anu, Enlil, and Ea saw him,
"Why are you come, Namtar?" "Your daughter sent [me], (45′)
"Saying, 'Seize that god, fetch him to m[e].'"
"Namtar, come into the court of Anu,
"Look for him ... and t[ake him]."
He went straight to the first, but did not see [that god],
He went straight to a [second, a thi]rd,
  [but did not see that god],   (50′)
He went straight to [a fourth, a fifth,
  but did not see that god].
[   ] made ready to speak, saying to Ea [   ],
"[Na]mtar the messenger, who has come to [us],
"[Let him dr]ink water, bathe, anoi[nt his body] ..."

(gap)

vi

"Let him not wrest away [   ].   (1)
"Erra, I shall make you go [   ] upon him [   ]
"I shall kill you ... [   ].
"Namtar, [   ] to [   ] your task.
"Erra [   ]   (5)
"All the authority of the great netherworld shall [I grant to you?].
"When you go from here,

"[You] shall c[arry the ...] of the throne[1]

"[You shall car]ry [   ]

"[You shall carr]y [   ]   (10)

"You shall [carr]y [   ]

"You shall [carr]y [   ]

"You sh[all c]arry [   ]

"[   ]

"[   ] your chest."   (15)

[Nergal] took the word of [Ea] to heart,

He [   ] and readied his bow.

[Down went Ne]rgal the long stair[case of he]aven(?).

When he re[ache]d the gate of Eresh[kigal],

"Gatekeeper, op[en] the gate [to me]!"   (20)

The gatekeeper hung up his [   ] at the gate,

And would not allow him to take it,

The second one of the g[ate] hung up his [   ],

    and would not allow him to take it.

The third one [of the gate hung up his ...],

    and would not allow him to take it.

The fourth one [of the gate hung up his ...],

    and would not allow him to take it.   (25)

The fif[th one of the gate hung up his ...],

    and would not allow him to take it.

[The sixth one of the gate hung up] his [...],

    [and would not allow him to take it].

[The seventh one of the gate hung up his ...],

    [and would not allow him to take it].

He en[ter]ed her broad court,

Approached her and burst out laughing.   (30)

He seized her by her coiffure,

He [pulled] her from [the throne],

He seized her by her locks,

[   ] his arousal(?).

They embraced one another,   (35)

Passionately they went to bed.

---

1. The implications of this episode remain obscure.

One day, a second day they lay,
    Queen Eresh[kigal and Er]ra,
A third day they lay, Queen Ereshkigal and Erra,
A fourth day they lay, Queen Ereshkigal and Erra,
A fifth day they lay, Queen Ereshkigal and Erra,   (40)
[A sixth day they lay, Queen Ereshkigal and Erra],
[A seventh day they lay, Queen Ereshkigal and Erra].
 [Anu made ready to speak], saying
[To Gaga his messenger] these words,
"[Gaga, I sh]all send you [to the Land of No Return],   (45)
"[To the house of Ereshkiga]l, who dwells in the netherworld],
"[Saying, 'That god] whom I sent to you,
"[Let him dwell with you] forever.
"[   ] upper regions,   (50)
"[   ] lower regions,

(breaks off about twelve lines from the end)

Text: A = C. Bezold, E. W. Budge, *The Tell el-Amarna Tablets in the British Museum* (London, 1892), 82 (+) B = Schroeder, VAS 12 195. C = Gurney, STT 28, 113-114; D = Hunger, SBTU I 1.
Edition: J. Knudtzon, *Die El-Amarna Tafeln*, VAB 2 (Leipzig, 1915) 357 (A+B); Gurney, AnSt 10 (1960), 105-131 (C); Hunger, SBTU I, 17-19 (D).
Translation: Speiser-Grayson, ANET[3], 103-104, 507-512; Labat, *Religions*, 98-113; Bottéro, *Mythologie*, 437-464; Dalley, *Myths*, 163-181.
Literature: Bottéro, Annuaire 1971/2, 97-110; Oppenheim, OrNS 19 (1950), 152; von Weiher, AOAT 11 (1971), 48-54; Reiner, *Poetry*, 50-60; Borger, HKL 1, 239-240; HKL 2, 92, 132.
*Notes to Text: (A+B 46) *a-mi-*[*ri?*]. (A+B 88) The tablet ends with *adu kinanna*. WLM suggests that this is a scribal notation, not part of the text, meaning something like "up to this point, so far." (C, D ii 34′) K. Foster, *Aegean Faience of the Bronze Age* (New Haven, 1979), 21; P. R. S. Moorey, *Materials and Manufacture in Ancient Mesopotamia* (Oxford, 1985), 133ff.

III.20 THE ADAPA STORY

(a) ADAPA AND THE SOUTH WIND

The story of Adapa reveals the goodwill and malice of the gods towards men. Adapa was the most perfect of mortals, a favorite of Ea's, whose cult he administered with wonderful assiduity. So great was his magical power that when a wayward breeze capsized his boat on an otherwise calm day, he cursed it and incapacitated it. When the absence of the wind was noticed in heaven, Adapa was summoned before Anu to give an account of himself. Ea admonished him to ingratiate himself with the vegetation deities standing at the door of the celestial palace. This he was to do by dressing himself in mourning for their seasonal absence from the land. These gods, amused, would put in a good word for him, and this is what occurred. Ea enjoined Adapa from accepting food or drink in heaven, though he might avail himself of the other offices of hospitality. Anu, after the intercession of the gods at the door, was so impressed that Ea would single out a man for his favor, that he offered him the hospitality fit for a visiting god. When Adapa declined the food and drink, which would have made him a god and released him from Ea's service, Anu was vastly amused by Ea's cleverness and his sage's stupidity, and so sent the swindled mortal back home.

The lessons of this simple text are numerous. Surely one is that if a man so perfect could not obtain immortality, despite his close relationship to a great god, who else could expect to? Even the apparent goodwill of the gods is limited; they will not gratefully manumit men from their service no matter how well performed.

Much has been written about this bitter little tale, as a perusal of Picchioni's volume (see Literature) will show, and many different constructions have been put on it. Later Mesopotamian scholars incorporated the story into incantations as a means of identifying and localizing the magical powers of Adapa for medicinal ends. Some Assyriologists see in this text an aetiology for the origins of magic, though others will read here a somber Mesopotamian statement on the lot of mankind.

A and A'

(about six lines lost)

Un[derstanding   ]   (1)
His utterance can command, like the utterance [of Anu],⋆
He made him perfect in wisdom, revealing (to him)
       the designs of the land.
To him he granted wisdom, eternal life he did not grant him.
In those days, in those years, the sage, the citizen of Eridu,   (5)
Ea created him as ... among men,⋆
The sage whose pronouncement no one gainsaid,
Able one, his perception of what pertains
       to the Anunna-gods was vast,
Pure, clean of hands, anointed one
       who was solicitous after divine rites,
He performed the baker's office with the baker,   (10)
He performed the baker's office with the bakers of Eridu,
Every day he (himself) made the food and drink for Eridu('s cult).[1]
He prepared the table with his own clean hands,
Nor without him was the table cleared.
He steered the boat, he made the daily fish catch for Eridu('s cult). (15)
At that time Adapa, citizen of Eridu,
At the drawing of the [bo]lt of Ea to its socket(?),⋆
Would each day set the bar himself.
[At] the sacred quay, the quay of "Heavenly Splendor,"⋆
       he boarded the sailboat.
[Without? a st]eering oar his boat would drift downstream,   (20)
[Without? a ru]dder he could pilot his boat (upstream).[2]
[Into the ... ocean, into the] wide sea

(fragmentary lines, then breaks off)

---

1. That is, he was so concerned with correct ritual observance that he assumed personally even menial temple duties, such as the baking of sacrificial loaves. An original interpretation of these lines has been offered by Talon, BiOr 40 (1983), 686f., whereby Ea is the sage who does the baking and so forth, not Adapa, but this is unconvincing.

2. I take these to be signs of superior ability, rather than poor seamanship, differently Talon, BiOr 40 (1984), 687.

Fragment B[1]

He ma[de ready to speak, saying to the south wind], (1)
"O south wind! [   ]
"I have done enough(?), let me [   ]
"O south wind, [gath]er against me your brothers,
     as m[any as there be],
"I will fracture your w[in]g!" (5)
As soon as he said it,
The south wind's wing was fractured.
The s[outh wind] not having blown
     for seven days towards the land,
Anu called to his messenger Ilabrat,
"Why has the south wind not blown
     for seven days towards the land?" (10)
His spokesman Ilabrat answered him,
"My Lord, Adapa, son of Ea,
     has fractured the south wind's wing."
When Anu heard this,
He cried, "(Heaven) help (us)!" He rose from his chair,
"Se[nd word and let] them bring him here." (15)
Ea, who knows the affairs of heaven, touched him,
[   ] made him wear his hair unkempt,[2]
[Had him put on] mourning weeds,
Gave him instructions,
"[Adapa], you are to go [before Anu] the king, (20)
"[You are to go up to heaven].
"When y[ou go up] to h[eav]en,
"[And draw near to Anu's door],
"[Tammuz and Gizzi]da will be standing at Anu's door.
"When they see you, they will ask you, (25)
    'Fel[low], for whom are you like this?
    'A[da]pa, why are you in mourning weeds?'
    'Two gods are disappeared from our land,

---

1. Fragment C is, for the most part, parallel to B, with minor variants, but because of its condition I omit it here.
2. A sign of mourning.

'That is why I am decked out so.'
'Who are the two gods
     who have disappeared from the land?'   (30)
'They are Tammuz and Gizzida.'

"They will look at each other and laugh and laugh,
"They will say a favorable word to Anu,
"They will help you see Anu's benevolent side.
"When you come before Anu,   (35)
"They will proffer you food of death, do not eat!
"They will proffer you waters of death, do not drink!
"They will proffer you a garment, put it on.
"They will proffer you oil, anoint yourself.
"Do not neglect the instructions I give you,   (40)
"Hold fast to the words which I have spoken."
Anu's messenger reached him,

    'Adapa, who fractured the wing of the south wind,
    'Send him to me!'"

He brought him along the [ro]ad to heaven,   (45)
He went up to heaven.
When he went up to heaven,
And drew near Anu's door,
Tammuz and Gizzida were standing at Anu's door.
When they saw Adapa, they cried, "(Heaven) help (us)!   (50)
"Fellow, for whom are you like this?
"Adapa, why are you dressed in mourning?"
"Two gods have disappeared from the land,
"So I am dressed in mourning."
"Who are the two gods who have disappeared from the land?"   (55)
"Tammuz and Gizzida."
They looked at each other and laughed and laughed.
When Adapa made his approach to Anu the king,
Anu saw him and cried,
"Come now, Adapa, why did you fracture
     the wing of the south wind?"   (60)
Adapa answered Anu,
"My lord, I was fishing in the depths of the sea,

"For my master's temple.
"The sea was like a mirror,
"Then the south wind blew upon me and capsized me.   (65)
"I spent the rest of the day in the home of the fish.
"In my fury, I cursed the [win]d."
There spoke up for [him Tammuz] and Gizzida,
Saying a favorable word about him to Anu.
His heart grew calm, he became quiet.   (70)
"Why did Ea disclose what pertains to heaven and earth
"To an uncouth mortal,
"And give him a violent temper?
"Since he has so treated him,
"What, for our part, shall we do for him?   (75)
"Bring him food of life, let him eat."
They brought him food of life, he did not eat.
They brought him waters of life, he did not drink.
They brought him a garment, he put it on.
They brought him oil, he anointed himself.   (80)
Anu stared and burst out laughing at him,
"Come now, Adapa, why did you not eat or drink?
"Won't you live? Are not people to be im[mor]tal?"*
"Ea my lord told me,

       'You must not eat, you must not drink.'"

"Let them take him and [ret]urn him to his earth."   (85)

(breaks off)

Fragment D

[He ordered bread of life for him, he did not eat],
He ordered [water of life] for him, he did not drink.   (1)
He ordered [oil] for him, he anointed himself,
He ordered a [gar]ment for him, he put it on.
Anu laughed uproariously at what Ea had done,
"Who else, of all the gods of heaven and netherworld,
       could d[o] something like this?   (5)

"Who else could make his command outweigh Anu's?"[1]
Adapa [surveyed] from the horizon to the heights of heaven,
He saw the awesomeness of [   ].
[At that ti]me Anu imposed on Adapa an observance,
[Aft]erwards Ea released him.   (10)
[An]u ordained that he be distinguished
        for his leadership for all time.[2]

(follows fragments of an incantation invoking Adapa's powers)

Text: A = Clay, BRM 4 3 = Picchioni, *Adapa*, Fig. 1; A′ = Schramm, OrNS 43 (1974), 162;
B = Schroeder, VAS 12 194 = Picchioni, *Adapa*, Figs. 2, 3; C (K 8743) = Langdon, PBS 10/1 3
= Picchioni, *Adapa*, Fig. 4; D (K 8214) = Strong, PSBA 16 (1894), 274-275 = Furlani, *Rend. della
Accad. Naz. dei Lincei, Cl. di Scien. Morali* 5 (1929), 132 = Picchioni, *Adapa*, Fig. 5.
Edition: S. A. Picchioni, *Il Poemetto di Adapa* (Budapest, 1981).
Translation: Dalley, *Myths*, 182-187; Speiser, ANET³, 101-103.
Literature: See Picchioni, *Adapa*, with bibliography, 14-23. For more recent contributions, see
P. Michalowski, "Adapa and the Ritual Process," RO 41 (1980), 77-82; M. Liverani, "Adapa
ospite degli dei," *Religioni e Civiltà* (Bari, 1982), 293-319; H.-P. Mueller, "Mythus als Gattung
archaischen Erzählens und die Geschichte von Adapa," AfO 29/30 (1983/4), 75-89.
*Notes to Text: (6) Translation uncertain; see Picchioni, *Adapa*, 127, with collation by Lambert.
(17) For the various proposals for this difficult line, see Picchioni, *Adapa*, 119. I follow Lambert's
suggestion, quoted there: [*giš*]-*ru* ᵈ*É-a*. Note the new proposal of CAD M, 118a: [MAŠ.S]UD =
"When [the w]ise Ea lies in his bed." This is epigraphically difficult. (19) For the problem with
this name, see Picchioni, *Adapa*, 130, whose reading I adopt. (B 83) The second part of the line
is obscure. The restoration implied here, *da-a-[ra]-ti*, is highly doubtful.

---

1. That is, by thwarting Anu's good intentions to give Adapa eternal life.
2. That is, he could not live forever, but would be famous forever.

(b) ADAPA AND ENMERKAR

This composition deals with the sage Adapa and Enmerkar, an early Sumerian king well known from Sumerian epic poems.[1] Sages and famous kings of the past were paired in other Mesopotamian texts,[2] while Enmerkar is also referred to in the Cuthaean Legend of Naram-Sin (III.7b(3)). Little of this text can be understood, owing to the broken condition of the manuscripts. The composition opens with Adapa apparently lamenting someone's death. Although the gods hear his lament, they do nothing to help him. Enmerkar, king of Uruk, becomes interested in the matter. An ancient tomb, deep in the earth, is excavated. They break into it but cannot see at first. Adapa does something rash, at which point the text breaks off. When the text becomes coherent again, Adapa engages the services of a smith to refit(?) the coffin they had broken into.

The moral of the story may have lain in Adapa's desire to see someone long dead. When he attains his wish, he is horrified at the sight, so makes sure to reseal the tomb forever. This text should perhaps take its place among those Mesopotamian compositions concerned with death and immortal life.

[   ]   (1)
He sets his [   ]
Adap[a   ]
... [   ]
He wailed to the lord, to [   ]   (5)
[When ...] heard [his] w[ail],
[He said] this [   ],
"[which] he has seized,
"This clamor [   ] how good."
At the speech of [   ] he wailed,   (10)
And the great gods [   ] his second 'hand,'[3]
[   ] to him.
His second 'hand' [   ]

1. For information on this king, see G. Komoróczy, "Zum sumerischen Epos 'Enmerkar und der Herr von Aratta'," AASH 16 (1968), 15-20. For another mention of Enmerkar in Akkadian literature, see III.7b(3), and p. 263 note 1.
2. Hallo, JCS 23 (1970), 62.
3. Unclear.

[reached] the [gate?] of Anu, Enlil, [and Ea],
[   ] the [ ] of the great lord Marduk.   (15)

Adapa [   ]
Enmerkar [exercised] king[ship] in Uruk.
When [he had   ] all the land of Akkad,
[He   ] his reign until the gods [   ].
Adapa [went down] nine cubits in the depths,   (20)
Enmerkar [   ] for the sake of [ ] of Adapa.
They lifted [   ] before [   ],
Enmerkar [   ] in order not to [   ].
An ancient corpse from remotest times [   ].
He made a terrible clamor in the palace(?) [   ].   (25)
They went down nine cubits [in the depths],
[Nine] cubits of earth they went down [   ].
He destroyed the door of the tomb
     [with]out(?) seeing the [corp]se.
Adapa [said to Enmerkar   ],

(two lines lost)

Adapa did not answer, but [   ]   (32)

(rev)

They buried [   ] minas of copper inside [   ],
The blacksmith who [ ] and(?) set up(?) [the do]or above,
[   ] and who fastened its latch(?) to the frame(?),   (5)
As [ ] Adapa was passing through the street,
He saw the blacksmith and said to him,
"[and?] is your latch(?) securely on the frame(?)?"

(fragmentary lines, then breaks off)

Text: W. G. Lambert, AfO 17 (1954/6), 321; Lambert *apud* Picchioni, *Adapa*, Fig. 6, 7; Campbell Thompson, GETh Plate 14 (K 9220); Hunger, SBTU I 4.
Edition: Picchioni, *Adapa*, 102-109.

III.21 ETANA

The legend of Etana enjoyed particular popularity in Mesopotamian tradition. What now remains of the story may be outlined as follows. In Tablet I the gods are building a city for the human race, the lesser gods doing the work, the greater gods making the plans. When the city is completed and surrounded with defenses, a king is needed. Enlil looks over all the cult cities in the realm for a suitable candidate. This turns out to be Etana. Kingship is created and Etana is made the first king.

In Tablet II Etana the king has built some structures, including a temple for Adad, and a poplar tree grows there. A serpent takes up residence in the roots of the tree, an eagle in its crown. The two creatures swear an oath of friendship to each other. They produce their young and share the task of feeding them. As his children grow up, the eagle conspires to devour the serpent's children. One of his own children attempts vainly to dissuade him, a reversal of the usual wisdom motif whereby an elder advises a youngster. The eagle devours his friend's children.

When the serpent returns and discovers his children gone, he calls upon Shamash, lord of the oath, to witness the eagle's perfidy. Shamash hears his plaint and arranges for a wild ox to die. He enjoins the serpent to hide in the belly of the cadaver to seize the eagle when he comes to feed. He can then pluck his feathers and throw him into a pit to die of hunger and thirst. The ruse is successful, despite the warnings of the eagle's youngster, for the greedy eagle plunges into the carcass to feed and is captured by the vengeful serpent. The eagle's pleas for mercy are rejected, first by the serpent and second by Shamash. He is left to languish in a pit. Shamash is moved by his continued pleas, but, since the eagle violated an oath, the god cannot rescue him himself. He decides upon an agent, whom he advises the eagle to expect.

Meantime, Etana, the king, has been praying to Shamash for an heir. All of his efforts to produce one have proved unsuccessful, so his last hope is to find a certain plant of birth. Shamash tells Etana of the eagle's plight, and advises him to save the eagle in return for the bird's assistance in finding the plant of birth. Etana sets forth and approaches the pit.

Tablet III opens with a fragmentary episode in which the eagle is trying to persuade some birds to help him. Just then he catches sight of Etana and asks him his mission. Etana, in his excitement, demands the plant, without even introducing himself. The following exchanges are fragmentary, but it seems that the eagle temporizes and promises other gifts instead, to no avail. At last he consents to help Etana get the plant, if only he will save him from the pit. Etana throws something into the pit that allows the eagle to flutter his way out. The rest of the tablet is lost, but Etana and the eagle become comrades. There is a considerable gap at this point.

In Tablet IV the eagle is recounting to Etana a propitious dream he had which suggests to him that their perilous mission to secure the plant may be rewarded with success. Etana grasps the eagle's sides and wings, in a posture well known from Mesopotamian seal engravings, and the eagle carries him aloft. Higher and higher they go, until they reach the first stage of their journey in the sky. There, as foretold in the eagle's dream, they make obeisance to the great gods through whose celestial gates they are passing. After a gap in the text, it seems that the next stage of the journey is about to begin. Eagle and man set off, the man looking behind and recounting excitedly earth and ocean's rapid diminishment into the distance. But, the instant he loses sight of them altogether, Etana's courage fails him, and he begs to return to his city. The eagle plunges earthward and they land, without the plant.

At this point the tablet ends, so no one knows how the story ended. Perhaps, like Gilgamesh and Adapa, Etana had tried the impossible and lost the prize. Etana is known to have had a son in Mesopotamian tradition, at least in the Sumerian King List, so it is possible that a subsequent venture was successful, or that Etana achieved his goal in some other way.

The manuscripts date to the Classical ("OV") and Mature ("MA") periods, and there is a diverse group of fragmentary manuscripts from Assurbanipal's library ("LV"). These last apparently constituted several editions of the text. Since even the latest manuscripts of the story, from one library, show considerable variation in style, content, and arrangement of the text, one can assume that numerous editions of the text were available. The three principal versions are translated separately below.

The earlier versions have interesting variations that show how both the motivation and details of the story were reinterpreted in the millennium that lies between the earliest and the latest versions. Note for example LV's expansion of the episode of the dialogue between Etana and the eagle in the pit, and how the eagle's impulsive offer of any favor in OV is made in LV into a demand by Etana that the eagle may be loath to grant, even in his extreme condition. Compare also the expansion of the hunting episode in LV. In OV only the serpent is portrayed as hunting, and the eagle feeds on his success, while in the later version the force of analogy expands the whole passage and robs it of some of the contrast the earlier shows between the behavior of the two creatures. Such comparisons illustrate the levelling-off and expansion so characteristic of the development of Akkadian literary texts.

(a) OLD BABYLONIAN VERSION (OV)

I/A

The great Anunna-gods, ordainers of destiny,	(1)
Sat taking counsel with respect to the land.*	
The creators of the world regions, establishers of all physical form,	
The Igigi-gods ...	
Ordained a festival(?)[1] for the people.	(5)
Among all the teeming peoples they[2] had established no king,	
Then no headdress had been assembled, nor crown,	
Nor yet scepter had been set with lapis,	
No throne daises at all had been constructed,	
Full seven gates were bolted against the hero.[3]	(10)
Scepter, crown, headdress, and staff	
Were set before Anu in heaven.	
There was no right counsel for their(?) people:	
(Then) [ ] came down from heaven.[4]	

(fragmentary lines, then gap)

(After a gap, serpent and eagle are making friends.)

1. Langdon, Speiser, and other translators have taken this to refer to a "fixed time," that is, mortality, but there is no philological basis for such an interpretation. If the Akkadian word used here really means "festival," the older version would still refer not to death but rather to a holiday. The line remains obscure.

2. Presumably the gods are meant.

3. This line expresses the absence of opportunity for the superior mortal (W. G. Lambert, JCS 32 [1980], 81-85). In the later version, the line is interpreted differently to imply that the lesser gods shut the gates at night, a task that was to be the king's.

4. Usually restored "[king]ship," though questioned by Wilcke (ZA 67 [1977], 157), who prefers to understand that Ishtar is coming down from heaven in search of a king.

I/C

"May the path vanish from him, may he not find the way,   (1)
"May the mountain hold back its pass from him,
"May the oncoming weapon make straight for him!"
(This was) the oath they swore to each other.
Together(?) they conceived, together(?) they bore.   (5)
In the shade of the poplar the serpent gave birth,
The eagle gave birth in its crown.
When the serpent hunted down a wild ox or a wild sheep,
The eagle ate, his children ate.
When the serpent hunted down a panther or a tiger(?),   (10)
The eagle ate, [his] children ate.
After his children had grown big and [flourished],
...
The eagle [plotted evil] in his heart.
"My children [have grown big and flourished],   (15)
"They are gone forth to seek [their own food?],
"To seek ...
"I shall eat the serpent's children [   ],
"I will ascend to [   ],
"I will dwell(?) [   ]   (20)
"Who is there that [   ]?"
The [littlest] fledgling, [exceedingly wise],
[Said] to the ea[gle, his father],
"My father, [do not   ]

(gap)

At dawn [the serpent went out to hunt?],
At nightfall [he returned?].   (30)
The serpent approached [his nest?],
The meat [he was carrying   ],
The serpent cast down before [his nest].
He looked, [his children] were gone!
[The eagle had gouged] the ground [   ] with his talons,
[   ] the sky.   (35)
[The serpent] set to weeping, sick (at heart),

[Before Shamash?] his tea[rs] were flowing down,
"I have put my trust in you, O warrior Shamash!
"I was the one who gave provisions(?) to the eagle, (40)
"I respected and honored you!
"I harbored no evil against my friend!
"As for him, his nest is safe, but [my] nest is scattered,
"The serpent's nest is turned into a moan of grief.
"His fledglings are safe, my children are gone!
"He came down and ate up my brood, (45)
"You know, O Shamash, the evil he did!
"Your net is the wi[de] meadow,
"Your trap [is the distant heaven]:
"May the eagle not [escape] from your net,
"Th(at) perpetrator of ev[il and ab]omination, (50)
"Who harbored e[vi]l against his friend!"

(After a gap, the serpent imprisons the eagle in a pit.)

I/D

The serpent [made ready to speak, saying to the eagle],
"Were I [to set you free   ]
"Your punishment [would come upon me   ]."
He ... [   ]
He plucked out (his feathers) [and cast him into a pit],
A place of dea[th by starvation and thirst].
The eagle ... [   ]   (10')
... [   ]
Daily [the eagle entreated Shamash, saying],
"O Shamash, ta[ke] my hand [   ]
"[   ] me!"
Shamash m[ade] ready to speak, [saying to the eagle],   (15')
"[   ] wicked deeds(?),
"[You have committed] an abomination of the g[ods ...]

I/E

He took him by the hand
    in his se[venth month (in the pit)],   (1′)
In the eighth month he brought him
    over (the edge) of his pit.[1]
The eagle took food like a ravening lion,
He gained strength.
The eagle made ready to speak and said to Etana,   (5′)
"My friend! Let us be friends, you and I!
"Ask of me whatever you desire and I shall give it to you."
Etana made ready to speak and said to the eagle,
"My eyes ..., open up what is hidden."

(breaks off)

---

1. Numerical parallelism, meaning that the eagle has been a long time in the pit, not that it took a month to get him out.

(b) MIDDLE ASSYRIAN VERSION (MA)

I/A

(The oath of friendship is sworn and betrayed.)

"May [the oath of Shamash] overcome him,   (1)
"[May the mesh of Shamash's oath] ensnare him,
"[May the mountains] turn their [passes] away from him,
"May the oncoming [weapo]n make straight for him,★
"May Shamash single him out for the slaughterer,★   (5)
"May Shamash deliver the offender to the executioner,
"May he station a malignant demon over him!"

At the top of the tree the eagle gave birth,
At the root of the poplar the serpent gave birth.
In the shade of that poplar,   (10)
Eagle and serpent became friends with each other.
They swore the oath together and became comrades.
They told each other their innermost desires.

The serpent would go out to hunt,   (★15)
Wild sheep(?) and aurochs(?) of the steppe(?)★
the serpent would hunt down.
The eagle would eat, turn away, his children would eat.
[Bu]ck, gazelle of the steppe the serpent would hunt down,   (★20)
[The ea]gle would eat, turn away, his children would eat.
[Beasts of?] the steppe, animals of the earth,
      the serpent would hunt down,
[The eagle] would eat, turn away, his children would eat.
[After the] eagle's [children]
[Had grown big] and flourished,   (★25)
Had acquired [   ] ... [   ],
[The eagle set his thoughts]
[Upon eating his friend's young].

(gap)

I/B

(The eagle is trapped by the serpent and denounced.)

They were hungry ... [   ],   (1)
They gathered [   ]
The littlest fledgling, exceedingly [wise],
[Said these words] to the eagle, his father,
"Do not go down!
       No doubt [the serpent is lurking in the wild ox]!   (5)
"The netherworld will h[old you fast]![1]
"[It is] the [serpent's] counter-plot,
"[His] wings are stretched out [to seize you],
"The netherworld [will hold you fast]!"

[The eagle] did not ag[ree   ]   (10)
Nor did he [listen to his sons' words].
He went down and [lighted on the wild ox],
With ... [the birds?]

A first time [inspecting in front and behind it],
The eagle lo[oked at the meat].   (*15)
A second time [inspecting in front and behind it],
The eagle loo[ked at the meat].
A third time [inspecting in front and behind it],
The eagle lo[oked at the meat].   (*20)

He plunged(?) into the inna[rds of the wild ox],
In search of the juiciest meat,
[He was working forward] into the belly of the w[ild ox].
[As he entered] into its vitals,
The serpent seized him [by his wings]!   (*25)

He brought him out and [   ]
"[You were] the intruder [   ]!

1. Kinnier Wilson suggests that the little one has seen the serpent's traces going to the wild ox, but not his "return" (here: "counterplot"). The passage is uncertain.

"Before Shamash [   ]
"May the king of the g[ods ...] be great!
"[May the] judge of [my] case [   ]   (*30)
"[   ] who binds fast [   ]
"You are the one, eagle, [   ]
"You flew down [   ]

(*gap)*

I/C

(Etana prays to Shamash for an heir.)
"[   ], open what is hidden."
"Take away (my) disgrace,* give me an heir!"

Etana [l]ay down* to see (a dream),
He had a dream [in] bed at night.   (*5)
"... go on the road, cross the highlands.
"As you traverse the [mou]ntains,
"[Loo]k for a pit, approach near to it.   (*10)
"An eagle is cast inside it,
"He will give you the plant of birth."

I/D

The eagle looked at him ...,
He said [   ] to Etana,
"You are Etana, king of the wild beasts,
"You are Etana, [   ] among(?) birds.   (*10)
"Bring [me] up from [thi]s [pi]t,
"Give me [   ] your hand,
"... [   ]
"I will si[ng] your [pra]ises for all time."

Etana [said] to the eagle (these) wor[ds],   (*15)
"(If) I save your life, [   ]
"(If) I br[ing you up fr]om the pit,

"[From th]at moment we [must be ...]"

(gap)

I/E

"[   ] to me ... [   ]   (1)
"From sunrise till [   ]
"From his rising, where [   ]
"... [   ]
"I will grant you the [plant] of life."   (5)

When Etana h[eard] this,
He filled the front of the pit with [   ].[1]
Next he threw in ... [   ].
He kept throwing in [   ] in front of(?) him,[2]
The eagle ... from the pit.   (10)
As for him, he flapped [his wings].
[A first time and a second time ...] the eagle ...] in(?) the pit,
As for him, he flapped [his] w[ings   ]
[A third time] and a fourth time ... [the eagle ... in? the pi]t,   (15)
As for him, he flapped [his wings   ]
[A fifth and a sixth time   ] ...

(fragmentary lines, then gap)

I/G

(Etana relates dreams to the eagle, who interprets them as propitious.)

"[   ] above
"[   ] at my feet."

1. Ebeling (AfO 14 [1941], 307) ingeniously restores pu[qulta] "thorn bushes"; Kinnier Wilson restores bu[rāšu] "juniper."
2. As understood here, Etana keeps tossing bushes into the pit for the eagle to scramble up on. The second dream in the MA version is perhaps based on this. Kinnier Wilson has Etana constructing a ladder of juniper-wood (63 and 74f.).

[The eagle made Etana] understand [the dream],
[   ] seated before him,   (*5)
"[   ] your [dream] is propitious,

"[   ] burden[1] is brought,
"They will give [   ]
"You have done [   ] of the people
"You will seize ... in your hand,   (*10)
"The sacred bond[2] [   ] above
"[   ] at your feet."

Etana said to him, to the eagle,
"My friend, [I saw] a second dream,   (*15)
"[   ] reeds [   ] in the house,
"In all [   ], the whole land,
"They heaped up loads (of them) in piles.
"[   ] enemies, they were wicked serpents,   (*20)
"[   ] were coming before me,
"[   ] they were kneeling before me."

[The eagle made Etana] understand [the dream].
[   ] seated before him,
"[   ] your [dream] is propitious,

(gap)

I/H

[Etana said to him, to the eagle],
"[The lan]d is a hi[ll],
"[And the se]a has turned into a brook(?).

---

1. Here and in the next dream "weight" (*biltu*) and "tribute" (*biltu*) are used with a play on the words. Etana's ascent is no doubt referred to, his weight being borne by the eagle. In the second dream there is a word play on *biltu* "weight" and *elpetu* "reeds," but the whole passage is too fragmentary to be understood.
2. A cosmic feature, being the linkage of heaven and earth.

He bore [him] up a [thi]rd league,
[The eagle said to] him, [to E]tana,   (5)
"[Look], my friend, how the land [is now],
"[Examine] the sea, [look for] its features."

[Etana] said to [him, to] the eagle,
"[The land] is set out (as if) for an orchard,
"[And the sea] has turned into an irrigation ditch."

(fragmentary lines, then gap)

(c) LATE VERSION (LV)

Tablet I

I/A

They planned the city [   ],[1]   (1)
[The gods? laid its foundations],
[They planned the city? Kish?],
[The gods?] laid its foundations.
The Igigi-gods founded its brickwork* [   ]   (*5)
"Let [ ] be their (the people's) shepherd,
"Let Etana be their architect, ..."
The great Anunna-gods, or[dainers of destinies],[2]
[Sa]t taking their counsel [concerning the land],
The creators of the four world regions,
     [establishers of all physical form],
By(?) command of all of them the Igigi-gods
     [ordained a festi]val f[or the people],
No [king] did they establish [over the teeming peoples].
At that time [no headdress had been assembled, nor crown],
Nor yet scepter [had been set] with lapis,   (15)
No throne daises(?)[3] whatsoever [had been constructed].
The seven gods barred the [gates] against the multitude,
Against the inhabited world they barred [the gates ...],
The Igigi-gods surrounded the city [with ramparts?].[4]
Ishtar [came down from heaven? to seek] a shepherd,   (20)
And sought for a king [everywhere].
Innina [came down from heaven? to seek] a shepherd,
And sought for a king e[verywhere].
Enlil examined the dais of(?) Etana,
The man whom Ishtar st[eadfastly   ]   (25)
"She has constantly sought ...

1. This passage has been discussed by Sauren, CRRAI 19 (1971), 460-461.
2. Old Babylonian version begins here, suggesting that the first eight lines of the Late Version were added as a prologue.
3. Text: "world regions," presumably a mistake; compare OV I/A 9.
4. See above, p. 439 note 3.

"[Let] king[ship] be established in the land,
　　　　let the heart of Kish [be joyful]."
Kingship, the radiant crown, throne, [　　　　　　　　　]
He(?) brought and [　　　　　　　　　　　　　　　　　]
The gods of the land[s　　　　　　　　　　　　　　　　]

(large gap)

*(Kinnier Wilson inserts here a fragment mentioning Etana and a plant of birth,
but its placement and interpretation are uncertain.)*

Tablet II

[   ] which he called [   ] ...
   the "High Water,"   (1)
[   ] he had built a tower(?) [   ]
[   ] shrine for Adad, the god [   ]
In the shade of that shrine a po[plar] was growing [   ],
In its crown an eagle settled,   (5)
A serpent ... at its root.
Daily they wa[tched the wild beasts].*
[The eagl]e made ready to speak, [saying to the serpent],
"[Co]me, [let us make] friend[ship],
"Let us be comrades, [you] and I."
[The serpent] made ready to speak, [saying to the eagle],   (10)
"[If indeed?] ... of friendship and [   ]
"[Then? let us swear a] mighty [oath of Shamash],
"An abomination of the gods [   ]
"Come then, let us set forth
      [and go up the high mountains (to hunt)],
"Let us swear [an oath] by the netherworld."   (15)
Before Shamash the warrior they swo[re] the oath,
"Whoever [transgresses] the limits of Shamash [   ],
"May Shamash [deliver him] as an offender
      into the hands of the executioner,
"Whoever [transgresses] the limits of Shamash,
"May the [mountains] remove [their pas]ses far away from him, (20)
"May the oncoming weapon [make straight for him],
"May the trap and curse of Shamash overthrow him
      [and hunt him down]!"
After they had sworn the oath by the netherworld,
They set forth, going up the high mountains,
Each day by turns watching for [the wild beasts].   (25)
The eagle would hunt down wild oxen and asses,
The serpent would eat, turn away, then his children would eat.
The serpent would hunt down buck and gazelle,
The eagle would eat, turn away, then [his] children would eat.
The eagle would hunt down wild sheep and aurochs,   (30)

The serpent would eat, turn away, then his children would eat.
The serpent would hunt down b[easts of the field,
 crea]tures of the earth,⋆
[The eagle would eat, turn aw]ay, then his children would eat.
… [   ] the food,
The eagle's children grew big and flourished.   (35)
After the eagle's children were grown big and were flourishing,
The eagle's heart indeed plotted evil,
Evil his heart plotted indeed!
He set his thoughts upon eating his friend's young!
The eagle made ready to speak, saying to [his children], (40)
"I will eat the serpent's children, the serpent [ ],
"I will go up and d[well] in heaven,
"If I descend from the crown of the tree, … the king."
The littlest fledgling, exceedingly wise,
 [said] these words to the eagle, his father, (45)
"Do not eat, my father!
 The net of Shamash will hu[nt you] down,
"The mesh and oath of Shamash will overthrow you
  and hunt you down.
"Whoever transgresses the limits of Shamash,
 Shamash [will deliver] him as an offender
 into the hands of the [executioner]!"
He did not heed them nor listen to [his sons' words], (50)
He descended and ate up the serpent's [children].
In the evening of the same day(?),
The serpent ca[me], bearing his burden,
At the entrance to his nest [he cast down the meat].
[He loo]ked around, his nest was gone!
He looked down, [his children were] not [ ]! (55)
[The eagle had gouged] the ground with his talon,
The cloud of dust from the nest [darkened] the sky.
The serpent …, weeping before Shamash,
[Before] Shamash [the warrior his tears ran down], (60)
"I trusted in you, [O warrior Shamash],
"I [was the one who gave provisions?] to the eagle,
"Now my nest [   ]!

"My nest is gone, [while his] ne[st is safe],
"My young are destroyed, [while his young are] sa[fe].   (65)
"He descended and ate up [my children]!
"[You know], O Shamash, the evil he has done me,
"Truly, O Shamash, your net is the [wide] earth,
"Your trap is the [distant] heaven.
"[The eagle] must not es[cape] from your net,   (70)
"Th(at) malignant Anzu, who harbored evil [against his friend]!"
[When he had heard] the serpent's lament,
Shamash made ready to speak, [and said] to [him],
"Go (your) way and cros[s the mountain],
"[I?] have captured for you a wi[ld ox].   (75)
"Open its insides, [rend its belly],
"Set an ambush [in its belly],
"[Every kind of] bird of heaven [will come down to eat the meat].
"The eagle [will come down] with them [to eat the meat].
"[As] he will not know [the evil in store for him],   (80)
"He will sea[rch for] the juiciest meat [   ],
        he will walk about outside(?),
"He will work his way* into the covering of the intestines.
"When he comes inside, seize him by his wings,
"Cut off his wings, his pinions, and tailfeathers,
"Pluck him and cast him into a bottomless(?) pit,   (85)
"Let him die there of hunger and thirst."
As Shamash the warrior commanded,
The serpent went and crossed the mountain.
Then did the serpent reach the wild ox,
He opened its insides, he rent its belly.   (90)
He set an ambush in its belly.
Every kind of bird of heaven came down to eat the meat.
Did the [ea]gle know the evil in store for him?
He would not eat the meat [with] the other birds!
[The eagle] made ready to speak, saying to his children,   (95)
"[Co]me, let us go down and we too eat the meat of this wild ox."
The little [fled]gling, exceedingly wise,
        said [these] words to the eagle [his father],

"Do not go down, father,
>   no doubt the serpent is lurking inside the wild ox."
The eagle said to himself,
"Are the birds afraid? How is it they eat the meat in peace?"   (100)
He did not listen to them, he did not listen to his sons' words,
He descended and perched on the wild ox.
The eagle looked at the meat, searching in front and behind it. (105)
A second time he looked at the meat,
>   searching in front and behind it,
He walked around outside(?), he worked his way
>   into the covering of the intestines.
When he came inside, the serpent seized him by his wings,
"You intruded ..., you intruded ...!*   (110)
The eagle made ready to speak, saying to the serpent,
"Have mercy on me! I will make you such a gift
>   as a king's ransom!"[1]
The serpent made ready to speak, saying to the eagle,
"If I release you, how shall I answer to Shamash on high?
"Your punishment would turn upon me,   (115)
"Me, the one to lay punishment upon you!"
He cut off his wings, pinions, and tail feathers,
[He pluc]ked him and ca[st him into] a p[it],
That he should die [there] of hunger [and thirst].
[As for him, the eagle], ... [   ]   (120)
He kept on beseeching Shamash day after day,
"Am I to die in a pit?
"Who would know how your punishment
>   was imposed upon me?[2]
"Save my life, me, the eagle!
"Let me cause your name to be heard for all time."   (125)
Shamash made ready to speak and said to the eagle,
"You are wicked and have done a revolting deed,
"You committed an abomination of the gods, a forbidden act.
"Were you (not) under oath? I will not come near you.

---

1. Literally: "I will give you a wedding present."
2. That is, there is no exemplary value in his solitary death; compare the passage in the penitential hymn III.29 lines 66ff.

"There, there! A man I will send you will help you."   (130)
Etana kept on beseeching Shamash day after day,
"O Shamash, you have dined from my fattest sheep!
"O Netherworld, you have drunk of the blood of my
          (sacrificed) lambs!
"I have honored the gods and revered the spirits,
"Dream interpreters have used up my incense,
"Gods have used up my lambs in slaughter.   (135)
"O Lord, give the command!
"Grant me the plant of birth!
"Reveal to me the plant of birth!
"Relieve me of my burden, grant me an heir!"   (140)
Shamash made ready to speak and sa[id] to Etana,
"Go (your) way, cross the mountain,
"Find a pit, [look insi]de,
"An eagle is cast within it.
"He will reveal to you the plant [of birth]."   (145)
According to the command of the warrior Shamash,
Etana went (his) way.
He found the pit, he looked inside,
[The eagle was cast] with[in it].
There he was for him to bring up!   (150)

Tablet III

III/A

The eagle made ready to speak, [   ]   (1)

(gap of three lines)

"[Whatever he shall say   ]
"[Whatever I shall say   ]."   (5)
[According to the command of Shamash the warrior   ],

...

[The eagle made ready to speak, saying to (E)tana],
"[Tell, O tell me why you are come]!"   (10)
[Etana made ready to speak], saying to the [ea]gle,
"[Friend, give me] the plant of birth!
"[Reveal to me] the plant of birth!
"[Relieve me of my disgrace], give me an [he]ir!"

(four fragmentary lines, then breaks off)

Tablet IV

IV/B

The eagle [made ready] to speak, [saying to Etana], (1)
"[My] fr[iend] ... that god [   ].
"[We] passed through the gates of Anu, Enlil, [and] Ea.[1]
"We did obeisance [together], yo[u] and I.
"We passed through the gates of Sin, Shamash, Adad, and Ishtar, (5)
"[We did obeisance together], yo[u] and I.
"I saw a house (with?) windows, [it had no] seal.
"I ... [   ] and went inside.
"A remarkable [young woman] was seated therein.
"She was imposing ..., beautiful of [fe]ature. (10)
"A throne was set out, the ground was trodden down,
"Under the throne [   ] lions were [c]rou[ching].
"As I went in, the lions [sprang at me?].
"I awoke with a start and shuddered* [   ]."
The eagle [said] to him, to Etana, (15)
"My friend, the [   ] are obvious,
"Come, let me take you up to heaven.
"Put [your chest] against my chest,
"Put [your hands] against my wing feathers,
"Put [your arms] against my sides." (20)
He put [his chest] against his chest,
He put [his] hands against his wing feathers,
He put [his] hands against his sides,
Great indeed was the burden upon him.
When he bore [him] aloft one league, (25)
The eagle said to him, to Etana,
"Look, my friend, how the land is now!
"Examine the sea, lo[ok for] its boundaries."
"The land is hills ...[2]
The sea has become a stream(?)." (30)
When he had borne [him] aloft a second league,

1. That is, they are passing across the major portals of heaven.
2. Text ununderstandable, perhaps corrupt.

The eagle said to him, to Etana,
"Look, my friend, how the land is now!"
"The land is a hill."
When he had borne him aloft a third league,   (35)
The eagle said to him, to Etana,
"Look, my friend, how the land i[s now]!"
"The sea has become a gardener's ditch."
After they had ascended to the heaven of A[nu],
They passed through the gates of Anu, Enlil, and Ea.   (40)
The eagle and E[tana] did obei[sance to]gether.
At the gate of S[in   ]
[The eagle] and Etan[a did obeisance together].

(gap, fragmentary lines)

IV/C

(different version of the preceding)

"[Wha]tever he shall say ... [   ],   (5)
"[Wha]tever I shall say ... [   ]."
According to the command of Shamash the warrior [   ]
... [   ]
The eagle made ready to speak, [saying to Etana],
"[Tell me] why you have come."   (10)
Etana made ready to speak, [saying to the eagle],
"My friend, give me [the plant of birth],
"Reveal to me [the plant of birth]."
"[Take away] my burden, [grant me an heir]!"
"[   ] was left [   ]."   (15)
"... [   ]
"I alone will [   ]
"I will bear for you [   ] ...
"[   ] went [   ] ... [   ]   (20)
"The eagle [   ] a bird [   ],
"There is no [   ]
"Come, my friend, [   ]
"With Ishtar, mistress [   ]

"Through the power of Ishtar [   ]. (25)

"Put [your arms] against my sides,

"Put [your hands] against my wing feathers."

He put [his arms] against his sides,

He [put his hands] against his wing feathers.

[When he had borne him aloft] one league, (30)

"Look, my friend, how the land [is now]!"

"The land's [circumference?] is become one fifth of (its size)."

"The vast sea is become like a paddock."

[When he had borne him aloft] a second league,

"Look, my friend, how the land [is now]!" (35)

"The land has become a garden plot [ ],

"And the vast sea has become a trough."

[When he had borne him aloft] a third [league],

"Look, my friend, how the land [is now]!"

"I looked, but could not see the land! (40)

"Nor were [my eyes] enough to (find) the vast sea!

"My friend, I won't go up to heaven!

"Set me down, let me go off to my city!"

One league he dropped him down(?),

Then the eagle plunged and caught him in his wings. (45)

A second league he dropped him down(?),

Then the eagle plunged and caught him in his wings.

A third league he dropped him down(?),

Then the eagle plunged and caught him in his wings.

Within three cubits of the earth [he dropped him down].* (50)

The eagle plunged, and ca[ught him in his wings].

The eagle [ ] and ..., while he, Etana, [   ].

(Two fragmentary lines, then breaks off. Nothing certain is known of the rest of the story.)

Text: Old Babylonian (OV I) = Clay, BRM 4 2; (OV II) = Scheil, RA 24 (1927), 106.
Middle Assyrian (MA) = Ebeling-Köcher-Rost, LKA 14; Ebeling, KAR 170, 335; VAT 10291, 10137, 10525 = Kinnier Wilson, *Etana*, Plates 7-10.
Late Assyrian (LV) Tablet I = Kinnier Wilson, *Etana*, pl. 11-12; Tablet II = Kinnier Wilson, *Etana*, pl. 13-19 (composite text); Tablet III = Kinnier Wilson, *Etana*, pl. 20-21; Tablet IV = Kinnier Wilson, *Etana*, pl. 22-29; Tablet V = Kinnier Wilson, *Etana*, pl. 30.
Edition: J. V. Kinnier Wilson, *The Legend of Etana* (London, 1985). The translation here follows Kinnier Wilson's line numbering where possible. Where there is a discrepancy between the numbering of his edition and his numbering of the text in the plates, I have preferred the plates and marked the line numbers in question with asterisks. I have also adopted his sigla for the tablets.
Translation: Speiser, ANET[3], 114-118; Labat, *Religions*, 294-305; Dalley, *Myths*, 189-202; R. J. Williams, "The Literary History of a Mesopotamian Fable," *Phoenix* 10 (1956), 70-77.
Literature: Borger, HKL 2, 170f.; H. Freydank, "Die Tierfabel im Etana-Mythus: ein Deutungsversuch," MIO 17 (1971), 1-13; B. Alster, "The Textual History of the Legend of Etana," JAOS 109 (1989), 81-86; see also Vogelzang, BiOr 43 (1985), 436-439; Horowitz, OrNS 59 (1990), 511-520. For Etana in Mesopotamian glyptic, see van Buren, OrNS 19 (1950), 160-162. Folkloristic aspects of the story have been discussed, for example, by J. Aro, "Anzu and Simurgh," AOAT 25 (1976), 25-28.
Notes to Text: (OV I/A 2) For the difficulties with this line, see Wilcke, ZA 67 (1977), 157. Is the *ša* distributive and paralleled in line 13? (MA I/A 4) *mul-ta[k-š]i-du* (WGL); for this obscure word, see CAD K, 283a. Kinnier Wilson reads *mul-ʾtarʾ-pi-du*. (MA I/A 5) Kinnier Wilson, *Etana*, 72. (MA I/A *16) Text corrupt, reading from LV II.30. (MAI/C *3) Moran, *Studies Tadmor*, 328f. (MA I/C *4) Borger, HKL 2, 171. (LV I/A *5). CAD N/1, 349b. (LV II 7) Kinnier Wilson, *Etana*, 88. (LV II 32) Kinnier Wilson, *Etana*, 129. (LV II 82) von Soden, WZKM 55 (1959), 61; CAD M/1, 349b. (LV II 110) von Soden, WZKM 55 (1959), 61; Kinnier Wilson, *Etana*, 132; Edzard, ZA 76 (1986), 137. (LV IVB 14) von Soden, WZKM 55 (1959), 61. (LV IVC 50) von Soden, ZA 45 (1939), 77-78; Horowitz, OrNS 59 (1990), 512f.

III.22 ANZU

This poem tells how the god Ninurta proved his valor and was acclaimed by the other gods as their deliverer. When the universe was still only partly organized, the Tigris and Euphrates rivers existed but no one worshipped the gods in separate sanctuaries yet, nor was there water for irrigation and rainfall. An eagle-like bird, Anzu, lived in a tree to the north of the land. His face was so horrible that even Enlil, chief of the gods, was taken aback when he saw it. Ea explains that he was a product of the flood waters, and suggests that his energies be harnessed by the chief god of Sumer. Enlil therefore puts the hideous bird in front of his own cella as a guardian.

The gods are given their responsibilities. The bird looks enviously upon Enlil's exercise of kingship and covets it for himself. While Enlil is in his bath, Anzu snatches and flies off with the tablet in which is the power to control all destinies, leaving Enlil and the other gods in disarray. The gods convene and seek a champion to recover the tablet and destroy the monster. Adad, god of rainstorms, is called but declines; Girra, god of fire, likewise. Shara, son of Ishtar, is no more eager than they. Throughout this portion of the story, as in the Creation Epic (III.17), suspense and a feeling of helplessness are conveyed by the verbatim repetitions of speech and action, mostly the former. Thrice turned down, the gods are at a loss (Tablet I line 157).

Ea, god of wisdom, offers a plan that is gladly acceded to. Mami, the mother goddess, is named by a new name, Belet-ili "Mistress of the Gods," because her son, Ninurta, is to be champion of the gods. Mami, now Belet-ili, accepts this honor and orders her dutiful son to avenge his father's dishonor, thereby to allow the gods to reassert their authorities.

Ninurta marches off on his mission (Tablet II line 28) and confronts his opponent. Since Anzu has the tablet of destinies, he has efficacious incantations against any attack, so Ninurta's onslaught is stopped. Anzu orders the oncoming arrows to return to their original elements. Ninurta sends Adad back to Ea to explain this impasse (Tablet II lines 85ff.). Ea sends him back with advice: cut off his wing feathers. When Anzu sees them fluttering about, he will order them to return to him. At that moment the arrow, which also has feathers on it, will find its mark. Again, lengthy repetitions are used to heighten suspense and delay resolution of the action.

In Tablet III Ea's suggestion is carried out. Ninurta succeeds in killing Anzu and regaining the tablet that controls destinies. The gods rejoice, but their festivity turns to uncertainty when the conquering hero does not return to yield the tablet back to Enlil. A messenger is sent to invite Ninurta's return. It appears, however, that Ninurta is not eager to return the tablet. At this point the text is damaged. When it resumes, Ninurta has returned and the gods are praising him as the most important among them. Various names of Ninurta are celebrated in a passage similar to Tablet VII of the Creation Epic (III.17).

The Anzu story is known in two versions. What survives of an Old Babylonian (Classical period) version corresponds to Tablets II and III of the later one. The later version is known from various Middle and Late Assyrian and Neo-Babylonian manuscripts (Mature and Late periods) that preserve most of Tablets I and II, as well as substantial parts of III. The Middle Assyrian fragments are treated here with the later version.

Of interest is substitution of Ninurta in the later version for Ningirsu in the Old Babylonian version; evidently the two were then considered equivalent. The basic story was borrowed and adapted by the author of the Creation Epic (III.17), who made major changes in it. For example, in the Creation Epic Marduk demands highest authority among the gods before the battle, as a plan already thought out by Ea before his son volunteers. Here Ninurta's supremacy is forced upon the gods by the mutinous hero after his victory.

Readers are advised to begin with the later version and then to return to the Old Babylonian.

(a) OLD BABYLONIAN VERSION

"Tablet II"

He snatched away supremacy, divine authority was overthrown, (1)
Their father and counsellor Enlil was speechless.
Panic spread,[1] deathly stillness reigned,
He threw all of the Igigi-gods into confusion.
The cella was stripped of its divine splendor. (5)
The gods of the land convened, one after another, for a plan.
Anu made ready to speak,
Saying to the gods his children,
"O gods, who will slay Anzu?
"He will make his the greatest name among them all."* (10)
They called the Irrigator, Anu's son.[2]
    Plan made(?),* he said to him,
"[   ] your battle, blitz Anzu with your weapons.
"[Your name shall be greatest] among the great gods,
"You shall ha[ve] no equal [among the gods your brethren].
"[Show yourself mighty] before the gods,
    your name shall be 'M[ighty One]'." (15)
[The Irrigator said to Anu his father these words],
"[My father, who would assault an inaccessible mountain]?
"[Who of your] children can defeat [An]zu?
"[He has taken control of the tablet of destinies],
    he has snatched away [supremacy] from (the) god.
"[He has soared off to his moun]tain, he has lifted high his head, (20)
"His command [has become] like that of divine Duranki.[3]
"[If he commands, the one he curses] will turn into clay."
At his [words] the gods were despondent,
[He turned away], he refused to go.
They called [Girr]u, first born of Annunitum. (25)
[Pl]an made(?), he said to him,

---

1. Literally: "was poured out."
2. Adad.
3. Enlil.

("... your battle, blitz Anzu with your weapons,[1]   (a)

("Your name shall be greatest among the great gods,

("You shall have no equal among the gods your brethren.

("Show yourself mighty before the gods,

    your name shall be 'M[ighty One]'."

(Girru said to Anu his father these words,   (e)

("My father, who would assault an inaccessible mountain?

("Who of your children can defeat Anzu?

("He has taken control of the tablet of destinies,

    He has snatched away supremacy from (the) god.

("He has soared off to his mountain,

    he has lifted high his head.   (i)

("His command has become like that of divine Duranki.

("[If he commands, the one he curses] will turn into clay."

(At his words the gods were despondent,

(Girru turned away, he refused to go.)

They called Shara, first born of Ishta[r   ],   (27)

Plan made(?), he said to him,

("... your battle, blitz Anzu with your weapons!   (a)

("Your name shall be greatest among the great gods,

("You shall have no equal among the gods your brethren.

("Show yourself mighty before the gods,

    your name shall be 'M[ighty One]'."

("Shara said to Anu his father these words,   (e)

("My father, who would assault an inaccessible mountain?

("Who of your children can defeat Anzu?

("He has taken control of the tablet of destinies,

    He has snatched away supremacy from (the) god.

("He has soared off to his mountain, he has lifted high his head.   (i)

("His command has become like that of divine Duranki.

("[If he commands, the one he curses] will turn into clay."

(At his words the gods were despondent,

(He turned away, he refused to go).

Being spent, the gods [left off making] proposal(s).

---

1. Lines a–m are not in the manuscript but were presumably indicated with ditto marks or omitted by the scribe to save effort.

The Igigi-gods were (still) assembled,
    [frowning?] and in a turmoil.   (30)
The lord of wisdom, who dwells in the depths,
    [Ea], the clever one,
Said [to Anu] his [father] the words in his mind,
"Let me give a com[mand],
    for then I will appoint Anzu's [conqueror]."
When the god[s of the land] heard [this] speech of his,
[Restored,* they did hom]age to him.   (35)
[He summoned] Belet-ili, mistress of divine plans,
    he proclaimed her supremacy in the assembly,
"[Give us] the mighty one, your superb beloved,
"Broad of chest, who leads the seven combats,
"N[ing]irsu, the mighty one, your su[per]b beloved,
"Broad of chest, who leads the seven combats."   (40)
When she heard this speech of his, she of surpassing
    greatness, Belet-ili, assented,
At her utterance the gods of the land rejoiced,
    And, restored, they did homage to him.
In the assembly of the gods she summoned
And commissioned her son, her heart's beloved, saying to him,
"Before Anu and Dagan, the valorous ones(?),   (45)
"They have discussed in the assembly
    what has h[appened] to their authority.
"The [Igi]gi-gods, I gave birth to all of them!
"[I bore] the assembly of the gods, I am Mami.
"I appointed [supremacy] to my brother,
    And to Anu the kingship of heaven.
"The kingship which I appointed [is overthrown]!   (50)
"[He has snatched away supremacy], he has spurned your father!¹

"[Make a way], choose the moment,²
"Make light come out for [the gods I made],
"Launch your [fullest] attack,

---

1. Addressed to Ningirsu.
2. The line may mean that the hero is to stop Anzu's forward progress and put an end to his usurpation.

"Let [your seven ill winds] go up* to the mountain.   (55)
"Conquer [soaring] Anzu,
"[   ] ... press hard upon his abode.
"[Let fear] weigh heavily upon [him],*
"[Let him tr]emble [   ]

(three lines fragmentary)

"[Draw the bow, let the arrows] carry [poi]son,
"Let the curse of your battle cry cast [gloom] upon him,
"Let him suffer darkness, let him become confused,
          his vision fail,   (65)
"Let him not evade you,
          (but) let his wings fall in the confrontation,
"Let your face change into a fiend's, send forth a mist so he
          cannot distinguish your features,
"May the ever-bl[az]ing one not blaze on high,
          the bright day turn to gloom for him!
"Cut short his life, conquer Anzu!
"Let the winds bear off his wing feathers as glad tidings*   (70)
"To Ekur, to your father,
"Let the winds bear off his wing feathers as glad tidings."*
The warrior heeded his mother's word,*
The valiant one of battle became mighty,
          [he made his way] towards [his] mountain.
She who harnessed seven [   ]   (75)
[The seven whirlwinds] who make [the dust dance],
[   ] who harnessed seven ill winds,*
[   ] his battle
[   ] ...
[   ] Anzu's mountain the god appeared.   (80)

"Tablet III"

Anzu [saw him] and shook at(?) him (in fury),⋆ (1)
He raged like a demon,
     his terrifying radiance enveloped the moun[tain],
[Anzu roared like a lion], carried away(?) with rage,
[In the fury] of his heart he shrieked at the hero,
"[I am] he [who carried off] all authority, (5)
"[You who] have come [for battle with me,
     account] for yourself!"
Ningirsu answered Anzu, [to the words] he spoke,
"[I am the son of Dura]nki, upholder of Duranki,
     ordainer of destinies,
"[   ] I am come, your crusher.
"[   ] whirlwind [ ] armor." (10)
[When he heard this], within the mountain
     he let forth in fury his shriek,⋆
[Armor's surface was] bathed in blood,
[   ] battle roared.
[The ..., son of] Mami, hope of Anu and Dagan,
     beloved of the Leader,[1]
[He shot a shaft] at him. It did not approach Anzu, (15)
[For he cried out again]st it, "Shaft who have come,
     go b]ack [to your thicket],
"[ ] shaft who have come, go b[ack to your reedbed]!"[2]

     (Gap of about forty lines. Ea is speaking.)

"Hurry to overwhelm [   ],⋆
"[you must not] spare Anzu's life!⋆
"[Let kingship return] to Ekur,
     let authority return to the father who begot you,
"Let [your?] daises [be built], (70)
"Establish y[our] holy places [in the] fo[ur world regions]."
[When the Lord heard the] command of his fathers,

1. Ninshiku (=Ea).
2. Magic words to ward off the arrow; see Later Version, Tablet II lines 63–65.

[The valiant one of bat]tle became mighty, and returned
    to [the mountain].
[   ] the four winds [   ] for battle,
[   ] the earth heaved, ... [   ]   (75)
[The su]n became dark, the heavens turned gloomy,
    [his vision] fa[iled],*
[An]zu [let fall] his wings in the confrontation with the tempest.

(tablet ends, continuation lost)

(b) LATE VERSION

Tablet I

Son of the king of the inhabited world, splendid one,
    beloved of [Ma]mi,   (1)
The mighty one will I ever sing, divine child of [En]lil,
Ninurta, the splendid one, beloved of Mami,
The mighty one will I ever praise, divine firstborn of Enlil.
Born (in) Ekur, leader of the Anu[nna-gods],
    Eninnu's[1] hope,   (5)
Who [wa]ters(?) pen, garden, ..., land, and city,
Wave of battles, dancing one, sash of valor,
Tireless one whose onset raging fiends dread,
Hear the praise of the mighty one's power!
It is he who in his fierceness bound
    and fettered the stone creatures,[2]   (10)
Overcoming soaring Anzu with his weapon,
Slaying the bull man in the midst of the sea.[3]
Doughty, valorous, murderous with his weapon,
Mighty one, fleet of foot, always leader in fight and fray!
Before that, no dais had been built among the Igigi-gods,   (15)
It was the Igigi-gods who knelt in their supremacy.[4]
Tigris and [Euph]rates rivers had been fashioned,
But the [springs] were not bearing [their?] waters to the land.
The very seas [   ]
Clouds were absent from the horizon [   ]   (20)
Then were the [Igigi-gods] convened from all parts,
To Enlil, their father, wa[rrior of the gods?],
Did his children bring [the news],
"Hee[d you well] the propitious word!

---

1. Temple of Ningirsu at Lagash.

2. A reference to a Sumerian poem called "Ninurta and the Stones," for which see J. J. A. van Dijk, *LUGAL UD ME-LÁM-bi NIR-GÁL* (Leiden, 1983), and Cooper, AnOr 52 (1978), 121.

3. Cooper, AnOr 52 (1978), 148-149; for the bull man, see Green, *Iraq* 48 (1986), 26 with Plate VIIC.

4. WGL: "though supreme gods." I take this obscure line to mean that the Igigi-gods worshipped but were not yet worshipped by anyone themselves.

"On Hihi Mountain[1] a tree [   ]   (25)
"In its fork the Anu[nna-gods   ]
"It[2] bore Anzu [   ]
"[His] beak a saw [   ]
"[Go] out and [   ]

(four lines fragmentary)

At [his] clamor [   ]   (35)
The south wind [   ]
The massive [   ]
The voluminous [flooding crest   ]
The whirlwinds [   ]
They met and [   ]   (40)
The four winds [   ]
When the fat[her of the gods] saw him [   ]
He took what [they] said of him [to his heart],
He inspected Anzu closely [   ]
Debated with [himself   ]   (45)
"Who bore [   ]?
"Why this [   ]?"
[Ea] answered the query of his heart,
The Leader [said] to En[lil these words],
"No doubt the waters of the fl[ood   ]   (50)
"The pure waters of the gods of the deep [ ]
"The [   ] earth conceived him,
"He is the one [born] in the rocks of the mountain,
"It is Anzu you have seen [   ]
"Let him serve you ce[aselessly],   (55)
"Let him always block the way to the cella [seat]."

(gap)

The god con[sented to the word] he spoke to him,
He took up holy places [   ]   (60)
And gave to all the [gods] their responsibilities.

---

1. See Erra and Ishum (IV.16) Tablet IV lines 139, 141, Jebel Bishri(?).
2. Antecedent unclear. Perhaps the flood is meant; see line 20 below.

He would reinstitute the decree (each morning?)
    and Anzu would hold [   ],
Enlil entrusted him with the entrance to the cella,
    which he had wrought.
He was wont to bathe in pure waters before him,
His eyes looked upon the trappings of supremacy,   (65)
On his lordly crown, his divine apparel,
On the tablet of destinies in his hands Anzu was wont to gaze.
He was wont to gaze, indeed, at the father of the gods,
    divine Duranki,
He resolved in his heart to make off with supremacy.
Anzu was wont to gaze on the father of the gods,
    divine Duranki,   (70)
He resolved in his heart to make off with supremacy!
"I myself will take the gods' tablet of destinies,
"I will gather to myself the responsibilities of all the gods,
"I will have the throne for myself,
    and take power over authority,
"I will be commander of all and every Igigi-god."   (75)
His heart plotted the assault,
At the entrance to the cella, where he was wont to gaze,
    he bided (his) time.
When Enlil was bathing in the pure waters,
Undressed(?),* his crown set on the throne,
He took control of the tablet of destinies,   (80)
He took supremacy, [authority] was overthrown!
Anzu soared off and [made his way] to his mountain,
Awful silence spread, deathly sti[llness] reigned.
Their father and counsellor Enlil was speechless.
The cella was stripped of its divine splendor.   (85)
[The gods] of the land converged, one after another, for a pl[an].
[A]nu made ready to speak,
Saying to the gods his children,
"[Which] one would slay Anzu?
"He shall make for himself the greatest name
    in [eve]ry habitation."   (90)
They called the [irrigator], Anu's son,

Plan [ma]de(?), he said to him,
They summoned Adad, the irrigator, Anu's son,
Plan [ma]de(?), he said to him,
"[O mighty] one, Adad, victorious Adad,
      let your battle not waver, (95)
"[Blitz] Anzu with your weapon.
"[Let your name] be greatest among all the great gods,
"You shall have no equal [among] the gods your brethren.
"Let there be daises to be built,
"Establish your holy places in the four [world regions], (100)
"Let your [holy places] come into Ekur.
"[Show yourself] mighty before the gods,
      for your name shall be "Mighty One."
[Adad] answered the command,
[To Anu] his father he said these words, (105)
["My father], who would assault an inaccessible [moun]tain?
"[Which] of the gods your children can overcome Anzu?
"He took control of the [tablet of destinies],
"He took away [supremacy], authority is overthrown.
"[Anzu] soared off and made his way to his mountain, (110)
"His [utterance] is become like that of divine Duranki.
"[If he commands, the one he cur]ses will turn into clay."
The gods were despondent [at his utteranc]e.
[He turned away, he refused to go].
[They called Girra, firstborn of Annunitum], (115)
[Plan made?, he said to him],
"[O mighty one, Girra, victorious Girra,
      let your battle not waver].
"[Blitz Anzu with your weapon],
"[Let your name be greatest among all the great gods],
"[You shall have no equal among the gods your brethren]. (120)
"[Let there be daises to be built],
"[Establish your holy places in the four world regions],
"[Show yourself mighty before the gods,
      for your name shall be 'Mighty One'."
[Girra answered the command], (125)
[To Anu his father he said these words],

"[My father, who would assault an inaccessible mountain]?
"[Which of the gods your children can overcome Anzu?
"[He took control of the tablet of destinies],
"[He took away supremacy, authority is overthrown].   (130)
"[Anzu soared off and ma]de [his way to his mountain],
"[His utterance] is become like that of divine Duranki.
"[If he commands, the one he curses] will turn into clay."
The gods were despondent [at his utter]ance.
[He turned away], he refused to go.   (135)
They [called] Shara, firstborn of Ishtar,
[Pl]an [made](?), he said to him,
"[O mi]ghty one, [Shara], victorious Shara,
        let your battle not waver.
"[Bli]tz Anzu with your weapon.
"Let yo[ur name] be greatest among all the great gods,   (140)
"You shall have no equal among the gods your brethren.
"Let there be daises to be built,
"Establish your holy places in the four world regions,
"Let your holy places come into Ekur.
"Show yourself mighty before the gods,
        for your name shall be 'Mighty One'."   (145)
Shara answered the command,
To Anu his father he said these words,
"My father, who would assault an inaccessible mountain?
"Which of the gods your children can overcome Anzu?
"He took control of the tablet of destinies,   (150)
"He took away supremacy, authority is overthrown.
"Anzu flew off and [made his w]ay to his mountain.
"His utterance is become like that of divine Duranki.
"If he commands, the one he curses will turn into clay."
The gods were despondent at his utterance.   (155)
He turned away, he refused to go.
The gods were spent and left off making proposals,
The Igigi-gods, (still) in session,
        were frowning(?) and in a turmoil.
The lord of wisdom, who dwells in the depths, the clever one,
Was devising an idea in his cunning mind.   (160)

Ea devised wisdom(?) in his heart,
What he thought of in his mind he explained to Anu,
"Let me give a command and so find the god,
"For then I will appoint Anzu's conqueror in the assembly,
"Let me be the one to find the god,   (165)
"For then I will appoint Anzu's conqueror in the assembly."
When the Igigi-gods [he]ard this speech of his,
The Igigi-gods, restored, did homage to him.
The Leader made ready to speak,
[Saying t]o Anu and Dagan these words,   (170)
"Let them summon to me the mistress of the gods,
        the sister of the gods,
"The resourceful one, coun[sellor] of the gods [her] brethren.
"Let them proclaim her surpassing greatness in the as[sembly],
"Let all the gods honor [her] in their assembly.
"[Then I will explain to her] the idea of my heart."   (175)
They summoned thither the mistress of the gods,
        the sister [of the gods],
The resourceful one, counsellor of the gods [her brethren].
They proclaimed her surpassing greatness [in the assembly],
The gods honored her in their assembly.
Ea [explained the idea] from his cunning mind,   (180)
"Formerly w[e called you]* 'Mami,'
"Now let 'Mistress of All the Gods' [be your name].
"Give (us) the mighty one, [your] superb [beloved],
"The broad-chested one who is ever leader in fight or fray.
"Give (us) Ninurta, your superb beloved,   (185)
"The broad-chested one who is ever leader in fight or fray.
"[He shall be   ] lord in the assembly of the gods,
"He shall be proud in the [   ]
"In all [   ]
"A holy place [   ]   (190)
"Lord [   ]
"A fes[tival   ]
"In [   ]."
[When she heard this speech of his],

[She of surpassing greatness, the most exalted
    mistress of the gods, assented].   (195)
[When she spoke, the Igigi-gods rejoiced],
[Restored, they did homage to her].
[She summoned her son in the assembly of the gods].
Commissioning her heart's beloved, saying to him,
"Be[fore Anu and Dagan   ]   (200)
"[They have discussed in the assembly]
    what has happened [to authority].
"[I bore] all the Igigi-gods,
"I made every [single one of them],
"I made all the A[nunna-gods].
"[To my brother I ...] supremacy,   (205)
"[I assigned] kingsh[ip of heaven] to Anu.
"Anzu has thrown into confusion
    [the kingship I appointed],
"The tablet of destinies, ... Anzu ... has taken control,
"He has snatched from Enlil, he has spurned your father.
"He has snatched away authority,
    he has turned it over to himself.   (210)

Tablet II

"Blitz the way, choose (your) moment,*   (1)
"Make light come out for the gods I made.
"Launch your fullest attack,
"Let your ill winds go against him!
"Conquer soaring Anzu,   (5)
"Flood the earth where he was made,
    bring chaos upon his dwelling.*
"Let (your) armor clash against him,
"Let your fierce battle keep raging against him,*
"May it have whirlwinds at their fullest to block him.*
"Draw the bow, let the arrows bear poison,   (10)
"Let your features turn into a fiend's,
"Send forth a mist so he cannot distinguish your face.
"Let your brilliant glow move against him,[1]
"Let your radiance be glorious,
    you should have an awe-inspiring sheen,
"Let the sun not shine upon him,[2]   (15)
"Let the bright day turn to gloom for him.
"Kill him, conquer Anzu!
"Let the winds bear off his wing feathers as glad tidings,
"To the temple Ekur, to your father Enlil.
"Flood and bring mayhem to the mountain meadows,   (20)
"Kill wicked Anzu!
"Let [king]ship (re-)enter Ekur,
"Let authority return [to the] fa[ther] who begot you.
"Let there be daises to be built,
"Establish your holy places [in the f]our [world regions],   (25)
"[Let your shrine] come into Ekur.
"Show yourself mighty before the gods,
    for your name shall be 'Mighty One',"
The warrior heeded his mother's word,
Seething with fury, he made his way towards his mountain.

1. Variant: "on high"(?) or: "against us."
2. Variant: "on high."

My Lord hitched up the seven battles,   (30)
The warrior hitched up the seven ill winds,
The seven whirlwinds that make the dust dance.
He launched a terrifying assault, made war,
The winds were ready at his side for battle.
Anzu and Ninurta met on the mountainside.   (35)
When Anzu saw him, he shook with fury at him,
He ground his teeth like a cyclone,
      he enveloped the mountain with his horrible glow.
He roared like a lion, seized with passion.
In his rage he cried to the w[arrior],
"I have carried off all possible authority,   (40)
"So I control the responsibilities all the gods must do.
"Who are you who have to come fight with me?
      Account for yourself!"
He advanced upon him, saying to him,
The warrior Ninurta [answered] Anzu,
"I [am the son of] divine Duranki,   (45)
"Upholder of the vast netherworld, of Ea, king of destinies!
"I am come to fight with you, your crusher!"
When Anzu heard what he said,
He let loose his piercing shriek within the mountain.
It grew dark, the face of the mountain was enveloped,   (50)
The sun, light of the gods, became dark.
Adad roared in great (thunderclaps),* the sign of Anzu was his clamor.
In the midst of the melee, the conflict,
      battle was joined, the deluge onset,*
Armor was on the move, bathed in blood,
Clouds of death rained down, arrows flashed as lightning,   (55)
Battle ran on,* thundering between them.
The Mighty One, the splendid firstborn of Mami,
Hope of Anu and Dagan, beloved of the Leader,
Mounted the bow with a shaft,
From the handhold of the bow he sent against him an arrow.   (60)
The shaft did not approach Anzu but returned!
Anzu cried out against it,
"Shaft which has come, go back to your thicket,

"Frame of the bow to your forests,
"Bowstring to the sheep's sinews, feather to the birds: go back!" (65)
Because he held the tablet of destinies of the gods in his hand,
The bowstring brought forth arrows,
    but they did not approach his body.
Battle die[d do]wn, attack was held back,
The fighting stopped,
    within the mountain they did not conquer Anzu.
He summoned Sharur[1]* and commissioned him, (70)
"Tell Ea the Leader what you saw happen,
"Say this:

    'Lord, Ninurta had surrounded Anzu,
    'Ninurta was enveloped with the dust of battle.
    'He readied the bow, mounted the shaft, (75)
    'He readied the bow, shot the shaft towards him.
    'It did not approach Anzu but returned.
    'Anzu cried out against it,

        "Shaft which has come, go back to your thicket,
        "Frame of the bow to your forests, (80)
        "Bowstring to the sheep's sinews,
            feathers to the birds: go back!"

    'Because he was holding the tablet of destinies
        of the gods in his hand,
    'The bowstring brought forth arrows,
        but they did not approach his body.
    'Battle die[d d]own, attack was held back,
    'Within the mountain fighting was stopped,
    'They did not conquer Anzu.'" (85)

Sharur did obeisance, received the command,
Bore the battle message to Ea the Leader,
He repeated to Ea all the Lord told him,
"O lord, he says this,

    'Ninurta had surrounded Anzu,
    'Ninurta was enveloped with the dust of battle.

---

1. Usually a deified weapon of Ninurta/Ningirsu, here a separate deity.

'He readied the bow, shot the shaft towards him, (90)
'The shaft did not approach Anzu but returned.
'Anzu cried out against it,

> "Shaft which has come, go back to your thicket,
> "Frame of the bow to your forests, (95)
> "[Bowstr]ing to the sheep's [sinews],
> > feathers to the birds: go back!"

'[Because he was h]olding the [tablet of destini]es
> of the gods in his ha[nd],
'[The bowstring brought forth arrows,
> but they did not approach his body].
'[Battle died down, attack was held back],
'[Within the mountain fighting was stopped], (100)
'[They did not conquer Anzu].'"

When [the Lea]der heard the words of his son,
He [called Sharur] and commissioned him,
"[Repeat] to him, to your lord, what I say,
"Remember every[thing] I say for him.

> 'Do not tire in battle, strive for victory, (105)
> 'Tire him out that he let his wings fall
> > to the brunt of the storm,
> 'Take, O lord, your darts towards the bottom,
> 'Cut off his pinions and hurl them, right and left,
> 'Once he sees his feathers,
> > they will take away his (magic) words.
> '"My wings!" to the wings he will cry; fear him still. (110)
> 'Ready your bow, let the lightning shafts fly from it,*
> 'Let pinions and wing feathers dance about like butterflies.*
> 'Kill him, conquer Anzu!
> 'Let the winds bear off his wing feathers as glad tidings, (115)
> 'To the temple Ekur, to your father Enlil.
> 'Flood and bring mayhem to the mountain meadows,
> 'Kill wicked Anzu!
> 'Let kingship (re-)enter Ekur,
> 'Let authority return [to the father] who begot you. (120)
> 'Let there be daises to be built,

'Establish your holy places in the four world regions,
'[Let] your holy places come into Ekur.
'Show yourself mighty be[fore the gods],
        for your name shall be 'Mighty One'."

[Sharur did ob]eis[ance] and received the command,   (125)
Bo[re] off the battle message [to] his [lord],
Every[thing] Ea to[ld him he repea]ted to him,

'Do not ti[re] in battle, strive for victory,
'Tire him out that he let his wings fall
        [to the brunt of] the storm.
'Take, O lord, your darts towards the bottom,   (130)
'Cut off his pinions and hurl them, right and left.
'Once he sees his feathers,
        they will take away his (magic) words.
'"My wings!" to the wings he will cry; [fear him] still.
'Ready your bow, let the [lightning] shafts fly from it.   (135)
'Let pinions and wings dance about like butterflies.
'Kill him, conquer Anzu!
'Let the winds bear off his wing feathers as glad tidings
'To the temple Ekur, to your father Enlil.
'Flood and bring [mayhem] to the mountain meadows,   (140)
'Kill wicked Anzu!
'Let kingship (re-)enter [Ekur],
'Let authority [return] to the father who begot you.
'Let there be [dais]es to be built,
'[Estab]lish your holy places in the four world regions.   (145)
'[Let] your holy places [come into] Ekur.
'Show yourself mighty before [the gods],
        for your name shall be 'Mighty One'.'

The Lord heeded the words of Ea the Leader,
Seething with fury, he made his way towards his mountain.
The Lord hitched up the seven battles,   (150)
[The warrior hitched up] the seven ill winds,
[The ...] whirlwinds [that make the dust swirl].
He launched a [terrifying] assault, made war,
[The winds were ready at his side] for his battle.

Tablet III[1]

(two lines fragmentary)

Armor ...
Constantly striking one another ... [ ]
The blazing of the fiery glare [   ]   (5)
[ ] to the four winds, the storm [   ]
The weapons he struck and struck, in horrible protection,*
Both were bathed in the sweat of battle.
Then Anzu grew tired,
     at the onslaught of the storm he dropped his wings,
The Lord took his darts towards the bottom,   (10)
He cut off his pinions, hurled them right and left.
When Anzu saw his wings, they took away his (magic) words.
When he cried "My wings!" to the wings,
     the arrow flew against him,
The shaft passed through the ... of his heart,
He made his dart pass through pinion and wing,
The shaft pierce through his heart and lungs.   (15)
He flooded, brought mayhem to the mountain meadows,
He flooded the vast earth in his fury,
He flooded the midst of the mountains,
He killed wicked Anzu!   (20)
The warrior Ninurta took control of the tablet
     of the gods' destinies.
The wind bore Anzu's wingfeathers
As a sign of his glad tidings.
Dagan rejoiced when he saw his sign,
He summoned all the gods, saying to them in joy,   (25)
"The Mighty One has outroared Anzu in his mountain,
"He has regained control of Anu and Dagan's weapons.
"Go to him, that he come to us,
"Let him rejoice, let him dance, let him celebrate,
"Let him stand with the gods his brethren,
     that he may hear the secret lore,   (30)

---

1. What follows is largely from R, based on the work of Saggs.

"[   ] the secret lore of the gods,
"Let [   ] grant him responsibilities ...
        with the gods his brethren."
[Ea?] made ready to speak,
Saying [to] Dagan (these) words,
"... he took the skin,   (35)
"When he killed wicked Anzu in the mountains,
"The warrior Ninurta regained control of the tablet
        of the gods' destinies.
"Send to him, let him come to you,
"Let him place the tablet of destinies in your lap."
Enlil made ready to speak,   (40)
Saying to Nusku his courier (these) words,
"Nusku, go outside,
"Bring Birdu[1] before me!"
He brought Birdu into Enlil's presence.
Enlil made ready to speak,
Saying to Birdu (these) words,
"Birdu, I am sending you ...

                    (gap)

Ninurta [made] ready to speak,
[Saying these words] to Birdu,
"O Birdu, why did you come furiously to ...?"   (5')
Birdu m[ade ready] to speak,
[Saying these words] to Ninurta his lord,
"My lord, [   ] to you,
"Your father Enlil sent me,
"Saying,

        'The gods heard [   ]   (10')
        'That [you killed] wicked Anzu in the mountain.
        'They were joyful and glad, but [   ].
        'Before you [   ] ...
        'Go to him [   ] ...
        'Let him rejoi[ce   ] ...   (15')

---

1. A god; see E. Ebeling, "Birdu," RLA 2, 31.

(three lines fragmentary)

Ninurta [made ready to speak, saying to Birdu],
"Why [surrender] the trap[pings of kingship]?   (20′)
"[My utterance has become] like that of the ki[ng of the gods].
"I will not re[turn] the tablet of destinies."

(fragmentary lines, then breaks off)

(A god is speaking to Ninurta.)

"Let [   ] not be built,
"[   ] Anzu in Ekur.
"[   ] the sign of the warrior,   (115)
"Let him look upon wicked Anzu
        [in] the greatness of his might,
"O warrior, you could slay mountains in your might,
"You defeated Anzu, you could slay his might,
"You could slay the might of soaring Anzu!
"Because you were valiant and slew mountains,   (120)
"You have made all enemies submit
        before your father, Enlil,
"O Ninurta, because you were valiant and slew mountains,
"You have made all enemies submit before your father, Enlil!
"You have gained lordship, each and every divine authority,
"For(?) whom besides you is the divine authority
        of the mountain?   (125)
"Greatness has been given you at the daises of the gods
        of destinies,
"They called your lustrations 'Nisaba',
"They called your name in the furrow 'Ningirsu'.
"They assigned to you full shepherdship of the people,
"As king, they gave (you) your name 'Guardian of the Throne'. (130)
"In Elam they gave (you) the name Hurabtil,
"In Susa they speak of you as Inshushinak.[1]
"In Ibbi-Anu[2] they gave you the name

---

1. Elam and Susa are in southwestern Iran (see III.11); the other cities and cult centers listed thereafter are Mesopotamian, so far as known.
2. Temple at Dilbat, a town in Babylonia (Moran, AfO 34 [1987], 29).

'Master of Secret Lore',
"[   ] among the gods your brethren
"[   ] your father,   (135)
"They gave you your name '[Pabilsag]' in Egalmah,
"They [called] your name '[   ]' in Ur,
"[   ] you ... Duranki,   (140)
"[In Der] they speak of you as 'Ishtaran',
"[In   ] 'Zababa',
"[   ] they call as his name.
"Your valor [   ] Enlil over all the gods,
"[   ] to make surpassing your divinity,   (145)
"[   ] I praise you.
"In NI.SUR [they gave (you)] your name
         'Lugalbanda' in E-giskalamma,
"[In] E-sikilla they gave (you) [your name]
         as 'Warrior Tishpak',
"In Bube in the E-nimmankur [   ],   (150)
"In Kullab they called (you) by your name
         'Warrior of Uruk',
"[   ] Belet-ili your mother,
"[   ] lord of the boundary,
"[   ] Panigingarra,
"They called ... [   ]   (155)
"[   ] 'Papsukkal, the vanguard'.
"O ... lord, your names are surpassing great
         among the gods,
"Lord of understanding, capable and dreaded one,
"[   ] Ea the Leader, your father,
"[   ] battle and conflict,   (160)
"He [   ] you '[   ] of their lands'.

(fragmentary lines, then breaks off)

Text: (a) = Scheil, RA 35 (1938), 20-21 = Vogelzang, BSD, 92-95, collated by the translator. These two tablets appear to be Middle or Neo-Babylonian copies that attempt to preserve faithfully an Old Babylonian text. Vogelzang reached similar conclusions independently. (b) Tablet I = Hallo, JCS 31 (1979), 106-115 (A); King, CT 15 39-40 + W. G. Lambert, CT 46 39 (G); W. G. Lambert, CT 46 36 (C), 37 (B), 40 (+) AfO 27 (1980), 81 (Sm 2195) (D); Saggs, AfO 33 (1986), 6-9 (R). Unfortunately there is no consistent line numbering for this tablet; I have used a continuous count based on R and BSD. Tablet II = 1-46 = Ebeling-Köcher-Rost, LKA 1 (E); 1-64 = Gurney, STT 21 (F); 26-41 = Gurney, STT 22 (H); 27-43 = W. G. Lambert, CT 46 38 (G); 41-90 = Gurney, STT 19 (I); 53-138 = Ebeling-Köcher-Rost, LKA 1 (E); 59-64 = K 18740 = W. G. Lambert, AfO 27 (1980), 82; 65-81 = W. G. Lambert, CT 46 41 (J); 82-88 = Gurney, STT 21 (I); 89-92 = K 19368 = W. G. Lambert, AfO 27 (1980), 82; 101-129 = Gurney, STT 21 (I); 131-142 = W. G. Lambert, CT 46 38 (G); 140-150 = Gurney, STT 21 (I); 141-150 = Ebeling-Köcher-Rost, LKA 1 (E); Saggs, AfO 33 (1986), 9, 20. Tablet III = i 1'-18' = W. G. Lambert, CT 46 42 (K); ii 1'-25' = W. G. Lambert, CT 46 42 ii (K) + AfO 27 (1980), 82; Saggs, AfO 33 (1986), 20, 26.
Edition: (a) Vogelzang, BSD, 96-118. (b) Moran, JCS 31 (1979), 65-102 (I); Saggs, AfO 33 (1986), 7, 8, 10; Vogelzang, BSD, 27-47 (I); Vogelzang, BSD, 48-67; Saggs, AfO 33 (1986), 10-19, 21 (II); Vogelzang, BSD, 68-72; Saggs, AfO 33 (1986), 21-25, 27, 28 (III).
Translation: (both versions) Grayson-Speiser, ANET³, 111-113, 514-517; Labat, *Religions*, 80-92; Bottero, *Mythologie*, 390-418; Dalley, *Myths*, 203-227.
Literature: B. Hruška, *Der Mythenadler Anzu in Literatur und Vorstellung der alten Mesopotamier* (Budapest, 1975); F. M. Wiggermann, "On Bin Šar Dadmē, the 'Anzu-Myth'," in *Studies Kraus*, 418-425; Vogelzang, BSD; Moran, AfO 34 (1987), 24-29.
*Notes to Text: (OB II 10) Wiggermann, *Studies Kraus*, 41. (OB II 11) Moran, JCS 31 (1979), 97, also AHw, 1386b. Other translators understand "the commander" (or the like), and make that the subject, but this is grammatically difficult. (OB II 35) Moran, JCS 31 (1979), 100; see p. 168 note 5. (OB II 52) Reading [*bi-riq*] from source F, though the reading *bi-šim* (WGL) can also be considered. (OB II 55) Vogelzang, BSD, 116-117. (OB II 58) AHw, 943b. (OB II 70) CAD B, 347a vs AHw, 885b. (OB II 72) Possible dittography, or, as taken here, a "pivot" construction (aba). (OB II 73) Moran, JCS 31 (1979), 67f. (OB II 77) ⸢*im-ḫul*⸣-*li*, collated CAD I/J, 116b. (OB III 1) [*i-mu-ur*/*mur-šu-ma*] *An-zu-um i-ru-ba-aš-šu* (collation). (OB III 11) For proposals on this line, see Moran, JCS 31 (1979), 93 note 45; Wiggermann, *Studies Kraus*, 419; AHw, 369a. My collation favors *šam*-ra*-x-x*, here read *šam-ra-t*[*am-m*]*a* by suggestion of W. Mayer. (OB III 67) *ri-ḫi-iṣ dú-ul-li-iḫ* (see CAD D, 45b). (OB III 68) AHw, 1221b, tablet has [*t*]*a-ši-it*. (OB III 76) Wiggermann, *Studies Kraus*, 419. (LV I 10) *šiknāt abni* (WGL). (LV I 79) Moran, JCS 31 (1979), 96. (LV I 181) Restoration WGL. NI is possible for the broken sign (collated), but the trace does not closely resemble the NI in the line above. (LV II 1) See to OB II 52. (LV II 6) AHw, 1035a; Moran, AfO 34 (1987), 24 (also to line 7). (LV II 8) Differently CAD N/1, 258b; see also AHw, 932b; Moran, AfO 34 (1987), 24. (LV II 9) Moran, AfO 34 (1987), 24-25. (LV II 52) Differently AHw, 1355b. (LV II 53) WLM: *ina birīt qabli tuqmāte ... aṣ-ṣ*[*er-ma*]. (LV II 56) George, *Nabu* 1991/19. (LV II 67) Saggs, AfO 33 (1986), 15. (LV II 70) Reading from Saggs. (LV II 110) Moran, AfO 34 (1987), 27. (LV II 111) It is unclear whether line 75, which should be repeated here, is a doublet there, or whether it has been accidentally omitted here. (LV II 112) CAD K, 564a, but see Wiggermann, *Studies Kraus*, 421. (LV III 7) Moran, AfO 34 (1987), 27-28.

III.23 THE SERPENT

A huge serpent has grown up in the ocean. The mother goddess is summoned and is asked who is the most valiant of her offspring. She names Nergal, perhaps referred to as "the Vanguard" in lines 19ff. The rest of the text may have told of Nergal's successful defeat of this monster and his exaltation among the gods. Most of the story is lost, owing to breaks in the tablet. There are obvious parallels with the Anzu story (III.22), as well as the Lion-Serpent (III.25) and the Creation Epic (III.17).

i

(lost except for a few signs)

ii

"[   ] there is no ... [   ]   (5)
"It was lying in the water, and I [   ]."

[   ] made ready to speak,
And said to [   ] his [   ] these words,
"Bring hither A[ruru], let [Arur]u [come here],
"Listen to me, Aruru, pay [attention to me].   (10)
"O ... Aruru, you are now "Mis[tress of the Gods],"★
"Among the sixty-six sons and brothers [of yours],★
"To which one did you grant strength?
"To which one did you give the fullest [   ]?"
"I granted strength to Nergal,   (15)
"To Nergal did I give the fullest [   ]."
"Bring hither the Vanguard, ... [ ] the Vanguard,
"I myself will tell the Vanguard about it ...
"Listen to me, O Vanguard, O Vanguard ... [   ]
"O Vanguard, listen carefully to what I have to say.★   (20)

"In the ocean a dra[gon]-snake was created,
"Its ba[ck]★ reached sixty leagues,
"Its he[ad] is thirty leagues high.
"Its blink(?)★ is half a league,
"Its [feet?] can go twenty leagues at a step.   (25)

"It ate the fish, creatures of [the sea],
"It ate the birds, creatures of [the sky],
"[It ate] the donkeys, creatures of [the steppe],
"[It ate] the black-headed folk.[1] [Go help?] the people."
The Vanguard, tamer of serpents, heeded the [   ],
[Nergal] made ready to speak,
[And said to   ] these words,

(five fragmentary lines, then breaks off)

Text: Ebeling, KAR 6.
Edition: Ebeling, OLZ 1916, 106-108.
Translation: A. Heidel, *The Babylonian Genesis*[2] (Chicago, 1951), 143 (partial).
*Notes to Text: (11) Restoration doubtful: *at-ti e-nin-na* ᵈ*Be-[let-ili]*. (12) WGL. (20) *si-qir* [*šap-ti-ja*] (WGL). (22) von Soden, AnOr 27 (1948), 107. (24) "Outer rim of the eye" (or the like)? See CAD L, 192a.

1. The Mesopotamians.

III.24 THE LION-SERPENT

This is another telling of what appears to be much the same story as the preceding. Various gods refuse to fight a huge monster. One does so at last in return for kingship and slays it with an arrow. The text as copied for Assurbanipal's library seems to the modern reader abbreviated or incomplete; note the absence of indication of speakers on the obverse and the abrupt ending.

Aside from its parallels with III.23, the basic plot of this text recalls that of the Creation Epic (III.17) and Anzu (III.22).

The cities had sighed, the people [had been moaning],	(1)
The people were diminished, [ ].	
No one [ ] to their lamentations,	
No one b[ent?] to their cries of woe.	
Who [produced] the serpent?	(5)
The ocean [produced] the serpent!	
Enlil has drawn [the image of the serpent] in heaven:[1]	
Its length was fifty leagues, [its height] was one league,	
Its mouth was six cubits, [its tongue?] twelve cubits,	
Its ear flaps(?) twelve cubits.	(10)
At sixty cubits [it snatches?] birds,	
It draws nine cubits water [ ],	
If it raises its tail, it [ ].	
All the gods of heaven [ ],	
The gods knelt before [Sin] in heaven,	(15)
And [seized] the hem of Sin[2] in has[te],	
"Who will go [to kill] the Lion?	
"[Who] will sa[ve] the vast land,	
"And exercise kingship [in the land]?	
"Go, Tishpak, ki[ll the Lion-serpent],	(20)
"Sa[ve] the vast land [ ]	
"And exercise kingship [in the land]."	
"You sent me, lord of the offspring of the river [ ],	

---

1. This line may be an aetiology for a constellation.
2. A gesture of entreaty.

"I do not know [the ways?] of the Lion-serpent,
"[   ] before [   ]." (25)
[   ] the people [   ]

(fragmentary lines, then gap)

[Ea?] made ready to speak, saying to [   ] (1′)
"Fling up a cloud, [   ] a storm,
"[Grasp] the cylinder seal at your throat,[1] before you,
"Shoot (an arrow), ki[ll] the Lion-serpent."
He flung up a cloud, [   ] a whirlwind, (5′)
[He grasped] the cylinder seal at his throat before himself,
He shot (an arrow) [and killed] the Lion-serpent.
Three years, three months, one day and night,
The Lion-serpent's blood flowed [   ].

(end of tablet)

Text: King, CT 13 34-35 (Rm 282).
Edition: King, STC 1, 116-121.
Translation: A. Heidel, *The Babylonian Genesis*[2] (Chicago, 1951), 141-143; Bottéro, *Mythologie*, 464-469.
Literature: Jacobsen, *Oriental Institute Communications* 13 (1932), 53-54.

1. Cylinder seals were often worn around the neck on a Lord.